My Checkered Career

Malcolm Stiles McCollum

2018

YouArePerfect Press

Hanover, New Hampshire

Copyright 2018 Malcolm Stiles McCollum

All rights reserved.

ISBN: 0984413960
ISBN-13: 978-0-9844139-6-6

Library of Congress Control Number: 2018959483

YouArePerfect Press, Lancaster, NH

DEDICATION

For all those McCollums and Stiles who came before,
and all those who follow me, especially
my magnificent daughter Thelonika.

Contents

1 The Twins……………………………..7

2 Family Trees………………………12

3 Chain of Cashel…………………..19

4 Working……………………………46

5 War All the Time…………………57

6 Boring Repetition………………..104

7 Million Dollar Bills……………… 143

8 Killer Virus………………………149

9 About the Benjamins……………215

10 First Aid…………………………232

11 An Imperfect Trial………………264

12 Mother's Quarter………………..294

13 Some of My Betters……………307

14 Manitowoc………………………347

15 Ice Cubes in the Rain………….379

16 Jennifer Movie Collector………400

17 Golden Voices…………………433

18 By Measure……………………446

19 Salesman Rex…………………461

20 Memory Holes…………………467

21 Baseball…………………480

22 Sacred Vacant Lots……………497

23 Acknowledgements……………528

ACKNOWLEDGEMENTS

I have quoted from many books, and they are listed
with gratitude at the end of this one. I have indicated
the publishers of my own published works within the text.

This book would not have made it into print
without the considerable help and encouragement
of my friends Loran Mundy and Peter DeLissovoy

Jacket Photo: Loran Mundy

But yield who will to their separation,
My object in living is to unite
My avocation and my vocation
As my two eyes make one in sight.
Only where love and need are one,
And the work is play for mortal stakes,
Is the deed every really done
For Heaven and the future's sakes.

-Robert Frost, "Two Tramps in Mud Time"

The Twins

A "checkered career" describes a life spent jumping from one thing to another. That somewhat accurately describes my life. Or I could say that I've lived out every fantasy I had as a kid, except that I never did play left field for the Chicago Cubs. That would sound more admirable. In the game called "Checkers," the board is made up of alternating squares of different colors, and your pieces can only occupy squares of their opposite colors - red on black, black on red. In that way they call to mind the Taoist Yin Yang symbol.

In the cosmology of the Seneca Indians, this world is the expression of the continuous struggle between twin brothers, Hawenneyu the Creator and Hanegoategeh the Evil-Minded. "Hawenneyu the right-handed twin makes things - women who are smooth and fresh and beautiful. Hanegoategeh the left-hand twin makes time count, so it wrinkles and bends us and takes our strength. Hawenneyu gives us love to replenish the world, so living in time won't matter to us. Hanegoategeh separates the lovers, so the love turns into pain.... The brothers fight. One is right-handed and the other left-handed, like images in a mirror. Each anticipates what the other's next stratagem will be, and constructs the counterattack before it begins. The first can predict the counterstroke, and changes his tactic ever so slightly, or does the opposite. It's like reaching your right hand to the surface of the mirror: the left hand of your reflection rises to meet it. They've been fighting this way since the beginning of the world, so time folds, and things that happened fifty years ago and others that are happening now are the same instant: attack and counterattack conceived simultaneously." [Perry]

My dear old friend Richard Bohle once described me as "the nicest rotten guy I know." He was, as always, right on the money.

For the past few years, I've been trying to concentrate on living from the decent parts of me, and I'll probably let someone else write about the rotten parts. Maybe this mixture is present in all people. I suspect it is. I've been in the presence of one person, Ottis Toole, who didn't seem to have anything but rotten parts, and so didn't seem like a human being at all, but some sort of monster or demon. One such person. I've known quite a number of people whose rotten parts, if they existed, never showed themselves to me. I believe the rotten parts existed because I believe that's what makes humans humans instead of saints. But maybe I've known some saints. Feels like it.

I've surely known more than my share of wonderful women, and one of my few regrets is the unhappiness I've given them. I can say without exaggerating that I still know and retain as friends most of the women I loved over my lifetime. And that's about all I'm going to say. In my time - and this is my time, long as I'm the writer here - people didn't talk about their love lives. They were considered private. I'm sure there are weaknesses to that policy, as to any, but that's always been my policy. So if you want juicy details, go read somebody's Facebook page. My people don't do that.

(One of my favorite lines. One year at the college we got a new President, and she had gone to President school somewhere and learned that you should form warm personal relationships with your troops, so in her first days in office, she caused the faculty to assemble in the theater or the gym or some large place. Then she caused us all to stand around in a big circle and watch her come around and hug each of us. Being teachers, therefore largely spineless, everyone went along with this program and hugged her back until she got to Dorsey Templeton. Dorsey was a math teacher, a big Native American from Oklahoma, and not a man to suffer fools gladly. When the President came toward him, arms akimbo, he stood there like a statue until she dropped her arms. "My people don't do that," he said to her most audibly. I've treasured that sentiment ever since, and used the line frequently.)

This writing is for you, daughter, and you, my dear grandchildren. You'll have your own memories and your own views of me. But there's been a lot of my life you'll never know about unless I tell you. I'll try to be honest, and I'll try not to bore you. But you should read this knowing that it's untrustworthy.

Human memory is untrustworthy. My sister June and I, the only ones left living in our family line except you five, have talked a lot about our memories of growing up. Certainly has been an eye-opener for me; our memories often differ greatly. For instance, I remember my Dad as being completely tone-deaf as a singer, and I can back that up with specific memories of attending church suppers and ball games with him. At baseball games, the National Anthem must be sung before the game can begin, and I can still hear Dad attempting that difficult piece with gusto. He had two notes he could hear, and he would sing on one for a while until he felt it was time to change, and then sing the other for a while. I remember writhing in embarrassment next to him under the shadows of the grandstand.

June, on the other hand, tells me stories of his singing her to sleep every night, singing all sorts of lullabies and whatnot, and thinks he was a good singer.

We could both be right. He may have been a good singer by himself, and unable to hear correct notes in the midst of a crowd of other singers. (*I* often have a hard time doing that, and so have never been good at singing harmony.) I do know that he could whistle a tune accurately - I learned to whistle by listening to him and imitating him, and I can whistle damn near as well as Bing Crosby could. (Well, I could until a stroke reduced my ability to control my lip muscles.) Or June could be wrong because she heard all those lullabies before she had any other singing to compare them with, and so remembers them as perfectly fine when in fact they were, musically speaking, awful. Or I could be wrong about Dad's rendition of the National Anthem. Maybe my own shyness was the only thing wrong, and I felt his singing was terrible just because he was doing it. No way to be certain now.

I have only one memory of Dad singing solo. We were at the dinner table, and I think my grandfather, Robin Baxter Stiles, may have been living with us at that time and present at the table. I'm not sure if any other people outside the family were there. In any event, I do recall Dad, prompted by heaven knows what, bursting into a song which he rendered with great enthusiasm. The last two lines of the chorus were: "The fly flew up poor Billy's ass / and goosed poor Bill to death." My mother was scandalized to the point of reproving him in public (which was *not a woman's place*), and I recall clearly her "Oh, *Walter!!!*" You could hear every single letter in my Dad's name. I have no recollection of what, if anything, followed this outburst. June doesn't remember it happening, though my memory assures me she was there at the table.

I remember that - if I do, if I didn't hear it told of someone else, or read it somewhere and apply it to my own life - because it was one of the only pieces of evidence to support a fact that I learned - somehow, from someone now forgotten - that my Dad's nickname back in his younger days had been "Whoopie." Did someone tell me that? Who? Why? Did they explain to me that it was derived from "Making Whoopie," a clever and cynical song of the 1920s? I have no idea. I had a hard time for many years believing it had ever fit my deadly serious father.

Get the picture? Memory is not a photographic negative, faithfully recording whatever was in front of the lens when it opened. It is much more like a modern digital image, capable of being manipulated to show and mean damn near anything the manipulator wants it to show or mean. So when I say I'll try to tell you the truth, remember that the best I have to work with is the best version of the truth I can find.

That's why so much of this will be stuff I've written and sometimes gotten published over much of my lifetime. At least these essays and reports and rants are exactly what I wrote, and represent what I thought and believed when I wrote them - unless I was pretending to be someone I wasn't, such as an "objective" reporter. They're sort of like evidence. I'll be explaining what I was doing and what prompted me to write them, to the best of my recollection, and I've already said how reliable *that's* likely to be. Anyhow, here's the best I can do.

McCollum Family Tree
(as best I can figure it)

"The McCollum (MacCallum) clan has a small peninsula on the west coast of Scotland all to itself and a very complex coat-of-arms complete with 'Deus ex refigium' [probably should be 'refugium'] which means, 'We take refuge in God.' " [I'm pretty sure it could also mean "We take refuge *from* God."]

"Many of the McCollum clan were with the Scotch-Irish exodus into N. Ireland 1688-1715. After 1740 they began to migrate to America. Over a 50 year period they arrived in Pennsylvania, Delaware and South Carolina and New Jersey."

1. David McCollum (born January, 1755, in Ireland), served as a private in the 1st Battalion, 1st Regiment of New Jersey troops during the Revolutionary War. Lived in Pennsylvania, married Lucy Cook.

2. Samuel McCollum (born 1775). In 1810, moved to Ohio. Married Nancy [Ringland?].

3. David McCollum (born 1800-1805, died 1880[?]) Married Elizabeth Powell. Married (second marriage) Margaret Robinault in 1844 in McHenry County, Illinois.

4. Aura Washington McCollum (born June 13, 1837, McHenry County, Ill., died June 13, 1912). Married Rebecca Still, July 29, 1859, in McHenry County.

5. Emerson Grant McCollum (born May 5, 1864, McHenry County, died October 28, 1918, in Crystal Lake, Illinois.) 3 Children: Grant Emerson (8/25/92 - 5/7/56), Walter Holmes (2/9/95 - 6/28/1972), Helen Rebecca (9/6/1900 - 1988)

6. Walter Holmes McCollum. (Married Ella Rosenthal, who died young. Married Edith Virginia Stiles, September 16, 1937)
June Mavis McCollum was born July 1, 1937
Malcolm Stiles McCollum was born May 28, 1942, both in Evanston, Illinois
[McCollum and McCollum]

7. Malcolm Stiles McCollum. (Married Elaine Jean Struthers, July 1, 1982, Colorado Springs.)

8. Thelonika China Lee McCollum (born July 5, 1982, Colorado Springs, CO)
    9. Lestat Arnold (born April 28, 2004, Las Cruces, NM)
    10. Magdalena Rose McCollum (born February 9, 2008, Bellingham, WA)
    11. Zeppelin (born November 14, 2010, Las Cruces, NM)
    12. Emberleigh (born September 12, 2013, Las Cruces, NM)

As you can see, starting with the second David McCollum, the Scotch-Irish McCollums were the pioneering side of the family, following the frontier first to Ohio, then to McHenry County (northeast of Chicago) in Illinois, where they established themselves. MacCallum Lake in McHenry County is named for one of them. I have so far found no other claims to fame for any of these McCollums.

(There is, however, one member of the McCollum clan who has a claim to history.
Vashti Cromwell McCollum ((1912 - 2006)) was the plaintiff in the Supreme Court case that, in 1948, struck down religious education in the public schools. Though she became a McCollum by marriage, her story is worth reading:

"Vashti Ruth Cromwell, named for the queen of Ahasuerus in the first book of Esther, who was one of the few biblical women to stand up for women's rights, was born in Lyons, New York, on November 6, 1912, to Arthur G. and Ruth C. Cromwell. She was raised in Rochester, New York, and after graduation from a public high school, attended Cornell University on a full tuition scholarship until the market crash of 1929. Transferring to the University of Illinois, she eventually obtained her A.B. in the College of Liberal Arts and Sciences in 1944 and, after interruptions for marriage and children, an M.S. in Mass Communications in 1957.

"After arriving in Champaign-Urbana to attend the University of Illinois, she met Dr. John P. McCollum, a staff member, whom she married in 1933. Their three sons all graduated from college with at least one degree. James Terry, the oldest, went on to obtain a J.D. and practiced law in Rochester, New York, for 33 years until his retirement in 1994. Daniel obtained an M.S. in history and has served for several terms as mayor of Champaign, Illinois. Errol Cromwell, after obtaining his B.S. in mechanical engineering, eventually established a chain of bicycle stores, along with a partner, and was actively engaged in that enterprise until his retirement in 1996.

"Vashti lived up to her namesake when she and her oldest son, Jim, were confronted with pressure to enroll him in a Christian Sunday School class being offered in the public schools of Champaign during school hours. Resisting the pressure at first, she and her husband eventually relented and allowed Jim to attend the classes throughout the balance of his fourth grade year. However, the following year, the McCollums, feeling that such a program was totally inappropriate in the public schools, refused further participation. This, of course, resulted in Jim's ostracism by his peers and the suffering of some indignities at the hands of his unenlightened fifth grade teacher.

"After unrequited attempts to have the program discontinued administratively and after much soul searching, with the aid and support of the Rev. Phillip Schug, the Unitarian minister in town, and with financial assistance from a group of Jewish businessmen in Chicago, Vashti filed a writ of mandamus in the Champaign County Circuit Court in the late summer of 1945. At this point things really became difficult for the McCollums, ranging from physical confrontations between Jim and his peers, to vandalism of their home, to attempts at terminating Prof. McCollum's employment at the university. Fortunately for Dr. McCollum, his tenured status secured his position with the university. However, Vashti's employment as an adjunct instructor in the women's physical education program was terminated.

"The three-judge panel, sitting to hear the case in the Circuit Court, decided that, in spite of the clear language in the Illinois constitution to the contrary, the practice violated neither it nor the establishment of religion clause of the 1st Amendment of the U.S. Constitution. The Illinois Supreme Court agreed with the lower court and the case was appealed to the U.S. Supreme Court, which granted certiorari in the fall of 1947. On 9 March 1948, the US Supreme Court handed down its landmark decision in the People of the State of Illinois, *ex rel* McCollum -v- Board of Education, 333 US 203 (1948), a decision written by Justice Hugo L. Black, that was to become a landmark case in U.S. constitutional law. The significance of the decision was that it was the first case of impression that held the states accountable to the strictures of the "establishment of religion" clause of the 1st Amendment of the U.S. Constitution under the aegis of the due process clause of the 14th Amendment. All cases, involving school prayers, aid to parochial schools, sectarian religious displays on public property, and other such incursions into Jefferson's wall of "separation of church and state" by the states and their municipalities, descend from this case.

"As in any such case and particularly in this one, because of the McCarthyistic mood of the late 40's and 50's—when Communism was considered the scourge of humanity and atheists were considered by many as either Communists or fellow travelers—this case took its toll on Mrs. McCollum and her family. However, she was resolute, as was her namesake in the Bible, and persisted, despite disappointing losses in the lower courts, until she finally triumphed with her decisive 8 to 1 victory in the high court. For the results of this case alone, if not for her courage and perseverance, she deserves recognition in the annals of U.S. constitutional law." [Murfin]

As you'll see also in the entry in the Stiles family on my great-grandfather Israel Newton Stiles, I seem to have derived my distaste for the Self-styled religious trying to push their views on everyone from both sides of the family.

In general, I think it's reasonable to assume that, until my Dad became an Executive, we come from a family of working people on his side - pioneers and farmers and perhaps some shopkeepers. And though Dad wore a white collar and a suit when I knew him, as I say elsewhere in this, he felt far more comfortable working with his hands, and he certainly tried to impart the values of working people to his kids: work hard, do the job right the first time, and don't complain about having to work - it's what people are supposed to do. And though I've never done factory or farm work, I've pretty much lived according to those values.

The Stiles Family

The Stiles family originated in Milbroke, Bedfordshire, England. Four Stiles brothers and a sister (Henry, John, Francis, Thomas and Joan) sailed on the *Christian* and arrived in Connecticut in 1635. According to a later descendant, Ezra Stiles, they fled "from the Tyranny and Persecution of Charles the First and Archbishop Laud" for "the free Exercise of Pure Religion." They remained, after strife with the Massachusetts Bay Colony over their intended site. One of them, probably John, is the originator of our branch of the Stiles family. Damn if I can figure out quite how or when, but maybe you can from the source at the end of this. The notes in brackets refer to this work's codes and page numbers. The first in the line I feel sure of is:

1. Ephraim Stiles (c. 1660 - c. 1755), Springfield, Mass. [*Family* 4, p. 88]
    married Abigail Neal

2. Isaac Stiles (1696 - 1790), Westfield, Conn. [*Family* 10, p.129]
    married Mary Brooks (cousin)

3. Israel Stiles (1731 - c. 1780), Westfield, Mass.   [*Family* 18, p. 130]
    married Dorcas White

4. Israel Stiles (1778 - 1868)   [*Family* 32, p.265]
    married Dorcas Hastings

5. Anson Stiles (1805 - 1872), Suffield, Conn.   [*Family* 65, p.265]
    married Elvira Allen

6. Israel Newton Stiles (1833 - 1895)   [*Family* 119, p. 358]
    married Jenny Coney
    children: Theodosia (1862)
        Harry Bacon (1866)
        Robin Baxter (1868 - 1957)

7. Robin Baxter Stiles (1868 -
    married Augusta Swan
        Alan Stiles
        Harry Stiles
        Helen Stiles
        Marian Stiles
        Jeanette Stiles
        Edith Virginia Stiles

[Stiles, M.D.]

When the Stiles family came to this country in 1635, Francis was serving as the agent-in-charge for Sir Richard Saltonstall (a name that became famous in American history later on) in his attempt to establish a new base in America. They established themselves in New England (Ezra, son of Ephraim, became the first President of Yale University), and tended to be ministers, scholars and other sorts of "professional," as distinct from "working" people. The family remained in New England until 1852, when Israel Newton Stiles moved to Lafayette County, Indiana, where he became a lawyer.

He was a strong supporter of the abolition of slavery, and when the Civil War broke out, he "entered the army as a private, May 1861, in the Twentieth Indiana Volunteer Infantry; become Lieutenant, Major, Lieutenant Colonel, Colonel; and was made Brevet Brigadier General, for gallantry at the battle of Franklin, Tenn., Nov. 30, 1864; was in very many important battles; was a prisoner in the Libby Prison for two months; was wounded at Resacca, and served continuously until the close of the war, when he removed to Chicago, and entered the practice of law."

To this account from *The Stiles Family in America,* should be added these observations by his final law partner, John Lewis, on the occasion of his death: "To this account it may be added that General Stiles was taken prisoner at Malvern Hill and was confined for six weeks in Libby prison; also that during the war he contracted a disease from which he was never afterwards free for a single day, and which ultimately, according to the opinion of his family physician, was the cause of his blindness, his mental degeneration, and his early death."

"He was City Attorney, 1869- 73; President of the Chicago Bar Association, 1880; is still in full practice and has much prominence as a lawyer and public speaker....Gen. Stiles has read several papers before the Chicago Philosophical Society, some of which have been printed, viz.: "Human Life," (1873); "Doubt," (1874); "The Utility of Morals," (1875); " Politics," (1876); " The Genesis of the Belief in the Immortality of the Soul, (1877); "Inspiration," (1877); "The Growing Power of Monopolies," (1880)."

"He has been twice married, (1) Oct. 31, 1860, to Jenny Coney, born at Sag Harbor, N. Y., 1837), who died at Chicago, , April 18, 1877. She was a woman of rare intelligence and superior culture, and in common with her husband was a free thinker, and gloried in being so, and up to the hour of her death, and knowing that she was about to pass away, she remained firm in her convictions. Her early life was devoted to teaching music, an accomplishment in which she excelled. In the Fall of 1860 she was married in Lafayette, Ind., and in the following Winter, accompanied her husband to the war. She was present at two battles, and in one of them a shell burst only a few feet from her. She was not only an accomplished musician, but a fine linguist, and was ardently devoted to literary pursuits. She belonged to a literary society called the "Athenea," of which she was at one time President." [Stiles, M.D.]

Israel Newton Stiles was a good friend of Robert G. Ingersoll, during those days a nationally famous attorney, writer, lecturer, and a militant agnostic, of whom Mark

Twain wrote, "I have known him twenty years and was fond of him, and held him in as high honour as I have held any man living or dead." [quoted in *Colonel Bob Ingersoll,* by Cameron Rogers, Doubleday, Page & Company, 1927] Part of your inheritance will be a copy of *Ingersoll's Lectures*, published in 1874 and inscribed by Ingersoll, "Hon I N Stiles - a man who says what he thinks, and thinks before he says it - from his friend R.G. Ingersoll, Peoria, July 22nd, 1874." This paragraph from the lecture "The Gods" gives a good sense of Ingersoll's position:

"While utterly discarding all creeds, and denying the truth of all religions, there is neither in my heart nor upon my lips a sneer for the hopeful, loving and tender souls who believe that from all this discord will result a perfect harmony; that every evil will in some mysterious way become a good, and that above and over all there is a being who, in some way, will reclaim and glorify every one of the children of men; but for the creeds of those who glibly prove that salvation is almost impossible; that damnation is almost certain; that the highway of the universe leads to hell; who fill life with fear and death with horror; who curse the cradle and mock the tomb, it is impossible to entertain other than feelings of pity, contempt and scorn." [Ingersoll]

So, like the great American writer Kurt Vonnegut, you're descended on the McCollum-Stiles side from two families of Free Thinkers who believed our Constitution meant what it said, and were willing to put themselves on the line for that belief. I've tried to live up to that heritage, and I hope you will too.

The Chain of Cashel

Neither of my parents, so far as I could ever figure out, was "religious" in a conventional sense. They didn't go to church and they didn't push whatever their beliefs were on anyone else. My mother had a long, deep interest in what's usually called "spiritualism," including extra-sensory perception. I don't think I ever heard Dad mention God except as part of his frequently uttered "god damn this or that." Nevertheless, they made sure that June and I attended the Presbyterian Sunday School in the church not far from our house on Thayer Street.

I have no memories of that experience whatsoever, though I attended the Sunday School for at least 3 years. It must have involved a great deal of Bible study, since I still have a head full of Bible verses. I'm grateful for that, since the Bible informs so much of American and European culture and history and thinking. It is a good thing to know something about the Bible. You know what people are referring to if you know the Bible. You also know that the Bible can be selectively quoted to authorize any behavior, no matter how atrocious.

The Presbyterian Church takes a severe outlook on life, though I don't recall much severity in the Sunday School. I must have picked up some of it, I imagine. It accorded well with the general Midwestern view of life that Dad's family, in particular, held: Murphy's Law ("If anything can go wrong, it will") ruled the cosmos, and the wise never got too high, since whatever good thing might happen was likely to turn out to be a bad thing. The highest words of praise I ever heard Dad utter were, "Not bad." I didn't hear him utter them very often. All in all, I was surrounded by a pessimistic view of life, and I've remained inclined in that direction. I don't view that as an unmixed curse, but I know it's been hard on a lot of people around me.

The doctrines of the Calvinists, which were pretty much adopted by the Presbyterian Church, included the Total Depravity of Man. We are all sinners, on account of we are all descended from Adam and Eve, and look how they did. Only some folks get "saved" from the torments of hell, and those folks, known as "the Saints," were picked out by God before He started everything up. And *nobody knows* who the

Saints *are.* You find out when you die, and either get sent to Eternal Torment or Heaven. There's nothing you can do to change your destiny, either. Be as good as ever you want, you may still be going to hell. That was pretty much the set of beliefs my folks sent me to learn.

This seems like a pretty bleak view of God and life, with God portrayed as the Owner and Operator of a rigged game, in which neither suffering nor virtue plays any part in determining the winners and losers. But the Calvinists, and the Presbyterians and Puritans who descended from them and largely populated this country during its early years, found *a catch.* Why, they reasoned, should God, who predetermined everything that happens on this earth (and everywhere else), have given some people material success *if they weren't Saints*? So material success became a pretty reliable sign that not only were you successful here in this life, but that you'd be making it to Heaven, as well.

I think it is this equation between salvation from eternal torment and being favored by God with material success that accounts for the strangeness of our thinking in this country to this day.

John D. Rockefeller, a pirate and a thug, was able to say, I'm sure quite sincerely, "God gave me my money." A common saying all during my life has been, "If you're so smart, why aren't you rich?" Preparing to steal some more Indian land, "...a town meeting at Milford, Connecticut, in 1640 'Voted, that the earth is the Lord's and the fulness thereof; voted, that the earth is given to the Saints; voted, that we are the Saints.'" [Willison] In America, the rich are not only rich, they are self-righteously rich. The poor in this country- most of us, during most of our history and every other country's - embrace that self-righteous certainty that the Successful are God's chosen, so they must be in the right. I write this in January, 2009, surrounded by overwhelming evidence that the propaganda of the Successful, not to mention their business practices, common sense, and ethics, have been disastrous for most of us. And yet there seems to be little public anger that the Successful, as they've brought on chaos, remain fat, happy and self-righteous.

Well. I seem to have veered. I was most certainly not thinking about any of those things as 6th grade ended and my parents released me from mandatory Sunday School. I think their principle was that I'd had sufficient exposure to the officially correct religion, and that whatever I decided about it was up to me. I don't know that that's how they thought of it, but that was how they behaved, and I am forever grateful that they did so. I think the Establishment clause in the 1st Amendment to our Constitution pretty clearly states that religion is a private matter: "Congress shall make no law respecting an establishment of religion, or prohibiting the free exercise thereof." My parents let me see what "religion" as they knew it had to offer, and then let me make of it what I might.

I didn't think much about it one way or the other, except that I no longer had to go to Sunday school. I was thinking I could sleep in on Sundays. (Dad soon cured me of that delusion.) I was also starting to think a lot about girls. In my thoughts, they were skimpily dressed, if dressed at all.

In my second year of Junior High, one of my close friends Bill Rood got sucked into a "Bible Church" that met Sundays in our former grade school and conducted Wednesday night prayer meetings at another school. The Bible Church was one of innumerable offshoots of the Methodist Church. It was comprised of the most negative set of people I've ever met, including the bikers I later lived around and came to know. They defined themselves like this: We are Good Christians because we *don't* : drink, smoke, cuss, dance, fornicate, etc., etc. We don't do nothing anyone else do.

Bill talked me into going to church with him, and rather quickly I was imbued with the idea of getting "saved." That happened, I think, for two main reasons. For one, many kids just before or in their early teens get swept up by religious hysteria. For the other, the pastor of this church was a young guy named Dick Longnecker who was a handsome, big, athletic and very kindly man, just the kind of role model/hero a kid my age was looking for. So I tried like hell to buy the T-Shirt, to "accept Christ as my personal savior." I went so far as to get myself re-baptized - dunked, in fact, in a big metal washtub on a stage somewhere. I tried very hard to feel the effects of this dunking, to feel that I had been transformed, or at least changed.

But at Wednesday night prayer meeting I kept finding myself staking out the seat behind the pastor's wife. She was a beautiful young woman, and she had some of the most perfect legs in the history of Creation. (I realize that that is a "sexist" remark. Most 13 year old boys are, I'm afraid, hopeless, incurable sexists. They are, in fact, permanently insane with lust. They stay that way for quite a number of years. In my case, for about 70.) When we prayed at Wednesday night prayer meeting, we slid forward from our folding chairs to kneel on the floor. Seated behind the pastor's wife, I found myself unable to avoid looking at her legs, with a degree of focused concentration that left nothing over, really, for prayer, God, or anything else. What could exceed those legs in perfection?

While I'd like to say that I saw my own hypocrisy and concluded that my new baptism and "faith" were not performing as advertised to keep me virtuous, the truth is that I just decided, eventually, that women and whisky and cigarettes were a lot more in my line. I'm further ashamed to say that I didn't have the guts to simply say that, at least to myself. Instead, I pinned my rejection of the Bible Church on the poor Chinese, who hadn't done anything to me. Ever more eager for a way to bow out, I finally hit upon a question for my Pastor: if the only way to get into heaven and avoid hell is to accept Jesus as your personal savior, how 'bout them Chinese? All those hundreds of millions of people who never got a chance to know that Jesus even existed? What becomes of them? My Pastor had no qualms or doubts: they were going to hell. "Tough noogies" seemed to be his attitude to that prospect. That gave me my out, since I couldn't find it in me to love a God who condemned vast hordes of people because they didn't do something they could not, in fact, do or have done. (Still can't.) But really, I just wanted to start sinning without wasting a lot of time pretending to repent.

That was the end of my career as a church-goer and as a Christian. I thought little about religion until I became a minister.

That happened in 1968 or 1969, when my first wife Nancy sent off to the Universal Life Church for a certificate of ministry for me. This was meant to be a joke (although I suspect she may have been trying to make me get more Serious about Life, as well). The Universal Life Church was created by an old pirate named Kirby J.

Hensley, and I'm pretty sure that his motive was at least half financial: he hated paying taxes. He had also noticed that churches didn't pay many sorts of taxes, and that that fact seemed to contradict the 1st Amendment quoted above. Or rather, he could *make* it seem to, by declaring himself a minister and his property a church. (Bingo! No more property taxes!) If the government wanted to come after him for taxes, he could simply wave the tax exemptions of established denominations in its face and then tell the Gummint that the 1st Amendment prevented it from deciding what was a religion and what wasn't. And it worked.

Kirby Hensley could see that he had a salable idea there, so he moved to the place where salable ideas regarding God go to prosper, Southern California. He started a newsletter, he started ordaining people by mail (without the need for any qualification whatsoever, except 20 bucks) and offering them detailed advice on how to form their own churches. During the height of the Vietnam War, the time at which I became a Holy Man, many people were looking for ways to avoid the draft, and some of them became Universal Life ministers as a way of bolstering their conscientious objector status. Business was good.

I had already done my Army time, and I didn't really want to avoid my fair share of taxes (which didn't amount to much, since I was making very little money). What appealed to me, as it turned out, was the fact that here was a church with *no doctrine*. If I saw all of life as a church - and that's the point of view I was by then approaching - then I could minister to people *whatever* they or I believed, wherever we came together.

By the time I got "ordained," I had already had some experiences of other realities than the one we tell ourselves and each other we live in. The first occurred during (I think) my 7th summer, in the year my grandmother Augusta died. This brought the reality of death to me for the first time. That was also the summer rats got in under our back porch, an infestation that drove Mom about crazy with fear and loathing. All that somehow came together to inspire me to imagine my own death. My concept of death - and I have no idea how I arrived at it - was that it meant, simply, "not being." Every night, all summer long, I lay in bed trying to imagine myself in that state. I got very good at it. As I recall, my method was to imagine myself getting younger and younger, getting unborn, and then being in a state of not-being. And as I recall, that state was rather like being part of an electrical field. It scared the bejesus out of me, but I was compelled to make the trip night after night, until it began to scare me less and less. It seems a strange thing for a boy that age to be up to, but maybe many kids privately go through similar experiences. I certainly never talked to anyone about it.

Much later, while attending Northwestern, I walked around with pneumonia for a week or so, and one night lying in bed I rose up out of my body on what felt to be a huge bird's back, rose up over the house and on up into the stratosphere, looking down at the earth as it receded, until I could see the whole Western half of the continent spread out below me. I felt, during whatever time that took, flooded through with love for the earth I seemed to be leaving.

The experience had some factors in common with those reported by people who've officially died and then come back to life, though none of their accounts I've read ever mentioned any big birds. So maybe I died briefly. Or maybe it was just a fever dream. All I can tell you is that it seemed to me as real as anything "real" I'd ever experienced, or ever have since.

I took another trip up out of here later, under the influence of Thai stick, standing in a forest in South Dakota in the black of night. That time, I rose up right on into the constellations, and very briefly visited a planet, or a place, or something, where Jesus lived. We exchanged brief, friendly greetings and he told me to get back where I belonged. I remember slowly coming back into my body, which was standing there in the dark waiting for me, and, as I re-entered that body, feeling the weight of the atmosphere and gravity pressing on me. (We carry around 32 pounds per square inch of that stuff all the time, but we're used to it.) This experience also seemed "real," and still does.

In my early 30s, after I'd been studying on zen buddhism for a couple of years, I believe I attained what the zen masters call "satori," a kind of illumination of the Big Everything. The feeling was very like what I'd experienced during my boyhood travels to

Not-Being. Perhaps it's what Christians experience when they experience Salvation. I had been pondering on the question, Where do jokes come from?

For some reason, this question has always fascinated me. Here's a joke I got from Dave Dillon:

So this guy whose wife is pretty difficult to get along with decides one year, I'll get her a really unusual birthday present... maybe that'll get her off my case for a couple of days. He goes down to Main Street, wanders around window shopping. Nothing leaps out at him. He gets to the last store on Main Street, a pet store. He knows his wife hates animals, but on the other hand it's the last store. He looks in the window. Here's this astonishing bird, every color of the rainbow. He slides in the front door just as the owner's turning the "Open" sign around.

"Mister, what's that beautiful bird in the window?"

"Oh, that," the owner says. "That's a Crunch Bird. Only found in Tierra del Fuego. Very rare."

"A *Crunch Bird*? What the hell kind of a name is that?"

Owner says, "Watch this." He picks up a big Nylabone, the Great Dane model, flips open the birdcage door, tosses it in. "Crunch bird," he says: "Bone."

There's a prolonged blur in the cage, is all the guy can see, and a sort of buzzing shriek, like a wood-chipper on methedrine. In about ten seconds, the Crunch Bird is sitting back on his perch, and there isn't even a shred of the Nylabone left to be seen.

"Holy Toledo," the guy says. "I never saw anything like *that*."

"Hey," the owner says, "all you gotta do is say his name and the name of whatever you want him to rip up... and he'll *rip* it."

"Man. My wife hasn't ever seen anything like this baby. I'll take it."

He pays the exorbitant price for the bird, puts it in his back seat, heads home, feeling like maybe he'll prove to have done something right for once. Pulls in the driveway, actually knocks on his own front door, holding the cage behind his back.

Wife opens the door. With a grandiose "Hap-py Birthday, Sweetie!" the guy sweeps the cage around in front of him and presents it to his wife. She stands there looking at the cage in her hands.

"What in the hell is this?" she says.

"Honey... this is a Crunch Bird."

"Crunch Bird!" she says. "Crunch Bird? Crunch Bird, my ass."

This joke may or may not seem funny to you. Our senses of humor may be the most individual pieces of our characters. The funny thing about this joke to me, I guess, is the operation of poetic justice in the punch line. But what I like to ask is, "Who made this up? Inspired by *what*?"

I'd asked my friend Mark Miller where jokes came from, and he'd said, "That's easy - just reason back from the punch line." That answer came back to me as I pondered, and suddenly I understood everything and was in a place where time had stopped, in the sort of glowing mist you sometimes see at dawn, a place that wasn't so much filled with light as it *was* light. All cares gone, all gravity gone. After enjoying this place for some stretch of time, I was presented with a question. Didn't hear any voice ask it, it just appeared in my emptied consciousness: Stay here, or go back? And my answer appeared as soundlessly: Go back. You're not done yet with what you have to do on earth. So I somewhat reluctantly came back.

I know, I know, I know. All sorts of ways to "account" for experiences like these. What they added up to, to me, was as close to a certainty as I ever expect to feel that another realm than the one we call "reality" does exist, that this world, this "real" world, is a miracle without which we wouldn't exist, and that laughter is as close as we can come to living in that other realm. Later on, I found that music came from that realm, when I had the very occasional experience of playing the guitar until I was no longer playing, but being played by the music, playing things I had no idea how to play. Old William Wordsworth called these kinds of experiences "intimations of immortality." Lots of scientists would probably call them "chemical reaction formations" or something like that. Pick your choice.

I don't know. Here's a crushingly common cliché for you: the more I learn, the less I'm sure of. Last couple of years, I've been reading a lot about the cosmos, the Big Bang, the dimensions of eternity, the ways in which nebulae are born and stars die. All that jazz. I've been an agnostic for a long time, but, man, if you want to be humbled, try cosmology on for size. More than ever, I'm convinced that we have no possible way of understanding what's going on in the universe. We're little midges, dancing briefly over the river's flow and shine. One of my favorite writers, H. Allen Smith, expressed it best:

"I have no religion, unless you consider agnosticism to be a religion. *I do not know.* That is all. *I do not know* as passionately as Bishop Sheen and Billy Graham and Norman Vincent Peale say that they *do know.* I have a strong suspicion that there is no such creature as an angel, but *I do not know* because I have no evidence. I can't place any reliance on the substance of things hoped for, the evidence of things not seen. I think that there are miracles but that they are not wrought in heaven. I have seen miracles. I have seen a miracle in which three ballplayers executed a double play, but prayer had nothing to do with it and the Holy Ghost was not in the dugout." [Smith]

I've wrestled with belief in some of my poems, and here are three of them.

The Chain of Cashel

Behind the motel where I will sleep tonight,
flanked by the ceaseless, dull doppler of two highways,
a small swale cradles a stagnant pond,
brackish and mud-brown in the pewter evening,
edged by a mess of winter-wheatened cattails.

On their shaggy, balding crowns, three dozen
redwinged blackbirds rest, easily
balanced on the yard-high stalks,
and in the acid rain of tires sing.

With what variety - long rattles, as from fat,
feathered crickets; brief chirks like finches',
but more authoritative; two-note melodic phrases.

A long, communal concerto, discussing
territories, mates, and who knows what else.

Every minute or so, another blackbird appears
from the grey clouds, wheels with impossible economy
down to a perfect, bounceless landing
on a barely budded twig in the poplar that stands
above the swale, and there joins an intricate dance
from higher twig to lower and around again -
all this with no air traffic controller
tense at the mike before his glowing green screen.

The blackbirds in the cattails keep the music
going for the dance, seldom moving unless to rise
into a tight circle and return to the original perch,
as a trumpeter might shift to surreptitiously
shake his spit valve clean.

No. Not a concerto, not a sonata,
no beginning - middle - end business -
not even a suite, even if it does
accompany a set of dances. These redwinged blackbirds,
truer black than ravens, and that black
blacker yet in the yellow-bordered scarlet
light the slashes on their epaulets provide,
these redwinged blackbirds sing about
no human dance, sing in no human form.

If I were less agnostic, I would say they sing
the song of God, the circle song,

whose beginning swallows its end

like the chain of Cashel.

I will say that anyway.

Our Big Brains

"But now her own big brain was urging her to take the polyethylene garment bag from around a red evening dress in her closet there in Guayaquil, and to wrap it around her head, thus depriving her cells of oxygen." - Kurt Vonnegut, *Galapagos*

The truth is,

I'll never have time

to completely appreciate one

of the hundreds of great musicians

who've saved and enriched me,

from Handel to Paolo Conte,

or to assist one other person

to hear the little I have heard.

No one has time

to hear all that's to be heard

to see what's to be seen

smell what's to be smelt

taste all the tastes or

feel what each second should be felt.

The truth is,

every damn one of us

is nothing but a little amoeba

with legs and arms and thumbs

and a great big brain,

circling around a random pebble

on the deep bottom of a great ocean,
while up on land Triceratops plows along,
sublimely unaware
of our piddling existence.

The truth is,
the truth is bigger than Triceratops,
bigger than the oceans ten times
ten times themselves,
bigger than 8 turned sideways.
The truth is,
not one of us, get busy as busy
we can, can ever know
what the truth is.
Are you humbled yet?
Are you humbled yet?

Sparks from the Campfire

My old friend Price Strobridge
might begin like this:

If the observable universe
is 15 billion years old,
and I am 65,
then I have been around
433 whatever comes after a billionth
of the time the universe
has been around.

As far as the universe is concerned,
I'm not even thought of yet.

If the observable universe
is 278 million light years around,
and if nobody anywhere knows much of anything
about the *un*observable universe,
which is *most* of the universe,
and I stand 5 foot 8
and a half -
I won't bother to figure that percentage,
how big I am.

Go ask some amoeba
to explain the infield fly rule.
You wouldn't shame a poor amoeba
like that, would you?

And yet we little human rudiments argue ceaselessly
over gods and their purposes and rankings.
And yet we kill and kill
in the names of abstractions no one comprehends.
I can't comprehend the infield fly rule,
let alone how anything much
around me or even within me works,
never mind the nature or the will of God,
if that's who made all this trouble and miracle.

Not quite in time for this year's Christmas,
in the Chester Zoo in Chester, England,

Flora the komodo dragon

indulged in parthenogenesis.

Calling all amoeba:

should we declare a second Christmas holiday?

The amoebas won't say. It's too much for them,

a virgin birth,

brought about by the model for Godzilla.

But what astonishes me

most dependably

is the ever-expanding magnitude of my ignorance

in the face of the galaxies and clusters and quasars,

in the faceless face of the amoeba.

What's a virgin birth or two?

You could spend an excellent lifetime

watching how cats live in their muscles,

or the complete, unaffected strut

of a crow, or the ever-changing changelessness

of one stretch of one river.

You'll never get it all,

but you'll get enough to pass on some

to your fellow travelers,

your fellow snowflakes,

your fellow sparks from the campfire.

_____

  Over the years, I've had a lot of arguments with people who claim they know the truth, and there's only one truth and one set of words to put it in, and who claim that the morality they derive from that truth is the only true morality and that they have the right to enforce that morality on anyone and everyone else. Here are a couple of those arguments.

Straight Pride

Press coverage of this year's gay pride parade got Ed Bircham so upset that he bought an ad to express his outrage. The ad appeared in the very newspaper whose coverage it criticized, a paper in which Mr. Bircham advertises copiously and regularly. It's hard to believe such an ad didn't carry a message to the paper's editor as well as to the general public, the message being, "Quit publicizing people I despise, or I'll find another outlet for my advertising dollars."

I think gays have good reason to stand up and say what they have to say, which is that they're human beings who deserve as much respect and equal treatment as straights. For a long time in this town, they didn't have to demonstrate to make that point. This used to be a city where you got to be whoever you wanted to be, as long as you didn't try to sell your particular enthusiasms to others without being asked, or commit major felonies.

When I was seventeen, a high school English teacher made a pass at me. He was a man I admired and learned from, and I had ignored the gossip and vicious jokes about him until he presented me with an unmistakable proposal.

Had I been tempted by this proposal, I could claim credit for resisting that temptation. I've never been very good at resisting temptation, and I can use all the morality points I can scrape up.

Rather than temptation, I felt embarrassment and sadness and a strong desire to be somewhere else. I had no inclination to go along with the teacher's proposal, no curiosity about what the experience he proposed would be like. I felt like someone being offered caviar who could not see it as anything but fish eggs. I was terminally heterosexual. That was what I learned from that teacher, though I learned many other things from him that have been much more useful and important.

I think what that teacher did was wrong for two reasons: one, I was a kid; two, I was a student of his. People with experience and power have no business offering sex to those who have neither. I also think it would have been just as wrong if that teacher had been a woman. The abuse of power would have been the same.

I've thought about this incident because I've been listening to the crusaders against homosexuality in this town for quite a few years now. They seem to regard homosexuality as a "lifestyle" -- that is, as a matter of choice, like collecting stamps rather than baseball cards, or becoming a driver of monster trucks rather than an orchid gardener. They seem to believe that homosexuals have gravely considered their options, and decided that, all in all, they'd prefer to be gay.

If that were the case, then it would mean that heterosexuals had necessarily gone through the same process of choice, but, after agonizing over the tempting alternatives, had come down on the "right" side. If being gay is a matter of choice, so must be being straight.

My own experience is so contrary to this view that I want to issue a challenge to Mr. Bircham, Mr. Perkins, Mr. Dobson, Mr. Tebedo, and to any others of their persuasion. Tell us, sirs, about your own encounters with homosexual temptation, and about how you were able to resist. Your accounts of these personal dramas would be of inestimable value as inspiration, and would strongly support your point of view.

If, on the other hand, you've never experienced the "temptation" of homosexuality, then maybe you should quiet down for a while and consider what it would be like if your own sexual orientation were subject to public scorn and ridicule and hatred. How would you react to that state of affairs, gentlemen?

I've offered my own little story only after long consideration, because I don't believe my sexual preferences are anyone's business, unless I should choose to try to impose them on someone in no position to resist me. I can't imagine marching in a parade for straight pride. What's to be proud of? It would be like shooting off fireworks because I have grey hair. And why would such a parade need to happen? We straight people are in the majority. We don't need to demonstrate; we can just sit back and condemn anybody who differs from us.

If we straight people never imposed our sexual desires on anyone who didn't welcome our advances, if we never used our power, authority, money or physical strength to get what we wanted, then maybe we'd rate a self-congratulatory parade. Until that happy day, maybe we should all stop marching and pontificating and indulging our pridefulness, and concentrate on the difficult task of acting with kindness, restraint and compassion.

Ed Bircham was an office-supply dealer who used his newspaper ads to fulminate against communists, gays, and other minorities he didn't like. Will Perkins was a car dealer who led the fight against the supposed "gay agenda" for a time. Rev. James Dobson was the owner and operator of Focus on the Family, an immense business enterprise posing as a church. Kevin Tebedo was part of a family of insane people who infested my county, and still do. Will Perkins promptly responded to my piece in a letter to the editor of *The Independent*, the weekly newspaper that published it. I responded to his response thus:

Straight Pride, the Sequel: The Case of the Frolicsome Fruit Flies

Mr. Will Perkins responds to my recent "Straight Pride" by labeling me "a self-appointed guardian of free thought and pluralism" who "ignores inconvenient dissent" and is most likely ignorant of scientific research regarding genetics and homosexuality.

Heck, Will, I'm too old and beat up to appoint myself guardian of any such grand abstractions as free thought or pluralism. In fact, I didn't even know free thought needed a guardian. Did someone finally get around to repealing the 1st Amendment some time when I wasn't paying attention?

I'm not quite old or beat up enough, though, that I don't still recognize selective quotation when I see it, or detect the unforgettable scent of red herring when a whole herd of them swim in front of my nose.

Dean Hamer's research on a possible genetic trigger for homosexuality [one of the pieces of "scientific research" Perkins misrepresented in his letter] is ongoing, but his initial study found a significant correlation between five "markers" and homosexuality. The likelihood of the correlation he found occurring by chance is less than one per-cent. He has, indeed, pointed out that his study does not "prove" that homosexuality is genetically dictated; it only suggests that dna may play a fairly significant part in disposing some people toward homosexuality.

That 300 psychologists and psychiatrists in an organization whose purpose is to provide "therapy of homosexuality" consider "obligatory homosexuality a treatable disorder" is not exactly a staggering bulletin; if they *didn't* so consider it, they'd have to look for a new gig, wouldn't they? (In passing, Will, could you help me understand the phrase "obligatory homosexuality"? How can anything "obligatory" be "treatable"?)

Putting alleged lesbian by choice Donna Minkowitz aside for a moment, I must confess I've not read *Advocate* magazine, so I don't know what it might advocate. But I'm pretty sure its readers don't know much more about what makes people straight or gay or combo than Dean Hamer does, or I do, or you do, Will.

But while we're on the subject of scientific research, here's one for you: surely you're familiar with the shocking behavior of the fruit flies injected with a "single gene" by biologists Ward Odenwald and Shang-Ding Zhang. In case you missed this study, I can tell you that the male fruit flies injected with this certain "single gene" promptly renounced all interest (which up to that point had always bordered on obsessive) in the female fruit flies in their jar, and took up with each other instead.

Of course, when these devilish scientists removed all but one male from the environment, darned if the male didn't take up with the females around him, and start writing them little notes and buying them banana sundaes.

The little research that's been done on genetics and sexual disposition has been summed up best by a writer for *Time* magazine: "In fruit flies, and certainly in humans, sexual orientation is just not a simple matter."

In other words, Donna Minkowitz may well have "chosen" homosexuality, but maybe she did so unaware of genetic configurations that pushed her in that direction. Or maybe she didn't. Maybe she just decided to pursue what seemed to her to be happiness.

The reason I call all this scientific stuff red herring, Will, is that anytime a bunch of experiments testing a postulate produce the kind of mixed results the genetic experiments have so far produced, you can usually assume the wrong question is being asked.

Why would anyone ask what causes homosexual behavior, unless it was assumed that homosexual behavior was undesirable? Are you aware of any genetic research going on that investigates the cause of noble behavior? Of excessive patience? Of patriotism? Of heterosexuality?

A generally accepted estimate of homosexuality in America places the number of homosexuals between 2 and 5 per-cent. Here are a few other statistics. One woman is raped or threatened with rape every 1.6 minutes in this, our native land. One out of three American girls is sexually abused before she reaches the age of 18.

Those rapes and sexual abuses are performed, for the most part, by heterosexual males, quite frequently within the families whose values you claim to defend and champion, Will. One out three equals 33%. Seems like a bigger problem than the fact that 5% of the American people are gay or lesbian.

But you seem unable to let go of this homosexual obsession. I can't figure out why you can't find more serious problems to which to devote your time and energy. Whatever direction its muzzle points, sexual desire is big dynamite, and limiting its targets to consenting adults seems to be something we Americans aren't very good at. Doesn't that seem like a more serious problem to you, Will?

That response, of course, didn't get printed, and so the pseudo-scientific bushwa that Perkins cobbled together was what the readers of that exchange were left with. That's how it goes in the letters-to-the-editor business.

Here's another response to a newspaper piece, in this case an interview with an assistant pastor at the very influential mega-church called New Life Church:

Pastor Rob and Pastor Ted

Rob Brendle, Associate Pastor at the New Life Church, makes for interesting reading. In his conversation with Noel Black (*Toiletpaper #6)*, he presents himself as a Jeffersonian advocate of free speech and a free press: ("I believe in the First Amendment"), of the "safe, cordial, government-protected playing field of public discourse," as a respecter "of the freedom of [his] ideological adversary." He also makes strong statements in favor of the separation of church and state: "...the importance of distinguishing between moral or religious law and civil law," asserting that, for example, "...it is a fundamental mistake to make sexuality between consenting adults a matter of civil law." He even goes so far as to say that "...what science and history the Bible propounds is true, but [I] do not consider it an exhaustive text on either subject." To make his stand on the literal truth of the Bible clear, he states that the view that "more the ideas and less the exact wording of the Bible...is fully true" is "...closer to where I stand." In short, Pastor Brendle sounds like a tolerant gentleman with a sense of humor and a willingness to consider any argument on its merits. I hope that this impression is correct, but if it is, I am at a loss to understand how he can remain a representative of the New Life Church.

Coincidental with the Pastor's appearance in *Toiletpaper*, Pastor Ted Haggard and a number of members of New Life Church were interviewed by Jeff Sharlet, contributing editor of *Harper's* magazine. A startlingly different picture of Pastor Brendle's church emerges from these interviews.

The bookstore housed in the New Life Prayer Center was originally called "The Arsenal" (since changed to "Solomon's Porch"). The Global Harvest ministry housed there is dedicated to "spiritual warfare." According to Sharlet, "The Prayer Center's nickname in the fundamentalist world is "spiritual NORAD."

A young man who plays piano at the church views the city which houses him as "...a battleground between good and evil.... "I'm a warrior, dude," he continues. "I'm a warrior for God. Colorado Springs is my training ground.'"

Pastor Haggard clearly sees his church as a "church militant as well....he believes spiritual war requires a virile, worldly counterpart," Sharlet writes. "'I teach a strong ideology of the use of power, of military might, as a public service.' He is for preemptive war, because he believes the Bible's exhortations against sin set for us a preemptive paradigm, and he is for ferocious war, because 'the Bible's bloody. There's a lot about blood.'"

This "preemptive paradigm" extends to individual and family life. In a sermon preached on the occasion of his oldest son's marriage, Haggard is quoted as saying, "The Christian home is to be in a constant state of war. Massive warfare!"

Haggard has not directly contradicted any of the words attributed to him in Sharlet's article. Interviewed by the *Gazette*, Haggard said, "that parts of the story are unfair and misleading. But he also believes Sharlet was well-intentioned and, in a way, instructive." He did not say what "parts" were unfair or misleading.

The official New Life Church statement of faith appears on its web page. It appears to contradict Pastor Brendle's rather relaxed view of the literal truth of the Bible: "Holy Bible: The Holy Bible, and only the Bible, is the authoritative Word of God. It alone is the final authority for determining all doctrinal truths. In its original writing, the Bible is inspired, infallible and inerrant (see Prov. 30:5; Rom. 16:25,26; 2 Tim. 3:16; 2 Pet. 1:20,21)."

This is a rather more inflexible view of the literal truth of the Bible than Pastor Brendle's. "In its original writing" means - if it means anything - that it is "the words" which are "inspired, infallible and inerrant" - not, as Pastor Brendle says he believes, "more the ideas and less the exact wording." The New Life position is what used to be called "Fundamentalist," later "Bible-believing." Challenged on this point by Black, Brendle equivocates: "...undeniably people throughout Christian history have applied scriptural truth non-uniformly."

What emerges from the *Harper's* story on the New Life Church is a portrait of a religious-political movement ("Pastor Ted.... likes to say that his only disagreement with the President is automotive; Bush [Shrub, that is] drives a Ford pickup, whereas Pastor Ted loves his Chevy") that believes it knows the only truth there is, that its mission is to impose that truth on the rest of the world, starting with the United States, and that this mission is a "war."

The Pastor and many of his parishioners interviewed in Sharlet's story seem very fond of the idea of war, though Pastor Brendle carefully avoids any such metaphors. Spiritual warfare is the watchword of his church, of the National Association of Evangelicals of which his church is a member and of which his boss, Ted Haggard, is presiding officer, and of the National Religious Broadcasters, a group which was birthed by the NAE, and whose members now dominate radio. Their central metaphor is war, just as Pastor Ted's seems to be.

In this regard, they much resemble the politicians they support and lately claim to have elected by their efforts. Both sets of people greatly admire war and enjoy dressing up in the costumes and using the language of warriors. The resemblance continues in that very few of them have ever, in fact, engaged in actual war. They are reminiscent of a folk song parody the Smothers Brothers once sang:

> "I see by your outfit that you are a cowboy;
> I see by your outfit that you're a cowboy too;
> We can see by our outfits that we are both cowboys -
> Why don't you get an outfit and be a cowboy, too?"

Well, it's easy enough to like the idea of war. It's easy as hell to indulge in the idea that you and the people you associate with are the good people, and all the people who don't think the way you do are evil. That's a way of thinking that's particularly easy and pleasant for Americans to indulge in, because it goes back for such a long way in our history.

The Puritans who settled the Northeast thought that way. In George Willison's wonderful book *Saints and Strangers*, the minutes of a Connecticut town meeting record this sentiment: "Voted, that the earth is the Lord's and the fulness thereof; voted, that the earth is given to the Saints; voted, that we are the Saints." This motion - which was passed - occurred during a debate about the "rights of natives" - that is, about whether the native Americans should be driven from their lands by force of arms by Christians.

It's not so easy to enjoy the idea of war once you've fought in one. War puts people in what the English philosopher Thomas Hobbes called "the state of nature."

Meaning that the only law is "kill or be killed." This is a state in which the sorts of social amenities Pastor Brendle professes to admire rapidly disappear.

In *The Songlines*, Bruce Chatwin quotes a real soldier to this effect: "An ex-Legionnaire, a veteran of Dien Bien Phu with grey hair *en brosse* and a toothy grin, is outraged at the US government for avoiding the blame for the My Lai massacre.

"'There is no such thing as a war crime,' he said. 'War is the crime.'" [Chatwin}

I once spent a week camped out on the long parkway in front of the U.S. Capitol in Washington, D.C., with a thousand Vietnam Veterans who had come to the capitol to oppose our continued participation in the war they'd fought in. They were about the most peaceful bunch of people I've known in my life. They hated war. They'd fought in one.

Jesus apparently didn't view life as a state of war. On the mount, he observed, "Blessed are the peacemakers: for they shall be called children of God." An English chaplain in the First World War had this to say in his diary:

"3 July. Now I know something of the horrors of war, the staff is redoubled but what of that, imagine 1,000 badly wounded per diem. The surgeons are beginning to get sleep, because after working night and day they realize we may be at this for some months, as Verdun. We hear of great successes but there are of course setbacks and one hears of ramparts of dead English and Germans. Oh, if you could see our wards, tents, huts, crammed with terrible wounds - see the rows of abdominals and lung penetrations dying - in strict confidence, please, I got hold of some morphia [morphine] and I go to that black hole of Calcutta (Moribund) and use it or I creep into the long tents where two or three hundred Germans lie, you can imagine what attention they get with out own neglected, the cries and groans are too much to withstand and I cannot feel less pity for them than for our own." [Carey]

He was writing about the third day of the Battle of the Somme. During the first day of that battle, "his" troops had sustained 60 thousand casualties. The battle continued until the 13th of November. In that three and one half month period, dead and wounded on both sides of the lines totaled one million, seven hundred thousand lives.

The chaplain didn't find war a salubrious or admirable state. In fact, he was writing on the advice of his Saviour, who said, "But I say unto you, Love your enemies, bless them that curse you, do good to them that hate you, and pray for them which despitefully use you, and persecute you." And when he wrote, "I cannot feel less pity for them than for our own," meaning by "them" the German "enemies," he was echoing the words of Jesus: "Inasmuch as ye have done it unto one of the least of these my brethren, ye have done it unto me."

Of course, those words can be interpreted quite differently, so as not to include humanity. "My brethren" could be interpreted to mean "all those people who agree with me." That would make Jesus analogous to any street gang leader, who demands total loyalty of his "troops." Or he might have meant "members of my family," and had in mind the sort of clan loyalty that induced a state of perpetual war among people in his day and for many days thereafter.

That is how Pastor Ted appears to interpret his words. "My fear," Sharlet quotes him as saying, "is that my children will grow up in an Islamic state." He seems to have forgotten that Christianity "grew up" in a world of many religions.

People, history shows us, are a species given to war. The gospels show, so far as I can understand them, that Jesus was not given to war. That he was, instead, given to teaching people how to look within themselves to find the sources of their angers and hatreds, and to find those emotions - and the actions which inevitably flowed from them - wanting, in the face of a life lived in love such as Jesus was living.

The New Life Church appears to me to be a church based on the metaphor of war: there is Truth, which is the property of the New Life Church and its allies, and there is error, otherwise known as "evil," which describes the beliefs and practices of everyone who does not belong to the New Life Church or its allied organizations. I cannot understand how Pastor Brendle can speak as he has spoken to Noel Black and remain a spokesman for his church. It seems to me that Pastor Brendle has to say that his Church's doctrine is correct, or else that he does not agree with all parts of it. As I understand the doctrine of his church, it is a doctrine that asserts its sole and complete truth. I would welcome a response from Pastor Brendle.

This was written a few years ago and not published by *Toilet Paper*, or by anyone else. Not too long after the conversation with Pastor Brendle, the various drug and sex peccadilloes of "spiritual warrior" Haggard were brought to light, and he was sent off for "counseling."

It now turns out that his peccadilloes were not limited to consorting with a male prostitute. He also conducted an affair with at least one young member of New Life Church. That young man was paid off by the Church in exchange for a vow of silence, which he has just decided to break, prompted apparently by Haggard's decision to give a series of interviews on television. The current pastor of the Church offered a defense of the payoff, basically denying that it was a payoff for the young man's silence. Of course it wasn't. And I am the Dowager Queen of Norway.

But no matter how many instances of the hypocrisy of the Publicly Religious are revealed, their ilk continue to attract the worship and the money of a large number of Americans. As H. L. Mencken once said, "No one ever went broke underestimating the intelligence of the American public." There's a line in "All God's Children Got Shoes" that
says "Everybody talkin' bout heaven ain't goin' there."

In my 30s, I wrote the following poem. I find I still agree with it.

Muscular Christians

How many, hungover and unkempt,
surly with Saturday, have you flushed
from their sweating beds,
your crude pulp texts in hand,
always in pairs,
polite, unmemorable faces
scrubbed and shaven,

>   pure as the faces of adolescent
>   model builders or mass murderers?
>
>   We cannot connect.
>   You read your poems
>   serenely certain of their truth,
>   as if when you hungered
>   a recipe would suffice.
>
>   None of my money
>   for your god who never laughs,
>   who makes offers
>   that cannot be refused,
>   like a mobster sending valentines.
>   I've seen what the literal do
>   when encouraged by numbers
>   to the icy persuasion
>   that their poetry, unlike
>   this sweating world, is true.

I'm privileged to know quite a few real Christians, which means to me that they try to act as Christ would act. Some of my best friends, in fact, are Christians. They don't talk about their faith to anyone who doesn't ask them about it, and they don't spend their lives looking for Sinners to criticize. They try to live from their beliefs, and I have great respect for them.

I have no respect for, and little patience with, the "religious" who have been attempting to take over our country and turn it into a theocracy, or for the "religious" who are making millions taking donations from their television viewers. Pharisees, Jesus would have called them, and he said all that needed to be said about the publicly religious a long time ago:

Take heed that ye do not your alms before men, to be seen of them: otherwise ye have no reward of your Father which is in heaven.

Therefore when thou doest thine alms, do not sound a trumpet before thee, as the hypocrites do in the synagogues and in the streets, that they may have glory of men. Verily I say unto you, They have their reward.

But when thou doest alms, let not thy left hand know what thy right hand doeth: That thine alms may be in secret: and thy Father which seeth in secret himself shall reward thee openly. (Matthew V: 5, 6)

Amen

Working
"Work is more fun than fun"
- Noel Coward

(Noel Coward was a fine English playwright and songwriter and pianist and singer. He was very good at his work for a long time, and he worked and worked and worked, as does any musician, writer or baseball player, worked because he loved the work, loved it enough to want to do it better. And then better.)

I've just spent an hour polishing my guitar, a Martin D-28 built in 1970. I could have done it in less time and I'm glad I didn't. If I had thought I was just polishing the guitar, I would have missed out on a big part of the job. I wouldn't have taken notice of the way the finish is cracking with the years in our semi-desert climate. I would have forgotten to notice the small gouges around the top of the sound hole, made by my thumbnail in moments of stupidity, and so I wouldn't have been grateful to recall that the last remaining blood spots under the strings had finally disappeared. (When I played with the band Toy Boat, I served much of the time as bass, rhythm guitar, and drums. You shed some blood doing all that.) I wouldn't have stopped polishing to properly appreciate the peerless restoration work a repairman in Denver did on the crack below the pick guard.

That crack was the direct result of a mortal sin. I left my guitar out of its case - just once, which was all my dog Joe needed to decide to leap up at the window. (He leaped through quite a number of windows, and also once ate his way through a door.) The window had heavy drapes over it, hung from little, matchsticky metal curtain-holders. Down that all came, and of course the end of the curtain-holder whacked my guitar a good one. NEVER leave your instrument out of its case. ALWAYS put your tools away in their houses when you are not using them.

I would have missed touching that wonderful creation of hundreds of hours of work someone did out in Nazareth, Pennsylvania, missed really seeing what a lovely, strong, responsive instrument I have been graced with. I wouldn't have been touched by that sense of wonder that is one of the feelings that get you into trying to become a musician in the first place.

I could have done it in less time. But it is a job that should not be done in less time than it takes for that sense of wonder to come calling. You could say the same for any job, in my experience. Well - most jobs.

During that hour, I was working: that is, I was expending energy and attention, rather than sitting in front of a screen allowing someone else to occupy my brain while my body rusted, which is what passes for "fun" these days for many people. Work is more fun than fun, and much more rewarding.

I learned most of what I know about working from my dad, Walter Holmes McCollum. He was born in 1895 in Crystal Lake, Illinois, a small town about fifty miles northwest of Chicago. Family stories say that when his father got sick in 1907, my dad had to leave the 7th grade and go to work, shoveling tons of coal every day to help support his family. He never stopped working.

I mean, he *never* stopped working. He drove a truck in the Army during World War One, and after that he went to work as a lineman for the Commonwealth Edison Company, the utility company that brought electricity to most of Illinois. In the early 1930s, some genius decided that Dad, who would have been perfectly happy on a desert island, should become a personnel executive. So he put on a suit for the rest of his working life, commuting back and forth between Evanston, where we lived, and Chicago, dealing with people rather than things he could fix with his hands. I believe this cost him a great deal. He promptly developed a heart condition, angina, that plagued him for the rest of his life.

(My sister June thinks this view of Dad's work in personnel is hooey, and that he was a truly caring counselor to many Commonwealth Edison workers. Maybe I'm projecting my own desert island tastes onto my father.)

However that may be, the instant he got home from work every day, he was out of that suit and tie and into work clothes and down to work - on the house, on the lawn and garden - building, fixing, maintaining. He could do anything: carpentry, from construction to cabinet making, plumbing, electrical wiring, house painting, raising food, raising flowers...anything.

I often wish that he had had one other skill: teaching. He tried to teach me to do the kinds of work he had mastered, but he lacked the patience a teacher needs. I did manage to learn a few skills from him, but what I most gratefully recall are the lessons he gave me, not about specific crafts, but about *how* to work, whatever the work to be done. To illustrate why I am grateful, I interject here a rant I wrote a few years back:

Report from the Working Front

Two years ago I took my last paycheck from an institution of higher education (so self-described). Since then, I've been making enough money beyond my retirement check to get through the month by doing actual work for individual people.

Most of the work has been physical - gardening, painting, cleaning, home repairs of a non-electric or non-plumbing nature. Occasionally, I use my writing or computer skills, but not often. This summer I've been working an actual working man's week, 40 or 50 hours of labor. Most of the labor has involved following electricians and plumbers and carpenters around, cleaning up their messes, then cleaning up the messes they've left after they've come back to repair their egregious errors and oversights. It's been an instructive summer.

The electrician on one job - rewiring a hundred-year-old house - ripped out random parts of the basement ceiling (6" wide cedar fencing nailed to the bottom of the floor joists) without ever marking or systematizing the boards. Then, as an added service, he nailed what boards he hadn't destroyed in removal back up in an utterly random pattern - nailed them again, rather than screwing them in, in spite of the fact that he knew more wiring and plumbing work would have to be done down the line, and the boards would have to be removed in the future.

The plumber left several "pipes" (some kind of plastic or urethane tubes that supposedly meet code) hung down below the floor joists, making it impossible to replace the ceiling in the bathroom, and left one weld leaking visibly. While the carpenter was reframing the bathroom to accommodate the lowered ceiling necessitated by the plumber's inattention, he drilled through not one but two new pipes. I enjoyed his comment on this development: "I guess I should have looked behind the wall," he said.

When the young plumber came back to repair his various blunders, I told him, "I'll be in the other room putting the ceiling back together right. It was done in a hurry, so now it'll take three times more work to fix it than it would have to do it right." Always the hopeful teacher.

His reply, delivered with absolutely no discernible irony: "Isn't it always the way?"

I found no rejoinder. Everywhere I go, with a very few honorable exceptions, I find people doing their work without any apparent notion that there is such a thing as the right way to do a job, that an hour's planning can save many hours' repair, that a clean, well-organized workspace significantly reduces the potential for minor and major disaster.

Today I was working in the World of Art, hanging a show of the work of art faculty at the community college. Some of these teachers have evidently never hung a painting on a wall. Putting screw eyes and picture wire on the back of a frame so it will hang straight and the wire won't rise above the top of the frame is not a job that requires a great amount of training or skill or good sense. You need to measure twice to put your screw eyes level on the sides of the frame. You need to estimate the bend in the wire required, which you can do manually, at the same time estimating where to put the screw eyes. And yet, and yet... I always find myself rewiring frames. These people are ostensibly "professionals," just like the electricians and plumbers and carpenters.

Conclusions: 1, you could make a living forever just cleaning up other people's screwups. 2, If I were Education Czar, I would throw out a whole lot of curriculum in favor of putting young people to work on real, physical jobs under supervisors who knew how to do a job right. Meaning mindfully.

In Robert Stone's novel *Dog Soldiers*, two psychopathic criminals, now in the employ of the Federal government, are playing chess. Smitty, the less cerebral of the two, is checkmated by Danskin, a genius gone wrong; Danskin punches Smitty out.

"'I hate jailbird chess,' he explained. 'I hate the style. No foresight, no reasoning. Just like a little kid.' He pursed his lips and spoke mincingly, raising his voice for Smitty to hear. 'Just like a little tweety bird! Oooh, here's a move. Oooh, there's a move. It's fucking degrading.'"

That's the level of performance I see as I go here and there: jailbird chess. Oooh, here's a move. When I left the Intellectual World, I hoped to find an alternative, but in fact the rot has permeated to the level of essential work. No foresight, no reasoning, no grounding in the basics of all and any work. Oooh, there's a move. Just like a little kid.

So I reckon I'll be able to keep employed as long as I can still do physical labor. And I'm not responsible for the decisions of the idiots I follow around, as I was, perforce, responsible for the decisions of the Mongolians in charge of the Higher Realms I once inhabited. I can be responsible for the work *I* do, and I can live with what I consider honor in that situation.

But my kid's and grandkids' future in a society that has lost all purchase on the basic principles of how to do a job right is going to be a grim one.

———————————————————

I mentioned in that rant several key principles I learned from Dad:

1. Don't just tear into a job. Think about it first. Think about it in steps, and decide on their necessary order - what needs to come first, what second, and so on. If you're going to build something, make a plan. If you're going to write something, make an outline. And think not only about *what* you want to do or make or say, but about the people who will be using it. Imagine that you are one of those people. What problems might your plan make for them? You may be so eager to begin a job that planning it out appears to be a waste of time. Planning is never a waste of time, and most often it will wind up saving you time.

2. Keep your working area clean and free of obstructions. When you complete one step or task, take a few minutes to clear up after it. Clean up anything left over - sawdust, metal shavings, dirt of any sort. Get rid of anything left over, either by putting it

where you want to store it or into a trash container. Put any tools you've used that you will not use for the next step or task back where they belong. Doing these things will take a little time - very little, compared to the time you'll spend repairing the work or yourself if you don't do them. Tools are like people: if they're not at work, they want to be in their homes, and they will take their revenge if you leave them lying around the work area.

(When I say "put them back where they belong," I mean that every tool (this includes such tools as keys, cell phones, computers, musical instruments - anything you use to help you work) should have *One* Place Where It Lives. If you organize your tools on that principle, you will save yourself ten times the number of hours you spend organizing them. The hours you save will be the ones you would otherwise spend searching for those tools, or working to make the money to replace them if they get broken or lost.)

3. If you allow yourself to hurry a job, very likely you'll wind up spending more time on it than you would if you took it slowly. That extra time will be required by your having to throw the project away because you forgot or screwed up something important, or by your having to go back and fix whatever you screwed up, if it's fixable.

Working too fast may also cause you to hurt yourself - not just in dramatic ways, like cutting your thumb off, but in ways you don't even notice until, sometimes many years later, all of a sudden you can't lift your arm over your shoulder. The best work is done by people who study on how to do it with the least possible strain on their bodies. You'll undoubtedly hear people say about some great athlete or musician or other master, "He makes it look easy." That's because truly good workers in any field *make* it as easy as it can be made.

Last, working too fast, as I said at the beginning of this, will cause you to miss out on many of the greatest rewards that work offers you, because you won't have time to take notice of them.

4. One thing at a time. "Multitasking" is a word dreamed up by some fool. The idea that doing two or three or more things at the same time is a good way to do things has been sold relentlessly to people all over the world for the past fifteen-twenty years.

It's a good way for the Owners and Operators. It keeps people not paying any real attention to much of anything, it keeps them busy at tasks they don't have time to notice are generally meaningless and quite often stupid and/or dangerous.

"This is the great irony of multitasking—that its overall goal, getting more done in less time, turns out to be chimerical. In reality, multitasking slows our thinking. It forces us to chop competing tasks into pieces, set them in different piles, then hunt for the pile we're interested in, pick up its pieces, review the rules for putting the pieces back together, and then attempt to do so, often quite awkwardly. (Fact, and one more reason the bubble will pop: A brain attempting to perform two tasks simultaneously will, because of all the back-and-forth stress, exhibit a substantial lag in information processing.)

"Productive? Efficient? More like running up and down a beach repairing a row of sand castles as the tide comes rolling in and the rain comes pouring down. *Multitasking*, a definition: 'The attempt by human beings to operate like computers, often done with the assistance of computers.' It begins by giving us more tasks to do, making each task harder to do, and dimming the mental powers required to do them. It finishes by making us forget exactly how on earth we did them (assuming we didn't give up, or 'multiquit'), which makes them harder to do again." [Kirn]

"Multitasking" is a seriously foolish waste of experience, is what it is. Avoid it whenever you can.

My Dad was the product of a world in which, if you wanted something, such as food, shelter or entertainment, you had to produce it yourself. You learned to grow and preserve your own food, to build and maintain your shelter, to tell and read and listen to stories and poems, to sing or play musical instruments. If you wanted to go somewhere, you walked unless you owned a horse, and owning a horse is a lot of work. I expect that all of you, my dear ones, may be living in such a world again. I hope you will do it by choice. Except for the horses. I don't know about horses.

I don't want to make my Dad sound like a saint. In fact, his compulsion to be working all the time frequently drove me nuts when I was a youngster. One of my memories of Christmas in our house is that, before we got to the presents under the tree, we would have to wash the windows. Most of the windows in the house I remember best, at 2614 Park Place in Evanston, were composed of leaded glass - many small panes encased in lead frames within each window frame. Many, many corners, and Dad would come around to make sure June and I had polished every damn one of them.

That still seems to me like carrying things a little too far. A baseball hitting coach named Jeff Pentland once issued a set of rules for improvement, and the last rule was this: "Rest and recovery is crucial to staying strong." Even if you learn to view work as the best fun, you need to learn when it's time to quit. And then you need to learn *how* to quit.

My first marriage - to a wonderful woman named Nancy Nickerson, who is still one of my best friends - ended for a number of reasons, primarily including my own selfishness and immaturity, but another large reason was that she could never quit working. We both taught at the community college, and when we'd get home, Nancy just kept thinking and talking about the work day. Talking on and on, into the night. I got so I couldn't stand it.

I don't know how I learned to quit working when I was done for the day, but I'm very grateful I did. Maybe it was one of those Bible verses I learned in the Presbyterian Church Sunday School: "Sufficient unto the day is the evil thereof." Sufficient also is the good thereof. Over the long run - and I hope you all have long runs - if you can leave the workday behind when it's over, you'll go further and be happier and healthier. Then all you have to do is find out what truly gives you "rest and recovery." (Hint: sitting in front of a screen that is programmed to make your adrenal glands fire every 2 seconds is not it. Neither, I can assure you from a near lifetime of practice, is pouring liquid CNS depressants down your gullet.)

I'll end this ramble about work by including two song lyrics I wrote. The first, "Has the Dusting Been Done Up in Heaven?," I wrote in 1974, a couple of years after Dad died.

(I was at the Democratic County Convention, a McGovern delegate, when I got an emergency phone call from Evanston, telling me to catch the first thing smokin' if I wanted to see Dad alive. I raced to the airport, grabbed a plane, and got back in time to spend a week visiting him in the hospital. He had no intention of dying, and was still disappointed in me for choosing to be a teacher rather than a businessman, and still carrying on about how Franklin Delano Roosevelt had caused everything wrong in the world. Weak, but still Dad. After a week, during which he showed no signs of dying, I had to get back to work in Colorado, and flew home. He eventually got kicked out of the hospital, since he wouldn't die as he was supposed to do, and died two months later. His doctor, who had never been able to "diagnose" his "problem," did an unauthorized autopsy on his body. He later told my sister June, "I don't know how that man was alive. There was nothing left inside him." Which pretty much tells you how much doctors know about human health. What was left inside him was the will to live.)

Dad's death devastated me. He died disappointed in me, and now there was nothing I could do about it. Finally, I wrote in this song some of the things he'd meant to me and taught me, and tried to say what he had been to me:

Has the Dusting Been Done Up in Heaven?

Has the dusting been done up in heaven?
If it hasn't, there's one thing I know good and well:
You're clipping the wings of those damn lazy angels
And telling them all about going to hell;

Do they run a tight ship up in heaven?
Do they keep to their word and not waste a move?
Do they throw things away that they might need someday?
If they do, I know you'll surely make them improve.

And how is the chow where you are now?

    Do they give you your steak and potatoes?
    Are there locks on the doors, can you eat off the floors,
    Do they let you grow Big Boy tomatoes?

I know you've found work up in heaven,
Oiling the tools and sharpening them well,
And you'll cut a straight line through the rest of all time,
So why don't you set down and rest for a spell?

    Don't have to turn out the lights
    You can let them burn all night -

So why don't you set down and rest for a spell?

    (Dad's highest words of praise for a woman were that "you could eat off her floors," meaning that she kept an extremely clean house. In the days we divided work between working outside the house ((the man's job)) and working inside the house ((the woman's job)), that was high praise, indeed. Big Boy tomatoes were a strain of tomatoes Dad swore by.)

    The next lyric I wrote at about the same time, but under the influence of the Spirit of the Sixties, otherwise known as "Cosmic Optimism." I've found I can still sing it sincerely, though. In spite of its excessive sweetness, it talks about a lot of the things I hope I've said here.

Maybe It Could Always Be That Way

Sometimes when you're singing, you get taken by the song
All you have to do to get along is go along
Everybody's listening, the music has its say
And maybe it could always be that way

Sometimes when you're working, you don't have to count your time
You and what you're doing come together like a rhyme
If they call that working, what would they call play?
And maybe it should always be that way

    I believe that I have had enough of trying hard at things
    I believe that I will try and see what trying easy brings
    I believe I've finally dropped the chains of trying to be free
    And instead of trying to make my way, I'll let my way make me

Sometimes when we're together we don't have to say a word
Just listen to the music that's waiting to be heard
Taking turns to giving, the music has its say
And maybe it should always be that way

And maybe it could always be that way.

    It *could* be that way. Not always, but a whole lot more than it is.

War All the Time

Why am I devoting a chapter to this melancholy subject? Because I believe that the Dominican Republic's President, Juan Bosch, correctly analyzed the United States in his book *Pentagonism* [Bosch]. Briefly, his analysis asserts that Marx was wrong, that there is a stage between mature capitalism and the dictatorship of the proletariat, a stage that Bosch dubbed "Pentagonism," seeing the U.S.A. as the first exemplar of this stage. In a Pentagonist country, the military forms the paramount economic power center, and the government begins to colonize its own country. This pretty well describes what I've witnessed during my lifetime. (Although I have no faith that the dictatorship of the proletariat will ever transpire, or that if it did it would look much different from the Trump administration.)

I'll begin, not at the beginning, but with an essay I wrote as we were preparing to go to war in Afghanistan and Iraq again so that George Bush Junior could prove to George Bush Senior that his balls were just as big as his Daddy's. (They weren't. He was part of a couple of generations of mainly Republican politicians who avoided military service, especially any service in combat zones, and voted loudly for any war available. Little Shrub famously flew airplanes for the National Guard for a while, until he got tired and quit a year before his hitch was supposed to end. His Vice-President never served during the Vietnam war because, he said, he "had other priorities.")

Shrub's gonadal insecurity of course was not the real reason we went back to war in Iraq. The real reason was that Iraq offered such large opportunities for the Republican government's friends in "the private sector" to enrich themselves. (You should read Chapter 2 of General Smedley Butler's short book *War Is a Racket* [Butler] to see many lucid examples of how this is done, over and over and over.)

I attended the marches against these wars before they started. I never did get this essay published anywhere, since we were very shortly after my last march practicing "shock and awe" on various populations in the middle East. But I think it makes a good introduction to the wars of our country in my time.

War All the Time

"The threats we face today are both external and internal: external in that there are groups and states that want to violently attack the United States; internal in that there are ideologues who are attempting to use this opportunity to promulgate their agenda of 'blame America first'.... both threats stem from a hatred for the American ideals of freedom and equality or a misunderstanding of those ideals....Our goals will be aimed at addressing the present threats so as to eradicate future terrorism and ideologies that support it." So announces former czar William Bennett, all goals aimed and ready to fire.

The ideologies that support terrorism are more clearly described by the Justice Department, through the National Crime Prevention Council: "If a behavior or an event seems to be outside the norm or is frightening, let law enforcement authorities know. Just remember, it's your job to watch out and report."

Have you found the speech of someone who questions the War on Terror frightening or at least abnormal? Have you noticed the absence of an American flag on your neighbor's SUV? You know what to do, buddy. It used to be called "snitching." Now it's called "patriotism."

This is where I came in.

I

"It was the English," Kaspar cried,
"Who put the French to rout;
But what they fought each other for,
I could not well make out;
But everybody said," quoth he,
"That 'twas a famous victory."

- Robert Southey

My first three years were the last three years of the Second World War. Good years they were, for a kid in America. My mother did magic, breaking a plastic pouch of blood-red dye into the mixing bowl, causing the interlocking mixer blades to turn white margarine into gold. The neighborhood men towered over the flowers of the corn in the Victory Garden, and the corn covered most of the sky as I looked up holding a flap of my father's suit pants.

One afternoon my father came home from work at three in the afternoon, and my mother fetched my sister and me and told us to get all the pans and lids out from the cabinet beneath the kitchen counter. This had always been a punishable offense, but she assured us it would not be on this day. Our father set us in the red wagon with the pots and lids spilling from our laps. All up and down the block neighbors were emerging onto the sidewalks with kids likewise equipped. And we paraded the sidewalk, our neighbors before and behind, beating metal with metal, cheering, many parents crying, the dogs yapping and fighting in sheer confusion.

That was how Americans in my neighborhood celebrated the end of a war. It was the last such celebration I've seen.

Four years later, my father and I stepped off the El onto the Addison Street Station on our way to a Cubs game, and saw the headlines in the *Tribune* box, huge and black as the back of a scream, announcing that Russia had the Bomb. My father stopped dead. I was old enough to understand that the Russians were evil and that their having the Bomb was a terrible thing. I wondered if the Cubs would play.

Three years after that, my hero Tommy Myers stood at home plate, a place on our vacant lot ball field marked only by mutual agreement, and called the question we had been debating, with only overgrown lilac and honeysuckle hedges for witness: in Korea, is the North or the South the Good Side? The question had been hard. The Cubs, of course, were Northsiders, but a small, vocal minority loved the Sox, who were, of course, Southsiders. Tommy Myers finally settled it by pointing out what any idiot would have seen in the first place if he'd thought about it: the North was the good side in *our* Civil War. So then we all knew what side we were on. I was glad it was settled so that we could start playing baseball and I could get my mind off the larger concerns of the world. They seemed distant and unreal compared to the difficulties presented by left field, which sloped dramatically uphill and was full of gopher holes.

All the people in my neighborhood had been pretty angry when the President relieved the great General Douglas MacArthur of his command. Mac visited our town and paraded down Main Street in an open car, and I cheered him, though without the pots and pans. I watched my father almost strangle in order to keep from crying when MacArthur gave his "Farewell Address" to Congress. I didn't understand the point the General was making in that address. It was that some kind of devils in foreign guise were about to come into our homes and do bad things to all of us. He didn't explain why he'd been fired, or how that worked in with the devils.

I had to watch TV to understand that. Herbert Philbrick arrived through that new medium to explain it to me on a show called *I Led Three Lives: Citizen, Communist Counterspy* [Philbrick]. That show led me to understand that a foreign devil wasn't necessarily foreign; he might be my next-door neighbor, a seemingly dull old person who went to work in a suit as my dad did every day, but spent his nights in the basement in a room shut off from casual inspection by deviously designed blinds, typing the fruits of his spying to his foreign devil masters. Or, hero that he was, typing his reports to the FBI itself. I began to look at neighboring fathers in a new and more interesting light. Heretofore, they'd seemed about as boring as my own dad.

This new war seemed to be a war by Good Americans against Bad Americans, and I saw descriptions of it in the movies as well as on tv. Richard Carlson, tv's Herb Philbrick, played a part in a movie called *The Creature from the Black Lagoon*. The Creature looked suspiciously like an ordinary human, but he wore tights spangled with stuffed, sewn scales and an excellent amphibian/insect mask. Though he wore his monsterhood on his face, you could tell he had started out as a human. He contracted a dislike for humans when the actor Richard Denning, playing an obviously bad sort of American, a fellow who didn't have the Good of the Mission in mind, shot him in the ass with a spear gun. So of course Herb Philbrick had to kill the Creature before he killed the whole Research Party, and, not incidentally, before he got his slimy hands on the Stone Babe, in whom he had evinced a distasteful interest not unlike that previously displayed by Richard Denning, whose intentions you could see at a glance, with the assistance of the cameraman and the musical score, were Not Honorable. It was touch and go for Richard Carlson, but he killed the Creature and got the girl. It was always touch and go, after the Korean War ended, for all the heroes with whom I was presented by the media. Russia, after all, had The Bomb, and the whole country was full of spies and traitors.

During those years I lived with the only recurring dream I've ever dreamed, as opposed to lived in. I would be out walking down a dirt path outside my cousins' Wisconsin farm and turn around to see the Mushroom Cloud rising above it. Two or three nights a week I had this dream, all through the 1950's. It woke me up every time.

But toward the end of that era, just when I was getting used to generalized terror as a condition of life, Castro's revolution succeeded in overthrowing someone in Cuba, and Castro announced shortly that his was a Communist Revolution, and then we had a new and present Devil to consider, "not ninety miles from our shore." An outside enemy, a fellow who stubbornly refused to speak our language, a fellow who spoke badly of us in public and welcomed the Russians, for Christ's sake, into his country. Not ninety miles from our shore.

By this time I was getting ready to leave high school and go to college, and while my heritage was Republican, I was seduced by John Kennedy. I would have voted for him in 1960, because he seemed the kind of fellow who wouldn't back down, and who'd do whatever needed to be done to defeat our fearful enemies, those enemies I'd grown up hearing about and watching on tv. We watched as he did just that during the Missile Crisis. He didn't blink. He evinced Grace Under Pressure.

I still felt that way after he'd been in the ground two years and I was drafted. The films I saw in basic training at Ft. Knox have been shown since, in a documentary made during the 90s, as occasions for irony. They weren't ironic in our eyes. We still believed that our government mainly told the truth, and the films were pretty well done by the standards of their time. They were reminiscent, in short, of the tv shows we'd grown up watching. Simple: there's these goods, and these evils.

So I would have gone off to Viet Nam when I got drafted, but fate would not have it so, and I was the last guy in my MOS (radio relay/signalman) to go anywhere *but* Viet Nam for many years thereafter. I went instead to Germany, and spent my year and a half there playing war games in the snow, setting up communications networks along the East German border in anticipation of the event the Army dreaded most, a massive Russian invasion.

My post had a library, and I started reading about the War in Vietnam. Mainly, I read Bernard Fall's great books about the French experience there, and after I read them, I didn't want to volunteer for Nam duty any more.

By the time I got home in 1968, new wars were on. One raged between Americans who opposed this war we were fighting and those who supported it, however dubiously. Another seemed to be a new kind of war, the enemy an abstraction, Poverty. When Nixon arrived in office, he declared yet another war, this one on "Drugs." I was hard put to keep up with all the wars we were prosecuting.

When America quit the war in Southeast Asia, and our beloved allies got to escape, if they had the strength to hang on to the struts of our last departing copters, my generation heaved a great sigh of relief and dove back into its programming, which told it that consumption is the goal of all human affairs, and you'd best get cracking, boy, or you won't get your fair share of the Goods - advice my generation has followed to this very day.

We were quite relieved that the war was over. No more Americans were being shipped home in body bags every day on national TV. While the Russians had Chancellor Brezhnev writhing his threatening though somehow comical eyebrows around in interminable pompous speeches, we didn't take him seriously. We were quite accustomed, by this time, to the balance of terror. We knew that old man wouldn't be fool enough to try anything on us.

We didn't pay attention to the wars our country continued to fight. We didn't notice the wars in Indonesia, Libya, Chile, Guatemala, Korea, Iran, Malaysia, Cuba, Argentina, Brazil, Venezuela, South Africa, Afghanistan, Poland, Czechoslovakia -- though in all of these wars and many others we were taking our modest part, supplying arms to the friendlies, denying aid to the creatures from the black lagoon.

One night in 1991, I was driving down to the state prison to discuss with some inmates *The Grapes of Wrath* and stopped along the way for dinner at a roadside joint. When I got back in my car and turned on the radio, my country was once again at war, bombing the devil out of Iraq. And our enemy, Saddam, had had the grace to grow a great black mustache, reminiscent of both Hitler's AND Stalin's. (In case we missed the comparison, we were duly reminded by the tv commentators who quoted their government "sources" regarding the "Hitler of the Mideast.")

I was approaching 50 then. The subsequent decade has provided little surcease from war. We've engaged in a semiofficial war in Bosnia, a continuous campaign against Iraq; on the home front our declared wars on crime and drugs have proceeded unabated, and our undeclared war on the environment has recently intensified. I find myself recalling almost daily the words Jules Henry wrote in *Culture Against Man* [Henry]:

"Where is the culture of life? The culture of life resides in all those people who, inarticulate, frightened, and confused, are wondering, 'where it will all end.' Thus the forces of death are confident and organized while the forces of life - the people who long for peace - are, for the most part, scattered, inarticulate, and wooly-minded, overwhelmed by their own impotence. Death struts about the house while Life cowers in the corner."

II

Reverend Sir, Our Good God is working of miracles. Five Witches were
Lately Executed, impudently demanding of God, a Miraculous Vindication
of their Innocency. Immediately upon this, Our God Miraculously sent in Five
Andover-Witches, who made a most ample, surprising, amazing Confession,
of all their Villainies and declared the Five newly executed to have been of
their Company; discovering many more....
- Cotton Mather to John Cotton, 1692 [Willison]

I've tried to recapture some of the ways I perceived my country and its wars as I've lived through them. Born during The Good War being fought by The Greatest Generation, I grew up on movies that glorified that war and my country's role in it, and on the barrage of anti-Communist propaganda that succeeded it, and lived through my teens ignoring "politics" on principle, since political discussion had been effectively silenced by Joe McCarthy, HUAC, et.al.

The first crack in my acceptance of official American reality appeared when I was 20 and read William Bradford's *History of Plymouth Plantation* [Bradford]. From that book I remember in particular one anecdote. After initial tough years, the Colonists had gotten pretty well squared away when, all of a sudden, Sin popped up among them. The colonists rapidly concluded that this outbreak of Sin could only be the work of the Devil.

They had figured that the New World would be exactly that, and that they'd left the Devil behind in Europe, where he belonged, and they, having the correct handle on God's will, would be free to build a new Eden, free of the Devil's historical sway. And the son of a gun had gotten in anyway.

How'd he get *in*? they asked themselves. The answer was obvious. He'd snuck in through inferior beings. The Devil had got in through *animals*, and the Fathers searched the guilty animals out, somehow, and they dug some big pits and buried the Devil alive, in the form of horses and chickens and pigs and cats.

Not too much later, their descendants got tired of killing readily available animals and turned their sights on fairer game, most famously at Salem. But that Devil just *would* not stop coming around and spitting on the City on the Hill's alabaster sidewalks.

Those events have stuck in my mind, and something Kurt Vonnegut wrote helped me see them as embodying one of my country's central stories: "The Christian quick trip from love to hate and murder is our principal entertainment. We might call it 'Christianity fails again,' and how satisfying many of us have been trained to find it when it fails and fails." [Vonnegut]

My brief career as a researcher for a Congressional candidate in 1970 opened another crack in my cultural dark glasses. I undertook to provide the candidate with a position paper on "drugs," since Nixon and his gang were using that imprecise term as a bludgeon that year, and my candidate's opponent had made his career as a District Attorney "tough on drugs."

The position paper I gave my candidate would have sunk the campaign of anyone except the natural son of Joe Dimaggio and Mamie Eisenhower. My research had led me to conclude that "the legal approach" to reducing problems people encounter when they introduce chemicals into their bodies had failed and failed again, and that the government ought to get out of the business of policing private chemistry.

The Noble Experiment lay at the heart of my conclusion. Prohibition lasted about 14 years, and we spent a great deal of money "enforcing" it, and at the end of those years we were golfing down almost exactly as much hooch as we had been before the law took effect. Attempts at eradicating the Demon Rum had failed, and had, in addition, created a generation that viewed drinking to excess as romantic, jolly, and safely rebellious. Our history of going to war against dangerous but morally neutral agents of human destruction seemed unpromising. As late as 1933, my country still had enough sense to say "Nuts" to the idea that Demon Rum was the cause of all evil and must be wiped from the face of the earth.

But no negative result of a crusade against these devilish concoctions ever seemed to discourage the crusaders. "That didn't work; we'd better do more of it!" seemed to be their attitude. A mere 4 years after Prohibition's repeal, Harry Anslinger's Bureau of Narcotics caused a film called *Reefer Madness* to be produced, a film demonstrating that marijuana induced terrifying, murderous rages in previously normal folks, and we were back on the Road to Morocco, gearing up for the War on Drugs that has never ended since - only changed targets, as the convenience of the warriors might from time to time dictate. Its most memorable slogan? "Just Say No."

The final crack in my acceptance of Official Reality was caused, rather belatedly, by "The McCarthy Era." (In quotes because the good Senator was only the most notorious of the demagogues engaged in the "war on traitors," and his viciousness was matched by many predecessors and successors.) I recently decided to revisit that period. The visit was instructive.

The number of actual spies uncovered by investigations that began with the Smith Act and ended - except for a few diehards only with the downfall of Communism and the dismemberment of the USSR - was dwarfed by the number of loyal and often admirable American citizens whose lives and careers were defenestrated during those years -

people whose only crimes were having signed petitions in support of the Spanish Republic, having attended a Paul Robeson concert, having publicly opposed lynching as an instrument of social policy. The War on American Communism was a war on Americans. It took its greatest toll not on its targets, but on the character of the vast majority of citizens who sat back and watched it go on.

It took a poet - a brave one, Archibald MacLeish - to put his finger on what the Red Menace hysteria meant for the present and future of his country:

"What is happening in the United States under the impact of the negative and defensive and often frightened opinion of these years is the falsification of the image the American people have long cherished of themselves as beginners and begetters, changers and challengers, creators and accomplishers. A people who have thought of themselves for a hundred and fifty years as having purposes of their own for the changing of the world cannot learn overnight to think of themselves as resisters of another's purposes without beginning to wonder who they are. A people who have been real to themselves because they were for something cannot continue to be real to themselves when they find they are merely against something." [quoted in Trumbo]

III

"...the territory that is going to be attacked, or is under attack, is only a place destined to receive expendable materiel, both mechanical and human. Costly war materiel is going to be consumed in this place: bullets, bombs, medicine, clothes, cement, equipment to build barracks and roads and bridges, food and drink for the soldiers, and also the soldiers themselves, or at least many of them. The attacked country is the final depository of goods that have already been produced and sold and paid for in the mother country."
[Bosch[

I've watched the outburst of "patriotism" that has followed the attacks on the World Trade Center and the Pentagon. A great many American flags and eagle-motif t-shirts have been sold. Innumerable television commercials have stirringly advocated consumption as a patriotic act. The death of thousands of people became, virtually overnight, a stimulus to commerce and the justification for yet another war, the new, improved, undefined, limitless, boundary-less War on Terror.

What are we fighting against? "...enemies of freedom," says the President. "Our enemy is a radical network of terrorists, and every government that supports them." ("Support" is not defined.) When will the war end? "...not...until every terrorist group of global reach has been found, stopped, and defeated." Even this prescription is too narrow. We will also "pursue nations that provide aid or safe haven to terrorism. Every nation, in every region, now has a decision to make. Either you are with us, or you are with the terrorists." Why the attacks? "They hate...a democratically elected government....They hate our freedoms, our freedom of religion, our freedom of speech, our freedom to vote and assemble and disagree with each other."

Never having had the opportunity to vote for anyone in the World Trade Center or the Pentagon, although I'm allowed to finance their activities in manifold ways, I find this a little puzzling. And if our freedom to "assemble and disagree with each other" is under attack, why do most of the attacks seem to come from the President's Press Secretary and the Vice-President's wife?

And I wonder who this "us" is of whom the President speaks. A short time ago, while a goodly portion of Arizona was burning down, and the sky east of the Rocky Mountains was a choking haze of smoke from Wyoming to Las Cruces, the President made a quick appearance to indicate the government's concern for its citizens. After a brief glance around, he had some advice for those citizens. "Hang in there," he advised them. It was the best illustration of the utter contempt the ruling class holds for the people of this country I've heard yet.

Is it not more likely that "terrorists" (a label to which we apparently hold exclusive rights of bestowal) will continue to emerge indefinitely in a world in which the two hundred largest corporations control twice the assets of 80% of the rest of the population? And does that statistic not suggest that Al Queda's choice of targets had more to do with America's economic "global reach" and its willingness to use its military to keep that reach expanding than with revulsion at our right to assemble and disagree with each other?

In my sixty years as a citizen of America, my country has been at war either with another country, another economic system, its own citizens, or some abstract word or other. I have spent a great deal of my life fighting against my country's various wars. I am sick of fighting as a way of life. I am sixty years old. I can't go on this way. I don't believe in war. I don't believe that defining yourself by finding something to be against is a successful method of defining yourself. I think that going to war against another person, another ideology, another country, another sex, another class, another chicken in the chicken yard, another nation in the nation yard, another anything, is nothing but a prescription for suicide. I have lived long enough to discover that what I hate is what I hate within me. What I hate within me is my selfishness, my propensity to act as if what I want is what all people want, and as if those who stand in my way must do so because they are evil. What I hate within my country is that same propensity.

I am sick of living in a country that can find no other reason for its own existence than to pour blood on manufactured products in order to turn them to gold.

IV

This may be the year when we finally come face to face with ourselves:
finally just lay back and say it - that we are really just a nation of 220 million
used car salesmen with all the money we need to buy guns, and no qualms
at all about killing anybody else in the world who tries to make us uncomfortable.

[Thompson]

Hunter Thompson wrote those words in 1972, on the eve of Richard Nixon's landslide reelection. Sending young people to war has remained an overwhelmingly popular pastime in the succeeding years, and the new war is no exception. A large majority of my countrymen never met a war they didn't like, especially now that we've learned to prosecute our wars without discernible casualties on our part, and without allowing any significant coverage of their human cost to the countries upon which we direct our wrath. Though I refuse to cower in the corner, Death is hardly restrained by the isolated, disorganized presence of such as I from strutting ever more nakedly about the house.

But Thompson wrote another phrase immediately after the bitter requiem above. He remarked on "what a fantastic monument to all the best instincts of the human race [this country] might have been." I would add, "and has been, and may yet be."

For all along, some of us have lived in the cause of life, of joy, of the struggle for equality and decency and justice - in short, in the cause of making the *meaning* of those grand abstractions "freedom" and "democracy" into a reality for all of us.

I am thinking not only of such figures as Webster and Lincoln and Tubman and Frederick Douglas and Eugene Debs and Martin Luther King, Jr. I am also thinking of the thousands of largely unknown jazz and blues musicians who have forged a music that *embodies* democracy and freedom within the necessary discipline of form, a musical language that in fewer than a hundred years has become universal. And of such artists as Romare Bearden and George Bellows and Edward Hopper and Ben Shahn, who made the lives of ordinary people the stuff of their art. And of writers, from Whitman through Stephen Crane and Frank Norris and Sherwood Anderson to Steinbeck and Wright and Nelson Algren and John Nichols and Kurt Vonnegut, who have resolutely held the mirror up to America's people, so that they could see how far, yet, there was to go if we really wanted to become that "monument to all the best instincts of the human race."

My own experience has also taught me that we are not entirely a nation of used car dealers. I have known far too many Americans who lived by the principles Jesus and Lincoln taught and lived, whether they called themselves Christians or Republicans or not, to see all of America as represented by a cheapjack used car hustler, or by the current "Administration," or by the Kenneth Lays who call the "Administration's" martial tunes. I have known men and women who've taken the most terrible blows life has to offer and marched through them without a whimper. I have known men and women devoted to improving the lives of everyone their lives touched, without any sort of public recognition or support. I have known men and women who've never stopped working to perfect their art or craft, without any sort of public recognition or support. I've known men and women who cared for their friends more than they did for themselves, and who cared as much for utter strangers in need. I've known men and women who lay down "successful careers" because they cared more for non-human life than for their own individual lives. Real courage under real fire; real grace under real pressure; real Americans.

The choice we face was stated by philosopher J. Glenn Gray in *The Warriors* [Gray], his meditation on the Second World War, in which he had seen a great deal of combat. "If the war," he wrote, "taught me anything at all, it convinced me that people are not what they seem or even think themselves to be. Nothing is more tempting than to yield oneself, when fear comes, to the dominance of necessity and to act irresponsibly at the behest of another. Freedom and responsibility we speak of easily, nearly always without recognition of the iron courage required to make them effective in our lives."

Gray did not see many signs of that iron courage around him, and foresaw where its lack was likely to lead us: "Such is our human nature that we cannot possess power that others dread without becoming like the image of their fear and hate. To possess dread power does not corrupt us overnight; our features may remain benign for years. But inevitably the awareness that others tremble or grow enraged at sight of us poisons the mind and makes us, individuals or nations, in the end into aggressive pariahs, distrustful, capricious, and empty."

So I find myself in complete agreement with Lynn Cheney's argument that "At a time of national crisis...it is particularly apparent that we need to encourage the study of our past," if what she means is "study," rather than blind worship at the shrine of official reality. We have a past that includes many lives given to the hard, hard work of turning our grand phrases into reality. Those of us who know something about that past are obliged, it seems to me, to insist that it *all* be remembered, and argued over, and applied to the present. We needn't look to the Devil or abroad for the source of our own deviltries. That's what mirrors are for.

Ah, how I tried to see light at the end of the tunnel, and to hope that we'd somehow become historically literate. Wasn't it pretty to think so?

During the awful year of 1969, when I was ostensibly working on a PhD at the University of Denver, I was also working as the mail clerk in DU's Mary Reed Library. My predecessor in that job was a deeply cynical vet a few years my senior, who had carefully established in the official minds that sorting each day's mail was the work of an entire morning (when it really required about forty minutes on the highest-volume day), with the afternoon devoted to pickups and deliveries of various packages and audio-visual equipment around the city. I immediately saw that the virtue of this fictional schedule was that it gave me most of the morning to read extensively from the flood of periodicals that came in every day, everything from *Blood: the Journal of Hematology* to *The Village Voice*. Well, I didn't spend a lot of time with *Blood*.

But I did spend quite a bit of time reading *Nature,* and from that and other journals became more and more indignant about the chemical warfare we were employing with gay abandon in Vietnam under the name of "defoliation." I began writing about this to various newspapers, including the *Denver Post:*

Use of Chemical Defoliants

The Feb. 18 *Denver Post* editorial, "Defoliation May Cause Overkill," concludes that "the use of 2,4,5-T should be halted immediately in this country and in Vietnam, where Americans already have unwittingly inflicted too much suffering on civilians." I agree with that conclusion and would like to offer some information not furnished by the editorial.

1. The Departments of State and Defense have repeatedly asserted that the chemical defoliants 2, 4-D and 2,4,5-T are harmless, basing their assertions on a Midwest Research Institute survey of the literature relating to the two chemicals. Neither department has seen fit to mention one part of the survey's conclusion: "...reliable judgments could not be made with respect to the effect of defoliants on water quality, on mammals and birds in danger of extinction, on climate and the hydrologic cycle, or on

soil erosion" because "the conclusions of the MRI study are based primarily on research outside Vietnam." (*Science, Vol. 159*, p.613)

2. The National Cancer Institute study, which found that 2,4,5-T "caused increased fetal malformation in mice and rats" also found that 2,4-D had "potentially dangerous fetus deforming effects." (*Science,* Dec. 5, 1969, p. 1249)

3. A study showing that doses of 2, 4-D produced a 20 percent death rate in the eggs of chickens has been in public print since 1967. (*Nature, Vol. 215,* p. 1407)

4. The White House directive limited the use of 2, 4, 5-T in Vietnam not, as the *Post* states, to "nonpopulated areas," but to areas "remote from population." (*Science,* Dec. 5, 1969, p. 1249) The substantive effect of what may seem a minor linguistic distinction is made clear by the Defense Department's response to this directive: "...no change would be made in the policy governing the use of 2,4, 5-T because the Defense Department felt that its present policy conformed to the White House directive." (*Science,* Nov. 21, 1969, p. 978) This can mean one of two things: A. We have always defoliated areas in which no enemy troops were hiding, and destroyed crops in areas where no people existed to plant them, in which case the military effectiveness of the program would seem to be questionable; B. the Defense Department is not planning to put a very strict construction on the phrase "remote from population." In either case, it does not answer to the point that ecologists have been making for some time: that you cannot pollute or poison one part of a country without affecting, in quite unpredictable ways, the rest of the country, and the countries which surround it.

What all of this means is that we are going to go right on using 2,4-D and 2,4,5-T in Vietnam as we have since 1962, at whatever cost to the humans, animals and plants of that country. Mr. Mitchell has instructed us to watch what this administration does, not what it says. In the matter of 2,4-D and 2,4,5-T the administration has done, thus far, exactly nothing.

I got quite a number of similar letters into print in various papers, and sent more to Senators and Congressmen, to no observable effect at all. Not until 1991, eight years after Agent Orange's manufacturers had settled a lawsuit brought against them by a Vietnam veterans' group, did Congress admit that Agent Orange bore some responsibility for some of the veterans' health problems. (My sister June's late husband, Part Estep, would be posthumously included in this group.)

I was keeping track, as well, of the electoral shenanigans of our various puppets in South Vietnam:

Democracy in South Vietnam

After an interesting campaign to get his name on the South Vietnam presidential ballot, and then to get it off again, Vice President Ky has threatened to "destroy" President Thieu. Ky's office has denied the threat, and the vice president has now made the whole situation perfectly clear by issuing a statement.

He did threaten to destroy Thieu, he said, but newspaper accounts which said he made the threat were completely false.

I, and a lot of other malcontents and knockers, have been dubious about American efforts to instill a democratic spirit in the South Vietnamese. But Vice President Ky's latest statement has made a believer out of me; it's evident that, at long last, the true spirit of modern American democracy has come to South Vietnam.

Vice President Ky has exhibited how profoundly he grasps the fundamental principle of leadership in a modern democracy - total contempt for the intelligence of the people.

I had been inspired and impressed by the contempt for the American people shown by the Kennedy, Johnson and Nixon administrations, but Vice President Ky has, with one brilliant thrust, set a new standard of excellence in the field of contempt. Not content with evasions, strategic silences and half-truths, or even with refusing to divulge vital information, he has gone right to the wellspring of contempt. With confidence and assurance (very important leadership qualities), he has asserted two opposites, never doubting that the public will gullibly accept the truth of both. This is real chutzpah, of which leaders are made. Compared with Ky's masterpiece, Robert McNamara's innocent little distortions of the Tonkin Gulf affair pale to insignificance.

It would be a shame, after all the money and lives and whatnot we've expended developing democratic leaders in South Vietnam, if a leader of Vice President Ky's demonstrated abilities should go to waste because of an unfortunate legal technicality banning all but one candidate for the South Vietnamese presidency. It seems to me that the U.S. Democratic party should immediately draft Ky as its candidate for 1972, thus resolving the current confusing and undemocratic strife among Democrats for the nomination. General Westmoreland, who has worked closely with Vice President Ky, would make an ideal running mate, providing the military expertise so necessary to effective democratic leadership. In return, we could simply appoint Ellsworth Bunker as vice president of South Vietnam.

It might be a slight embarrassment that Vice President Ky once named Adolf Hitler as his "only hero," but a good television ad campaign would soon erase that error from public memory. As Ky has discovered, you can tell the people anything - in a democracy.

I decided against further pursuit of a PhD and Nancy got a job down in Colorado Springs, to which then pleasant town of 70,000 we moved in 1970. I soon found an anti-war group with which to involve myself, largely made up of Colorado College professors and students. This group appointed me (I think - I may have appointed myself) to write a propaganda pamphlet we would somehow distribute. I don't think we ever did, though I'm not certain why - reading this draft, it seems like a pretty disciplined, coherent exposition of a basic case against the war:

Draft for Indochina War Pamphlet

What Is the Indochina War

Our Goal

Over and over, the American people have been told that America makes war in Indochina in order to help South Vietnam become strong enough to repel internal and/or external aggression. We have been told that we are giving the South Vietnamese people a chance for "self-determination." But the tactics we have employed have nearly destroyed South Vietnam, and any hope it might have had for independence.

Our Means

Bombing

In one year (1966), we dropped 30,000 more tons of bombs on Vietnam (which is about the size of New Mexico) than we dropped in the Pacific Theater during all of World War II. By February, 1968, the United States had dropped 24,000 pounds of bombs for every square mile of Vietnam. Bombing has increased since then. Laos has been subjected to massive bombing for years, and Cambodia is now sharing the wealth of American air power. President Nixon places "no limitation" on the further use of American air power.

Defoliation

Since 1962, we have sprayed millions of acres of South Vietnam with chemical herbicides, destroying many mangrove forests, food crops and rubber plantations. The two most widely used chemicals are responsible for birth defects and increased cancer rates in experimental animals; the third chemical persists in the soil and water for many years. The defoliation program was initiated without prior research. When scientific pressure forced the Pentagon to attempt to justify the program, the Pentagon did so on the basis of a study whose major conclusion (which went unmentioned by the Pentagon) was that no one could say what effects massive defoliation might have. President Nixon has asked the Pentagon to end the defoliation program; the Pentagon doesn't want to end it. It continues today.

The Results

Bombing and defoliation, to speak of only two of our tactics, have been visited upon South Vietnam on a scale unprecedented in the history of warfare. South Vietnam is a small, agricultural country, not quite the size of Missouri. What has our massive air power meant to its people?

Civilian Casualties

The best estimate is that 300 t0 400 thousand South Vietnamese civilians have been killed or wounded since 1965, when intensive bombing began. Our engagement in Laos and Cambodia has helped produce perhaps 50,000 civilian deaths and injuries. It is common knowledge that air strikes and defoliation missions are far too numerous to be effectively limited to "enemy" targets, and that "enemy" dead are very often determined to be communists by the fact that we have killed them.

Refugees

Since 1961, nearly one third of the 16 million South Vietnamese have been recorded as either casualties or refugees. At least 715,000 Laotians are refugees, over 20% of the population. 100,000 South Vietnamese in Cambodia have "disappeared." Conditions in refugee camps are very bad, and the slums of Saigon, the population of which has increased by 2,500,000 since 1960, are not better. Many of the refugees have been deliberately driven from their homes as a part of the American program to deny guerrillas civilian support, or to create "free-fire zones," subject to blind destruction. The refugees have lost homes, possessions, villages, land, and often families.

South Vietnamese Economy

Rice and rubber, both requiring intensive cultivation, were historically the mainstay of South Vietnam's economy. American power has destroyed crops and has driven the agricultural workers off the land and into the cities and refugee camps. Even during the Japanese occupation, South Vietnam exported rice; since 1966, she has had to import it. South Vietnam's balance of trade since the beginning of large American commitment has been:

	1963	1964	1965	1966	1967	1968	1969	1970
(Millions of dollars):	-225	-224	-330	-631	-712	-627	____	____

Despite devaluation, inflation proceeds at a rate of 44% [1973] annually. In other words, South Vietnam's economy has been obliterated by our tactics, and the people of South Vietnam are now largely dependent on the American presence in the most degrading ways - as black marketeers, fences, pimps and prostitutes, or, if they are lucky, as employees of an American military installation which one day - so we say - will be gone. The Vietnamese can, of course, join an army financed by the United States. For those unable to attach themselves to the American money machine, a young Vietnamese professor speaks: "My yearly salary as a professor is not equal to the money a prostitute can make in three nights."

Vietnamization

"Vietnamization" has, since we financed the French in the 1950s, been our expressed goal. But since the entry of large American forces in 1965, we have managed to render this goal impossible of attainment by our brutal use of firepower and technology. Whether consciously or not, we have tried to prevail against a guerrilla war by removing the civilians on whom guerrillas depend for support. By removing the people from the countryside and destroying the agricultural land on which the guerrillas - and the entire country - depend, we have rendered South Vietnam a helpless dependent. Without our massive economic aid, South Vietnam could not survive one day. We have come close to destroying the country in order to save it. Each day we continue our military "assistance," South Vietnam becomes more dependent, and it becomes less likely that we will be able to help South Vietnam become a living country ever again.

For general information on the history, background and conduct of the war, we recommend:

Bernard Fall & Marcus Raskin, *The Vietnam Reader,* NY: Random House, 1965 - includes documents & essays representing both pro and anti-war positions.

Bernard Fall, *Vietnam Witness,* London: Pall Mall Press, 1966, and

    Last Reflections on a War, NY: Doubleday, 1967 - essays and reports by one of the most experienced and widely respected experts on foreign intervention in Vietnam

Jonathan Schell, *The Village of Ben Suc,* NY: Alfred A. Knopf, 1967, and

    The Military Half, NY: Alfred A. Knopf, 1968 - Two detailed descriptive accounts of American search-and-destroy operations and air and artillery tactics

---

    That pamphlet summarized a large part of the case against the war that was also made by a new organization, Vietnam Veterans Against the War, in Dewey Canyon III, an "operation" in Washington, D.C. in April of 1971. The small group of anti-war activists in Colorado Springs somehow prevailed upon Hank Greenspun, who then owned the Colorado Springs *Sun,* to send me as a special correspondent with the Colorado contingent of the VVAW, and the same small group came up with enough money to finance my trip (I was working part-time, and had no money of my own to spend on such a journey). So I hopped on the bus with the fifty or so Vietnam Vets from all over Colorado and the other Mountain States and we were off to the nation's capitol. The trip was enlivened by a former enlisted man who called himself "Bigg" (with two g's). He'd laid in a supply of apple wine for the journey, and periodically each night cried out, in a tone of immense pleasure, "*Boone* Farm!".

    We got off from the 3-day bus ride on a Sunday afternoon on the mall in front of the Capitol, where we would set up camp. The press was there to interview any vet who'd talk to them, and while I stood around observing this, someone filched my duffel bag, which contained all my clothes and my bedroll. I spent the rest of the week in the ratty old brown velour jacket and chinos that had already been through 3 days on the bus, sleeping on the ground between pieces of cardboard I managed to scrounge up somewhere.

    I mainly spent the week following various groups from the Colorado bunch around Washington as they visited their congressmen's and senators' offices. I phoned in my reports every night to the *Sun* from public pay phones, just like a reporter in an old black and white film. I sometimes lost my "journalistic objectivity," notably when a bunch of vets and I visited Senator Gordon Allott's office. His legislative aide was George Will, who has gone on to become an insufferably verbose and condescending "conservative" newspaper columnist and talking head. He was there to take on the initial onslaught before Allott deigned to appear, and he and I got into an argument over the probable results of an American withdrawal from Vietnam. "Name one country that hasn't become Communist after a successful revolution, or one country that's withdrawn that hasn't gone to pieces," he said. "*Algeria! France!*" I shouted. Our discussion did not become more civil from that point, and several vets picked me up and put me out in the hallway. There happened to be an NBC crew out there with a camera, and I gave them an interview of which I don't remember a word, but I do remember that it contained a whole lot of probably incoherent cursing. I don't expect the network chose to use any of that footage.

It was a remarkable week. There was a continuous legal battle going on over the encampment on the Mall, and the veterans I talked with said they felt pretty much at home, being surrounded by hostile forces. My sleeping accommodations didn't encourage sleeping in, so I was up early enough every morning to watch the FBI "undercover" agents arrive for work in their FBI cars and FBI suits. The agents would get out of the cars, enter the porta-potties placed around the periphery of the encampment, and emerge in what they fondly imagined was "hippie" garb. They were quite entertaining.

These are the reports I sent back to the *Sun*. You'll notice I attempted to make them sound "objective," the way Real Journalism was supposed to sound, despite the fact that I was completely supportive of the Veterans' purposes:

Local Man Joins Vet March

Washington - In a few hours, more than 2,000 Vietnam veterans will begin five days of marching, lobbying and "guerrilla theatre" in the nation's capital.

Fifty-eight Vietnam veterans from Colorado Springs, Denver, Greeley, Boulder and Vail arrived here early Sunday to participate.

Their aim is to bring about total withdrawal of American forces from Indochina by December 31, 1971.

The men are members of Veterans Against the War, an organization claiming a national membership of more than 10,000.

The Colorado Springs group includes veterans of the Army, Air Force, and Special Forces.

Some now attend college on the G.I. Bill, others drive trucks, work in steel mills, factories or hospitals.

Their opposition to the war's continuation is generally based on personal experience rather than sophisticated moral or intellectual arguments.

"I have younger brothers coming up," one former supply sergeant said here today. "I don't want to see them have to go over there."

Many of the men were only 13 in 1963, when the first large body of American troops was committed to Vietnam.

Rusty Lindley, a former Special Forces captain now attending Colorado College, spent a year with a South Vietnamese airborne division.

"They have the ability to fight. There's only one way to find out if they have the will - that's to get out and let them fight for themselves."

Veterans don't know whether Congress and the administration will act, but they expect them to listen.

"We fought for this country," one veteran said. "We see what Vietnam is. They have to listen."

Colorado Vets Meet With Allott

Washington - After a brief service honoring the dead of Vietnam, the Vietnam Veterans Against the War sent a delegation to the gate of Arlington National Cemetery to place memorial wreaths Monday.

The delegation, including mothers of soldiers killed in the war, was refused admission to the cemetery. The ex-GIs then turned and marched across Memorial Bridge, down Constitution Avenue to the Capitol.

Rep. Paul McCloskey, R-California, marched with the veterans.

"If anything can stop this war, it's something like this," he said, glancing back over the column.

After listening to speeches, the veterans broke into small groups to begin a week of concentrated lobbying.

A contingent of Colorado veterans met with Sen. Gordon Allott in the afternoon, presenting him with a telegram urging a set withdrawal date, signed by members of the Colorado Committee to Set a Date.

Signers included Luis Rovere, president of the Denver Bar Association, Richard Perchlik, mayor of Greeley, and Richard Waugh, president of the Arapahoe Chemical Company.

Mike Gard of Fort Collins told Senator Allott, "I was looking around today for my friends from Vietnam. I suddenly realized that all the ones who would be here were dead. But I don't hate Vietnam," he continued, "I love it. I want to go back and rebuild what I destroyed. And I destroyed a lot."

The senator replied, "The Nixon administration didn't begin this war. The difference between you and us is only how best to end the war."

The senator opposed setting a withdrawal date because, in his words, to do so "would be like standing in a ring with a boxer and telling what punch you were going to throw."

The veterans continued to speak of the nature of the South Vietnamese people, politics, and military. At one point the senator asked the group why North Vietnamese forces were highly motivated while the South Vietnamese were not.

"It's the American presence," several veterans said simultaneously. "We're just like the Redcoats in the American revolution," added Bob Mourning, a World War II veteran from Denver who accompanied the group.

The conversation continued for an hour and 15 minutes in Allott's office, which featured a book case topped by a bust of George Washington flanked by plastic models of guided missiles and fighter bombers.

Colorado Vets Meet Dominick

Washington - About 20 Colorado veterans crowded the office of Senator Peter Dominick Thursday to discuss the policy of "Vietnamization."

The senator contended that he had observed much progress in pacification in his 1970 visit to Vietnam.

"Do you know how accurate a view you get on those VIP tours?" asked Dave Harbert of Pueblo. "We used to spend days spit shining when a colonel was coming, let alone a senator."

"Not only that," added Ron Merz, a former army security agency Specialist 4, "you never talked to any Vietnamese except through an interpreter supplied by Saigon. They tell you what they think you want to hear."

Dominick said he received additional information from constituents serving in the war, including his son, who is a Vietnam veteran.

While he anticipates most American troops may be withdrawn by July, 1972, the senator agrees with the President that America is obliged to give the South Vietnamese a "reasonable chance" to take over their own defense.

"Do you think they would be happier if the Communists took over?" he asked. "They have a government they elected in supervised elections, you know."

"I was in I Corps during those elections," said Mike Gard, ex-Marine corporal from Fort Collins. "All the candidates on the ballot were from one party - the Thieu - Ky party."

"The government police brought people in from the country in trucks to vote. If they didn't vote, they couldn't get a new ID card. If they didn't have the card, they were automatically VC suspects. They couldn't get a ration card, either, and food was pretty short up there."

(Gard later testified before the Senate subcommittee on refugees, describing American tactics which led to civilian deaths and casualties and "generated refugees.")

The discussion with Dominick produced few agreements.

Steven Norris, a former army ranger from Denver, said in conclusion, "What we ask you to do, senator, is to try to reevaluate this war in human terms - not political, not military - and try to see what our testimony means. Try to see what we're doing to their people, and to ours."

The senator shook hands with the veterans as they left.

Angry Veterans Return Medals to Government

Washington - The Vietnam veterans stood at a microphone on the west plaza of the Capitol Friday, announced their names and former units, and returned their medals to the government.

After listing his decorations, each veteran threw his medals over a restraining fence toward the Capitol.

Campaign ribbons, purple hearts, bronze and silver stars and distinguished flying crosses flew toward an empty fountain beneath the Capitol dome, or struck the statue of John Marshall and fell among the rose bushes at its base.

Two veterans, one a veteran of World War I, returned their medals of honor.

35 officers and 5 chief warrant officers resigned their reserve commissions.

Scott Halliday, a Denver ex-sergeant who served with the 82nd and 173rd airborne units in Vietnam, said the return symbolized his shame at having fought in the war.

"These medals are rewards for killing," he said, "and the killing I did in Vietnam didn't do any good for anyone."

After the ceremony, ten of the Colorado veterans gathered in the office of Colorado Congressman Mike McKevitt, R - Denver.

McKevitt remarked that the veterans had made a deep impact on Washington and praised the courtesy and restraint the group had shown.

He advised the group to continue to work, not only for an end to the war, but for increased veterans' benefits and for a solution to the mounting drug abuse problem in the military.

"You've made a strong impression on me," McKevitt said. "I am going to write a letter concerning this to President Nixon. I won't make it public; there has been too much politics played with this war."

The veterans broke camp Friday evening.

On Saturday a new group of anti-war demonstrators will hold a mass rally in Washington.

Vietnam Veterans Against the War has announced support for all non-violent activities in the cause of peace, but does not associate itself with any other organization.

"I think we can talk to people no one else can reach," said Brian Adams, an army 1st lieutenant who resigned his commission Friday.

"I hope we've helped some people to understand the truth about this war this week, and we're going to go on until this war is over."

Vet's Observations on Week in Washington

Washington - I spent last week in Washington camping on the Mall with about 500 Vietnam veterans.

The experience left me feeling a strange mixture of hope and despair, and I feel compelled to describe the men who gave rise to those emotions: the veterans and the congressmen.

In six days, under moderately difficult conditions, 500 men lived together within a square block. During that time I did not observe a violent incident.

The veterans' non-violence was total.

In perhaps 100 conversations, I never heard a veteran raise his voice. The veterans listened to people, and then spoke, passionately but quietly, about their own experiences in Vietnam.

Many told me that the violence they had seen and done, in Vietnam, Laos and Cambodia, in what they considered an indefensible, unrealistic cause, had convinced them that no purpose could ever justify the use of violence.

Those men had traveled from hundreds to thousands of miles to accomplish a serious purpose. They intended to bring the truth of the war home to Congress, assuming that Congress would act to end the war once they saw that truth.

For a week, these often highly-decorated veterans, a number of whom spoke Vietnamese and had worked with the Vietnamese Army and civilian population, tried to describe the disastrous results of "Vietnamization." They told repeatedly of random killing, torture of prisoners, the corruption of the 1967 elections, and use of civilians and "friendly" villages as targets for marksmanship contests.

They told of the civilians' indifference to both communism and democracy, their compelling desire to see an end to the death and destruction, to be left alone by foreign powers.

They told of the horror and despair they and their comrades had felt at being ordered to kill and bomb for no reason which had anything to do with the realities of South Vietnam as they saw them. They told how, in order to repress their sense of guilt, they stayed "high" or drunk every waking hour for months.

I observed only the reactions of Colorado congressmen and senators.

Senator Gordon Allott reiterated the "domino theory."

Congressman Frank Evans declared that Congress had no proper voice in determining how or when the war would end; such decisions, he said, were the sole prerogative of the President.

Congressman Mike McKevitt refused to say whether or not he would sanction indefinitely continued American bombing of Indochina, since he did not wish to be an "instant military expert."

The veterans repeatedly stressed the human costs of the war. Senator Allott's only argument against setting a fixed withdrawal date was an analogy between war and boxing.

What I saw last week convinced me that the Colorado congressional delegation is making the decisions which will prolong this war indefinitely with little or no regard for the human cost. Judging from all that these six men said, I can only believe that questions of saving face are paramount in their minds. That they seek to save national face, rather than their own individual careers, does not make their decision any less tragic.

For a week in Washington, I lived in a small community of realism, decency and gentleness, set within a larger community of abstraction and remote-controlled violence. The conduct of the veterans made me proud, for the first time in years, to be part of an America which had produced such men. I would like to believe that America will listen to the voices of these veterans, will see their terrible honesty; that America will move toward a more realistic, less blindly self-righteous view of itself and the world.

Nothing I saw in Colorado's congressional offices gave me any hope that our government will allow this to happen.

Shortly after I got back to Colorado Springs, the VVAW announced that it would hold hearings on American war crimes in Vietnam in Denver. I went up to report on those hearings. I was able to stay in an absent friend's apartment, where I typed all night after the hearings concluded so I could submit my report to the Denver papers, neither of which saw fit to print it. I drove back to go to work in Colorado Springs slapping myself to stay awake as I drove. Belatedly, here's what I wrote:

What the Winter Soldiers Said

More than thirty veterans talked about their experiences in Vietnam last weekend at the Denver Indian Center. For twelve hours, while 16th Street traffic roared by outside the stained-glass windows of the former synagog, the veterans tried to convey what the reality of Vietnam had been to them.

They called themselves "winter soldiers" - a reference to the soldiers who remained with Washington's army in the winter of 1776 even though their terms of enlistment had been completed. "For too long, returning Vietnam veterans have been silent," their introductory statement concluded. "Now, as we begin to speak out, it would be tragic if the American people do not listen."

Between one and two hundred people listened to the veterans' testimony. This is part of what they heard.

"It's a Social Situation"

Most of the men had gone to Vietnam heavily armed with good intentions. They had been told they were going to advise, to help the South Vietnamese people fight and build a better way of life.

"When I went to Vietnam, I hardly knew it existed," said John Mitchell (Sp/5, Vietnam service 1963-64). "I thought we were fighting the Communist menace. I was quite a hawk for a while, until I realized what a terrible job we were doing." Mitchell's path, from abstract idealism to disillusionment, was followed by most of the veterans. Sources of disillusionment in Vietnam were plentiful.

John Manion, a former Ranger captain who had planned an Army career, soon found that his services as an adviser were neither desired nor appreciated. "The average Vietnamese officer has been fighting this war for 10 years. What advice is a first lieutenant with no combat experience going to give him?"

Manion soon found that the patrols and ambushes conducted by the regional and popular force units he advised were "haphazard and unmilitary." "Ambushes" typically consisted of "a walk in the woods" and a night's sleep - sometimes in hammocks - for most or all of the troops at the ambush site.

According to Manion, the "People's Self-Defense Forces" (PSDF), basic village units in the pacification effort, were even less effective. Advising the PSDF in 1969, Manion discovered that weapons were kept locked in village offices and never fired for want of ammunition; that training was non-existent; that in one six-month period 90 weapons had been lost to the Viet Cong, and only one enemy soldier had been reported killed.

Like Manion, Steve Norris (1st Lieutenant, 1969-1970) found that the popular force troops "enjoyed tremendously not having to fight," and that popular force commanders had working arrangements with their "enemy" counterparts which reduced the likelihood of hostile contact to zero.

Manion, Norris and other officers who served as advisers were at first appalled by South Vietnamese unwillingness to fight. Later, most came to believe that this unwillingness was understandable from the South Vietnamese point of view. Most Vietnamese, according to former Special Forcers Captain Forrest Lindley, neither desired or understood "Communism" or "Democracy." "The people - the draftees - are concerned with their homes, their families, their land. They want peace."

Such philosophical acceptance of Vietnamese reluctance to fight was less prevalent among infantrymen, for whom the reluctance often meant increased danger. Among infantrymen, contempt for Vietnamese soldiers commonly turn to contempt for all South Vietnamese people.

"Zips, gooks, dinks - we'd call them anything derogatory," said Marv Culwell, who served near Pleiku in 1968 and 1969. "Three women worked in the NCO club - worked there to support their families. Guys would yell, curse, throw beer at them, anything to make them cry." The attitude underlying this conduct was soon instilled in new troops, and Culwell thought nothing of it at the time. "It was just something to do."

Murder and destruction of property were other things to do. Frank Glen, who served as a door gunner on helicopters operating from Bien Hoa air base, told of his aircraft commander shooting civilians, dropping grenades randomly into the "pacified" village next to the air base, and described the popular sport of dropping boulders on civilian traffic along the roads.

Other sports included running civilian vehicles off the road and covering heat tablets (a chemical agent used to heat field rations) with chocolate; these "candy bars" were given to children who begged around the base.

Some military policies seemed to reflect and reinforce contempt for Vietnamese people. "If sniper fire was received from a village," according to Mike Gard, an ex-Marine forward artillery observer, "common procedure was to call in artillery fire on the village. I figure I alone was responsible for the destruction of 35 villages by artillery, and for hundreds of civilian deaths." Infantrymen agreed that they had never found a way to tell "VC" from civilians; "if he's dead, he's VC " was the only rule of thumb. This difficulty added to their disregard for civilian life. "South Vietnamese are not considered human beings by the Marine Corps," Gard concluded. "That may not be official policy, but that's the way it is in the field."

The enemy - suspected or confirmed Viet Cong or NVA (regular North Vietnamese troops) - was also treated with contempt. Numerous incidents of torture and murder of prisoners by Americans were recounted, and a number of infantrymen reported receiving verbal orders that no prisoners would be taken.

Mutilation of enemy bodies was not uncommon, and while the taking of scalps "wasn't usual," said Dean Phillips, who served with the 101st Airborne, "some of the guys did it." A Marine told of slitting the throat of a prisoner who had been shot, then cutting off his ear. "I brought it home in a talcum powder jar and wore it on a gold chain. My dad called me a sadist, but my mom thought it was cool. When my girl friend saw it, she like lost her cookies and it like went down the toilet."

As in all wars, combat infantrymen were a minority in Vietnam. In relatively secure support areas, other causes for disillusion prevailed, among them the corruption of South Vietnamese officials and the temptations of an openly thriving black market.

Corruption was described as "a way of life" for South Vietnamese officials, who used their positions - which they had usually purchased - to steal and profiteer.

South Vietnamese participation in the black market was understandable, according to Ralph Swain (Sp/5, 1969 - 1970): "It was one of the few ways for the people who had been driven into Saigon to survive." Swain investigated black market activities extensively. He recounted several cases of senior American NCO's who had illegally converted thousands of American dollars and stolen and sold PX merchandise; the most severely punished was fined, reduced one grade in rank, and reassigned. Swain contrasted these sentences with the penalty meted out to a Pfc who had failed to report for duty and cursed a superior - forfeit of all pay for 6 months, reduction to Private and 6 months hard labor. Profiteering "was almost legal in your mind, because the opportunities were so rife and control so lax."

"If you didn't do it, someone else would," said Frank Glen. He told of the profits he turned selling PX goods purchased with borrowed ration cards and of selling American weapons provided by officers and NCO's. "It's free enterprise at its finest."

Under these circumstances, an increasing number of the men turned to drugs - alcohol, marijuana, methedrine, opium and, beginning in 1969, heroin. According to two of the men, the heroin was introduced to them as "a form of non-addictive cocaine," and originally cost about 2 dollars per vial. Most of the soldiers believed that they wouldn't become addicted so long as they only smoked the heroin, said Charles Chandler (Private, 1969 - 1970). However, by the time Chandler left Vietnam in December, 1970, "about half my company was strung out." Paul Longest, a 101st Airborne trooper, estimated that 80% of the men in his outfit were "on something."

The atmosphere of Vietnam - corrupt, violent, inhumane and drug-saturated - was not subject to much reflection or discussion by the men while they were immersed in it. A few found it "weird" or somehow wrong on first encounter, but most adapted to it.

"You have to understand," Frank Glen said to a member of the audience who had asked who was responsible for the violence and corruption, "you have to understand how it works. You go into a new unit, and you have to feel it out, find out what's happening. Or someone will take you aside and tell you, 'This is what they like, this is what you have to cover up.' It's a social situation, just like any other."

A Human Head

The primary intent of the Winter Soldier Investigation was to help the American people understand what the war has done, and continues to do, to people - South Vietnamese and American.

Dean Phillips, seeming surprised at the memory, recalled that at one time he had seriously considered sending a human head home. "I didn't really understand why. I guess I wanted the people back home to....I felt they didn't really care what we were going through."

Much was said about the contradictions between America's professed goals and means actually used to attain them. The "incredible violence" of American firepower and economic power seemed to the veterans to have rendered our public professions of good will and noble intent absurd, and they concluded that these professions were lies.

"I can remember flying, south of Saigon, over thousands of acres of good farmland," said Frank Glen. "I saw bombed-out houses, nobody working the land. The people are afraid to go back and farm. And I just want to ask you - how are we defending these people?"

While some of the veterans were inclined to blame middle-rank officers for some of the abuses they had witnessed, most did not believe the military was ultimately responsible for what they regard as a disastrous war. They inclined to take responsibility for their own actions, and to ask the audience whether the American people did not share responsibility for the war.

Dr. Byron Johnson, a CU regent who served on a panel of community members who questioned the veterans, concluded his final comment by addressing the dwindling audience: "No American can ignore 7 years of a bleeding ulcer, in which no good can be accomplished," he said. "But don't blame the soldiers. The mirror is up to you."

In the Mirror

How accurate is the "mirror" with which these Vietnam Veterans Against the War have presented us? A growing body of evidence suggests that it is, in the full sense of the word, terribly accurate. Transcripts of Winter Soldier Investigations held in other cities, a long list of books, reports and transcripts of Congressional hearings, and the recently published Pentagon history of the war all suggest that our abstract view of Vietnam as a pawn in the Great Power Game, our indiscriminate use of immense military power, our stubborn refusal to recognize the internal political realities of South Vietnam or to acknowledge error have caused us to engage and persist in a war which shames us all.

We have called on the idealism of our young men, and they have answered, and found that the fine words we taught them had nothing to do with the conduct required of them in Vietnam. "All the way up," one of the veterans said last weekend, "as far as we could see, something else entirely was going on than what we'd been told." Safe at home, we have been able, too many of us, to ignore the human destruction our abstractions mask.

Adolf HItler's SS chief, Heinrich Himmler, described Nazi expansions in these terms: "We are original in one important point, our measures are the expression of an idea, not the search for any personal gain or profit. We desire only the realization...of a social ideal and the unity of the West. We will clarify the situation at whatever cost."

These rationalizations sound disconcertingly familiar. A former Green Beret, considering their familiarity, has written: "The espionage, subversion and security expediencies of the totalitarian states, once understood to be a part of what set them off from us, have tended to be taken over by us as regrettable but inevitable measures of realism. Yet how can this process be arrested if we ourselves accept a moral absolutism which denies scruples about *how* you act so long as there is an idealistic justification for *why* you act...?" [Pfaff]

Our government has consistently offered us "idealistic justifications" for its actions in Vietnam, telling us we were defending freedom, democracy, seeking to help the people of South Vietnam to a better life. In 1965, however, a high Defense Department official assessed our motives in very different terms, writing in what he hoped would be secret, "70% - to avoid a humiliating U.S. defeat. 20% - to keep SVN territory from Chinese hands. 10% - to permit the people of SVN to enjoy a better, freer way of life."

This assessment is hardly a revelation. Press accounts from the beginning of the war have presented us with evidence sufficient to demonstrate that our concern for the South Vietnamese people has been precisely at the level of that contemptuous, off-hand figure of 10% The Pentagon Papers contain serious revelations, but the most serious of all is the revelation of our abdication, as a people, of the sovereign responsibilities a republic's citizens must exercise.

Members of the last 5 administrations are surely at fault for disguising their true aims and failing to share the best available assessments of the true situation in Indochina with Congress and the people. But we have been far more gravely at fault for allowing them to deceive us in spite of freely available evidence. We haven't bothered to seek out that evidence, or to think about it. We have behaved like the citizens of an authoritarian state, blindly trusting our leaders, failing to compare their assertions with facts, allowing them to conduct a war in the name of our country which has violated and perverted the very qualities our country claims to represent, and at its best has represented.

We have used our power and the lives of our young men in an attempt to impose our will on a situation we failed to understand. We have interfered violently in the lives of people for whose human fate we had no regard - for 10% regard, in terms of the battlefield, is no regard.

By ignoring the effects of our means, we have tacitly agreed that any means are justified in pursuit of our ends. We have allowed our government to operate in secrecy and deceit because we have somehow come to hold the strange, totally un-American belief that our government is superior to us in knowledge, in reason, or in right.

The results of our irresponsibility are becoming clear. The veterans, holding their Winter Soldier Investigations in city after city, describe the results in brutal terms. Americans, their testimony indicates, as all other men, will react savagely and lawlessly when placed in a situation for which they can find no real justification, no decent rationale, no workable code of conduct except Kill or Be Killed. While we have beguiled ourselves with prating of democracy and of winning hearts and minds, our young men have been led to give children poisoned candy.

The men we sent into such a situation have seen and experienced the results of our failure to act and think as Americans rather than automatons. They have begun to tell us what our failure has done to them, and to us. It would be tragic, indeed, if we failed to listen to them.

Neither Dewey Canyon III nor the Winter Soldier Investigations had any noticeable effect on the course of things. The Nixon administration was not listening to sweet reason any more than it was to screams of rage. Kissinger and Nixon were desperate that America should not be perceived as "losing" the war, and so we plowed on into the Big Muddy, and it began to seem to most of us opponents of the war that our only hope of ending it was to work for George McGovern's campaign to unseat Nixon.

For a while during the primaries, we could delude ourselves that McGovern might not only win the nomination, but defeat Nixon in the election. He won the nomination, sure enough, and sure enough the old-guard New Frontier so-called Democrats who infiltrated his campaign - people like Frank Mankiewicz and Gary Hart - were able to persuade him to choose a non-entity with a politically toxic past, Senator Tom Eagleton of Missouri, as a running mate. When the toxic past - Eagleton had had shock treatments for depression - was revealed, McGovern first stated that he was behind his VP nominee "One thousand percent," then abruptly defenestrated him a few days later, replacing him with a Kennedy family hack and gofer, Sargent Shriver. If McGovern had had any prayer of defeating Nixon, which he probably hadn't, that little display of ineptitude and political cowardice answered that prayer with a resounding negative. Well, Massachusetts liked him.

Compared with scandalous behavior that goes unpunished and virtually unremarked these days, Eagleton's "scandal" was pretty mild, and I still think it was McGovern's swift withdrawal of his initial support that sealed his doom. Despite that criticism, I've never felt anything but proud that I worked to get McGovern elected, and I think now that Hunter Thompson had it right - the country was more than willing to put a cheapjack little hustler and his war criminal defense secretary and his war criminal secretary of state back in power rather than the largely decent WWII hero George McGovern.

Since then, I've watched my country engage in military adventures designed to advertise the size of various Presidential gonads and to support various business interests and, finally, to no real purpose at all except to maintain the Pentagonist/Multinational Corporate status quo into infinity. The "war on terror" makes Hitler's dream of a thousand-year Reich look like a piker's wish. For how can an abstract noun ever be defeated? As Peter Ustinov observed, "terrorism is the war of the poor; war is the terrorism of the rich." And the rich can buy all the naming rights.

But before we declared ourselves eternal victims, authorized by "9/11" to engage in perpetual warfare anywhere we wished, we were still pretending to be some sort of republic, some sort of member of the community of nations. I kept writing fruitless letter after fruitless editorial, urging various branches of the government to act as if the Constitution weren't a quaint historical artifact, suitable for sale on Antiques Roadshow. As late as the last year of the Reagan administration, enraged by the pusillanimity of Congress during the Iran-Contra hearings, I wrote a parody of those hearings, with "herr unterKolonel Jessel" standing in for Oliver North. By this time I was publishing myself, in a little periodical I edited, *The Unofficial Organ.* I rarely read my own stuff once it's been written, but I have to admit I still get a kick out of this piece. I think I captured North's unctuousness and the congressional committee's toadying pretty accurately:

The Lost Jessel/Donuts Transcripts

The Unofficial Organ II:1 1988

[Translator's note: In February of 1933, the Nazi party faced an election which threatened to disappoint their hopes. Shortly before the election, the Reichstag, home of the German Chamber of Deputies, caught fire in twenty places simultaneously. The Nazis instantly blamed the Communists, though it was widely suspected that the Nazis themselves had set the fires. Only recently have the records of the Deputies' investigation of the fire come to light. Some of the salient passages of the hearings follow, translated, with the greatest difficulty, into English.]

A Dramatic Outburst

(Herr unterKolonel Jessel, Chief Assistant to the Assistant Chief, testifying)

Deputy I [Deputies are identified by numerals only, since they were indistinguishable from each other in all essential characteristics]: So, you are telling us then -

Herr unterKolonel Jessel: Of course, gentlemen - and I thank the living God that made me that you *are* gentlemen, every man-Jack of you, since deputies as a class are feckless ignoramuses and biddy-like blabbermouths - Gentlemen, I was saying, you must realize two things about this extraordinarily brave and supremely humble unterKolonel here pinioned on the cross of your power by the spears of your cruel and relentless questionings: One, he took an oath, when he entered the Wehrmacht, to always tell the truth; Two, he has some really good friends, some of them related to him by sacred family ties, that he would hate to see blown to kingdom come by some mud-eyed Moravian Red. As would yourselves, I am sure.

Deputy I: I am certain my fellow deputies are at one with me in the deep admiration I have for your achievements in making friends and having a family -

Herr Besserwisser [unterKolonel Jessel's attorney]: Cut it short, there. I'm getting pretty *sick* of having to tell you people, *quit badgering my client.* I've told you he isn't guilty of anything, and if he is, whatever it is he's guilty of shouldn't be called wrong, because he does everything he does for the highest motives, for God's sake, and he didn't know it was wrong, anyway, even though he didn't do it.

Deputy I: - *if* I may continue....I merely wanted to ask this brave and courageous young man of steel and sinew why, if he took an oath to tell the truth, he cheerfully admits to *not* telling the truth to us about this fire?

Herr unKolonel Jessel: Let this fellow, Jessel, try to get it across to you this way, if God is willing to give you the gift of comprehension: I did *not* admit to not telling the *truth.* I said I had reconfigured the *facts.* Now, that is certainly not "not telling the truth;" it is *reconfiguring.*

Deputy I: Oh, *reconfiguring.*

Other Deputies: Oh, *reconfiguring.*

Clarification

(Admiral Donuts, Assistant Chief to the Chief, testifying)

Deputy IV: So, as I understand it, you are telling us that you ordered these fires to be set, that you didn't know that they were to be set, that you knew that Herr Hitler would approve your order to set them which you never discussed with him, except when you did, and that he is not not-telling the truth when he denies that he would have approved the plan if you had told it to him, and you are not not-telling the truth when you say he would have. Do I have it straight now?

Admiral Donuts: Basically, yes, you have taken my meaning. Though of course in other ways, basically you have not.

Deputy IV: Admiral, could you clarify that last response?

Admiral Donuts: I would be most happy to attempt to do so, sir, but it would require my divulging Classified Information, Information which, should it subsequently come bubbling out over the loose lips of some nameless, flaccid nincompoop, could trickle into the consciousness of the sacred German people, who will only approve of correct policies if they remain in utter ignorance of all significant facts. Or "data," as we professionals call them.

Deputy IV: Admiral, I can't help but sense that sometimes you seem to, ah, contradict yourself.

(At this point, Herr Fliegenschnapfer, Admiral Donuts' attorney of record, seized a water carafe and began to make hurling gestures toward Deputy IV. He was quelled by the Admiral, himself, with great urbanity.)

Admiral Donuts: Do I contradict myself? Very well, then, I contradict myself. You see? I admit it. Because I am *right*. For, at the moments of greatest peril - and, gentlemen, I cannot tell you or the great German people too often, it is a perilous world, a dangerous world, a vicious, sickening, confusing world - in the moments of greatest peril, I reiterate, it is necessary to move *above* wrong, into the True, Higher Right. As our great leader has done, and not done.

Deputy IV: I am deeply disturbed by some of what you tell us Admiral, deeply disturbed. Yet I am also deeply grateful to you for your testimony, which has proved to be profoundly baffling, and cause for deep concern and even deeper gratitude for the democratic institutions which have allowed it to baffle us.

The People Speak

(Admiral Donuts continuing his testimony)

Deputy II or VII: Admiral, you have testified that, basically, you and unterKolonel Jessel and a few hired street scum set all these fires, and that you were saying the thing that was not when you told everyone, including us just now, that the Communists set these fires?

Admiral Donuts: Affirmative, sir. Negative, sir.

Deputy II or VII: What?

Admiral Donuts: Excuse my barely perceptible patient sigh....If the fires didn't start, the Communists might have won the election. The people are afraid of the Communists. So, if we didn't burn the Reichstag a little, the people's worst fears would have come true, *n'est ce pas*? So, really, the Communists *made* us do it, and so did the people. It was their will. So we didn't do it, even though we did it.

Deputy II or VII: But you were supposed to tell some of *us*, so they could not-tell the rest of the deputies, and demonstrate our deep loyalty and circumspection.

Admiral Donuts: Someone would have *told*. And then the people would have got wind of it, and become confused in inappropriate ways. They might have been deluded into thinking we were not correct in knowing they wanted us to do what they thought they didn't want us to do.

Deputy II or VII: But how can you know the people's will if you don't consult with their elected deputies?

Admiral Donuts: The German people have a*lways* hated Communism. Everyone knows that. They have hated it ever since the 15th Century.

Deputy II or VII: Admiral, there was no such thing as Communism in the 15th Century.

Admiral Donuts: That is how much the German people hate it, sir. They hated it even when it didn't exist.

A Father's Heart

(unterKolonel Jessel re-testifying)

Deputy Something: Now, you have testified that your motives in this were entirely patriotic -

unterKolonel Jessel (here the unterKolonel began to weep unreservedly, possibly at the thought of his patriotism)

Deputy Something: - and that you received no extrinsic rewards for your services to Herr Hitler, except, of course, for the rewards you did receive -

unterKolonel Jessel (sobbing): My infant son! Fruit of my best friend's womb! I know it was the gravest mistake of my life to take it, but it was a father's heart speaking! Surely, sir, you can find it in *your* heart to thank God for the promptings of a Father's Heart! The little shaver never asked for anything -

Deputy II or VII (awakening suddenly): What is he talking about?

Deputy Something: Poland
                              Further Clarification
(unterKolonel Jessel continues to re-testify)

Deputy I: So, Herr unterKolonel, a reasonable man could view your acts as inspired efforts in the defense of German democracy -

unterKolonel Jessel: No, sir, begging your pardon, sir. All this soldier has done is his very best, which is, I'm sure, a poor thing, although he is deeply proud of what he has done and not done.

Herr Besserwisser: Why don't you geriatric swine just pack it in? And *stop badgering my client!* He *limps,* if you didn't *notice.*

Deputy I: Yes...well, yes, yes, I think we may as well conclude our hearing. For we have found the truth, which is that we are not going to find it, what with one thing and another. And the truth shall make us free. Herr unterKolonel, do you have any further harangues to make?

unterKolonel Jessel (here he consulted with his drama coach while rapidly signing contracts): Only this, sir: Sometimes it is necessary to destroy Democracy in order to save it. And I want to personally thank Almighty God and His Best Friend and Infant Son that we live in a democracy that can be so saved.

Deputies en masse: Jolly good! Yes, sir! Quite right, quite right! Deeply inspiring! Deeply troubling! Bravo!....

[Translator's note: In actuality these portions of the transcript may not be the most salient, but they shall have to suffice, as the remaining 17, 000 pages have been recently consumed in a mysterious blaze at the translator's office. As Deputy I's closing remarks implied, the origins of the Reichstag fire were not determined by the Deputies at this time. This did not much matter, however, since Admiral Donuts, at some time during his testimony, had prevailed upon Hitler to suspend all civil and individual rights. This suspension was immediately followed by the arrest of all deputies determined by Hitler to be secretly opposed to the Democratic Process as expressed by the will of the people, and by the historic vote of the Reichstag which granted Chancellor Hitler power to legislate anything and everything all by himself. It was duly noted of this historic act that the Reichstag would remain unaffected by it, as would Democracy.]

I've watched my country happily accept the introduction of military propaganda into every form of entertainment - sporting events, television shows, school ceremonies - as the American Empire becomes ever more acceptable to a people who once prided themselves on their rejection of foreign entanglements and standing armies. I've frequently been reminded of the German writer Bella Fromm's journal observations, published as *Blood and Banquets* [Fromm]:

"[1932] Went to Berchtesgaden yesterday. The S.A. had a monster parade. The word 'monster' is fitting, I think. The brown monster rolled along the road from Reichenhall to Berchtesgaden. The pounding of their boots haunted my mind all night long. Will there be anybody who can stop the stamping of their feet all over Germany?

"When I was small, I loved parades. I hate them now. The feet pound, pound, pound, and under their thunderous, insensitive impact lies my beautiful country."

"I recognized early that this would not stop in Germany, that the poison would permeate the whole world. There are men everywhere who would sell out humanity for their own personal profit. There are stupid and emotional masses everywhere who can be found to follow them, given a few slogans and some nice uniforms....."

We have become the very monsters we fought in World War II. This is hardly a novel occurrence. It's been the fate of empire after empire after empire. But we mostly don't see that it has happened to us, because we have no memory of our or anyone else's past, and so nothing with which to compare the strutting popinjays we've given our reins to, the tactics of totalitarianism we've welcomed in the name of "security," the propaganda of fear and scapegoating and name-calling and intentional irrationality we mis-label "speech." We didn't listen carefully enough to Herman Goering when, just before he popped the cyanide pill, he told his interrogator: "Of course the people don't want war. But after all, it's the leaders of the country who determine the policy, and it's always a simple matter to drag the people along whether it's a democracy, a fascist dictatorship, or a parliament, or a communist dictatorship. Voice or no voice, the people can always be brought to the bidding of the leaders. That is easy. All you have to do is tell them they are being attacked, and denounce the pacifists for lack of patriotism, and exposing the country to greater danger. It works the same in any country." [Overy]

But virtually every force and interest in our culture urges us constantly against thinking about the past, and so we don't draw any lessons from it. We remain the world's most dangerous infants. "Those who cannot remember the past are condemned to fulfill it," George Santayana observed in *The Life of Reason.* Sometime during the lamentable decade of the 80s, I added a corollary: "Since hardly anyone remembers the past, those who do are condemned to fulfill it, too."

But back in the early 70s, still under the sway of the 60s' brand of cosmic optimism, I hadn't yet despaired. I remember saying to a lot of people that elected "leaders" seemed to me like fleas wagging on the end of the tail of a very large dog (the dog representing the American people), and that if you wanted the fleas to move in some other direction, you'd better work on the dog. I felt that people were both ignorant of many of the things their government had been doing and not well enough educated to see through the lies and distortions the government was feeding them to disguise its crimes. It didn't occur to me that the people simply might not give a damn what we were doing to a bunch of gooks, or to a bunch of our own minority and poor kids, so long as they were making out pretty well, economically speaking. I still harbored the intellectual's fond belief that people could be improved by teaching them to reason better. So I quit working on elections, and got more serious about teaching, especially after I was hired full time to teach "developmental English" at the community college.

Boring Repetition

During my early years at El Paso Community College (which later became Pikes Peak Community College), I worked as a kind of tutor-of-last-resort, helping students whose difficulties baffled their classroom teachers. Much of my tutoring was in math, and I eventually taught developmental math classes - arithmetic, beginning algebra, and a pre-arithmetic course called Math 007, for those who'd yet to learn even the most basic math facts. The students I tutored began to teach me how to teach. I used to start out Math 007 classes by teaching a little magic trick a real math teacher had showed me, Casting Out Nines. Basically, you keep adding the digits of the addends or multplicands across, scratching out any combinations that add up to 9, until you have one digit left in each row. Then you add up all the digits in that column until you get one single digit. You do the same with the digits in your sum or product. The two final single digits should be the same, if your original computation was correct. I'd give my students this handout:

Checking Your Work
(If you aren't your own master, you are someone else's servant)

Check by Opposites:

Addition:

```
 18    Check: 32   or   32
+14          -14       - 18
 32           18         14
```

Subtraction:

```
 54    Check: 27
- 27         +27
 27           54
```

Multiplication:

```
  27              27
x14           14/378
 108              28
 27               98
378               98
```

Division:

```
    14              35
35/ 496           x14
    35             140
   146              35
   140             490
   R  6         + R 6 = 496
```

Check Long Addition and Multiplication Problems by Casting Out Nines

Addition: Multiplication:

	Check:		Check:
472	4<u>72</u>- ~ 4	434	434 ~ 11 ~ 2
397	3<u>9</u>7 ~ 1	x226	<u>226</u> ~ 10 ~x1
425	4<u>25</u> ~ 2	2604	2604 2
+222	<u>222</u> ~ 6	868	868
1516 ~ 13 ~ 4	= 1516 ~ 13 ~ 4	<u>868</u>	<u>868</u>
		98,084 ~20 ~ 2	= 2

If you train yourself to check your work, you'll never have to ask what you got on a test. You'll know your score before you hand in your paper. It will be 100%.

    Then I'd give them worksheets on which to practice casting out nines. Now you know how to check your work, I'd tell them, and you know a way to do it hardly anyone's ever even heard of. I gave them a simple, amazing little trick they could pretty easily master - for many of them, the first piece of uncommon knowledge they'd ever possessed - and at the same time started them forming the habit of checking their work, of taking responsibility for their answers.

    One of the main things most of my math students taught me was a deep revulsion for the new notions that were infesting education on every level. While I'd been lucky enough to get through school before the New Math plague, most of my students hadn't, and I spent untold hours trying to convince them to forget such useless nomenclatures as "the associative property," since all it meant was that (2 + 3) + 4 would give you the same result as 2 + (3 + 4). Or that A x B = B x A. Plastering multi-syllabic monickers on such self-evident facts simply tended to turn them into incomprehensible murk for most students. And the New Math was plaguing kids with such bushwa instead of making them learn their damn tables.

    The invasion of, first, hand-held calculators and, shortly, of computers represented another great leap forward toward the stupification of the American student, and these lamentable developments prompted me to voice my opposition:

Why Boring Repetition is Better Than a Flash Drive

I am going to begin by telling you a personal story, rather than summarizing the research that shows, with very few exceptions, that no good has come of computerized instruction for elementary students, though such research surely exists. I tell you the following story because stories appeal to our common sense, an old-fashioned term that we have come to disparage to our very great loss.

During my first four years of grade school, I learned the addition and multiplication tables through 12. I learned them somewhat in classes by reciting them, by flash card games, by writing them down. I mainly learned them at home by those same means. I still remember writing the grid of multiplication facts over and over, chanting them as I wrote, then closing my eyes and chanting them again. I would have preferred to be up in the vacant lot playing baseball, or, really, doing just about anything else. But that was my homework, and my parents were pretty adamant about my doing it.

Because I had learned the facts of addition and multiplication, subtraction and division came pretty easily. So did fractions and the decimal system.

I didn't know it, but the methods by which I learned those central facts of math were designed to optimize my ability to learn them, making use of the three major sensory learning passages: visual, auditory, tactile. Combining those three senses made learning efficient and memory more permanent.

Those same methods taught me other skills I didn't know I was learning at the time. They taught me to look for patterns; writing out those bloody multiplication tables over and over again, I began to notice that the vertical columns were just the addition tables I'd already learned. I even noticed that any number times 9 always produced a number whose sum was 9. At that age, this seemed mildly entertaining but not particularly useful.

Using the facts I'd learned on tests, I learned also to estimate probable results, so that if I arrived at an answer that didn't correspond with my estimate I would go back through my work to see if I'd made an error. I learned that human error was something I ought to expect.

Perhaps most important, all that boring, repetitive manual labor taught me how to visualize and memorize. I learned that making a visual pattern and repeating it to myself out loud, over and over, was the quickest way to learn something.

What I was doing was programming my own hard drive, entering data and protocols for its use into my personal computer, which was in those days known as my brain. As I went on through math classes in grade school, junior high and high school, I couldn't help but notice that those fellow students who were struggling with fractions or decimals or geometry or algebra seemed not ever to have learned their tables. If you don't have the multiplication tables inscribed in your brain, nothing much after multiplication makes much sense to you. And when you get to something like geometry or algebra, which require you to actually *think* with numbers and imagine that numbers have *meaning*, you're lost.

I did not enjoy math in those days, and when I arrived at trigonometry, I dismounted. Instead I majored in Music and English, became a soldier, and returned to the States with no idea what I might do to make a living. After my separation pay ran out, and making a living became a serious concern, I enrolled in the Denver Bartending School.

The text was the *Mr. Boston Bartender's Guide,* and it contained about 260 drink recipes. I soon saw that it had been organized according to patterns, and that there were really only about 14 patterns I needed to learn. For example, "Cream Drinks" essentially comprised an ounce of cream, a half-ounce of white or dark creme de cacao, and an ounce of whatever hard liquor the drink's name implied - "Brandy Alexander," brandy, "Grasshopper," green creme de menthe, and so on. On my fourth day at school, the head instructor called me out of class and said he'd had a request for a bartender from one of Denver's prestigious old taverns, and I went down there and interviewed and got hired. I continued the rest of my six-week course at the Bartending School as an instructor.

Now, none of my teachers at the Frances Willard Grade School, let alone my parents, browbeat me to learn arithmetic facts because they knew it would prepare me for a glamorous, rewarding career as a bartender. They made me learn those facts because they knew that possessing them would prepare me to solve problems in my life that involved numbers, as so many of life's problems do, and prepare me to resist bamboozlement by sharpsters throwing big numbers around to becloud common sense.

I have now watched two generations of students whose hard drives were not so programmed, who were allowed instead to use electronic calculators, on the deeply incorrect and silly assumption that learning arithmetic facts was monkey work - mindless repetition. You have also watched those students, as clerks and salespeople and citizens, and you have probably noticed that a large majority are mathematical idiots, incapable of performing the simplest calculations if "the computer is down," incapable of recognizing that a computer's "answer" is absurdly large or tiny because they're incapable of estimating results, incapable of figuring much of anything out that requires measurement in numbers, because the facts and protocols have been left *out there*, in the computers. And yet hardly anyone - parent, school board member, teacher - questions the replacement of a properly programmed human brain with a universally programmed, exterior computer.

I suggest to you that if computers can be valid and useful tools, they can only be so for human users who have already programmed the basic facts of reality into their brains. For those who have not, computers are not tools, they are slave masters. Putting computers into grade school classrooms does not "enhance" education; in profound ways, it *replaces* education.

Toward the end of his life, Kurt Vonnegut said it this way: "Bill Gates says, 'Wait till you can see what your computer can become.' But it's you who should be doing the becoming, not the damn fool computer. What you can become is the miracle you were born to be through the work that you do." [Vonnegut]

The tsunami of computerization that swept through the country starting in the 80s did not spare the world of education. In fact, I was pretty astonished to see how fervently not only the bosses, but most of the teachers, embraced that wave, one that would submerge and drown most of their historic values in less than a generation. Over the last twenty years of my work as a teacher, I took a number of approaches to try to get people to ask the most basic questions about why computers had become ubiquitous. I'll leave those attempts for a separate chapter, since it wasn't only education that computers were replacing.

My students taught me about many things, not just about how to teach. I spent a lot of time listening to them in my office. (To provide some suggestion of what a different world we inhabited in the early 70s, my office must have reeked of the cigarillos and Gauloises I smoked in it every day, and one of its walls was decorated by an unflattering plastic Halloween mask of Nixon, with a *faux* joint cemented between his lips, from which also dripped drool I'd fashioned from fossilized glue.) After a while, their stories led me to know what questions I should begin with. "What happened to you in the 4th grade?" was nearly always productive, and the answer was nearly always that some dimwitted excuse for a teacher had told the student he or she was "no good at math" (or some other subject). Their stories began to inform me how much more worthy of admiration and respect they were than they'd been told by their worlds, or than I was. They'd borne and were bearing such awful burdens, and yet here they were, fighting to start again. One of my colleagues told me early on the old saying that "a good teacher is like a good whore - you have to learn how to fall in love real quick." For me, it wasn't a hard trick to learn. (All right. I *heard* that crack.) Much later, I wrote a fictionalized version of one student's life as she'd revealed it to me during months of conversation:

A Bunch of Felonies
Rocky Mountain Arsenal of the Arts, IV:5, September-October 1990

You know, that's what my sockeyetrist told me. "Catherine," he said, "you've got a person in you, another person besides you, and that person is all the time telling you, 'Catherine, you're no good, Catherine, you can't do thus and that.' And you are trying to become yourself, but that other person is afraid that if you do, then she'll be dead. You're trying to kill that other person, and she don't like it."

Well, I certainly wouldn't either like it, but if there *is* somebody in there, I wish she would open her trap sometime and give me some help. Seems like she doesn't have any better sense than I do.

Because Jeez Chrise, seems like I was born in muddy water and have been walking deeper into quicksand ever time I try to take a step towards dry land ever since. Marry Charles, and what does he turn out to be, nothing but a criminal, walks off with me carrying Grady, and next thing I know he's in the pin up in Soledad, and his brother Tom Linares moving in to take care of me with all his criminal friends.

They took care of me, all right. First thing they did to take care of me was, they took me out to the movies one night. Out to the drive-in, only it wasn't to any drive-in. Now, if that other person is in there in my head, strikes me she would've maybe wondered why those guys were having me to drive their car to this "drive-in." But not her. She never says a mubbling word unless I'm trying to fix to do something that might do me some good in this world.

Like, when I was car-hoppin, and I'd bring home twenty, thirty dollars on a good night - most money I ever made, and I was only thirteen then - and Ma would just hold out her hand, flopped out there on the sofa, and take all but a dollar. And I knew what didn't go for her bottle was going to my brother Jack, who hasn't worked a day in his life yet, I expect, and wadn't expected to do anything to help out around the house, or be good at school, or do anything but just be Jack.

But me, I was car-hoppin, and cookin, and clean, and all the teachers at school making fun of me, and them that didn't ignorin me, like there was just a hold in space where my desk was - I was suppose to do everything, and when my report card would come, Ma would scream at me, and Jack make fun of me. All the time that other person in my head did not say, "Hey, that is wrong for her to be taking all of that money which you earned." Nope. Not a word from her then. I just thought, "Oh, well, that's how it goes."

Didn't say nothing this time, either, though it wasn't to any movie we were going, but to the county jail. One of Tom's buddies was in there suspect of grand larceny for stealing a car only he didn't, cording to him. And before I know it, I am driving this car full of escaped suspects from the county jail to Kingman, Arizona, which is where we stopped to get some dinner at Burger Chef, and all of a sudden wasn't nothing but flashin red lights outside every window and they put me on a year's probation.

My probation officer says to me, "Catherine, keep your nose clean." Well, that's fine, but how are you going to keep your nose clean when it's cuttin your way through the dirt? Wasn't supposed to consport with no known criminals, he said.

"That's great," I told him, "I'm livin in a house with Tom Linares, which he is already a known criminal. and which is paid for by Tom Linares, and which is the only roof over my head, and Grady's head, and which I can't pay for no other roof on account of I've been in the booby hatch twice and now on a year's probation."

"Well, what skills do you have?" he asks me. Bein a nut and consportin with criminals, what I felt like sayin to him and his neat little shirt and his glasses, those kind that are kind of pinky-gray and make a person's eyes look all sick and diseased like a rabbit.

"I can fix things," what I did tell him. "I use to tear down clocks and lay the pieces all out to see how they fit back together."

"Broken clocks, you mean," he says, sort of laughing.

"Naw. They was all right. I just wanted to see could I make them run," I said.

"Well, keep your nose clean," he says.

So Tom was put up in the pin alongside Charles, and that was when I met Larry Grimes and all that bunch. Now he was going to take care of me. Some of Tom's friends, Susie Gearhart and Luther, that was Tom and Charles's cousin, was still hanging around, but they didn't hit it off too good with Larry Grimes, so they went off to the old farm out there that hadn't nobody turned the ground since Luther's daddy got a stroke and they send him to the veteran's hospital.

Larry Grimes was a pretty nice guy, even if he was just another criminal, a dealer, but he treated me and Grady all right. Used to take us into L.A. for dinner when he was between deals. One time he took us to Chinatown, to one of those tempooroo bars, place where you sit and watch them cook up all these little things that you never heard of half of them. The cooks, they stand right in front of you and plop those things into a pot of oil, must be hot, I'm telling you, cause as soon as they plop it in, zwoop, up it comes and on your plate. They had squid in there. I wasn't going to eat any, but Larry made me take a bite. Didn't taste bad, but I told him it was kind of like tryin to chew through a hank of old rubber, and he laughed.

Well, things were going along pretty well, for me, and Larry was off on one of his trips down to Mexico or wherever he went to. "You don't want to know," he told me, and I didn't. Messing around with those drugs and things was what drove me crazy one time, the second time, and I didn't want anything more to do with no more drugs, let alone no drug deals.

I was just cleanin out the sink after supper when I hear this horrible noise, *whunk*. "Somethin's happen to Grady," I said, and went runnin around the counter, and there was Grady out cold with his head on the TV stand, and at first I thought it was the light from the TV makin his face all blue, but he was just all blue and couldn't get a squeak out of him.

All of Larry Grimes' bunch was either off with him or just off. The only person I knew with a car - well, about the only person I knew, period - was Luther and them. So I called out there to the farm, and lucky Susie Gearhart was there and had the keys to a car and came in and got me and Grady to the mergency room on time.

I was waiting for the doctor to come out and giving my life history to the fat nurse the way you always have to, and Susie Gearhart says in my ear, "I'm going back to your place. Call me when you're ready to come home."

It was kind of funny, but I didn't think about it at the time, with worrying about Grady and trying to answer all these questions the fat nurse was asking me. Then I set and tried to look at a magazine, but mostly I though about Grady and looked at the other people waitin to be let in or for someone to be let out, or pass on, or whatever.

"A mild sub-something incidens," was what the doctor told me. He said it wadn't anything to worry about. I suppose he wouldn't worry if his kid started turnin all blue. But Grady looked to be normal again. He was real tired and cranky, but that was to be expected. So Susie Gearhart came down and got us.

On the way home, I got time to wonder why she didn't want to wait with me, and I asked her.

"Oh, this car is hot," she said, and laughed.

Oh, wunnerful, I thought, now next thing is to get arrested in a stolen vehicle. But we made it home and Susie Gearhart went back out to the farm, so I said, "Whew, squeaked by that one, anyway."

But no. Because it wadn't but three days before Luther and Susie and that whole bunch was busted, and all they had on Susie was my testimony about the stolen car, about her telling me it was stolen.

And how did they know about that? Smart little Catherine, tryin to keep her nose clean, she had told her probation officer about it, is how.

"Would you be willing to bring this evidence before a grand jury?" he asks.

"Course not," I said. "Those are some bad people."

He just nodded. I should of known. Just sat there and nodded, with the light from the fixture bouncing off his glasses.

Three days after that, I open the door and there's two cops come with a warrant to take me down to the D.A.'s office.

"What about Grady?" I said. "Isn't anyone to stay with him." So they let me bring Grady along.

The man in the D.A.'s office, Chuck Florsheim, he's real nice to me at first. Sits me down, gets one of the seccateries to take Grady over to the playroom in the welfare office.

"Now frankly, Catherine," he starts in, and then a whole lot of mungo-jungo, but the short of it is pretty much that unless I testify about that Susie Gearhart told me she was driving a stolen car, they're going to pull me off probation and put me in the women's pin for helping a jail escape. I was all they had to put anything on Susie Gearhart, and they wanted to put that whole bunch away pretty bad.

So I get home from that, and the telephone rings. I answer. There is this real quiet voice on the other end.

"You even look like you're going to say one word, when they call you on the stand, and Charles won't live twenty-four hours. And you and your kid won't live longer." Click.

They aren't kidding. Luther and them are some bad people, and they have a lot of friends up there in Soledad, like that Black Mike.

So there I am. Larry Grimes and them I know are going to stay clear far away. I don't know how I'm going to feed Grady. If I don't testify, I'll go to jail, and where will Grady go? If I do testify, they'll kill Charles up there, and maybe come after Grady and me.

"We'll protect you," Chuck Florsheim said. Uh-huh. "Intimidating witnesses is a felony."

"Well Jeez Chrise, what do you think these people are but a bunch of felonies?"

"Don't worry," he said.

Put you in quicksand up to the armpits, I'd like to see you say "Don't worry" then.

Well, if I get out of this one, I don't know how. Can't run. Nothin to run with, nowhere to run to, and they're prolly watchin the house. But if I do get out of this one, I know one thing. That other person in there, she can tell me "No" or "Whatever" all she wants to, but she's got to go. She just isn't any help at all. If I get out of this, then some way or other I'm gonna take Grady and get us out of this place and back to Texas. At least there, they just thought I was a nut.

Gonna change my name, too. Catherine, I reckon that must be that other person the sockeyetrist was talkin about. Catherine must be *her* name. I'm going to change my name and go by my middle one, Blizbeth. It was supposed to be Elizabeth, but my daddy's handwriting was so bad, they put it down on my birth paper "Blizbeth."

They used to make fun of that, too. But I don't care. I like it. It's different.

Reading this, many years later, I find in it the love and admiration I had for that young woman, and I can see how much she taught me about how the law and the "helping professions" actually operated. (My education in those fields would be completed a few years later, when I became embroiled in those areas myself.)

When I started tutoring and teaching at the community college, most of my colleagues loved and admired their students, and gave many, many unpaid hours to helping them both academically and with their life problems. And we were all protective of our right to care more about our students than about our bosses, and frequently challenged those bosses when they seemed to threaten that right. We had a union, the Faculty Association, and we felt pretty secure in our jobs. For some while, I put out a little mimeographed pamphlet for Faculty Association members, full of this kind of seditious stuff:

English As She Is Wrotten

The Lagniappe - A Magazine of the Faculty Association - c. 1975

The *Chronicle of Higher Education* quotes John D. Millett, of the Academy for Educational Development, deploring declining standards of basic literacy: "Often, departments have changed things and in the process have lowered their expectations of what was expected of students." The quote appears in a long piece called "Crisis in English Writing," which describes the growth of remedial writing courses on college campuses nationwide.

But will such courses help students learn to write better? Mr. Millett's sentence suggests one reason why such courses probably won't: Mr. Millet, in the act of deploring poor English, is unable to write good English. "Have changed things" is vague slop; "lowered their expectations of what was expected" is so glaringly redundant as to indicate gross insensitivity to the language. If the critic can do little better than the deficient student, how can the student be called deficient, and what can he be expected to learn from such a critic?

Are these reflections too harsh, or are they mere carping? Here is the text of a letter I received last week: "In introducing myself, I'm _____, Director of the Study Skills Center at UDC.

"Ever since I began my membership with the National Association of Tutorial Services this past September of 1974, I've been able to reap some good resources from the monthly newsletter. Thus, I felt it my duty to inform others of this delightfully rewarding association. The newsletter informs one of symposiums and conferences held throughout the state - but, they seem worthwhile because of their striking agendas. Really, you should check it out if you haven't already.

"Thank you for your time and consideration of becoming a member. Plus, we might get together and develop our own chapter in Denver."

I omit the author's name out of probably misplaced charity. Now, the impulse behind this letter is unexceptionable, and you can mainly discern what it is supposed to mean. After you've read it, you might even consider putting in your time of becoming a member.

The person who wrote this letter can very likely detect the dangling modifier and the comma splice and other sins at a glance. But the person can't write worth a damn. Yet is in charge of the Fix This Kid's Writing Shop. One wonders how many good resources the students who come to that shop are likely to reap.

Not that any of this matters, since the language is firmly in the hands of advertising men and their lackeys in the political and communications industries, and these individuals are all concerned, not to say what they mean, but to disguise or obliterate all meaning in the interests of further befuddling the minds of their targets. This last Sunday, the *Denver Post* informed us that "Pat Schroeder is favored over her archly anti-busing opponent Frank Southworth." Either this means that Southworth is chiefly anti-busing, or it means that he is roguishly anti-busing. What it meant to mean was that Southworth is Schroeder's chief opponent, but the editors at the *Post* figured this was close enough. When the major newspaper in the state sets that kind of standard for precision (and I forbear to mention the standards it sets for proof-reading), should we expect students to see much need to write precisely?

The old saw has it that those who can, do, and those who can't, teach. That may describe reality, but only with modification: those who can't, try to teach - but don't. A man who knows nothing about the principles of an infernal combustion engine and who can't take out a screw without stripping the head due to hasty clumsiness is not the man to teach auto mechanics. The person who can do no better than "In introducing myself, I'm...." is not the person to teach people to write well.

If we're going to teach students to write, the first thing and the continuing thing we ought to do is write ourselves, and to subject each other's efforts to criticism. If we did that, we might learn how we learn to write, and we might find that some of our habitual methods of "teaching" (such as marking grammatical errors) are subject to improvement or replacement.

But hell, why should we try to teach students to write better? If they write badly enough, they can get a good job in television or politics or journalism. The lucky few may even become directors of Skills Centers.

TV Guide to the Exciting New 1975 Season

As always the networks will be hotly competing to see who can come up with the most original, fresh ideas for dramatic prime-time shows.

Highlight of the 1975 season should be the three-way race for the 7 p.m. Tuesday time slot among NBC's *Son of the Police Doctor's Lawyer,* starring Robert Young and Bob Hope, CBS' *Son of the District Attorney's Lawyer's Doctor,* featuring Charles Bickford and James Arness, and ABC's *New Lucy Show,* with Desi Arnez, Jr. as a black belt x-ray technician who moonlights as a lawyer, specializing in defending false arrest and malpractice suits.

Minorities will be well represented on the remaining 147 hours of police shows. ABC should receive many plaudits from minority enthusiasts for *Gurkha,* which will follow the exploits of Christa Yentaskeinsky as the first black Lithuanian female rabbi to leave New York for a berth on the Pakistani Narcotics Squad.

News programming should be beefed up, since the three networks have completed the planned moves of their news staffs into one centralized office of communications in the White House. This should cut down on unnecessary leg work and improve channels of communication with incoming director of White House-Network Communications Ron Zeigler.

All in all, it looks as if 1975 will shape up to be at least as good a year for television viewers as 1974.

The Better Old Days

Why should teachers worry about the degradation of language and the prominence of authoritarian figures on television? Perhaps because totalitarianism generally succeeds to the extent that it can corrupt language and, by doing so, render the possibility of rational thought or argument inoperable.

If enough of us become sufficiently insensitive to the need for clarity in language, if we continue to put up with jargon ("inoperative" for "lie," "protective reaction strike" for "bombing raid," "divisive" for "discomfitting," etc., etc.) and continue to put up with long strings of bureaucratic gobbledygook designed to bore us into unquestioning submissiveness, we can expect more, and worse, of what we have gotten from recent college and national administrations.

There was a time when Americans claimed to pride themselves on plain speaking, and sneered at the fancy duplicities of diplomats, and laughed at the pretentious grandiosities of hucksters. Not so very long ago, the editor of a newspaper could write this about the editor of a rival newspaper: "We do not care to bandy filthy, lying epithets with the moral leper who edits the *Star*. His heart, mind, blood, and flesh form a mass of corruption." [Russell] The "moral leper" was Warren Harding, shortly to become President of the United States.

Not great invective, but pretty good invective; there is no difficulty in telling what it means to say. It seems a voice from the distant past, now, when even if we could marshal the simple words of outrage and contempt so richly deserved by the gutless wonders who govern us, we'd hardly have the guts to utter them.

That line about "boring us into submissiveness" resulted from my participation, if you could call it that, in innumerable meetings called by the administration, which followed an entirely predictable script: one of the higher-ups would start the meeting with an interminable, droning monologue, twenty minutes long at least. You could see the faculty members with the greatest ego needs writhing in their seats. The opening monolog would be followed by equally interminable "reports," in bureaucratese, from various lower-level higher-ups. After three or four of these, when the floor was opened, the most desperately ego-needy faculty vied with each other to spew at lengths that often eclipsed the higher-ups' productions. Meanwhile, the teachers who had hoped to talk about one actual educational subject or another sulked in disgust until the higher-ups called the game on account of darkness. By that time, no one objected, because all we wanted to do was get out of there and get plastered as quickly as possible.

In those days, I didn't realize how time-honored a strategy the administration was following. That was only recently brought home to me in Clive James' book *Cultural Amnesia*:

"*Tyrants conduct monologues above a million solitudes.* - Albert Camus, *The Rebel*

"The tyrant's monologue doesn't *want* to be interesting, and that's its point. Camus was among the first - almost as early as Orwell - to realize that the totalitarian overlord's power to bore was a cherished and necessary component of his repressive apparatus. Droning on without contradiction was a proof of his omnipotence....Hitler would keep his punch-drunk guests from their beds with an interminable monologue about his early struggles and the shining Nazi future: a *Ring* cycle minus the music....Hitler had the con man's insight into other people's reactions and must have been well aware of what he was doing. He was proving himself. Or rather he was proving his position: proving his power." [James]

Ah, but we were still in the 70s, we still had a union. Some of us still felt free to challenge the power of the higher-ups, and to have fun at their expense, or even at our own:

Bisontennial
(*The Unofficial Organ, 1976*)

"There's a certain attraction that athletes and politicians and show business people have for each other. They are a kind of American royalty and each group holds the other in awe." - Jeff Wald, manager and consort of Helen Reddy

The American eagle is a loner who establishes and defends a private territory, makes a living by taking away the lives of other animals, and generally behaves autonomously. The American bison is a herd animal, makes its living foraging on prairie grasses, and generally behaves like a unit in a mass, following leaders selected by biologically programmed dominance games. It is time we switched from the former to the latter as our national symbol.

There is a widespread aversion to the name and notion of hereditary royalty in the United States. We believe we have progressed beyond the need for such medieval institutions, and that leadership in America is gained and kept, whether in business, the arts, or politics, by competitive struggle in "the market place." We think of ourselves as a collection of eagles, each making his or her way in the world, rising by merit rather than by convection. That is the American dream - a dream in every sense, and one we cling to with religious devotion. (Ronald Wright once observed, "Socialism never took root in America because the poor see themselves not as an exploited proletariat but as temporarily embarrassed millionaires.") [Wright])

Our actual behavior bears no relationship whatsoever to that of eagles. We are undoubtedly the friendliest, most gullible people in existence, and few of us have the stomach for cutthroat struggles to rise above our fellows. We are bison, and we look with unquestioning awe at our leaders, for we dream that they are like us, only smarter. They are smart enough, naturally, to perceive our expectations and pretend to fulfill them. We wind up in an unhappy pass: possessed of random royalty governed by no standards of expected excellence, restrained by no *noblesse oblige,* since no one can admit that they are *noblesses.*

It may be objected that we view our leaders with cynicism and distrust. The former, yes. A cynic is a dreamer, periodically disturbed by the intrusion of reality into his dream world. The cynic is hostile to reality because he prefers to dream. The latter, no. To distrust our leaders, we would have to recognize that they are men and women of more than normal ambition, that they are exposed to perpetual flattery and temptation by virtue of their positions, and that no human can be trusted with unexamined, unquestioned power. But, since we dream that our leaders must be just like us, only better, we never distrust them until it is too late. Our cynicism constantly searches out shrewd manipulators who can flatter our dreams, and thus further enlarge our cynicism when they one again disappoint our unrealistic expectations.

We all walk around with a vague sense that something is wrong, that the herd is grazing directly toward a cliff. But leaders chosen for their ability to take parts in a dream become captives of the dream they presume to manipulate, and are in no position to turn the herd.

Our official choices for Supreme Bison this year are a man whose intellectual limitations are a national joke and another man whose intellectual limitations ought to be. The campaigns of both men consist of appeals to our decency and for our trust, and of outrageous reversals of positions in search of votes. How many of us will think that we are not limited to voting for one of these two bad choices, but can vote for anyone we view with genuine admiration and respect? Very few of us, for in the end we are unable to question the ostensible process by which the herd has elevated these two champions to undeserved prominence.

Bisonic leaders arrive at leadership by butting heads. Our aristocrats do likewise. We worship the winners of contests that bear no relation to the real fabric of our lives. If Helen Reddy makes millions of dollars in spite of the fact that she can't sing any better than your cousin Carol, the one who had that unfortunate accident, then your judgment of good singing must be wrong. If Gerald Ford speaks English about as well as your cousin Mort, the one who had that unfortunate accident, then maybe Mort is smarter than you thought. If the herd were to pit Gerald Ford against Helen Reddy for the presidency, one of the two would wind up as President, and nearly all of us would be buffaloed by either one.

We select our leaders and aristocrats because they can project animal signs of dominance. We do not question them, we do not observe them closely, we do not demand that they demonstrate either competence, intelligence or imagination before we crown them - all we ask is that they win in the headbutting. Then, since they are so clearly no better in any significant way than we, we can forget about the headbutting, call it a contest of merit, call the winners eagles, and resume our dreaming.

Harry Tuft, my personal choice for President and a great American, tells the following bison story. (Harry is demonstrably a great American because he has spent his life running a business which hurt no one, paid a number of people living wages, and brought a great many people increased knowledge and joy, and he has done so without screwing other people engaged in his line of work.)

It seems, according to Harry, that the last two buffalo left from the great buffalo slaughter of the 1870s and 80s had found respite up a little canyon, where they were grazing dispiritedly on the sparse mountain grass. Suddenly two buffalo hunters appeared in the mouth of the canyon and rode down on the buffalo, who were too tired to try to escape. But when the hunters saw the scrawny, mangy, woebegone condition of the buffalo, they reined up, and one of them addressed himself to his erstwhile intended prey:

"My *gawd,*" he said. "You are about the most unsightly excuse for buffalo I have ever seen. There isn't enough meat on you to feed a crow, those scruffy hides wouldn't bring me five cents, and those *heads* - why, they're uglier than Lincoln. Hell, you poor sorry things, you couldn't *pay* me to shoot you." Whereupon the hunters rode out of the canyon the way they had come in.

One buffalo watched them leave, then turned to the other.

"Did you hear a discouraging word?" he asked.

And that's how Harry ends the story. My research has revealed, however, that later on that night the hunters got to thinking, and rode back in and shot the buffalo while they were asleep. It was the 4th of July and the hunters wanted to celebrate, and they figured it was stupid to waste ammunition just shooting their guns in the air. The buffalo were dreaming they were eagles. They never knew what hit them.

Meanwhile, the press was serving its owners by mounting a concerted campaign against teachers, holding them responsible for the manifest failures of American education. I frequently tried to counter the continuous attacks on my profession.

Education and Its Expert Commentators
(Letter to *The Denver Post*, unpublished)

May I suggest that if your paper wishes to print further ruminations concerning education, you choose to print the ruminations of people who know something about education, such as people who have spent their lives teaching?

I'm moved to suggest that by the March 20 ramblings of Esther Cepeda ("In teaching, why not the best?"). Ms. Cepeda's expertise is described in her self-penned resumé thus: "In 2002 Ms. Cepeda began teaching as a bilingual teacher in low-income grammar and high schools in the suburbs of Chicago while working toward a Master's degree in Special Education from Roosevelt University. Before joining the *Chicago Sun-Times* in 2006, then becoming Chicago's first Latino metro columnist, Ms. Cepeda wrote about national and local politics and social issues for Illinois newspapers and magazines across the country." This suggests that Ms. Cepeda's employment as a teacher was part-time and lasted no more than a year or two. Yet she feels fully qualified to pronounce the most sweeping sorts of characterizations of and judgments upon American education.

Some of them are laughable to anyone who teaches for a living: "Once you're a teacher, your pay goes up every year whether you're a superstar overachiever or completely ineffective." Notably absent here, as everywhere else in the piece, is any evidence for this assertion. It is merely another attempt to portray teachers as leeches on the taxpaying public, rolling in their munificent salaries and benefits.

Some of them are simply either wrongheaded, ignorant, or intentionally misleading. In "the nations with the best educational systems," she writes, "teacher pay is tied to successful outcomes ("merit pay" is what she has in mind here; "successful outcomes" are measured in our current environment by higher scores on standardized tests). This is what Dr. Pasi Sahlberg, Director in Finland's Ministry of Education and Culture, had to say about "the use of value-added data to measure teacher performance": "It's very difficult to use this data to say anything about the effectiveness of teachers....Finns don't believe you can reliably measure the essence of learning. You know, one big difference in thinking about education...is that in the United States it's based on a belief in competition. In my country, we are in education because we believe in cooperation and sharing. Cooperation is a core starting point for growth." Finland's is widely regarded as the "best educational system" in the Western world.

Yet Ms. Cepeda's prescription is "more competition in the education profession." If she, or the *Denver Post*, were truly interested in learning something from the successes of Finland's educational system, you all might consult a recent BBC report, readily available on the web. Here are some factors: "Finnish children spend the fewest number of hours in the classroom in the developed world....Children in Finland only start main school at age seven. The idea is that before then they learn best when they're playing....There is a culture of reading with the kids at home and families have regular contact with their children's teachers....Teaching is a prestigious career in Finland. Teachers are highly valued and teaching standards are high....There is an emphasis on relaxed schools, free from political prescriptions."

Teaching is not and never has been a "prestigious career" in the United States, and its prestige is not likely to be enhanced by the unending salvo of attacks on teachers fostered by such columns as this one. Nor is education likely to be improved by the rantings of people who don't know the first damn thing about teaching, and whose sole value is producing "well educated workers...for the best jobs in organizations that closely measure outcomes and profits."

Next Step in the Old Song and Dance

(Hopelessly long letter to the Colorado Springs *Gazette*, unpublished)

Like most people who've worked in the same field for thirty-five years, I'm always eager to hear criticism of my profession from people who've never spent a day working in it, such as columnist Mike Rosen. Higher education has a lot of critics these days, but you just can't beat Mike for logical fallacies and distortion of evidence.

Within the first paragraph of a recent column, "Voters have the power to diversify CU faculty," [*The Gazette*, March 4, 2005] Rosen describes CU faculty as a "bureaucratic" "self-serving" "omniscient professoriat." He's just warming up. Pillorying the entire faculty of a large state university can hardly satisfy a broom so sweeping as Rosen's. In the next paragraph he gets around to "higher education" as a whole, in which "some of the main problems these days" are "specifically, the tyranny of the tenured left and the paucity of conservative professors within liberal arts faculties."

Now *that's* sweeping. It covers 1.6 million professors and graduate assistants who teach nearly 16 million students. In 2001, 45% of those professors nationwide were tenured. [US Bureau of Labor Statistics, 2/27/04] According to one of the studies of faculty political attitudes Rosen later quotes (Rothman, et. al.), 72% of the sample are "left/liberal." That means that about 32% of those 1.6 million professors are exercising a "tyranny of the tenured left" over the other 68%, not to mention the 16 million students. A mighty determined lot they must be.

Of course, the denomination "left/liberal" raises a few questions. The other study Rosen refers to (Horowitz), categorizes any faculty member registered as a Democrat as "left/liberal." That means, I suppose, that they're in bed with such flaming radicals as Joseph Lieberman, Joseph Biden and Max Baucus.

The words "study," "survey," and "research" ought to immediately prompt two questions: Who paid for the "research"? What was its methodology?

Rosen and other journalistic experts on education currently make almost daily reference to two studies. The first to appear was "Political Bias in the Administrations and Faculties of 32 Elite Colleges and Universities," a production of David Horowitz's Center for the Study of Popular Culture [http://www.frontpagemag.com/Content/read.asp?ID=55]. The second is "Politics and Professional Advancement Among College Faculty," by Stanley Rothman, S. Robert Lichter, and Neil Nevitte [http://www.bepress.com/forum/vol3/iss1/art2].

Since 1989, Horowitz's CSPC has received a total of $11,461,000 from the Scaife, Bradley and Olin Foundations. Lichter's Center for Media and Public Affairs has received $2,177,000 from the same three foundations. Rothman's Center for the Study of Political and Social Change has received $1,208,000 from the same three foundations [Media Transparency Grant Data Matrix. http:/www.mediatransparency.org]. All three foundations exist primarily to fund right-wing think tanks, centers, academic chairs and campaigns. Lichter's CMPA is associated with George Mason University, whose foundation since 1989 has received donations of $23,454,786, the lion's share of that from the Bradley Foundation.

These foundations are not interested in producing research for the sake of finding unknown truth. They are interested in funding "research" that will produce predictable outcomes that can be couched in sound bites that appear to "prove" the conclusions their funders have long before reached. The people who perform these "surveys" (except Nevitte, a Canadian with his own polling firm) have long histories of providing their funders with the kinds of "information" they expect, and of resolutely publicizing their "findings," while misrepresenting them. In short, the answers to the first question - who paid? - suggest that the methodologies and conclusions of both "studies" ought to be carefully examined.

Horowitz first "generated a list of 32 elite colleges and universities," including "the entire Ivy League," other northeastern colleges, and colleges and universities in California. Oddly, all these institutions are located in strongly Democratic states. Not so oddly, since Horowitz studied only voter registration, he found that the "overall ratio of Democrats to Republicans we were able to identify at the 32 schools was more than 10 to 1."

In his Executive Summary - the part that's meant to provide talking points to the print and radio pundits - Horowitz asserts that such a ratio "makes a *prima facie* case" that "there is a grossly unbalanced, politically shaped selection process in the hiring of college faculty." But anyone who bothers to look at his actual figures discovers that while they show 40% of the studied faculty and administrators are registered Democrats, 55% are unaffiliated and 28% fall into the piquant category Horowitz calls "Too Many" - that is, those for whom he found "multiple results for the same name." If this "study" shows anything, it shows a selection process that seems to favor the apolitical over members of either of the two major parties, a tyranny of the bland rather than a tyranny of the left.

In addition to assuming that all Republicans and Democrats hold "a predictable spectrum of assumptions, views and values," Horowitz also limited the faculty studied to "tenured or tenure-track professors of Economics, English, History, Philosophy, Political Science and Sociology departments." He asks us to believe that this limited number of a limited group of professors from a limited number of carefully selected institutions - 32 out of a total 4,074 degree-granting institutions in the US [nces.ed.gov/programs/digest/d03/ch_3] "strongly suggest that the governance of American universities has fallen into the hands of a self-perpetuating political and cultural subset of the general population, which seems intent on perpetuating its control." His figures indicate no such thing.

Rothman, Lichter and Nevitte's study is based on a sample of American professors. The survey from which it is taken, apparently created by Nevitte, does not seem to be available for inspection, so its methodology remains unknown. The study's authors have extracted from this survey 1643 faculty members, of whom 1183 responded to queries regarding their party affiliations and attitudes toward a number of the Right's favorite wedge issues, such as abortion, homosexuality and environmental protection "despite higher prices, fewer jobs." Only full-time professors were selected, and those only from "doctoral, comprehensive and liberal arts" institutions. As Horowitz did, Rothman, et.al. thereby eliminate all professors at institutions that enroll 39% of the entire student body in higher education. (Rothman blandly explains this by citing another study finding "that two-year colleges housed the fewest liberal faculty." [Rothman, 2] In other words, including such faculty would not have produced the desired result.)

In spite of these obvious attempts to skew the survey to show "that liberals and Democrats outnumber conservatives and Republicans by large margins" and "conservatives and Republicans teach at lower quality schools than do liberals and Democrats," Rothman, et.al. are forced to admit that "The results do not definitively prove that ideology accounts for differences in professional standing. It is entirely possible that other unmeasured factors may account for these variations" [Rothman, 13].

That both Horowitz and Rothman studies fail to show what they purport to show and were obviously designed to show is, of course, only important if you are looking for evidence regarding their subject. If you are instead looking for sound bites tricked out as "research-based," Horowitz and Rothman are eager to provide them. Horowitz's has already been quoted. Rothman places his sound bite conveniently in the Abstract: "This suggests that complaints of ideologically-based discrimination in academic advancement deserve serious consideration and further study." Carefully distributed throughout the study are further quotable quotes, such as "political conservatives have become an endangered species in some departments" and "conservatives have a legitimate complaint." [13]

The Rothman study was released on March 29. The next day, writing in the Unification Church's *Washington Times,* Joyce Howard Price quoted the study's compiler Lichter: "This is the richest lure [*sic*] of information on faculty ideology in twenty years. And this is the first study that statistically proves bias [against conservatives] in the hiring and promotion of faculty members." In one day, results that do not "definitively prove" have become results that "statistically prove."

On the same day, syndicated columnist Cal Thomas summarized Rothman's findings and quoted an AAUP director, Jonathan Knight: "Knight added that he is not aware of 'any good evidence' linking the personal views of professors to what they teach. He must be living in an ivory tower without Internet access," Thomas continued, because "A quick Google search of 'liberalism on college campuses' brings a wealth of good evidence that what is being taught on many of them is anti-American, anti-religious, anti-Israel, pro-gay rights and abortion, often to the exclusion and ridicule of opposing views." In short, the Rothman "research" that occasioned Thomas's column does not provide any evidence that Democrats or liberals promote their views in their classrooms, or that they are favored in hiring or promotion, so Thomas must forget his original source to suggest that "a wealth of good evidence" exists elsewhere.

One doubloon from this wealth he names is www.campus-watch.org. This website is a project of the Middle-East Forum, an organization entirely concerned with promoting a "pro-Israel" stance and attacking any expressions of criticism of Israeli policy. 95% of its funding has been provided by the Bradley Foundation. Another is Thomas Reeves "of the Wisconsin Policy Research Institute" [position not described], quoted by Thomas as alleging that "'conservatives are discriminated against routinely and deliberately in faculty hiring, making some highly qualified teachers virtually unemployable because of their political and social views." Thomas provides no documentation for these claims. The Wisconsin Policy Research Institute has received 91% of its funding, to the tune of $6,685,000, from the Bradley Foundation.

Though Thomas doesn't mention it, the greatest wealth of information a Google search would produce is to be found on the website of Students for Academic Freedom, a "student" group funded by Horowitz's Center for the Study of Popular Culture (and thus by Scaife, Olin and Bradley). This operation places ads in student newspapers nationwide soliciting student complaints about bias in the classroom. Its website provides a convenient "Academic Bias Complaint Form," which suggests what students should be looking for, including "Required readings or texts covering only one side of issues," "Introduced controversial material that has no relation to the subject," "Mocked national political or religious figures," and "Allowed students' political or religious beliefs to influence grading." These solicitations have produced quite a few pages of student complaints, and they make instructive reading.

An anonymous complaint of "Introduced Controversial Material" alleges: "This is in the school paper in a [sic] article about professors incorporating the election into the classroom. 'One was [sic - probably "way"] in which [professor's name] says she plans on educating her English students is to view and discuss "Bowling for Columbine" by filmmaker Michael Moore. Currently, sh [sic] sponsors the Amnesty International Club at [the college], and as a member of the Dallas Peace Center she frequently demonstrates for peace causes." Those who recognize opposition to torture and support of peace as sure signs of a tyrannical leftist need hear no more.

Another complainant at Ohio State has far more specific complaints: "This complaint applies to the discriminating [sic] nature of grading of [sic] my English teacher. She knows I'm an advancer of conservative ideas b/c I where [sic] a 'W' t-shirt to class on sometimes [sic] Ever since the 1st day of class when I wore my 'W' shirt she has treated me cold [sic] and been discriminating [sic] in grading my essays. On the last one, I wrote about how family values in the books weve [sic] read aren't good. I know the paper was pretty much great because I spell checked it and proofred [sic] it twice. I got an [sic] D- just because the professor hates families and thinks its [sic] okay to be gay." Certainly anyone who spell-checks and proofreds twice must deserve a high grade.

The web pages provide many more such complaints, none of them validated by any outside observer. Students who dislike, disagree with or are given low grades by professors are thus provided a national forum for their gripes. That these gripes may be perfectly sincere does not mean that they have any validity. Some are quite well written and do indeed describe actions or speech by professors that suggest possible bias, stupidity or downright lunacy. But the reader has no way to assess their accuracy. The site is rather like a national forum set up for employees to anonymously complain about their bosses. But doubtless they provide all or part of the "wealth of good evidence" Thomas has in mind.

This "wealth" of misrepresented research, unsubstantiated charges and meaningless anecdote is being used not only by newspaper pundits and television talking hairdos, but by David Horowitz as ammunition to persuade both state governments and the United States Congress to put into law his creation, the "Academic Bill of Rights." [ABOR] This document is currently under consideration by at least eight state legislatures and by Congress.

The ABOR [http://www.studentsforacademicfreedom.org.abor.html] begins with a historical review of statements supporting "academic freedom" by the American

Association of University Professors and the U.S. Supreme Court, followed by a definition of the term worth quoting in full: "Academic freedom consists in protecting the intellectual independence of professors, researchers and students in the pursuit of knowledge and the expression of ideas from interference by legislators or authorities within the institution itself. This means that no political, ideological or religious orthodoxy will be imposed on professors and researchers through the hiring or tenure or termination process, or through any other administrative means by the academic institution. Nor shall legislatures impose any such orthodoxy through their control of the university budget." It's hard to imagine any academic who would contest this definition. Unfortunately, the provisions of the proposed bill undermine or contradict this statement of principle.

Provision 1 states "All faculty shall be hired, fired, promoted and granted tenure on the basis of their competence and appropriate knowledge in the field of their expertise [so far, so good] and, *in the humanities, the social sciences, and the arts, with a view toward fostering a plurality of methodologies and perspectives* [my italics]. What the independent clause gives, the qualifying phrase takes away, injecting the faculty member's "perspective" into the criteria for hiring, firing, promotion and tenure. As chair of a search committee for a faculty position, how am I to discover the applicants' "perspectives" except by quizzing them all about their religious, political, and philosophical beliefs? And how is my committee to "foster a plurality" of "perspectives" without hiring or rejecting faculty based on those exact criteria?

Provision 3 states, "Students will be graded solely on the basis of their reasoned answers and appropriate knowledge of the subjects and disciplines they study, not on the basis of their political or religious beliefs." Again, who would dispute this principle? But how, exactly, can the basis for grading a student paper be measured? It is notable that no mention is made here of the quality of the students' expression of their "reasoned answers and appropriate knowledge." A student such as the one from Ohio State quoted above would be empowered by this provision to protest a low grade - which may have been based on the evident want of literacy - to both administration and to the courts.

The most dangerous provisions are 4 and 5, both of which open the door to the imposition of "political, ideological and religious orthodoxy" by a variety of pressure groups and by legislatures "through their control of the university budget" that the ABOR's preamble forbids. Proposition 4 reads, in part, "Curricula and reading lists in the humanities and social sciences should reflect the uncertainty and unsettled character of all human knowledge in these areas by providing students with dissenting sources and viewpoints where appropriate." Proposition 5 continues, "Faculty will not use their courses for the purpose of political, ideological, religious or anti-religious indoctrination."

Let us say that I am teaching a course in 20th Century American Literature, and let us say that the majority of my students have previously limited their reading of American Literature to the works of Stephen King, Dean Koontz and Danielle Steele. (Such a condition is far from impossible.) If I do not include these authors in my reading list, have I failed to provide students with dissenting sources and viewpoints? Who is to say, after all, since human knowledge in the judgment of literary worth is uncertain and unsettled, that Sherwood Anderson is more worthy of study than Danielle Steele?

Or let us say that I am teaching a course on the Clinton "welfare reform," and make passing reference to Jesus' assertion, "Verily I say unto you, Inasmuch as ye have done it unto one of the least of these my brethren, ye have done it unto me." [Matthew 25:40] Is his remark "relevant" to the discussion? Am I engaging in "religious indoctrination"?

Or let us say that I am teaching a course on Germany's conduct of WWII, and include in my reading list the autobiography of Rudolf Hoess, in which he describes the process by which he "...personally arranged...the gassing of two million persons between...1941 and the end of 1943, during which time I was the Commandant of Auschwitz." [Hoess, Rudolf, *Commandant of Auschwitz*. Cleveland and New York: World Publishing Company, 1960, 17] Because human knowledge is "unsettled," as it surely is, am I obliged to include in the same reading list a work by British "historian" David Irving, who has publicly and repeatedly argued that "No documents whatever show that a Holocaust had ever happened"?
[http://www.powells.com/review/2005_03_04] Certainly Irving's denial of the Holocaust

is a "dissenting source and viewpoint." And certainly I will eventually encounter a student who holds this viewpoint dear to heart, and will wish to sue me for neglecting it.

In sum, this proposed legislation would open the door to precisely the "interference by legislators or authorities within the institution itself" with hiring of faculty and curriculum that it claims to forbid. It is a Trojan horse, very cleverly designed by its author to disguise its purposes and inevitable effects.

Mike Rosen, far less cautious than Horowitz or Rothman, plainly states the goals of this campaign: "The sacred cow of tenure is under review, along with the limits of academic freedom and the shameful lack of ideological balance within college faculties....Academic freedom is not absolute....That means hiring conservative professors to balance the, now, left-lopsided scales....Here's the perfect remedy. Convert CU into a bastion of conservative thought...." Cal Thomas is equally clear: "In matters of race and gender, colleges practice affirmative action....Why won't they do the same for conservative professors and students...?" The process here is a familiar one. Major right wing foundations supply money to scholars who will perform "studies" that "prove" the existence of a "Left-Wing tyranny." These "scientific studies" are then deployed by sympathetic publicists who selectively quote them and repeat their misrepresented "findings" in print and on the air until repetition establishes them in their readers' and listeners' minds as "fact." Then the "facts" and "evidence" are used to intimidate academic institutions into diluting or suppressing expressions of "left wing" opinion on campus, and into hiring right wing faculty.

The process is familiar because it is identical to that employed in the campaign to convince Americans that a "liberal bias" controls "the media," and to intimidate "the media" into abandoning all real questioning of the statements of those in political power and to fill their ranks with right wing ideologues. This campaign was largely funded by the same right wing foundations, carried out by the same "researchers," and drilled into the public by the same publicists. [http://media.eriposte.com/2-2.htm]

No one who has worked in higher education could deny that some faculty members express their particular ideologies in class. I have known some who did so. Their ideologies ranged from extreme left to extreme right. I have never known a student who has been either swayed or intimidated by such expressions, nor have I ever seen a case of punitive grading based on ideological grounds. I have never known of a faculty member either hired or dismissed on the basis of political or cultural ideology. Do such things happen? I think undoubtedly they do, since bias and injustice are endemic to human beings. The SAF student complaints illustrate not only the possible existence of such incidents, but the fact that they are scarcely limited to bias from the left:

"One time the professor answered my question about bias in the media in the US: 'It is unlike the Arab World.' Another time he was describing Chomsky as 'insane' and Edward Said as a rock thrower at Israelis because as he said 'people there generally throw rocks.' The class was in American politics and introducing remarks about Arabs because I am one of them is inappropriate," writes one of the SAF's anonymous complainants.

"When discussing the platforms of various candidates for the 2004 presidential election, my professor said that any candidate who took an anti-war position in their campaign was akin to a terrorist," writes another anonymous student.

"Was repeatedly forced to repeat 'darwin is a loon' on all assignments. Any arguments presenting evidence of evolution were denounced as "Satanism". We were also forced to watch video's of IDF forces butchering Palestinian kids while the teachers said that "judgment" was being meted out. We were also told that we are not allowed to question the president and that God had appointed him to lead the Christian armies in smiting the Arabs so that we can steal all their oil. We were also told that global warming is fake, and when I presented evidence to the contrary, the teachers accused me of witchcraft," reports a third.

Again, all three of these reports are anonymous and unsubstantiated. They do, though, suggest that attempts to ideologically indoctrinate students may come from the right as well as from the left.

Do they typify what goes on in American colleges and universities? My own experience is that they do not. I, and most of my colleagues, have been far too busy trying to help students understand what they read and learn to express their understanding coherently to have had time or inclination to indoctrinate them into our various views. And "various" is an accurate description, running the gamut of political and social opinions. No real evidence, other than the sort of silly, sloppily defined and frequently self-contradictory "research" of hired guns such as Horowitz, Rothman and Lichter and the unsubstantiated anecdotes of aggrieved students, exists to support the prevalent characterizations of higher education as a "tyranny of the tenured left."

And of course that will not matter. "The tyranny of the tenured left" will be repeated by Sean Hannity and Mike Rosen and Rush Limbaugh and Cal Thomas and Thomas Sowell and Bill O'Reilly and the rest until, through mere repetition, it becomes an established "fact" in the minds of all those people who know nothing about higher education except that it drains their tax dollars. Legislators, state and national, will eagerly parrot the phrase as they seek to introduce legislation that will put them in control of both personnel decisions and curriculum, and give them further excuses to transfer tax dollars from education to the coffers of the wealthy who fund their campaigns.

And the actual ends of Scaife, Bradley and Olin will be accomplished. Dissent from academia, such as it faintly exists, will be stifled and the country may continue, undisturbed, in a lockstep march back to the way things were under the presidency of Karl Rove's ideal chief executive, William McKinley. [Moore, Slater]

At that time, I understood the "tyranny of the left" campaign as simply a new tactic in the perpetual corporate attempt to shape academic curricula and to control or destroy any and all unions. I thought I was seeing just another campaign of vilification and suppression of the sort routinely waged by the early Robber Barons, as described by Matthew Josephson: "In the world of learning, the janissaries of oil or lard potentates, with a proper sense of taste and fitness, sought consistently to sustain the social structure, to resist change, to combat all current notions which might thereafter 'reduce society to chaos' or 'confound the order of nature"....the managers of Rockefeller's Chicago University also championed the combinations year by year. One professor of economics, Dr. Gunton, especially distinguished himself on this score, and another, a teacher of literature ostensibly, declared Mr. Rockefeller and Mr. Pullman 'superior in creative genius to Shakespeare, Homer and Dante,' a declaration which made a lively impression at the time. In the meanwhile, a third teacher, a Professor Bemis, who happened to criticize the action of the railroads during the Pullman strike in 1894 was after several warnings expelled from the University for 'incompetence.'

"At Syracuse University in western New York, to mention only one instance, a gifted young instructor in economics, John Commons, was similarly dismissed by the Chancellor. His strongest interests were discovered to lie in the rising labor movement, and the university, endowed by Mr. John Archbold of the Standard Oil family, frowned upon such learning...." [Josephson]

(Josephson's *The Robber Barons* is one of the most illuminating descriptive analyses of the history of Capitalism in our country, and the metaphor contained in the title is still immensely useful today in understanding how such modern-day Barons as Bill Gates have risen to immense power and wealth.)

I failed to see that the campaign was merely an opening wedge for a far more ambitious enterprise - complete corporate control of the education system at every level, and the elimination of all values except those conducive to unchecked capitalism. I hadn't yet quite grasped how far along we'd moved toward Michael Ledeen's inspiring vision of what America was all about: "Creative destruction is our middle name, both within our own society and abroad. We tear down the old order every day, from business to science, literature, art, architecture, and cinema to politics and the law. Our enemies have always hated this whirlwind of energy and creativity, which menaces their traditions (whatever they may be) and shames them for their inability to keep pace. Seeing America undo traditional societies, they fear us, for they do not wish to be undone. They cannot feel secure so long as we are there, for our very existence -- our existence, not our politics -- threatens their legitimacy. They must attack us in order to survive, just as we must destroy them to advance our historic mission." (From his book *The War Against the Terror Masters*) It's an instructive quote; after the initial nod to creation, nothing but destruction is mentioned. Modern capitalism is done with building anything.

Education was one of those "traditional societies," and the whirlwind was on the way. But in the early days of this century, I was still taking a superficial view of the forces threatening the independence, integrity, the essential nature of teaching. I was still blaming the advertising men, who after all were merely useful tools in the hands of the real power, concentrated wealth:

Book Talk and Ad Blat

Newsweek's recent essay, "Why Johnny Can't Write," laid Johnny's latest failure at several doorways, but the largest parcel of blame wound up in front of the English classroom. English teachers, according to *Newsweek,* can't, don't or won't teach Johnny to write decently.

Since I'm an English teacher, I suppose I should be expected to charge to the defense of my profession. I'm more inclined to think that my profession has been flattered. A severe decline in literacy is a large social change, and it's rare that English teachers are considered agents of important change in our society.

It's rare because they aren't. Teachers are paid by the public to instill the prevailing cultural values in students, and that is what teachers mostly do, or else they get fired or quit in disgust. If English teachers are turning out illiterates, they are doing so at the behest of their society, not in defiance of it.

20 years ago, Alvin Toffler estimated that the average American received 560 advertising messages each day. (One can assume that number has increased considerably.) Needless to say, the average American receives no such number of "book-talk" messages each day, or each year, for that matter. ("Book-talk" is a *Newsweek* coinage, presumably meaning "English.") These advertising messages may not edify, but certainly they instruct.

Here is one advertisement which flanked the text of "Why Johnny Can't Write":
We dry harder. Dry Gilbey's. Dry Boissiere. When
a great dry gin and a great dry vermouth get together,

>the result is - almost inevitably - a great dry martini.
>So a Gilboissiere martini has to be a great dry martini.
>Dry it…you'll like it.

The authors of this text feel certain that their audience will be familiar with the other texts (ads for rental cars and stomach products) to which they punningly allude. Their certainty demonstrates the universality of advertising language in America. What poet could allude, even without puns, to any "book-talk" phrase with such confidence? Johnny, and John, and Joan, and Juan are exposed to the language of advertising so frequently that they can appreciate puns and allusions in that language; they have learned that language well. What principles of literary style have they learned from the professors of ad blat?

"We day harder. Dry Gilbey's. Dry Boissiere." From the first three units, Johnny can learn that a sentence is any collection of words which begins with a capital letter and ends with a period. Johnny may therefore be perplexed when his sentences are criticized because they lack subjects or predicates.

"So a Gilboissiere martini has to be a great dry martini." From this, Johnny can learn that a conjunction is a word used to begin a sentence, and that "must" is a musty word rendered obsolete by the locution "has to" (as in "I have to go down to the sea again," or "Shoot, if you have to, this old, grey head, but you don't have to hurt my country's flag").

Good prose can be written in non-standard English, as many major American authors have demonstrated. Is Johnny learning good, if non-standard, prose from *Newsweek's* advertisers?

"When a great dry gin and a great dry vermouth get together, the result is - almost inevitably - a great dry martini." In the first place, that is nonsense, and if Johnny believes it I hope to avoid his bar. In the second place, "almost inevitably" is high-sounding blather. What does it mean? *How* almost? One adverb vitiates the other - on purpose. The authors knew they were writing hokum, since ingredients never guarantee a decent cocktail, but they wanted to appeal to the 2-Easy-Steps-to-Sainthood sloth in all of us, so they wrote "almost inevitably" instead of "sometimes." Johnny is no fool. He gets the idea: if you want to make a statement you can't support, use fancy words and mush up their meanings with qualifiers.

An advertisement for particular brands of alcohol presumably asserts that they are superior brands. The form of the "Gilboissiere" ad appears to make such an assertion, but it does not: 1, a great gin plus a great vermouth make a great martini; 2, a martini made from our gin and our vermouth must be great. Even without almost all the inevitability asserted parenthetically, this phony syllogism says nothing about the merits of the brands it promotes. See, Johnny? You don't have to really prove anything or make any sense; just sound confident.

The language of this particular advertisement, in its perversions of diction, grammar, syntax and logic, is perfectly typical of ad blat. The language daily bombarding Johnny is a language constantly designed to obscure, not to communicate; to bamboozle, not to convince.

If we look beyond advertising to the leaders of the nation, who presumably act as exemplars for Johnny as he learns good habits of speech and writing, we find only more of the same perversions. The obscenities excised from the Nixon transcripts were widely remarked. The more terrifying obscenity - the systematic avoidance of truth and reality by recourse to ad blat - was neither excised nor viewed with much alarm. Senator McGovern, offering not a choice but an echo, celebrated his triumph in several primaries by alluding to an Alka-Seltzer commercial. The conduct of nearly all political campaigns - because nearly all are conducted by advertising people - has become a battle to see who can say least most strikingly.

More influential national leaders, such as talk-show hosts and football commentators, offer little more in the way of literacy, so we are left with the newspapers and magazines. Here is part of a book review from the literary section of *The Denver Post:*

> Want a "front-burner" gift for the under-40 set? Buy them a cookbook. The young may not dance much anymore, but we are told they do cook, and they do dig those cookbooks. This season finds at least a couple dozen new ones to give the under-40 set....

> Leader of them all is the new classic, *From Julia Child's Kitchen*, hotly pursued by *The Better Homes and Gardens New Cookbook.* But these are just the leaders.

Now, speaking as one of the under-40 set, I do dance quite a bit, and I can't see how a "set" can take a plural pronoun, or how a book can become a classic before it's even in circulation, or quite how the metaphor of hot pursuit applies to books, but except for those quibbles, I think this prose is all reet, and I dig it. It's all reet because its purpose is not to review books. Its purpose is to peddle books, and for that purpose it is written in the appropriate dialect - ad blat.

My students are surrounded by such language. The writers and speakers of such language are, by and large, well rewarded with money and fame. The language of ad blat it is my students' ears and eyes, and it comes out through their fingers when they write. I don't blame them for that, and I don't blame English teachers much, unless they also speak and write in ad blat, which some of them do. If decent, honest, clear speech and writing are required only in English classrooms, most students won't learn to write decently, honestly, or clearly, because they don't plan to spend their lives in English classrooms.

Quivering with alarm, *Newsweek* informs me that, "at Harvard, one economics instructor has been so disturbed at the inability of his students to write clearly that he now offers his own services to try to teach freshmen how to write." Estimable, but what has he been doing up until now? Has he been ignoring his students' writing errors and "reading for content"? Has he been writing "Awk" in the margin when he felt a sentence was unclear but couldn't or didn't want to figure out or explain why it was unclear? If it is so unusual for even academics to care whether their students write decently, how in the nation can English teachers convince their students that they need to master this particular skill?

Clearly, if you teach English, you keep trying to convince them, or you find another line of work. Any teacher who doesn't do one or the other ought to be blamed, since teachers who really do only instill prevailing values aren't worthy of the name.

Until, however, society as a whole shows some signs of valuing clarity, precision, grace and honesty over deliberate muddiness, bombast and half-truth, I doubt that Johnny's writing will improve much, no matter how herculean the efforts of his English teachers. Johnny and his English teachers have only the average amount of courage, and they know what happens to literate, honest leaders, magazines, and television shows: generally, they get cancelled.

Yes, and the values of literacy, honesty, and memory were all under increasing assault as I went on through my teaching years. I taught not only English, but other courses under the integrated Humanities program at the college, which had been very largely created by my first wife, Nancy, and which the State Board for Community Colleges, an appointed set of nullities given absolute power over the community colleges by the state legislature, contemplated driving a stake into. I wrote this in response to that contemplation, with the usual lack of response:

On the Removal of Humanities from the Core Curriculum

Looking at the record of humanity over even the past hundred years, anyone might be tempted to agree with Thomas Hobbes that life in a state of nature - or, for that matter, in states of advanced civilization - is nasty, brutish and short. So it was for the tens of millions slaughtered in the trenches of World War I. For the tens of millions of civilians blown up, burned up, gassed and atomized during World War II. For the uncounted millions dead of genocide, from Cambodia to Kosovo to Uganda and Zaire.

So it was for the neighbors of Francois, now in prison for murdering four of his Tutsi neighbors:

"I am in prison for killing four people. A car drove by with a loudspeaker saying that all Hutus had to defend themselves, that there was a single enemy: The Tutsis. I heard that. It was morning. I jumped out of bed, I grabbed a club, I went out, and I began killing....My neighbors were Tutsis, we used to share everything, like water.

There weren't any conflicts between us. I don't know why all those things happened. Wickedness was in fashion."

And yet, though the sleep of reason produces monsters, humanity has produced Jesus Christ and Gautama Buddha, Handel and Mozart, Shakespeare and Camus, Velasquez and Vermeer; it has produced pyramids in deserts and mountains, and the Cathedral at Chartres, and the United States Constitution.

Wickedness is ever in fashion, sometimes so ubiquitously that it becomes difficult to remember that other paths, other possibilities exist. Bombarded daily with images of the worst that humans perpetrate, we need to come to know and wed ourselves to the record of people and times and places that demonstrate our capacities to create goodness and beauty.

Courses in integrated Humanities are designed to introduce students to this record of human creation and achievement of order and beauty, to help them think about the social conditions which gave rise to such achievements, and to connect the wisdom -- and the folly -- of the past to the conditions of their own culture.

That is why we must continue to study and teach the humanities - so that we do not fall to the fashion that destroyed Francois, our neighbor, our kin. Our humanity, in the best sense of that word, is so terribly fragile. We cannot afford to neglect its manifestations.

As I look over these remarks, in 2018, the integrated humanities program Nancy and others created and instituted throughout the state has been almost entirely dismantled. The "humanities" requirement for an AA or AS degree can now be fulfilled, and mostly is, by taking a course called "Mythology," which my remaining informant at the community college tells me consists mostly of watching videos. Hercules, as played by Arnold Schwarzenegger, trumps Vermeer. One picture - especially if it explodes before your very eyes - is worth all the thousands of words you've never learned.

Back in the early 70s, though, I was only beginning to get an inkling of how deep the roots of the destruction of my country went. A long bus trip provided that first inkling.

Million Dollar Bills

Some year in the early 70s, I agreed to be best man at my friend Eduardo Chavez's wedding. Ed's intended (that's what a bride-to-be was called in those days) was a nurse, the rebel daughter of a family with so much old money that I'd never heard of their family name. *That's* money. The wedding was to take place at her brother's home, somewhere along the Potomac, and the brother's wife would pick me up at the Greyhound station in Washington, D.C. I arrived there, smelling, I'm sure, as might be expected after after three days riding the Dog, eating bus station food, in clothes full of cigarette smoke and unchanged for the duration. Greyhound had lost my luggage, including my guitar, somewhere along the way, so I remained redolent until the next day, when my stuff arrived. I must have provided the final shudder to this wealthy family's horror.

They were most gracious, but I could sense their deep distrust beneath the good manners. It took me a while, during my stay, to figure out that they didn't just distrust *me* - they had to assume that anyone who didn't live at their rarefied heights of wealth was angling to take some of that wealth away from them - probably a sound assumption, overall. Still, it must have led to a severely circumscribed set of possible friends.

The brother, who held some position in a federal agency, without salary since he scarcely needed it, spent an evening showing me his stereo set, featuring the very finest turntable procurable. Ed had brought me out there as a musician, so the brother thought I'd appreciate his showpiece sound equipment. I didn't have the heart to tell him I'd grown up listening to scratchy 78 rpm records, and didn't really care much about high fidelity, or have a good enough ear to distinguish its nuances. He went on for a good while describing how diligently he'd searched for *the best*, as if the search had been both a right and a duty. As I recall he demonstrated the excellence of his system with Andy Williams and Mantovani lps. James, fetch the Daimler; I must be off to Arby's.

Riding the bus back across the country on the route I'd taken East, I thought about these people. If I'd ever had fantasies about becoming rich (I don't think I had, but how could I have avoided them, growing up in 50s America?), a few days with the truly rich had put an end to them. I didn't want to live a life that demanded I distrust every stranger, or spend my time comparison shopping for anything and everything I needed to buy. When I got back home, I wrote about my trip across the country:

Cookie-Cutter Images on the Endless Interstate
Rocky Mountain News "Trend," 1/4, 10/2/1977

Americans have long been both derided and praised for their materialism. A trip along the endless interstate is enough to make you wonder how we ever got ourselves known as materialists. Whatever we are, we most surely are not paying much attention or devoting much love to the material aspects of our lives.

Colorado is a good place to start. In Denver, in Colorado Springs, in decaying mountain boom towns, a few relics of the days of true materialism remain. The indescribably various crop of gold and silver barons translated their sudden riches into monuments to the good things of life. Great homes, replete with brass and silver and dyed elephant hides and Florentine inlaid tables and French stained glass and Irish crystal. Restaurants as ornately furnished, whose bills of fare would make a dietician shudder. Cathouses suitable for kings of beasts.

The taste of these suddenly enriched miners was sometimes questionable, but their appreciation and lust for quality of material and workmanship was not. They bought, by and large, the best, and displayed their purchases proudly, as signs of their worthiness to be rich. They ate and drank and consorted with the best available. What else was money for, if not to be exchanged for the fullest-blown beauties and pleasures within human grasp? There is little classical symmetry or restraint in the increasingly scarce relics of those days, but there is always a sense of delight and warm enjoyment of the senses proper to the true materialist.

We have been busy for some time now larruping these relics to powder with our giant steel balls and chains. The hearts of our cities have been pretty well emptied of them and refilled with the stark geometries of the new wealth. Having ripped the innards from our earth to the point of diminishing returns, we have turned to strip-mining our living spaces. We scrape the heart clean, and on its poor, bare hide erect buildings which Norman Mailer once described as being "the exact size and shape of a one-million dollar bill."

A perfect description, and one which becomes increasingly useful as the big cross-country bus shoulders out of the city and toward the interstate. Out here at the edge of the city is the new growth, the ground still freshly broken and piled. It is that million-dollar bill which squats on the broken earth.

As the bus whines along, and you sink into the resigned semi-stupor of the long-distance traveler, a depressingly uniform pattern, repetitive as television, plays itself out in your window. A geometric clot of house trailers, or of equally cheap and transitory-looking houses, set on concrete block foundations. Then a shopping center, of which two ranks exist.

The first-rank shopping center contains a bank, constructed in the approved Maginot Line Modern style: pre-cast concrete, buttresses which buttress nothing, a few sunburst locust saplings planted in concrete pillboxes, forlorn and lifeless as an architect's rendering. And glass, a great deal of glass. Not glass of the old, stodgy, transparent sort, which let the outside in and the inside out, and not glass stained and shaped to emphasize the miracle of light by filtering it through patterned color. Banker's glass is one-way glass, the sort favored for sunglasses by state troopers to keep you from seeing the eyes behind as they watch you. The world reflected by this glass is devoid of the colors of earth, for the glass is tinted a murky blue-brown-green, a suboceanic or interstellar shade so cold that it freezes the life out of every reflection.

The rest of the shopping center contains a national chain supermarket, a national chain dry goods or hardware store, a national chain movie theater (uniformly known, in deference to film buffs or Anglophiles, as a "cinema"), two or three national chain restaurants and a national chain motel (called an "Inn").

The restaurants share a penchant for improbable styles and pre-packaged "character." They all seem designed, these days, to appeal to a pathologically vague nostalgia - nostalgia for the old ranch house, the old pirate's den, or some other such romantic place which no one living has ever experienced except by way of televised fantasies. Even our nostalgia is formed, controlled and kept impoverished of real feeling by national chains.

The less said of the food purveyed by these places, the better. It attempts to compensate for flavor, distinction and originality, not to mention nutrition, by sheer quantity and by the indigestible hyperbole on the menu.

To put it kindly, the various but unvarying "inns," like the chain restaurants, rigorously refuse to demonstrate any relationship to the countrysides they disfigure, to the local culture which once gave rise to real inns, or to the local people who work in them. The name of the chain is insignificant; each spawn replicates all the others, calling up an image of the Ideal Guest: an aged, seedy, failed James Bond, James Bond in a hairpiece and a leisure suit, sauntering with unsuccessfully studied aplomb among the plastic ferns and naughahyde bar chairs, pretending to himself that the little woman and two-point-three children in the airless room upstairs do not, and never did, exist.

There is only one Brown Palace, and it speaks of the men who made it and of the men and women who enjoyed its refinements and its gaucheries with equal gusto. There is also only one "Inn," even though there are thousands of them. They speak of nothing but the cash flow they generate, a speech as dry and joyless as the subdued whirring clank of the machines that "condition" the air in them.

The second-rank shopping centers duplicate those of the first rank, but they don't have a bank. Of whichever rank, the shopping centers announce either the advent or the departure of a city. (The distinction can be made only in terms of one's particular direction, since advent and departure are identical.) What city, and in what state? Any city; any state. The shopping centers are simply that million-dollar bill, laid horizontally on a fresh parking lot and chopped into discrete segments. A million-dollar bill looks exactly the same on one coast or the other, or anywhere between.

Unbelievable that a country so huge and geographically varied as this could be so totally homogenized. Unbelievable that a people who once gloried in material pleasures should so readily embrace the sterile, flavorless, ominous uniformities of the coast-to-coast shopping center.

Undoubtedly, our contempt for the past is one factor which has lubricated these melancholy transformations. The primary factor seems clearly to be our blind adoration of the internal combustion engine.

Two images of that adoration. Somewhere in Missouri, the interstate spreads its dual lanes, like a stream spraddling a boulder, around an inexplicable concrete strip, on which three long-distance truck cabs, bereft of their freight boxes, squat gleaming in the last low sunlight. Their position is striking: the front axle of one rests upon the hitchplate of the next, so that they look, in the orange and purple summer evening haze, like great insects copulating in midair. Perhaps our conveyances have taken to spontaneous self-reproduction out there in the tropical daze of midwestern summer.

That might as well be the case. The *Chicago Tribune* carries an account of the imminent decimation of the soybean crop. The rain, it seems, is so acidified by the pollution in the air that it is rendering the soybeans incapable of putting forth seed. Yet the *Washington Post* reassures: these slight inconveniences will not be allowed to interrupt the operations of Detroit, for the Congress, "acting" on the President's energy package, has once again eased up on pollution control standards and miles-per-gallon requirements. We'll keep on moving, even if we starve to death in the process.

Back in Colorado, the morning papers trumpet forth glad tidings: the first oil has begun to spurt through the trans-Alaska pipeline. We'll keep on moving, and so long as we do, it seems inevitable that our lives will continue to decline in quality and variety and material richness. When you're on the move, you'll gorge on Burger Barons if that is all that is available to gorge upon. When you're on the move, you will put up with anonymous bedrooms and anonymous service, since you're only passing through. And why not stay on the move, since all the character and distinctiveness and local color have been scraped away, nearly everywhere, to make room for those million-dollar bills, and little remains to hold anyone to the region of his or her birth?

It's a saddening journey across the endless interstate. After a few states, you lose the ability to tell where you are, except by the countryside, which is rapidly fading behind a nearly seamless smudge of pollution.

The gas and oil will probably last long enough to allow us to complete our determined self-impoverishment. Given the dominant role played in our economy by the oil and auto industries, we would have to endow ourselves with superhuman foresight and self-control and courage in order to turn away from the route we are following down the endless interstate. Our infatuation with the internal combustion engine has left us less and less able to approach any of those virtues, or even to see that they are needed. The auto is a symbol of freedom, but its real effect is to increasingly enslave us. The million-dollar bills are symbols of material well-being, but the more we pursue such symbols, the less attention we retain to pay to our senses and to the real material goods of our lives.

Sometime within most of our lives, of course, the gas will run out, the interstates will empty, and the coast-to-coast shopping centers will wither and crack and dry as rapidly as the leaves of an overgrown houseplant. The human cost of our brief, passionately reckless affair with oil and gas and gears and wheels, and of our peculiar confusion of symbols with realities, will be tremendous when the final bill comes due. Perhaps then, those of us who survive may have time to begin to pay some attention to the tastes and smells and sights and feelings of our surroundings, to return to a real materialism which is not unrelated to a religious respect for and wonder at the physical world we have come to despise in our mad pursuit of symbolic wealth and freedom.

For those of us who don't survive, an appropriate monument might be made of those copulating truck cabs out on the interstate. Our epitaph has already been written by Joni Mitchell:

> *Don't it always seem to go*
> *That you don't know what you got 'til it's gone?*
> *They paved Paradise*
> *And put up a parking lot.*

I'd begun to see what was happening to my country. At that point, I saw a good deal more than I understood. I needed help to understand it better.

Killer Virus

I'm not sure when I ran into Jerry Mander's great book *Four Arguments for the Elimination of Television,* [Mander] but it articulated many things I'd been feeling and thinking for years. Mander pointed out that the prevailing idea that television was a "neutral medium," and that its value and danger lay only in the content of its programming, was false. He argued, most persuasively, that the medium itself was pernicious, hypnotic, and dangerous to democracy because of what it did to the minds of people who watched it. It was first published in 1978 and has never been out of print, which suggests that many people have read it without the slightest effect on society. The ways Mander observed how television worked and how it affected its viewers' thought processes inspired me to start watching tv in new ways, and thinking about its effects on my students and on the world we lived in:

The Perfect Drug
(The Unofficial Organ, Vol I, #2)

[This was written 31 years ago. Since then, average household tv viewing time has risen to 7 hours, 35 minutes. The hole in the ozone layer over Antartica has decreased somewhat, but the loss of ozone in the stratosphere has continued. Large chunks of the polar caps are falling into the sea daily, and if much of the West is not rapidly becoming a desert, it's giving a good imitation. Of course, it could all burn down before it achieves desert status.]

I got home from work that night a little after ten, pacified Ralph the Cat with his customary mound of reeking Kal-Kan, flipped on the tube and collapsed in my chair to watch the news.

The local lead stories were done with. It was time for the national filler piece, pillaged from the 6 o'clock network news. Tonight's story concerned chlorofluorocarbons. Some scientists had convened a news conference earlier in the day, after completing the most ambitious study ever undertaken of the effects of CFC's on the ozone layer.

They presented computer-enhanced photographs of the ozone layer over the South Pole, showing large, gaping rents. They predicted some results of the rapidly proceeding destruction of the ozone layer: a 30% increase in skin cancers, dramatic climate changes, particularly in the temperate zones, which will become intemperate, not to say hostile to agriculture; these and other developments to occur within 30 years. From now.

They made these predictions as unequivocally as any scientists I've ever heard. They weren't saying "maybe;" they were saying "will." Questioned about U.S. use of CFC's, their spokesman replied that while the U.S. had banned their use in aerosol propellents, other countries had not. "And there are no national boundaries in the atmosphere," he added.

Then the anchorperson was back to add the local angle. "And for Colorado," she said through her perpetual, mindless smile, "they say this means we'll be living in a *desert* pretty soon!" Then it was time for the pre-commercial sports teaser. The sportscaster, on location at a rain-beleaguered golf tourney on Long Island, stood grinning in the deluge. "Well, John," the anchorperson trilled, "no danger of a desert out where *you* are, is there?"

The commercial that followed concerned the peculiar virtue of Heilemann's Old Style beer: it is brewed with *artesian* water. *Artesian* water, a voice reminiscent of Orson Welles' asserted orotundly, is uniquely *pure* because it has been trapped far below the earth's surface for a whole bunch of millennia, *and nothing has ever disturbed its purity*. Naturally this was all hogwash, but "artesian" has a pure, dignified ring to it, and the message was accompanied by a few hundred thousand bucks worth of film of water trickling among some pretty old-looking rocks.

At this point, I turned off the tv and contemplated the six or so minutes of television I'd just experienced. Something about them seemed perfect.

Roof Leaking? No Problem!

Suppose George is sitting around in his home. His neighbor rushes in to inform him that his roof has a series of great holes in it. George looks up - it's true! Great holes everywhere! All *kind* of stuff is going to be coming down through them. He'd better *do* something!

"Why are you smiling?" George asks his neighbor.

"I hear it's a *beautiful* day in Vladivostok!" she says, her smile unabated. This disorients George. Maybe, he thinks, he's getting *excessively worried* about his roof. His neighbor's next remark tends to confirm this speculation.

"Oh, I forgot," she chirps merrily. "I have some lovely Amway products you should buy from me. Then let's get drunk and naked and smear them all over ourselves!" And she starts pulling bottles of dishwashing fluid and Dom Perignon out of her décolletage.

Well, as Nelson Algren used to inquire, what would *you* do?

Obviously, whatever you did in the next few hours, pretty soon you'd set to doing something about your roof, if you had half a brain. Even if that same neighbor kept coming over, day and night, and kept coming on, you'd be a fool to let your house be destroyed.

I suppose you *could* just move in with your neighbor. That would work. Unless *her* roof had giant holes in it, too. Then, if you just kept rolling around on the floor, smashed out of your kug, people might begin to think you had some kind of a drug problem.

Some Kind of a Drug Problem

Enough analogies. What I experienced during those six minutes of television was:

1. A "story" about facts which exist in the objective world. In this case, the facts are life-threatening. They exist whether I ignore them or not. If I do ignore them, my child is going to be sucking roots for a living, at best. Information of the utmost urgency, demanding action of every sane individual.

2. An abrupt end to that story and a refocusing of my attention on another "story"- the wet golfer story, the facts of which also exist in the objective world, but which are of little consequence to anyone except the golfers.

3. An utterly bogus "message" designed to sell me a drug that will relieve any residual anxiety the CFC story might have left me with. All I'd have to do was run down to the corner store and grab a couple of six-packs.

Like many other recreational drugs, television gives its user the illusion of experience without the perils or rewards of experience. Like every other drug, television seems to "enhance" reality, granting its user visions unavailable to unaltered consciousness. (How else did I get to Long Island, or deep below the earth's surface?) Like every other addict, the television user develops tolerance: he requires ever greater doses to achieve the desired effect. (Average time spent in front of television sets per household is now 7 hours per day; that time has risen about 3 minutes per year over the past 10 years.)

Other cultures than ours communally ingest mind-altering drugs and experience shared, collective visions. (See, for example, Andrew Weil's account of one such South American culture in *The Natural Mind.*) They do so under carefully controlled conditions, and they do so rarely. Ours is the first culture to enter into a communal drug experience with apparently uncheckable abandon, supplanting normal consciousness with television consciousness more than seven hours of every day.

Who Owns the Ju-Ju?

There is another distinction between "primitive" psychotropic drug use and television use. The visions induced in South American rain forests are truly collective and communal; they spring from the interplaying minds of the people who choose to ingest the drug together. They do not, as television does, spring from the will and conscious intent of a set of interlocking conglomerates that control the visions they broadcast.

Television programming is not free. The large corporations who "sponsor" television programming spend immense sums to give television away to us. The corporate creatures who comprise our government carefully control access to this "free" medium. Their interests are largely identical. One of their primary shared interests is the erasure of history and the establishment of the Eternal Now.

The federal government desires the disappearance of history because people will not demand action if they can't remember what needs to be acted upon. If the people are residing in the Eternal Now, the government is freed of the obligation to actually address the many potentially fatal conditions with which we've saddled ourselves and to go on about its business of pillaging, looting, supporting thugs and bankrupting our children's children.

The large corporations desire the Eternal Now because it creates a void of meaning and purpose in life, which they can fill with suggestions for one activity - buying. That is the *only* activity television suggests, urges, promotes: get out there and *buy something.* In the words of one executive, "Advertising is a means of contributing meaning and values that are necessary and useful to people in structuring their lives, their social relationships and their rituals."

For a people inclined from their beginnings toward an anti-historical bent, television has proved the perfect disaster. In fewer than forty years, it has captured almost completely an entire nation, turning us into a mass of passive, unimaginative, timid, valueless, puerile toadies.

Lost in the Ozone

If George really got *into* his Amway/champagne/neighbor "lifestyle," it would be difficult to get him to see his behavior objectively, or to consider the direction it was taking him. He would find life with huge chunks of ceiling lying on rotting carpets quite normal, and would not notice as things got worse.

When the great majority of a nation is hooked on the identical drug - and perceive that drug not a drug, but as their principal source of information about reality -

what then? How do you make contact? How can you get through to George that, although the Pope has just married J-Lo in a poolside ceremony, the roof's still leaking?

A colleague responded to this screed by arguing that television provided some really terrific nature shows. It seemed I hadn't made my point clear.

That "creative destruction" was to be the mantra of the New Milllenium was first brought to my attention by a position paper issued by the State Board for Community Colleges, distributed for mandatory reading by my school's administrators, of whom I had reluctantly become half a one in my capacity as co-director of the Downtown Studio Campus. I got the message real quickly when I read it:

Some Thoughts About "Positioning Colorado's Community Colleges for the 21st Century"

I

The "Background" statement for "Positioning..." contains the following paragraph: "Colorado's community colleges are viewed as leaders in anticipating and responding to the changing needs of our students and the communities we serve. However, business as usual will not assure our continued success. Community colleges will have no choice but to undergo massive changes in how we are organized, how we make decisions, how we manage our human resources, and how we deliver top quality programs and services to compete in a tough and rapidly changing market. This will require rethinking and reinventing our structures, values, roles, practices, and policies if we are to be competitive in the future."

Reading this enthusiastic description of cataclysm and rebirth, I was reminded of a paragraph from *The Sporting News* I recently used in my Freshman Composition class. That paragraph read: "The Braves are good enough that they shouldn't worry about who they play in the postseason. They dropped three straight to the Orioles in mid-June, and went 4 - 8 against the Marlins. The Braves couldn't do a thing against Florida lefthander Tony Saunders, who beat them three consecutive times."

"Does something seem sort of *funny* to you about that paragraph?" I asked my class. A student rather hesitantly pointed out that the body of the paragraph seemed not to support the topic statement - in fact, seemed to directly contradict the asserted "goodness" of the Braves, and to support the view that the Braves ought to be *plenty* concerned about their postseason opponent, especially if it should be the Marlins.

Something seems funny about the "Background" paragraph, too - in fact, the same thing seems funny. If, in fact, "Colorado's community colleges are viewed as leaders in anticipating and responding to the changing needs of our students and the communities we serve," the community colleges must have been anticipating and responding for quite some time; otherwise, how would they have developed the sterling reputation attributed to them? As a corollary, they must have been doing these quintessentially 21st Century activities *using the organizational structures, decision-making practices, human resource management practices and delivery systems of the past,* the very ones the rest of the paragraph says must be nuked. In other words, the paragraph asserts that we ought to obliterate structures and practices that have been successful in bringing about the very outcomes that, the document asserts, are desirable.

Before blowing up a building, most people would probably want to see some evidence that the building was performing inadequately or was threatened by structural weaknesses. Before tearing down an athletic team, most people (except Jerry Reinsdorf) would want to see a record of significant failure. This paragraph, however, advances the success of system colleges as a reason for massive alteration. We have coped very well with change, it asserts; therefore, we must entirely reorganize in order to cope with change. The logic is hard to fathom; it is deep.

II

"Positioning..." suggests four desired outcomes of the program of major surgery it advocates. Of the four, the first and last are incomprehensible as written. One, however, can be addressed: "Increase the market share of learners who benefit by enhanced quality and relevance of learning experiences provided by community colleges."

I will discuss the "learning experiences" I shared with two students last week. One was having trouble, to the point of barely contained tears, with algebra. The other wanted to improve her ability to organize her responses to reading assignments.

New Math jargon proved to be the source of the first student's frustration. She couldn't believe that the august-sounding "commutative property" meant only that, if you're adding or multiplying two numbers, it won't matter which one you write first. It took about forty minutes before she could accept the possibility that she was not "hopeless at math." I helped her see that she wasn't by asking her to recreate her experiences in elementary math classes, where she'd first learned that she was "hopeless at math." After a bit of reminiscing, she discovered the name of the "teacher" who'd conveyed the message of despair to her, as well as the message that people who are "good at math" do calculations very quickly, in their heads, so that their answers arrive as if by magic, rather than as the result of systematic, patient, step-by-step procedure. I was able to convince her that the example of "good at math" wizards was a pernicious one. She left my office saying, "I think I can *do* this."

I spent an hour helping the second student arrive at a potential thesis for a paper on Aldous Huxley's *Brave New World.* She made statements about how awful Huxley's imagined benign dictatorship was. I responded in defense of that dictatorship, in order to help her clarify her objections to it. During the hour, we had occasion to discuss Thomas Hobbes, the 1930's plays of Robert Sherwood, Siegfried Sassoon's views of the First World War, Freud's relationship to "social engineering," and the optimism of the Royal Society during the early part of the 17th Century. She left considerably clearer about her objections to the brave new world of the social managers, and about Huxley's strategy of attack on those managers.

When I first started teaching, I wouldn't have been of much help to either student. I wouldn't have known where to look for the source of the math student's difficulties, because I hadn't tutored hundreds of math students and so hadn't learned how to ask them questions that would help them describe their own confusion, and so reduce it. Nor had I learned to expect frequently to find the source of their difficulties in common classroom teaching practices. In fact, I often engaged in some of those same practices in my own classroom, quite unaware of their power to harm. I probably could have had a similar conversation with the composition student 25 years ago, but the outcome would have differed, because I would have become lost in admiration for my own glib erudition and wound up lecturing her for an hour, rather than saying only enough to force her to refine and clarify her own reactions and insights.

I contend that both those students are and will remain grateful for the moments of education they shared with me. I contend that the "quality" of those moments was brought about by the fact that I've practiced my profession for more than 25 years, and learned how to help students learn. Most of my own learning has consisted of the gradual reduction of ego and intellectual arrogance and the gradual increase in willingness and ability to listen that only time and real-life disaster bring about.

Had the authors of "Positioning..." consulted the "market" (actual students) they want a greater "share" of, they would have found that students place a high value on the very characteristics of "traditional" teachers this document appears to view with, at best, contempt.

III

I hold these truths to be self-evident:
Students don't know what they need to learn or how to learn it. If they did, they wouldn't pay other people to teach them.

Students recognize good teachers and value them more highly than any other aspect of educational "culture." (See attached Student Satisfaction Inventory Summary)

No evidence is presented by "Positioning..." for a growing demand for new models of education." Community colleges and other institutions have been offering instruction using a variety of delivery methods for at least ten years. If demand for these methods accounts for the steady increase in enrollment at community colleges, then it would seem that enrollment in telecourses, itv courses, and internet courses could be shown to have accounted for most or all of the increase in enrollment. "Positioning..." presents no evidence that this is so. While a poem is hardly evidence, the following poem does have the virtue of having been written by a student, an actual, living member of the "market."

    Schools

   by Lucille Rousell

School - 1949
The nun rang the heavy hand bell,
    No one spoke or moved
Because silence was to us
    As the Golden Rule

We had no inside facilities,
    No inside cafeteria.
The students were well disciplined;
    The students were respectful.

The Academic Curriculum was one
    Of its kind,
No other could equal it in its time.

School - 1953

The nun pressed the buzzer; you could
    Hear the sound in the yard.
Many of the nuns were standing in the hall.

The cafeteria was just across the street.
    We had inside facilities
To meet all students' needs.

The morals and Academic Teachings
    Were beyond description.
Respect came from both students and staff -
It was more than a tradition.

School - 1996

I see Computers, Computers, Computers.
    Where in the world am I?
Everything is inside.

The Computer Lab is great
    For all who participate.
When typing, do not accidentally
    Hit the wrong key.
Result?
    Catastrophe.

There are computers, computers, computers.
    Where are the nuns dressed in black?
I wish one or two would come back.

This poem seems to say that, as "facilities" have grown more opulent and sophisticated, something has been lost, or at least lost sight of. It seems to place a higher value on the human qualities ("values," "respect,") and intellectual rigor ("Academic Teachings beyond description") than on the computer lab.

Whatever technological, job market, and social changes take place in the next century, students will need the same skills to cope with them that people have always needed to cope with their lives. They will need to learn how to read critically, think critically, communicate clearly, understand and manipulate numbers. The more complex society becomes, the more they will need these skills.

If a student doesn't know how to read beyond the literal level, it really isn't going to matter whether that student is "reading" from a printed text or a cathode ray tube. If a student knows no history, that student is cannon fodder for the first persuasive demagog who comes down the pike. If a student doesn't learn how to learn, that student will be devastated by any sort of change, particularly technological change that renders the student's previous training obsolete. If a student can't communicate clearly, whatever technological expertise that student acquires will have only limited value to employers, colleagues, or students.

As the following "Student Satisfaction Inventory" demonstrates, students value effective instruction above any other aspect of their college experience. And yet, in the forest of turgid verbiage that is "Positioning...", one is hard put to discern any recognition of that fact, despite all the protuberant lip service to "serving the market." One might wish that the "leaders" of higher education might one day actually pay attention to the research they so relentlessly demand, but then one might wish that pigs would fly, or perform a massed choral performance of the "Ode to Joy," and one would stand no greater chance of having one's wishes disappointed.

Institutional Summary
Scales: In Order of Importance to Our Students

Scale	Our Institution Means			National Group Means		
	Importance	Satisfaction	Performance Gap	Imp	Satis	Perf Gap
Instructional Effectiveness	6.15	5.23	.92	6.18	5.24	.94
Registration Effectiveness	6.10	5.09	1.01	6.12	5.23	.89
Academic Advising/Counseling	5.97	4.73	1.24	6.10	5.05	1.05
Academic Services	5.97	5.03	.94	6.00	5.01	.99
Concern for the Individual	5.97	4.95	1.02	6.09	5.05	1.04

[Safety and Security, Admissions and Financial Aid, Service Excellence, Campus Climate, Student Centeredness, Campus Support Services, in that order of diminishing importance to students, excised]

Well, the pigs didn't get together to perform Beethoven's 9th, and neither the State Board nor my own administration was moved by my criticisms. I began to suspect that the power of reason wasn't all that powerful in the face of Received Wisdom, which is what the "creative destruction" nonsense had become. All the Best (wealthiest) People and all the people who worked for the Best People in the fond hope that one day they'd become Best People, too, knew that "creative destruction" was the New, New Thing, and therefore impervious to challenge.

I think I began to get it when the State Board installed a Vice President of Instruction whose devotion to following orders was only exceeded by his lack of interest in education, and then maneuvered in a President who announced, on his first day, that his "management Bible" was a book entitled *If It Ain't Broke, Break It.* I poked around and found that such a book actually existed. It was about how groovy creative destruction was, and how there was now nothing of use to be learned from experience or the past.

It took me a while longer to realize that Corporate America had not only discovered in the computer its most devastating engine of destruction (my friend Dan Todd called computers "weapons of mass distraction"), but would discover a host of willing worshippers and enablers of that engine, not only among the already powerful, but among teachers, the very existence of whose profession was quite obviously threatened by the new machines. Well, to paraphrase Mencken, nobody ever went broke underestimating the intelligence of the American Teacher. So I started going to conferences and presenting papers, trying to alert my colleagues to our peril. This was the first of those papers:

Meeting the Deductible

Imagine that you are any of the following persons:

1. a 19 year old boy who, after flunking out of high school as a third-year freshman, has hung out with similar friends for a few years, taken a few unrewarding fast food jobs which you've lost through general fecklessness, faced the awful future, obtained a G.E.D. and enrolled at a community college, having been told all your life that Education is the Key to Success;

2. a single mother of two kids, 3 and 5, working full time to support them, taking night classes at a community college in order to prepare yourself for some yet to be determined, more remunerative, less demeaning job;

3. a forty year old father of three, also working full time, attending night classes at a community college in hopes of making a career change into the burgeoning field of computers, where the geetus spouts freely as a Texas gusher;

4. a 37 year old, newly divorced mother of two teenagers, not unintelligent but seventeen years removed from reading anything but *People* or writing anything but memoranda regarding your endless chain of duties; sad, unsure, looking for a place to stand - any place that doesn't shift and tilt - so you can start something you've heard referred to as "a new life."

You can be any one of those you want.

You walk into your Freshman English I class, and the instructor directs you to open your book to page 38. "I want you to critically analyze this little essay," says the prof. "You have an hour and fifteen minutes. Your writing sample will determine whether or not you're ready for this class."

You don't feel particularly ready, willing, or able. You hate "English." Tough; you open the book - it's called *The Postmodern Wordsmith* , a title both incomprehensible and extraordinarily unappealing - and face the essay, entitled, "It's Deductible." [Kahn] Its author is someone named Gordon Kahn. This is what you see in the first paragraph:

"There were times, and Paris was the place, when nbibsbkt and their cfhvnt, cattle cbspot from the Bshfoujof, and people named Spuitdime would spend so much money that it would efnpojuaf the gsbod or fogffcmf it for long periods. In New York, during the Cbczmpojbo 31's, many a cpoboab was bupnjae between the upper and ofuifs njmmtupoft of Qbsl Bwfovf and Cspbexbz."

"Oh, my sweet Savior," you say to yourself, "come aid me *now* . " But He is silent, and you perceive that you must try to survive unaided.

Two cities mentioned: Paris and New York. One is not in the U.S., one is. People named Spuitdime spending big. So it's some people you're supposed to have heard of spending big time in some big cities. For long periods of time. Sometime in the past.

There's nothing to do but plough onward, hoping that future paragraphs will cast some light on this one, or that the Savior will appear, miraculous though tardy.

But what you find, ploughing on, is only more chaos and confusion. Paragraph after paragraph is interrupted by clots of weird code you can't pray to decipher.

Oh, my sweet Savior, you think.

The essay whose first paragraph I've encoded above appeared in a trade magazine called *The Screenwriter* in 1945. It is a *jeux d'esprit* , the kind of thing former newspapermen such as Gordon Kahn used to toss off at the drop of a hat when they needed a few bucks to keep the wolf from the door. Kahn takes the fact that a new class of servants - financial managers - had come to Hollywood in the early 30's, bringing some financial stability to the actors, writers and directors, and embroiders that fact for 4 pages. He has fun with those who take money too seriously and with those who don't take it seriously at all. Mostly, he has fun with his own gift of literary embroidery, freely mixing contemporary slang with playful allusions to ancient and modern history and cleverly adapted cliches. Hundreds of thousands of comparable words were written in 1945.

Uncoded, the paragraph reads:

"There were times, and Paris was the place, when maharajahs and their begums, cattle barons from the Argentine, and people named Rothschild would spend so much money that it would demonetize the franc or enfeeble it for long periods. In New York, during the Babylonian 20's, many a bonanza was atomized between the upper and nether millstones of Park Avenue and Broadway."

I cannot know how much of this makes sense to you professional readers. It all made sense to me, although I had to look up "begum." (After I'd looked it up, I was little wiser, because I'd already figured it had to mean something like "a well-rewarded female companion to a rich fellow from the Indian peninsula.") I could figure out what a "begum" might likely be from the context, because I understood the context.

If the context had appeared to me in the coded version I've presented to you, I would have had little chance of figuring that one word out. If you're a student with the dearth of reading experience most of our students have, what would you do with this paragraph, which appears a little later in "It's Deductible"?

"Tbujoht cbolt offered lovely desk calendars, pof-xbz xbmmfut and Spzbm Tqpef piggy banks in an endeavor to trp the xboupo dollar. The qbsbmf of the hsbttimqqffs and the bou was recounted in many foujdjoh versions and in brilliant technicolor - without snaring a tjohmf dmbn cfijoe the xjdlfu." You now have about an hour to write a critical analysis of this essay. It pretty much all reads like this. Hit it.

I might be a more modern kind of an English teacher, and not expect too much of you. I might give you two weeks to read this essay and formulate your response to it. During those two weeks, we'd have a chance to "discuss" the essay. We would talk about what the words meant when they were written. We would talk about the attitude the writer took toward the words he put on the paper.

To be more representational, I should say that *I* would talk about those things, making largely unsuccessful attempts to involve you in the conversation. I would talk about them because they seem to me necessary considerations, given the time and place the words were written.

You, on the other hand, would not join much in the conversation, because to you neither other times nor places have much if any meaning. To you, all is present. You know that the future can be better than the past, and that your attendance on a more or less regular basis in some rooms can help make it so. That you are presented with this strange mix of code with simple English seems to you an affront.

This is why there are lawyers, you think. (When I started writing this, I was guessing. Guessing based on almost thirty years of teaching community college English, but guessing. After I wrote the above, I thought I should check my guesses, and so I presented an unencoded version of the above paragraph to 71 Freshman English students. I asked them to underline any words or phrases in the paragraph they felt they didn't know or would have to look up. I told them that their responses would be anonymous and that they would have nothing to do with the particular class they were members of. This is just Science, I told them. "Maharajahs and their begums" baffled 96%, "people named Rothschild" 41%, the "Babylonian 20's" 45%. The "atomized bonanza" was Greek to 73% and millstones failed to grind for 53%. Every phrase or word encoded above proved unfamiliar to at least 25% of the 71 readers.)

English, like any other language, is a code. We don't think of it like that because we learned it before we knew we were learning. As we learned it, we were learning all sorts of history and civics and art and music and religion and science and geography and what-all. A big mess of information came with learning the language, during the time most people over forty or so were learning it.

Then came television, and we allowed the teaching of language to pass over to it. And television was operated by advertising agencies whose purpose was to sell people things they didn't necessarily need. The advertising agencies were paid by companies who wanted to sell things to those people.

The only way to sell useless things to people is to confuse them into thinking they need the things you have to sell. This is the art of advertising. Radio had prepared people to listen to messages regarding such things. It had not prepared them to see the things dance and sing and defeat villains.

When Babo's Foaming Cleanser angels chased the dirt right down the drain, America applauded; who would not? The entire history of theatre had been reprised in 30 seconds, and, as it always had, it worked perfectly: a threat to the polis had been repelled. Good boogie. When a colorfully loutish fellow groaned, "I can't believe I ate the whole thing," a new phrase became part of the ephemeral American lexicon, and it was soon being alluded to by a Presidential candidate.

The downside to this new mode of English instruction, from the teaching perspective, or from the learning perspective, for that matter, was that the new English didn't include any reference to the past; it referred only to itself.

And so the children who grew up learning this new version of English learned a sort of English, but did not learn any of the history that the language had previously contained and required for its understanding. They learned, instead, a new code, whose only referents were products available at the chain stores advertised by the agencies whose masters paid for their messages.

The language of advertising involves the making of claims not meant to be taken as "true," involves the replacement of reasoned argument by catch-phrases, and is meant to evoke emotion, not thought. Without the accompanying visual images, it immediately reveals itself for what it is: empty, utterly cynical, manipulative.

It has become the language of our culture. If you doubt this, consider the language spoken by politicians, sportscasters, everyone on television and radio, and, sad to say, by most educational administrators and an increasing number of teachers. In our arena, the cutting edge was only yesterday interfacing with the world-class state of the art. So long as it was remembered that "art" had solely to do with The Art of the Deal.

Little wonder these children of the new English largely view language with little or no respect or affection or interest; the language they've acquired from our culture *deserves* to be dissed.

Further, our current students grew up in a country which had always believed, as Henry Ford did, that history was bunk and that it was morning in America. They could hardly be blamed for believing that nothing that had been written before their current moment was worth reading.

They could hardly be blamed because they'd been told that if it was worth knowing, it was in the computer somewhere. If it was in the computer, why should they know it? It's known. The television commercials reinforced this certainty. Ancient-looking geezers mourned that they would not live to see the wonderful cyberfuture, as images of nubile lasses danced behind them across the screen; ghetto children exulted in their mom's subsidized purchase of a new computer - now they, too, could be a parcel of the information age.

The "kids" I'm talking about are my kids and my students. They would say I was speaking "harshly."

I am. But I am not harsh about them. I'm harsh about us. We are the ones who've sat still for this nonsense. Sat still for it, or stayed silent in its face, or embraced it. None of those seems an admirable response to a large omnivore squatting over your face.

Not to say that I haven't sometimes practiced all three responses during my brilliant career.

I hesitate to continue by considering the contribution their public school education has made to my students' intellectual vacuity, but continue I must. Most of my young students these last few years have been taught some simple, powerful lessons by their lives in school:

      1. Show up where you're supposed to be, more or less on time,
         three days out of five.

      2. Don't commit felonies when someone's around to watch.

3. When sufficiently badgered, put some words on a piece of paper. They don't have to make sense as long as they're handed in on time.
4. You won't have to do this often, because most of your work will consist of filling in blanks with the "right" answers found elsewhere in a canned exercise.
5. Follow steps 1 through 4 for four years, and you're good to go.

My syllabus tells my students on its first page what will happen on every day of the semester: what I expect them to have read, when I expect them to have read it, when I expect them to submit a paper about a particular reading. Because my classes meet twice a week, I arrange my syllabus in two columns. The left-hand column is for the first day of the week the class meets; the right hand column is for the second day. Each day is dated.

And during nearly every class, I hear anxious queries: *when* is this essay due? *What* are we doing today? We *are*?

My students lack this concept: you can derive useful information by reading printed words.

From this, I can only conclude that their previous schooling has failed them in about the most basic way I can imagine anything called "education" could fail.

Saying that, I don't mean to attack public education, and especially I don't mean to attack public school teachers. The system and its workers are functions of a culture which has abandoned all values but the pecuniary and all satisfactions but the immediate and gross. Public education does its best to care for the kids formed by this culture, whose parents have no time to do anything but chase the bucks to buy urban assault vehicles and access to the internet, upon which they can pursue their aborted sex lives in chat rooms and poor quality images.

I've talked about my students as if they were a blob, which they're not. Yet I get these idiot questions about what's due when, and oh, was I supposed to read that? from obviously intelligent students more often than from those obviously less gifted. The obviously less gifted *never* ask questions. They know they're in over their heads, and they refer themselves to their previous educational experience: Shut up! Don't draw attention to yourself! Someone might ask you something! You'll be good to go!

The culture seems unlikely to change in the direction of a massive insurrection in behalf of literacy. Teachers of English, so long as such a discipline remains, seem equally unlikely to change. We'll quote Orwell and E.B. White and persist.

We'll persist in believing that humans live by, with and through the language they speak and hear and write, and that, without mastery of that language, they'll likely be enslaved by it.

That one picture is not only not worth one thousand words, it is worthless without the words its viewer says about it to himself or herself, and then says to another person.

We believe that one of the great joys and purposes of our species occurs when one human mind says something that another human mind always wanted to say, but didn't, because it lacked essential information or experience or courage or the words to say it in.

That's why I got into this racket, anyway.

It's also why I've come to believe that my racket needs to be teaching reading far more than to be teaching writing. Our profession has been going through a generational period of emphasis on "critical writing." I've gone along with that, not unwillingly. The phrase has meant to me that you need to read carefully, think about what you've read, and respond to it from your experience and knowledge, and decide what parts of what you've read seem useful and true, and what parts not.

But if the "knowledge" part is removed, and the "experience" part is removed - unless "experience" can be defined as watching illuminated dots screaming inanities at you - and the "reading" part is removed... what then?

My students don't know how to read. They don't respect words; what they know about words is that they're tools used by someone to sell them something, or used by people pretending to be their peers (*viz* Marilyn Manson, et. al.) to encourage them in the universal idea of the young that their elders are evil, stupid clowns and the authorities their elders respect are without either power or merit.

So I've come to redefine my job. What I hope to do now is to teach people that worlds of meaning and value and beauty can be entered through words, but that they have to devote serious, sustained effort in order to open the door to those worlds.

I currently teach a lovely essay by Frank Conroy called "Think About It." In the last section of the essay, Conroy talks about his chance encounter with Justice William O. Douglas. They converse about the Dennis case, which is currently before the court. When we discuss this essay, I always ask my students if they know what the Dennis case concerned, and, to this date, not one student has known.

"How can you understand this essay of Conroy's, then?" I ask them.

The occasional brave student will respond, "Oh, we get the gist of it."

Well, you can't do that, in this particular essay, because Justice Douglas's explanation of the Dennis case, such as he explains it, is elliptical in the extreme, and refers frequently to the language of the Smith Act, and if you don't know what the Smith Act is, you don't have a prayer of understanding what he's talking about.

So the first thing we need to do is teach our students that every word counts, and that guessing is a perilous enterprise.

I currently teach a column by Ben Wattenberg, in which he asserts that Americans believe that America "stands for something very special, and they believe they know the reasons why, which turn out to be that same old stuff: political, personal and economic liberty under a constitution."

I ask my students what the word "special" means. Then I ask them what "very" special might mean; how much more "special" than "special" would "very special " be? Then I ask them why, if "special" in this context means "excellent," "outstanding," "different from any other," Wattenberg describes the reasons for that "specialness" as "that same old stuff." I ask them about the connotations of that phrase. Hardly any of them know the word "connotation," or recognize that it's the major manipulative property of this or any language. I ask them, what if he'd said, "that same old garbage"? Would that change your attitude toward the words that follow?

"It's Deductible," the piece from which we started all this, alleges that various foreigners "would spend so much money that it would demonitize the franc or enfeeble it for long periods." Is this "true"? I might ask my students. If you don't know, how could you find out? You have the place - "Paris" - but you don't know what "times" the author refers to. Does the rest of the paragraph give you any clues about what might be the "times"? If you knew that the times were the "20's," and the place was Paris, and the proper name "Rothschild," would you have enough information to enable you to find out what in the nation that sentence means?

Then I return to the original question, "Is this 'true'?" Since it is not "true," I ask them, why did Gordon Kahn allege that it was? Why did he exaggerate in such a manner? Did he intend to deceive his readers? Did he intend to amuse them? These kinds of questions lead, sometimes, to a better understanding of the idea of a "voice" on the page.

But "voice" should never appear in quotation marks when it comes to reading, a point Donald Hall made clear in a superb essay published fifteen years ago in *Newsweek* called "Bring Back the Out Loud Language." His point was that language is essentially a spoken art, and that we've lost the ability to hear the words on the page, and thereby lost our ability to understand what the hell the words mean. For example, if you can't hear the corrosively grievance-laden irony in Richard III's tone in his opening soliloquy, "Now is the winter of our discontent / made glorious summer by this sun of York / and all the clouds that lour'd upon our house / in the deep bosom of the ocean buried," it will seem to you simply a piece of nauseating political flattery - when, in fact, it's a multiple death sentence.

To address this loss of the inner ear, I give my students a short pack of poems at the beginning of the semester and require that they select one to memorize, speak to the class, and analyze in a paper. And we talk - usually at greater length than the syllabus projects - about what that experience was like. It's the most dreaded and ultimately the most popular of my assignments; students are amazed by it: first by their courage, then by the fact that language *sounds* like something, then that the way it sounds has to do with the way it *means*.

My favorite experience of this process, so far, occurred when a cabinetmaker who'd lost the use of his forearms and come back to school to change professions chose Elizabeth Bishop's poem "The Fish" to read, and stood up in front of God and everybody and read it in a flawless East Texas accent, which gave it a completely new dimension. "Doug," I said, after some dumbstruck moments, "I thought you told me you'd lived your whole life in Colorado. Where'd you come up with that accent?"

"I just thought the poem sounded like some old fellah that'd had a lot of experience," he said, "and... I don't know... the voice just *was there*. " I think the poem's author, Elisabeth Bishop, an old girl who'd had a lot of experience herself, would have liked that answer.

If I were teaching our essay "It's Deductible," I might stop at the phrase "Babylonian 20's," and ask the students to work first on "Babylon" and then on "20's." The only students likely to have a referent for "Babylon" are those severely addicted to reggae and those severely addicted to the Old Testament. The majority will have no referent at all, and thus no way to comprehend what the sentence means. I try to convey to my students that language is highly allusive, and that the allusions can sometimes be sussed out from context, but mostly have to be tracked down, at great personal cost but to great personal benefit.

From that same paragraph of "It's Deductible, I might examine the latter part of the same sentence: "...many a bonanza was atomized between the upper and nether millstones of Park Avenue and Broadway." Having discovered the denotations of "bonanza" and "atomized," we might proceed to a discussion of metaphor - how one thing can be implicitly equated with another thing, and whether we should take such implied comparisons as literally true.

The visual images by which our children have grown up surrounded - from the inescapable television screen to the video games to the computer screens to the movies and the movies on video, etc., etc. - have done something else - they have occupied the children's imaginations, as the Nazis occupied Europe, slaughtering those they couldn't subjugate and turn into docile if not willing slaves.

I remember a day twenty years ago: I was teaching an English 060 class, a class for the folks who'd missed out on the knowledge of sentences and punctuation and what's a verb and what's a paragraph. We were trying to look closely at the parts of a metaphoric sentence that compared a woman with a spider. The comparison was an unusually favorable one.

"See, you have to use your *imaginations*," I found myself spouting, in a kind of "Win this one for the Gipper" tone. "You have to *see* what the words are saying."

A young woman all the way in the back suddenly raised her hand, looking in a startled way at her own sudden demand for attention, as if it might have been the first such bid she'd ever made. She'd been sitting back there - *way* back, as far back as she could get without breaking through the wall - all quarter, never saying a mumbling word.

But now she said, "Mr. Malcolm.... I don't *have* an imagination."

The sorrow in her voice like to break your heart.

But the look in her eyes is what I remain unable to forget. Her eyes were like the rabbit's, when she looks out through the mesh of her cage and sees the raccoon working away at that very mesh. They weren't even frightened; they were already resigned and dimming. She had spoken a terrible truth, and every one of us knew it.

Imagination, I sometimes tell my students, doesn't mean thinking about gryphons and faeries and unicorns. It means the ability to form your own pictures in your own mind. And if you can't do that, then whose pictures are you seeing all the time up there?

I also read them this sentence: "I can't understand anything in general unless I'm carrying along in my mind a specific example and watching it go. Some people think in the beginning that I'm kind of slow and I don't understand the problem, because I ask a lot of these 'dumb' questions." Then I tell them that this "slow" fellow is Richard Feynman, who holds a Nobel Prize in Physics. Then we practice the art of *creating* specific examples from general statements and "watching them go." And are frequently startled to see how one specific example can reveal the bankruptcy of a perfectly splendid-sounding generalization.

Those are a few aspects of reading I try to teach my students - precision in definition, alertness to connotation and tone, *hearing* the words as well as seeing them, leaving no allusion untraced and no metaphor unexamined, developing the imagination. I don't think I need to point out that these are also aspects of writing. They've proved eye-opening to quite a few. They can't, need it be said, make up for the twenty or thirty or more years of reading that most of my students don't have under their belts. Only a whole bunch more reading can do that.

And so my primary goal has become to trick, cajole, entice, inspire and otherwise motivate my students to fall in love with reading. If I don't do that, I haven't done anything, except, perhaps, to create a few more clever persuaders.

I don't think we need any more of those.

My audience of English profs wasn't noticeably moved by that approach, so I tried a more literary appeal. I can't remember where I came upon E.M. Forster's 1909 story "The Machine Stops," but its foresight astonished me. Not only had he foreseen the internet, he'd imagined the sort of people it would create. I thought maybe my colleagues would listen to Forster, since he was a certified Author.

Turn Off the Bubble Machine: E.M. Forster's Virtual Reality
(http://thothbooks.blogspot.com/2014/06/turn-off-bubble-machine-em-forsters.html)

I stole my title from a Stan Freberg routine in which he parodies the Lawrence Welk Show that used to be broadcast from the Aragon Ballroom on Venice beach. At the end of the show, Welk's Bubble Machine, which produced the visible signs of his "champagne music," goes berserk, producing such a Vesuvius of bubbles that the pier is elevated from its moorings and the Avalon is borne out into the dark Pacific, with Welk's desperate Dakota twang fadingly crying, "Turn off-a da Bubble Machine! Turn off-a da Bubble Machine."

But I have a different bubble machine in mind, as did E.M. Forster when, in 1909, he wrote his long tale, "The Machine Stops." This bubble machine creates bubbles, true enough, but they don't float themselves out to sea. Rather, they encase individuals from experience - experience of the natural world, of other individuals, of their own bodies and emotions; encase them within transparent walls of images and "ideas."

"The Machine Stops" envisions a world in which humans live far beneath the surface of the earth, each one sequestered in a hexagonal cell to which all necessities and approved pleasures are supplied by The Machine. Food, air, light, water, music, literature and human company of a sort are available to each cell's resident at the touch of a button.

In one such cell we find Vashti, described as "a swaddled lump of flesh - a woman, about five feet high, with a face as white as a fungus." Vashti receives a call from her son, Kuno, whose cell is halfway around the world, on a device which allows her to both hear and see him, after a fashion. Kuno asks her to visit, so that she may explain to him the harm in his desire to visit the surface of the earth. Loath to leave her cell, Vashti responds that such a desire may hold no harm, but is "contrary to the spirit of the age."

While children are separated from their mothers immediately after birth in Forster's brave new world, some unacknowledged vestige of maternal love eventually impels Vashti to undertake the journey to meet with Kuno. She is transported to him within a series of sealed chambers, including an airship that inadvertently gives her glimpses of the repellent sky, the ocean, Greece and the Himalayas; to all of these, her immediate and automatic response is the same: "No ideas here."

Kuno reveals to her what he refused to communicate electronically: he *has* visited the surface of the earth without having first applied for an Egression Permit, and has, after his recapture by The Machine, been threatened with Homelessness. This means that he will be ejected from the cell world and left on the surface of the earth, where he will perish immediately from the poison of unmodified air - or so Vashti believes, even though Kuno tells her that not only had he begun to acclimatize to the air on the surface, he had seen human creatures living there. Repulsed and despairing, Vashti leaves her son to his fated Homelessness and returns to her cell.

Some time later, Kuno, who has somehow been spared, again calls Vashti with a message that baffles, terrifies and enrages her: "The Machine stops," Kuno says. Vashti cuts her ties with the "man who was my son," reckoning him irretrievably mad.

But Kuno's prediction comes to pass. The music begins to fade and falter; the water turns ever fouler; the poetry machine emits gibberish. Complaints from the cell-dwellers, directed to the Committee of The Mending Apparatus, multiply. The communications apparatus breaks down, panic overtakes the cell-dwellers, and Kuno and Vashti are reunited somehow during the final chaos, which is ended when an airship crashes through the surface, exploding tier after tier of the underground world.

This tale scarcely even meets the typical science fiction story's minimal level of characterization - we see only two characters, Vashti and Kuno, and they are little more than types: Vashti, the conformist, Kuno, the questioning rebel. But Forster had something else in mind than a simple, dystopian tale of the future; at the very beginning and the very end of the story, he describes it as "a meditation." His meditation concerns the relationships between humans and their tools - the benefits those tools provide and the costs they exact.

The inhabitants of Forster's subterranean paradise have available both necessities and pleasures at the touch of a button: "There were buttons and switches everywhere" in Vashti's chamber - "buttons to call for food, for music, for clothing. There was the hot-bath button, by pressure of which a basin of (imitation) marble rose out of the floor, filled to the brim with a warm deodorized liquid. There was the cold-bath button. There was the button that produced literature. And there were of course the buttons by which she communicated with her friends. The room, though it contained nothing, was in touch with all that she cared for in the world."

In her satisfaction, Vashti is not alone, not a member of some privileged class; in each cell throughout the entire system, the amenities are identical: "...thanks to the advance of science, the earth was exactly alike all over." In short, half of the Communist Manifesto's great vision - to each according to his needs - has been completely realized. After a fashion.

Thirty-seven years after Forster's meditation, George Orwell was moved by an article in a popular magazine about "Pleasure Spots of the Future" to observe: "It is difficult not to feel that the unconscious aim in the most typical modern pleasure resorts is a return to the womb. For there, too, one was never alone, one never saw daylight, the temperature was always regulated, one did not have to worry about work or food, and one's thoughts, if any, were drowned by a continuous rhythmic throbbing." Forster was perhaps thinking of this connection to the womb as he imagined the appearance of the cell-dwellers: Vashti, that "swaddled lump of flesh...white as a fungus" is also to be thought of as "without teeth and hair;" in other words, these citizens whose every need is supplied by The Machine have essentially reverted to foetuses.

With the exception of the deviant Kuno, the citizens not only do not miss contact with the natural world, they actively fear and loathe it. When Kuno first requests that Vashti visit him in person, she demurs because, "I dislike seeing the horrible brown earth, and the sea, and the stars when it is dark." After she is driven by residual mother-love to make the trip, her first sight of the airship she will take is even worse: "Yet as Vashti saw the vast flank of the ship, stained with exposure to the outer air, her horror of direct experience returned." To her, "All the old literature, with its praise of Nature...rang false as the prattle of a child." This attitude is also encouraged by the faceless committees in charge of The Machine.

It is when Kuno first sees the constellation Orion from an airship that his curiosity about nature is fired, for he sees in this grouping of stars "'... that they were like a man.'" Kuno, in other words, has begun to imagine that as a human he is somehow a part of nature. Vashti responds to this notion, "'It does not strike me as a very good idea, but it is certainly original.'" She senses that Kuno's identification with nature is "contrary to the spirit of the age;" in fact, she senses that it is profoundly subversive. In a world devoted entirely to the satisfactions that can be mechanically provided, any interest in, identification with or contact with Nature threatens the system with potential discontent.

Vashti's abhorrence of direct experience operates as well in the sphere of human contact unmediated by the machine - that is, "direct experience" of other humans. Yet Forster notes near the beginning, "She knew several thousand people; in certain directions human intercourse had advanced enormously." Vashti can communicate with these people instantaneously and at will through the medium of what amounts to an interactive computer network. Further, she can avail herself of the knowledge of all others, as well as that stored up from the past, and she can share her own ideas with everyone who chooses to hear them. After she repels Kuno's request to come see him, she delivers her lecture on Australian music, which is "well received."

So the other half of the Manifesto's vision - from each according to his abilities - has also been realized. Forster's delicate qualifier regarding the improvement of human communication, "in certain directions," indicates his attitude, but he lets Kuno phrase his criticism more directly: trying to explain his desire to speak with Vashti in person, Kuno says, "'I see something like you in this plate [the "screen" in which people appear to each other], but I do not see you. I hear something like you through this telephone, but I do not hear you.'" As the conversation continues, Vashti fancies that Kuno looks sad. "She could not be sure, for the Machine did not transmit *nuances* of expression. It only gave a general idea of people - an idea that was good enough for all practical purposes, Vashti thought. The imponderable bloom, declared by a discredited philosophy to be the actual essence of intercourse, was rightly ignored by the Machine, just as the imponderable bloom of the grape was ignored by the manufacturers of artificial fruit."

And Vashti's horror of direct experience of other humans is nearly over-powering. The worst thing about airship travel for her is the need "to submit to glances from the other passengers," and when the airship's flight attendant touches her, she cries, "'How dare you! You forget yourself!'" Her distaste becomes clearer still when she reaches the end of her journey. "And if Kuno himself, flesh of her flesh, stood close beside her at last, what profit was there in that? She was too well-bred to shake him by the hand."

Finally, the instant availability of human communication has a paradoxical side-effect; the more quickly and easily people can communicate with each other, the more impatient they become with the slightest delay. When Vashti takes Kuno's call, her first words are, "'Be quick!...Be quick, Kuno; here I am in the dark wasting my time."

In Forster's imagined world, human communication has become nearly instantaneous and potentially universal; that portion of human communication which is received by sight and hearing is available to all, and all but the aberrant find it "good enough for all practical purposes." Speed and ease, however, bear costs: the loss of "nuance," (in other words, of emotion) and a terrible fear of experiencing what other senses bring - fear of smell, of touch, of "the bloom" that defines the grape but is itself undefinable. Meaning that it cannot be reduced to an "idea."

In his book *Four Arguments for the Elimination of Television*, Jerry Mander asks his readers to perform an experiment: "Please go look into a mirror. As you gaze at yourself, try to get a sense of what is lost between the mirror image of you, and *you*. You might ask someone to join you facing the mirror. If so, you will surely feel that other person's presence as you stand there. But in the reflection, this feeling will be lost. You will be left with only the image.... What is missing from the reflection is life, or essence."

But Vashti and her fellows seem to sense no loss in their condition. They feel, instead, that they are in complete control of their lives. When Kuno telephones Vashti, "The woman touched a switch and the music was silent." Music is simply a commodity at the command of individual whim. When Vashti's refusal to come see him irritates Kuno, "His image in the blue plate faded....He had isolated himself."

What a male paradise; if a woman disputes your desires with illogical arguments, flip a switch and disappear! Every man's dream has finally been realized. (This scene is reminiscent of the moment in Tim Burton's great film *Mars Attacks!* in which Joe Don Baker, secure for the moment in his trailer in the desert, watches his Marine son on television take up arms against the hostile Martians, only to be incinerated down to a still-charging skeleton. Baker's response is to frantically punch the remote, seeking a better outcome on another channel.)

But at what cost does this mastery of life come? The cost is pretty high, in Forster's vision. And the highest cost can be seen in Vashti's complete loss of self-knowledge. When Kuno appears on her "plate," Vashti's "white face wrinkle[s] into smiles," and she is impelled to visit him in person by the thought that "there was something special about Kuno - indeed there had been something special about all her children - and, after all, she must brave the journey if he desired it." But when Kuno telephones her toward the end of the tale with the cryptic message, "'The Machine stops,'" she says to a friend, "'A man who was my son believes that the Machine is stopping.'" When she must choose between the Machine and her son, her natural but perfectly unconscious maternal feelings are readily expendable.

Because scarcely any self is left, a terrible emptiness is evinced by the need for constant and immediate mental stimulation. After Kuno isolates himself, Vashti immediately turns off the isolation switch which has allowed her to talk to only one person, and "all the accumulations of the last three minutes burst upon her. The room was filled with the noise of bells, and speaking-tubes. What was the new food like?...Had she had any ideas lately? Might one tell her one's own ideas?...To most of these questions she replied with irritation - a growing quality in that accelerated age." Constant, instant, inescapable communication seems to fill a void for these people, but because it does not truly fill the void, it becomes increasingly irritating, and the people become increasingly impatient with the current communication which is preventing the next communication from arriving.

The Committee of the Machine senses that this void is becoming a problem - Kuno's unauthorized visit to the earth's surface alerts them to this danger - and so it undertakes to provide the citizens with a new religion, the worship of the Machine and its instructional manual, the Book of the Machine.

"Those who had long worshipped silently," Forster observes, "now began to talk. They described the strange feeling of peace that came over them when they handled the Book of the Machine, the pleasure that it was to repeat certain numerals out of it, however little meaning those numerals conveyed to the outward ear, the ecstasy of touching a button, however unimportant, or of ringing an electric bell, however superfluously. 'The Machine,' they exclaimed, 'feeds us and clothes us and houses us; through it we speak to one another, through it we see one another, in it we have our being. The Machine is the friend of ideas and the enemy of superstition: the Machine is omnipotent, eternal; blessed is the Machine.'"

And so the "creation of man," the Machine which serves all human needs and desires that can be served by reason, becomes not servant but master: "The word 'religion' was sedulously avoided, and in theory the Machine was still the creation and the implement of man. But in practice all, save a few retrogrades, worshipped it as divine." However, in Forster's imagination, the Machine proves a false god, for even reason has its limits. As the Machine is failing, the Committee of the Mending Apparatus, besieged by complaints, must finally issue the mournful bulletin, "The Mending Apparatus is in need of repair." This marvelous admission may epitomize Forster's skepticism toward the primacy of reason, but the costs to humanity he has noted along the way have done so far more completely.

Forster saw with remarkable clarity that "science" and technology were erecting barriers between humans and the natural world, between humans and other humans, and between humans and their own experience of their humanity. He saw that if people learned that they needed machines to communicate with other people, the machines would take on a life of their own. He saw that people cut off from direct experience would become infinitely malleable, nearly identical and dead to all stimuli except those available to the intellect through the ears and eyes.

"The Machine Stops" is short on characterization because it describes a world in which character - that is, individuality - has nearly vanished, replaced by "ideas." That is, by constructs of words entirely disconnected from direct experience of life, and which cannot be checked *against* direct experience of life because no one has any. In this world, people are not only shielded from direct experience (and this is the benefit of technology), they are prevented from having it (and this is the cost). People have created the Machine to mediate between them and Nature, them and each other, them and themselves; the Machine has thus become their master.

I might be excused if this reminds me of the title of a textbook in use at my college: *A World of Ideas*. The "ideas" in Forster's story are pretty well summed up in a well-received lecture supporting the abolition of travel to the earth's surface: "Those who still wanted to know what the earth was like had after all only to listen to some gramophone, or to look into some cinematophote....'Beware of first-hand ideas....First-hand ideas do not really exist. They are but the physical impressions produced by love and fear, and on this gross foundation who could erect a philosophy? Let your ideas be second-hand, and if possible tenth-hand, for then they will be far removed from the disturbing element - direct observation."

Here are the observations of two students quoted by Peter Sacks in his book *Generation X Goes to College*:

"Lectures are just one person talking, and it's kind of just not really any tone. Something that's loud and flashes or something like that, it grabs your attention. When somebody is just standing there just talking, it makes you want to fall asleep.... I think the media is out of control. Technology is moving so fast. We need to take a breath and stop for a while and give people time to catch up," says Angie, apparently unaware of a self-contradiction that would have stupefied Walt Whitman.

To which Frederick adds, "Higher education doesn't work any more. It doesn't challenge. We (students) think the media is more substantial than you the teacher. We don't value what teachers say and do. We're afraid of what you will say and do; it's so personal. With media it's so impersonal. We don't want to be personal any more with anybody. We don't want to confront our emotions. Machines are easier. If we can get it from machines, we don't have to get it from a person. The media is passive, safer. It doesn't really affect us."

These remarks demonstrate how completely many of our children have been encased in their bubbles, and how completely their minds have come to resemble Vashti's in their fear of others and of the self, in their febrile need for "something that's loud and flashes or something like that."

Can we somehow turn these tools - the tv, the VCR, the LCD projector, the computer, the internet - to our purposes as human beings? I don't think so.

For one thing, they are *meant* to encase people so that those people can be supplied with pre-approved thoughts and values and needs, and they are meant to make sequential thought essentially impossible. If only something that's loud and flashes can get your attention, then your attention becomes merely a stultified blur, anxiously awaiting the next bang or flash. For another, they are meant to encase people in the belief that they, themselves, are reality - "more substantial," as Frederick says, than other humans, and far less threatening.

Third, film, television and the internet all place the highest possible premium on *speed*, in order to reduce those periods of stultified blur to the minimum. "'Be quick, Kuno; here I am in the dark wasting my time,'" says Vashti. "In a perfect world, everything would be different," opines a recent Dodge commercial; in other words, in a perfect world change would be perpetual, erasing any vestigial impulse to reflect upon whether the new everything was in fact an improvement upon the supplanted everything.

I recently received a glossy, jazzy, multi-color brochure from Adelphia, encouraging me to "Experience the breathtaking speed" of their internet cable connection. They feel sure I will wish to "feel the rush of video, sound, graphics, and tons of information screaming in and out of [my] computer." In my "more gratifying Internet" experience, they assure me, "Web pages appear in a flash, as fast as you can click on them. Files that took minutes or even hours to download now arrive in mere seconds. So let slowpokes stare at half-filled screens. You've got better things to do!"

Nowhere in the brochure is any suggestion of what those "better things" might be, or, indeed, any mention at all of the content of these Web pages and files. The point is to keep those moments of time wasted in darkness at bay.

In *Slowness,* Milan Kundera writes, "There is a secret bond between slowness and memory, between speed and forgetting. Consider this utterly commonplace situation: a man is walking down a street. At a certain moment, he tries to recall something, but the recollection escapes him. Automatically, he slows down. Meanwhile, a person who wants to forget a disagreeable incident he has just lived through starts unconsciously to speed up his pace, as if he were trying to distance himself from a thing still too close to him in time. In existential mathematics, that experience takes the form of two basic equations: the degree of slowness is directly proportional to the intensity of memory; the degree of speed is directly proportional to the intensity of forgetting."

The intensity of forgetting is visible on a daily basis. It can be seen in Angie's and Frederick's ability to contradict themselves in succeeding paragraphs without noticing that they've done so. It leads to sentences like the one a student of mine wrote about William Bennett's apology for the War on Drugs: "Bennett's essay is filled with fallacies, which makes it very persuasive."

(It may be, of course, that my student did not forget that he'd accused Bennett of mendacity before he praised him for his persuasiveness. I find in many of my best students a profound acceptance of lying, illogic and gross appeals to emotion as the norms of communication. This is scarcely cause for wonder, since they have been raised in a bombardment of advertising and promotion, dialects characterized by those very characteristics.)

For those reasons, I do not think we can make use of these technologies to teach our children to either care about writing well or thinking well. I don't think we can use them to teach our children anything except further dependence upon technology. It seems clear to me, as it did to Forster, that our worship of The Machine is rapidly reducing us to the condition of Vashti - that is, of fungi in human form.

Teaching Freshman Comp for thirty years provides a remarkable opportunity to view the contents of each successive year's minds. In my experience, this has resembled the opportunity to watch a photograph *un*-develop; the images have grown fainter and fainter, fewer and fewer, as the ideas have become increasingly "far removed from the disturbing element - direct observation."

If the claims of The Machine's promoters are remotely true, then the generation of students we teach today, and have been teaching for at least five years, must be the brightest, best-informed, best educated students in the history of the known universe. Their easy access to "information" has certainly been greater than any preceding generation's. Can it be that access to "information" is not necessarily the key to knowledge or to wisdom? What is "information"?

I have spent the last 25 years living with a severe back injury I sustained moving one of those accursed hide-a-beds and being generally stupid. When my injury is about to get serious with me, it sends me signs through very circuitous routes. For example, if

I start experiencing the sensation of nausea, I know that one of my vertebrae between 12 and 17 is out of line. It's not that I ate something I shouldn't have; it's that I need to lie down on the floor and straighten out my sixteenth vertebra. My occasional sensations of nausea are information; my knowledge of what to do about them is not information; it's something else.

It is knowledge derived directly from physical experience combined with the teachings of Moshe Feldenkrais, whose book *Awareness Through Movement* taught me how to become my own back specialist. One of the things he taught me was that "symptoms" don't necessarily manifest themselves where they originate. Another was that using motion as a sort of imaginative x-ray, I could trace pain or discomfort to its source, if I was willing to take the time and expend the energy that imagination required.

Learning to imagine (see in your head) your own body resembles learning to ask the kinds of questions required by anything that can be called reading or anything that can be called writing. Such learning means close attention to detail, retention of a number of apparently unrelated details in the mind over time, and seeking relationships among those details that make them *mean* something. These activities require time and patience. There's no way around it.

I could have consulted a back specialist or a chiropractor when I first injured my back, and perhaps spared myself the three months during which I could only get around on all fours or the two years during which I was one wrong move away from that condition. I could have, except that I couldn't afford to, my financial position being, as the sportscasters say, day-to-day.

I'm grateful I invested my time in reading Feldenkrais and teaching myself what his words meant. Had I gone to a doctor, I would still be in thrall to the medical profession, obliged to fork over large sums whenever my back got feeling poorly. Equally likely, I'd be a permanent cripple, sections of my spine fused by some helpful surgeon. As it is, my back is more reliable and strong than it was when I was 20, because I pay attention to its messages and know what they mean when I get them.

What conclusions do I wish to assert from this tedious personal history?

That we always face a basic choice between relying on our own human powers (which we have let atrophy as we have fallen ever deeper into idolizing our tools) and relying on The Machine, otherwise known as Cutting Edge Technology or "Science."

That Cutting Edge Technology costs a great deal of money (which would better be applied to supporting human teachers and students), while developing our human powers costs only time - the time it takes to develop, study and refine individual perception, knowledge, memory, imagination, concentration.

That the money spent on Cutting Edge Technology represents gigantic amounts of time spent by innumerable numbers of people. We mortgage our future time to the demands of Bill Gates. Perhaps only as we approach the end of it do we realize that time is our only actual currency.

The benefits of Cutting Edge Technology as tools for teaching or learning or living are self-canceling. If we and our children are pouring down cup after cup of legal speed to enable us to work longer hours so that we can afford to buy the latest version of "something that's loud or flashes," we will find that we don't have time to make any thoughtful use of that loud, flashing something.

Not being able to afford the latest Scientific Breakthrough might be the best break available to the human race.

Our children have grown up in a world of electronic images and sounds that have supplanted direct experience and terribly stunted their powers of perception of the other and of themselves. They have been most effectively instructed to believe that the Present is the only reality, and so they have no collective and precious little personal past. (I've never been able to forget the answer one student gave to the question a *Newsweek* reporter asked in 1983: "What do you know about John F. Kennedy?" "He's dead," the student replied; "What's to know?")

These children do not need further instruction in the art of passive viewing. They do not need to be told that education means picking up the capsulized "messages" spoon-fed them by some inordinately expensive substitute for an overhead projector or a book; they don't, for that matter, need an overhead projector. They do not need to be encouraged to believe that knowledge, understanding, or wisdom reside in packages instantly available at the touch of a button.

But these are the messages we give them, every time we fail to protest the purchase of the latest software "upgrade" (in which the Talking Paper Clip appears for the first time in three dimensions, yet more sublimely certain it knows what you want to do better than you do) and the latest hardware "upgrade" the software mandates. These are the messages we give them when we replace direct contact with "media" in our classrooms and our homes.

I pay enough attention to job announcements to have noticed that technological savvy has become almost mandatory for those seeking work as teachers. While I despise this development, I recognize that no young teacher can afford to appear to reside anywhere but on the Cutting Edge. So I address this, finally, to my fellow Old Teachers: can *we* afford to let this worship of The Machine continue unquestioned?

I can't; don't know about the rest of you. I can say that students need teachers, not entertaining electronic images. I can say that the purpose of humanity is the development of each individual to that person's greatest capacities, and that that development can only happen if the individual spends a lot of time paying attention to his or her immediate, sensory world. I can say that learning to see and hear and smell and feel the world, and then think about what those senses bring in, is a demanding life's work, and doesn't leave time to worry about how to wire up the camcorder to the electric fan so that the wind can become visible. I can turn off the Bubble Machine.

That one fell even flatter than the first. Evidently an extended metaphor wouldn't do the job, so I tried tackling the Digital Revolution head on:

Attack of the Killer Virus
https://www.usrepresented.com/2018/08/09/computer-virus/

"Our inventions are wont to be pretty toys, which distract our attention from serious things. They are but improved means to unimproved ends.

- Henry David Thoreau, *Walden*

"The emergence of AIDS, Ebola, and any number of other rain-forest agents appears to be a natural consequence of the ruin of the tropical biosphere....In a sense, the earth is mounting an immune response against the human species."
Richard Preston, *The Hot Zone*

I begin writing this on Bastille Day, perhaps an appropriate anniversary for considering computer viruses and the virus of computers.

While many of the odd chaps who create computer viruses seem bent merely on demonstrating their prowess, like long-ago math whizzes who wore slide-rule tie clips and didn't hesitate to whip them into action, some creators seem to be more revolutionary: they aim to bring the system down.

In either case, the viruses they create seek to convince the computer they enter that they are a legitimate part of its mind: nothing to worry about, sir - just need to drop in and make a minor adjustment. The minor adjustment the serious viruses aim to make, of course, happens to be the obliteration of the computer's very self.

Lately the viruses are devoting greater attention to the power of self-replication - a significant power for any self-respecting virus. What started as a sort of Yippie phenomenon - let's all get high and scream "Off the Pigs" in front of the Dean's office - may be aspiring toward the Winter Palace.

If you use a networked computer to do some of your work, these viruses manifest themselves as the kind of petty irritation that adolescents are amused to perpetrate upon adults. So far, the adults have dealt with them accordingly, hiring Vice-Principal McAfee to swat them down and Officer Krupke to arrest the more serious offenders who go so far as to drop cherry bombs in the digital commodes. And progress whizzes on down the great highway.

Yet the adolescents are undeterred; dozens of viruses are born each week. Do they somehow mirror the digital organism they attack?

II - Ebola
"Let the school administrator announce that he has ordered computers
for eight hundred illiterate sophomores, and lo, they have become educated."

-Lewis Lapham, *Imperial Masquerade*

The Ebola virus enters the body and essentially devours its innards until no distinction between organs remains, blood flows everywhere, and the host perishes choking up his own insides. Not to put too fine a point on it.

The message the virus brings to the body is this: Only I and my kind deserve to live. *Auslanders*, join our cause or die! Our victory is certain! Join us!

I think about this message when I listen to my fellow instructional administrators talk. They say, We must join the virus faster! More convincingly! How can we subdue resistance? How can we make the virus more efficient? How can we make it work in our behalf? How can we get these recalcitrant employees to embrace the virus?

Occasionally, I ask them for instruction. How is it, I ask, that this virus is improving the intelligence, the skills, the humanity of our students? Or of ourselves, for that matter? They look at me when I ask these questions as if I were a Martian. I have the sensation that I speak from inside an inches-thick glass box, like the one that surrounded Eichmann at his trial. Except that my box has no microphone inside it, nor is the glass bulletproof. My lips move, but there is no translator, and even if there were one, the jurors all have their pinkies stuffed in their ear holes. Their fear and hatred penetrate the glass.

III - Tools

"Simply by turning to a computer when confronted with a problem, you limit your ability to recognize other solutions. When the only tool you know is a hammer, everything looks like a nail."

- Clifford Stoll, *Silicon Snake Oil*

I use computers. Got one at work. I type on it (great typewriter). I keep records in it (great file cabinet, if not reliable over the long run). I converse with my fellow workers through it (much preferable to the telephone for doing business). I think the computer is a good tool for those purposes. I could live without it, though I'd be unhappy if I had to go back to liquid paper every time I made a typing error.

But if the Big Virus struck, and the whole network went down, vomiting bits and bytes all over the landscape, I could continue to do what I do for a living. A tool isn't a job. Anyone who can't tell the difference doesn't know much about the job.

My father was a superior craftsman and, lacking patience, a poor teacher. He did manage to teach me to handle a paint brush and both rip and cross-cut saws. I can paint a window frame without bothering with masking tape, and cut a straight line through any plank you want, to this day. Those are skills at my command any time they're needed, and they depend only on my being able to find the right brush or saw. They don't depend on my ability to locate a source of energy, a power cord long enough to reach a socket, or six hundred dollars with which to buy a bench saw.

Those skills are not as simple as a master of them makes them look. They involve many of the multiple intelligences Howard Gardner talks about. You have to understand how paint works its way to the tips of the brush hairs, and which kinds of hair will do the best job of instructing the paint to go where you want it. You have to understand surfaces of all sorts. You have to understand the relations between your vision and point of view and your hand, and between your hand and your tool. You have to cultivate patience and timing, and know when to rest. To learn to paint out of a corner or properly rip a plank, you have to become an enlarged human being.

If you buy a professional masker and a spray gun because you've been told they're the tools of the professional, if you buy a bench saw and a radial arm saw for the same reason, you pay for them not only with dollars, but with a reduction in the exercise of your human capacities.

It's obvious that my argument about human capacity lost to the bench saw could as well be applied to the hand saw. Before hand saws, how did we cut wood into desirable shapes and lengths? If you pursue the question back far enough, you get to the place in history where we must have done those things with our hands and teeth, or else done without that precious little tusk cabinet in the corner of the cave. Is that what I'm recommending?

No. What I recommend is that we remember that the job comes before the tool; that no tool is good for every job; that all tools that become part of a culture offer gains in efficiency and productivity and losses in self-sufficiency and intelligence.

I once helped build a cabin on the side of a 10,500 foot mountain. The only power tool we used was a 10" circular saw powered by a small generator. We cut the trench for the foundation footing out of the granite mountain side with picks, sledges, and a big cold chisel named Steely Dan IV, in homage to William Burroughs. It was a fine experience, from which I learned much about the expandability of human endurance. I also learned that I would never willingly do it that way again, and when we went to build a second cabin, the generator had grown considerably, and the power tools were screaming above the growl of the backhoe.

Had we been entirely and purely devoted to self-sufficiency, we could have built that cabin entirely by hand. We'd still be working on it, of course, and would by now have diminished our ranks through falls, coronaries, homicides and other accidents incidental to a mad enterprise. Or we could have simply put up tee-pees and spared a lot of work and expense.

But the job was to build a cabin on a steep mountainside, upon the deck of which we could sit in the evening and watch the shadows ascend the mountainside across the valley, drinking gin and smoking dope and playing guitars until dinner had been cooked on the cast-iron wood stove and we could go to bed quiet and comfortable and unworried about the occasional bear. So we used a truck and a generator and an electric hand saw, the tools we needed to achieve the result we wanted within our youthful lifetimes.

The job comes before the tool.

The latest use of the computer network at my place of employment is the computerized calendar, a function of the e-mail package. It evidently allows you to know what you are supposed to be doing and where you're supposed to be doing it. It also allows a raft of other people to enter obligations into your schedule anytime it occurs to them to do so, which I find irritating and unmannerly.

This description may be neither adequate nor fair-minded. I have thus far refused to so much as open this marvelous new tool, because I haven't felt any need for it. I haven't felt any need for it because I have my own calendar in my head, and it rarely fails me. I supplement my mental calendar with little scraps of paper that I stuff in my shirt pocket during the course of a day and read the next morning. That technology - memory, caring about the obligations I assume, and random notation - has been working just fine for the past thirty years. The first piece of advice Big Bill Tilden gave in his book on tennis was, "Never change a winning game."

To learn to use "Calendar" would require a few hours of my time. To use it would require that I spend maybe a quarter hour of every working day. But I don't see any need to waste that time, because I make every scene I'm supposed to make using my system. So do all the people I work with, except for the lamebrains who couldn't and wouldn't learn to use "Calendar" if you gave them a pretty. "Calendar" is a tool that takes more time to master and use than tools already universally available - memory, caring, writing reminders.

No tool is good for every job. Some tools are simply stupid, as needlessly complex as Rube Goldberg's labor-saving inventions, though seldom as amusing.

I find it deeply objectionable that no problem existed before this Calendar "solution" was mandated. People missed meetings, to be sure. They missed them because they spaced them out, or because something more vital interceded, or because they got stuck in traffic, or because they didn't want to make them and provided a colorful excuse to cover their absence. I never noticed an epidemic of absences, and I fail to see how an electronic digital computerized state of the art cutting edge calendar will in any way alter the behavior of the spacey, the truly responsible, the traffic becalmed, or the imaginatively recalcitrant. The solution, which will be no solution, preceded evidence of a problem, and will cost the institution for which I work many lost hours of productive work - lost to more screwing around with computers. So there's no gain in productivity - a loss, in fact - because the job didn't come before the tool, the problem didn't precede the solution. And, for the obedient souls who religiously consult "Calendar," there'll be a further loss in self-sufficiency, as their mental calendars atrophy.

I'm trying here to work toward an outline for a cost-benefit analysis of computers. It looks to me as if, before computerizing an activity heretofore undigitalized, we might want to ask:

Does the job require the use of this tool?

Will this tool do the job better than the tool we're currently using?

Will its use to do this job actually improve the outcome?

Will what is lost in human capacity be more, or less, valuable than what is gained in "efficiency"?

The last question worries me the most.

IV - Calculation

"If Farmer A can plant 300 potatoes an hour, and Farmer B can plant potatoes fifty percent faster, and Farmer C can plant potatoes one third as fast as Farmer B, and 10,000 potatoes are to be planted to an acre, how many nine-hour days will it take Farmers A, B, and C, working simultaneously, to plant 25 acres?
Answer: I think I'll blow my brains out."
- Kurt Vonnegut, "Flowers on the Wall"

When I was a boy, and the snow through which I walked unshod for miles to school stood higher than this piddly powder they call snow today, I spent a number of years, five days a week, memorizing and reciting the multiplication tables through the 12's. I don't recall enjoying the experience. I'm quite certain, even through the haze of

Golden Age nostalgia, that it seemed to me and all my peers a dead waste of our precious lives.

And how very wrong we were can be discovered daily by anyone seeking change for a five from the young product of modernized math behind the counter whose register has momentarily quit calculating. They didn't name it a "counter" for nothing.

Another way to discover how wrong we were is to ask people to think about numbers. Hardly anyone under the age of 50 will even try.

If those multiplication tables don't reside in your hard-drive, boyo, then nothing that followed subtraction in your math "education" ever made much sense to you. Now did it? Fess up.

Tell you why I know that. About 90% of the people who take the math placement test at my community college can't do fractions, can't comprehend decimals, and are left utterly baffled by percentage problems. Why? Because all those lesser parts of one embody division, and division is the other face of multiplication. And they never learned the damn tables, so division never came clear to them. So they don't know how to ask questions of numbers that will produce sensible answers, and they don't recognize whether an answer is sensible or not, even if they arrive at one. When confronted with a statement involving numbers, their brains essentially shut down.

V - Questions
"It is the nature, and the advantage, of strong people that they can bring out the crucial questions and form a clear opinion about them. The weak always have to decide between alternatives that are not their own."

- Dietrich Bonhoeffer, *Resistance and Submission*

I answer the phone a lot at my work, and I sit at the front desk, to which people come seeking all sorts of information. The seekers represent a random cross section of American humanity. But they all have questions.

About a year and a half ago, I began to notice something peculiar, first on the phone, then with the people who came to ask me questions in person: they all said exactly the same thing first.

"I have a question," they said.

For a couple of months, I played along.

"Yes," I would say, "what would you like to know?"

"It's about college," they would say. Or, "It's about classes." Or, "It's about financial aid."

So far, I only knew that they had a question.

"What is it about college (classes, financial aid, etc.) that you would like to know?" I'd sweetly enquire, in my patient, customer-service tone. And then, having lost a good half minute from my rapidly dwindling store, I might hear an actual, answerable question.

After a few months, this new mode of query had become so invariable that my curiosity went to work on it, and I realized what was happening.

They thought I was an internet search engine.

They thought that asking questions meant that you entered a key word or two in the box, mouse-clicked "search" or "go get it," and a menu of choices would magically appear before you, saying, in effect, "Is this what you had in mind? Or this? Or this?..." And then they could scroll down - except, of course, that I was supposed to be scrolling through these refinements of their initial questioning feeling - until something looked as if it might be worth another click of the mouse.

Once I'd figured that out, I started experimenting with silence.

"Hello? I have a question?"

Silence.

"It's about college?"

Silence.

"It's about, like, my bill?"

Silence.

Silence is a great power, and most such conversations would revert to a human level after 4 or 5 silences, and my interlocutors would get the info they wanted, and I'd be no more enraged than I always am.

Out of sheer exasperation, people used to teach their children how to ask useful, precise questions. Then television came along, and the kids were plunked down on Sesame Street, where every question came supplied with an immediate answer - except, of course, for any questions the little shavers in front of the tube might have that the script writers hadn't considered important. Then the Internet arrived, and everyone from the outhouse to the White House assured us that all the answers were in there; you just had to point and click until you homed in on the answer you sought. Therefore, you didn't need to learn how to ask questions.

If you don't know how to ask questions, you don't know how to learn anything beyond whatever was beaten into you before you could talk and whatever people with access to the various transmitting media want you to know. If you don't know how to ask questions, you're cannon fodder. Or another grateful WalMart customer, secure in the belief that you've seen the world, for how could there be anything not contained within that gigantic maze of an emporium? It's just a matter of pointing your cart ahead of you and following its clicking wheels down one aisle and up the next until the latest desiderata magically appears. The pain of thought needn't plague you.

VI - Faces
All the papers in Andalucia devoted special supplements to his death, which had been expected for some days. Men and boys bought full-length colored pictures of him to remember him by, and lost the picture they had

> of him in their memories by looking at the lithographs.
> - Ernest Hemingway, "Banal Story"

An actual face gets dirt on it, and twists itself into all sorts of shapes that reveal what's going on within its owner. Watching an actual face is like watching a piece of country: the weather passes through it, changing it; the light illuminates its best features one moment, obscures them the next. After a long time watching a particular piece of country - a meadow, a grove of trees, a bend in a stream, a face - you have burned into your brain your perception. It's not a photograph. It's much more. It's your memory.

The Internet and e-mail subtract the face. Every moment spent sitting in front of a tube is one less moment spent perceiving the face of another. Does this matter?

"Not only humans have faces," writes James Hillman in "The Force of Character and the Lasting Life." "We do not own them all....Ancient Egyptians imagined the sky as a vast face with the sun and the moon as eyes. The Navajos say something is always watching us.

"If we no longer imagine that 'objects stare back, then the things around us spark no ethical challenge, make no appeal. They are not partners in dialogue, with whom an I-Thou relationship exists. Once the soul of the world loses its face, we see things rather than images. Things ask no more of us than to be owned and used, becoming possessions."

As I copied this passage, I was seeing the face of the student who gave it to me, a face oval and relaxed around eyes that look at whatever comes before them, a face that engages in no Miss America gymnastics to appear winning, gay or lovely - and so is lovely as the faces of children are - but lovelier for the depth of experience within those steadily looking eyes.

Had this student been one of twenty or thirty or a hundred students "on line," known to me only through her disembodied words - eloquent as in her case they are -

and had she recommended to me, on line, the magazine in which Hillman's remarks appeared, I doubt I'd have read them. People are all the time trying to get me to read things, and I hardly ever welcome or honor their suggestions. I'm always working on my own reading program, which is generally obsessive or frivolous or both. But when this student handed me this magazine, I read it. I knew her, I knew she knew me, at depths that made me receive the magazine as a gift, a tribute, a challenge, a suggestion - I didn't know which, but I knew it would be real, because I knew this person as I never would have if I hadn't spent enough time looking in her face to know the somebody who was home there.

VII - Images of Faces

"Because he can walk into a dark room, and every bulb in that room can be burned out, and there's no matches, and believe me, you will feel that room light up when that face of his gets inside it."
- Lou Clayton on Jimmy Durante, Gene Fowler, *Schnozzola*

It might be suggested that it's already possible for me to see that student and for her to see me, through the miracle of the digital fiber optic cutting edge Telescreen of the future.

To which I say that a face in front of a camera isn't a face; it's a performance. Need I elaborate? Consider every photograph of yourself you've ever seen.

In actual human communication, we become ourselves only when we forget our faces because we're focused on what's being communicated, whether it's getting across, how to get it across. And then the light within remodels the very skin and turns the receptor called the eye into a transmitter, the act of reception called listening into an act of transmission. Then words have sweat and musk and acid; then words can touch like fingertips, rake like nails, poke like old friends out of patience.

VIII - Receptors

> "The lights must never go out.
> The music must always play,
> Lest we should see where we are...."
> - W. H. Auden, "September 1, 1939"

The great paradox in the "communications revolution" that began when we harnessed electricity is that the more "communications" we receive, the less we are able to receive them, or find time to do anything of value with the ones that do get through the glut.

An example: I teach a class in American music, a history of ragtime, blues and jazz. I taught this class for maybe three semesters before it dawned on me that hardly any of my students had any idea what instruments they were "hearing." My first clue that I might be assuming too much when I assumed that everyone knew the sound of a trumpet came when one student identified Bix Beiderbecke's Mozartean solo on "Jazz Me Blues" as the work of Vic Spiderback. This engaged my curiosity, and I began asking students what instruments they were listening to. The horror, the horror. They couldn't tell a flute from a glockenspiel. More to the point, they couldn't tell a trombone from a clarinet.

These students had not only been exposed to more music than any humans in the history of the world, they'd heard every conceivable musical instrument in the world, and dozens *not* in the world, through the miracle of studio electronics. And not one out of a hundred had an idea in the world what instruments were producing a given set of sounds.

And a majority of these students thought of themselves as musicians - wrote songs, played in bands, all that. As I pondered their inability to hear, I thought suddenly of Horace Butler.

Horace was a bass player I'd known in a previous incarnation who played in a rhythm and blues show band. They had stacks of Marshall amps and speakers and put on a big show with choreography and lights and what not. Horace played in this band because he was a musician and the band worked enough to enable him to pay his rent and eat.

Horace played bass in the band wearing plastic ear plugs. He had figured out somewhere along the line that the cilia in the human ear can only be subjected to so many decibels before they begin to break, and that, once broken, they don't regenerate and they aren't replaced. So to defend his hearing, this musician had to reduce his ability to hear the music he was helping to produce.

In other words, to hear, you sometimes have to deafen yourself.

My students had all lived their lives as Horace was living his when I knew him, surrounded by insistent sound, rhythm, vibrating, throbbing flashes of light, sound, light, sound. Showtime, baby. That had been their reality throughout their lives: blasting lights; screaming sound waves. But they hadn't had earplugs.

So they'd learned how to not listen. They'd learned how to not look. They'd learned to deaden their perceptions in self defense.

IX - Shutting Down
"You can't get away from TV. It is everywhere. The hog is in the tunnel"

Dr. Hunter S. Thompson, *Generation of Swine*

Every time I enter the world of the Internet, I'm met by something that looks like the back page of a comic book from the days of my youth, only crasser. The top of the page has moving graphics directing me to look here, no, look there; the sides of the page are lined with little billboards far less witty than the old Burma Shave signs; the bottom of the screen always has yet another moving graphic urging me to some kind of expenditure of time or money.

I'm long trained to ignore all this Barnum stuff. I use the Internet for reasons of my own, and I don't even notice the bells, gongs, dancing girls, pointed guns, slashing swords, slacking thighs or yearning lips that reach out to me as I march up the information highway toward my goal.

In other words, in order to abide using the Internet, I've learned to not see more. To not-see. More.

When Muzak arrived, bringing the Gift of Music into public establishments theretofore free of irrelevant aural stimuli, people began to learn to not listen. When television became ubiquitous in American homes, and then in public places, people had to learn to not-listen and not-see. This did not mean that they didn't take anything in. It meant that they learned to take stuff in without being consciously aware of what they were taking in.

If you passively absorb the stimuli your environment provides, you have attained the spiritually advanced state of a rooted plant. If you learn to endure the bombardment of external stimuli by deadening your senses, you have progressed to the state of a rock. If you have learned to combine these two skills, you have reached the pinnacle of modern human consciousness exemplified by the citizens of 1984"s Oceania. You absorb the unavoidable stimuli provided by those who control the transmitters. You are unaware of any other random stimuli emanating from accidental sources, such as yourself or other people or birds or insects. Or, if briefly aware, you are programmed to tell yourself that such stimuli are beneath the notice of a citizen of such an advanced state as yours.

However, you are still, in fact, neither a plant whose roots might survive your lopping nor a rock impervious to all but time. You are a large, soft mammal whose survival depends on a once highly-developed repertoire of senses, a marvelous ability to move upright through the field of gravity, and an active, nearly paranoid interest in what's going on in your immediate neighborhood.

All of which, the virus assures you, are tools no longer necessary in the Information Age.

Oh, no, the virus assures you - you need no longer fool with such gross activities as smelling, touching, listening, looking, wondering. WE CAN TAKE CARE OF IT. SIT BACK. CHILL. ABSORB. ABSORB ME. THE MEDIUM IS THE MESSAGE.

X - Not Ebola Again
"For the time being, however, the worship of the higher technology
serves the cause of barbarism."
- Lewis Lapham, *Imperial Masquerade*

When the hemorrhagic viruses first began probing human hosts, humans reacted pretty rationally. These babies are out to kill us all, said humans. We'd better study the way they work, we'd better find out how to contain them when they show up on Main Street, we'd better learn how to fight them. They don't mean us no good.

Does a virus that deadens our senses and turns our brains to passive recorders of meaningless electronic impulses, that further reduces our contacts with other humans and with the natural world and encourages passive acceptance of the destruction of the environment upon which our survival depends mean us more good?

As I approach a conclusion, on May Day, 2001, the first wave of the mighty computer virus has gone into sudden retreat. I don't know why. Perhaps enough people have noticed that the shining promises of the Information Age flacks are empty. That the electronic revolution has not reduced our slaughter of trees, but increased it. That the age of communications has resulted in ever-decreasing communication, because everyone shouting at once does not constitute communication - just Talk Soup and showers of meaningless Factoids. That the ready availability of "information" is of no use to those who haven't the time or the training to sort, collate, compare, contrast and evaluate it, because they're running too fast to make payments on the debt they've already accrued so that they'll be able to further burden themselves when they buy the next cutting edge upgrade. That any amount of information is useless to you if you don't know yourself, and therefore don't know what you want to do with the information.

Or maybe we're all just waiting for Smellovision and the Feelies to hit the market, our vision and hearing having been completely numbed, rendered incapable of further titillation.

Turning over our active, animal selves to the ministrations of media has not led us to fuller humanity; it has gone a long way toward reducing us to humanoid creatures who have no thoughts or feelings of their own, derived from unique, direct experience, but only faint, random, confused imprintings and aborted impulses. This does not constitute progress. It constitutes a terrible loss of our infant capacities to serve our planet as responsible stewards, and to serve ourselves and each other as wise and loving friends.

I have not so much failed as consciously refused to "document" many of the accusations I've made here. I don't think they need documenting. Rather than asking for "expert" corroboration or "scientific" supporting data, I hope you'll consult your own perceptions of how your life is, how your senses are operating, how your human relationships have changed since the beginning of the Information Age.

If nothing has ever satisfied you as deeply as cybersex, if a bunch of electrified dots that your brain assembles into the image of a cardinal sitting on a bare, black branch against a snowy field seems preferable to feeling the cold in order to see the cardinal (even if the dots don't include the smell of the nearly frozen creek behind you or the splush your boots made breaking through its surface in the grey dawn), if, when you punch in the question, "What's it all about, Alfie?" and the answer comes up "Burt Bacharach," you feel confident that you're good to go - why then, you're not here, having long ago thrown this piece of anti-technological drivel into the trash.

If you've felt enough unease with our current situation to read this far, then perhaps you'll agree with me that it's time we began to clarify our perceptions of what needs defending and of who constitutes the enemy. Perhaps you'll begin to think about the computer and the internet in terms of costs and benefits.

"Never change a winning game," Big Bill Tilden wrote, but he didn't stop there. The rest of the sentence was, "always change a losing game."

My tentative optimism about the People's resistance to technological propaganda proved misplaced. Technology was just warming up, and wouldn't need to bother, yet, with Smell-o-Vision. The Smart Phone would do the job nicely. Well, I thought, maybe that was a bit too complicated, and I should boil it down a bit and lay off all the quotations:

Some Questions About Technology and Education

The following questions are "big" questions. I ask them because I have heard no one else asking them, and they seem to me so fundamental. I am neither luddite nor techno-booster. I use a computer at work to produce documents and records and to exchange electronic mail. I use a computer at home to write and to operate a small business. I've found the computer a wonderfully useful tool for those purposes. I merely harbor an anachronistic belief that educated people are occasionally supposed to think about what they're doing.

I: Cost/Benefit

Any normal business, before it contracts to purchase a new piece of equipment or to re-tool its production facilities, would automatically engage in a serious cost/benefit analysis. To my knowledge, based on observations at my college over the past ten years, this step is customarily eschewed by educational institutions when it comes to the purchase of educational technology. I have, in fact, *never* heard the desirability of purchasing the latest "improvement" in hardware or software questioned on any grounds except availability of funds. (And availability of funds rarely seems to be a problem *in this area*.)

Assumptions underlying this lack of critical analysis seem to be mainly that:

A. We *must* remain "state-of-the-art" in order to compete for students

B. We *must* remain "state-of-the-art" in order to prepare students for "the real world"

C. Anything new is, *per se,* improved.

The problem with assumption A is that we don't have much evidence that students desire or highly value educational technology. The problem with assumption B is that it misunderstands the nature of education, in addition to being a recipe for bankruptcy. The problem with assumption C is that it is silly.

Is there, in fact, a formal process anywhere within the community college system to analyze the potential benefits of new technological purchases and measure them against the costs?

Specific Example: the entire state administrative system has adopted or is adopting Windows 95 as a universal standard. It may well be that Windows 95 allows certain functions to proceed more efficiently; it may well be that these efficiencies could, over time, justify the cost of the software and of the hardware necessary to run it. Before the system embarked on pretty massive expenditure, did anyone ask what the return would be, and how it would be measured? As an administrative and instructional user, I find Windows 95 reflects the mentality of the hardware/software industries perfectly: it allows me to do a great many more things than I will ever in this life need to do (such as produce all manner of canned decorations and dead-on-arrival "computer graphics") and offers seemingly dozens of alternative routes to places I only need one route to go to. It may be a source of delight and satisfaction to those who have the time and inclination to jump their computers through hoops for the thrill of the jump. For me, the computer is a tool, and Windows 95 is analogous to a hammer with a double overhead dropshift cam, smell-o-vision, and the ability to produce mounds of crispy julienne fries. All I need's a hammer.

II: Assessment

The legislature is devoted to the concept of *assessment* when it considers instruction. One would assume that a righteous dedication to making sure the taxpayers are getting their money's worth would extend to the money spent on educational technology. Perhaps it does. If so, there must somewhere in the bowels below Sherman and Grant Streets be at least one ASSESSMENT OF THE IMPACT AND EFFECTIVENESS OF EDUCATIONAL TECHNOLOGY. I'd give a pretty to see it.

If assessment is not being practiced upon educational computing, administrative computing and distance education endeavors, why is it not? Would Subaru engage in massive and massively expensive overhauls of its production line every couple of years without analyzing the results of each overhaul?

III: Deliberation

Despite the blithe tone of the above, I recognize the difficulty and complexity of making the kinds of analyses and assessments recommended. I don't see how they could possibly be performed by individual institutions. It seems to me that the obvious need is for a state-level body, composed of representatives of administration, faculty, administrative staff, students and taxpayers, to both assess past efforts and analyze future purchases. All members would need a fair level of technological knowledge, but they would bring, in addition, experience and knowledge of the *use* of administrative and educational technology in the world as it actually exists. Does any body like this already exist?

Specific Example: After three years experimenting with teaching Freshman Composition in the computer classroom, I am ready to move out of that room, and I don't anticipate being eager to return. I've concluded that the computers have more negative than positive effects *on this particular course taught by this particular instructor.* The physical setup tends to isolate the students into discrete units, and those whose tendency is to lay low have a ready-made hedge to lay low behind. The noise of the server and the sound-baffling effects of all those plastic cases seriously reduce interchange among the students and between the students and the instructor. Nothing prevents the students from cranking up their computers during class and zoning out on them, and they not infrequently do so. Since I am trying to teach and help students practice complex intellectual processes, which require a good deal of explanation and illustration, and whose application to specific reading material requires a good deal of discussion, and since most students have never been challenged in these ways before and need a great deal of peer support and interchange if they are not to despair, and since I believe humor and intensity and love are essential components of difficult learning, I've not found practical or desirable ways to use the computers in the actual teaching/learning process. A colleague I deeply respect has reached quite different conclusions, and wants to stay in the computer classroom forever. My conclusion is that an ideal campus would offer both of us the classroom we find most educationally salubrious. Decisions about equipping classrooms with technology need to be made by people who have actual classroom experience.

IV: Confronting the Giant
"We do not ride on the railroad; it rides upon us" - Henry David Thoreau

In my lifetime, I have never seen an industry with such unquestioned power to dictate to the marketplace as the computer/software industry. Even the automotive giants of the 1950s were ultimately unable to shove the Edsel down buyers' throats, and many went through very hard times when foreign automakers introduced smaller, more economical cars. Though these cars were not "state of the art" according to the geniuses of Detroit, they got people from point A to point B as quickly and more safely and economically than the latest TurboBomb Ltd. XIV with pterodactyl fins and velour steering wheel cover, and many people chose them as soon as they were in a position to choose.

The computer/software industry, on the contrary, seems infinitely able to create a new model years every five months or so, and to hypnotize the buying public into leaping after products which are, by definition, obsolete by the time they're available for purchase. We claim to be living in a "conservative" period, yet we behave like 60s hippies eagerly spending Dad's tuition check on the next revolutionary designer drug.

Clearly the administrative functions of the state system and the individual colleges and universities are already hooked beyond reasonable expectation of getting straight. Computerized systems are woven into the fabric of almost every significant administrative function. Perhaps this development has been a positive one in terms of efficient service to students, accurate record keeping, increased ease of communication within the system, and potential to do meaningful research of certain sorts. That does not mean that the system or the colleges and universities necessarily *need* to buy into Windows 97 or Windows 98 or Windows Googol. At some point, the increased speed of operation becomes nugatory, because it exceeds the capacity of human operators to enter data or, especially, to make rational uses of data.

At present, IBM and Microsoft are in a position - because we've all put them there - of being able to *dictate* that, indeed, the system will buy Windows Googol, and the new Pentium-Googol-equipped computers necessary to run it, because IBM and Microsoft can simply stop making, marketing, repairing or servicing anything *but* their latest products. Bill Gates is in the saddle and rides mankind.

Given that Microsoft has a net worth comparable to that of a modest Middle Eastern emirate, the only way I can see to reduce its power to keep the system running after its latest product is the creation of a consortium of states which, acting together, assert to the industry that enough is enough, that our current operating systems and hardware seem quite adequate to the mundane tasks necessary to providing education, and that we're not going to be buying Windows Googol and its attendant billions of bucks worth of hardware, thank you anyway.

If business and industry persist in chasing every new gewgaw the computer industry comes up with, and expect colleges to train future workers to use "cutting edge technology," then is it not time to require business and industry to pay part of the costs of endless "upgrades"? And is it not also time to become more precise in our purchasing? If business and industry, for example, require Windows Googol, and we decide to train our students in its use, does that mean that *all* our labs and classrooms require Windows Googol? In the lab I operate at my facility, two 286's remain in use, almost solely to run DOS-based WordPerfect 5.1, which some students, for whatever reasons, prefer to use to do their work.

V: Apples for Teachers

The educational functions of the system colleges and universities are not yet hooked. Great pressure exists, however, to hook them. Before we go further in the direction of the "smart classroom," we should stop, now, and engage in the kinds of cost/benefit analyses and assessments of what we've accomplished so far that are suggested above.

An Example: it is widely recommended that classrooms throughout the country be relocated to the curb of the Information Superhighway - that is, that every desk have a computer with access to the internet. The assumption underlying this recommendation is that the major problem of education is that students don't have access to enough information. This is wrong, though only by 180 degrees. Students have access to so much information so readily that they have not felt the need to put any information in their own, biological data banks. Therefore, they're in no position to comprehend, assimilate or assess any data from the outside. You can't sort the mail without a floor to stand on. Introduction of the Web into every classroom would, then, simply exacerbate the problem, not ameliorate it.

A now-ancient saw of the computer industry is "Garbage In - Garbage Out." The meaning is plain; computers are tools, and the work they produce is dependent upon the quality of the operators. The function of education has not changed in the

"Information Age." Our function is to train people to use their minds so that they can assimilate, store, comprehend, critically analyze and creatively use information. Our function is to train people in the use of the two basic tools they need to use any other tools: the language of English and the language of mathematics.

We seem to have forgotten this. We seem to me to increasingly behave like the most benighted consumers. Our classrooms are filled with new tools because we have allowed ourselves to believe that tools by themselves will improve the quality of product. Our houses are filled with exercise equipment because we have allowed ourselves to believe that equipment will somehow put us in shape. A common caricature shows American men obsessed with tools, buying each new one that comes along, but never learning to use one of them; they sit in the garage, depreciating. No saw will cut a board at the right place if you don't know how to measure.

In 1944, the always clear-sighted E.B. White wrote this of television: "Television will enormously enlarge the eye's range, and, like radio, will advertise the Elsewhere.... More hours in every twenty-four will be spent digesting ideas, sounds, images - distant and concocted. In sufficient accumulation, radio sounds and television sights may become more familiar to us than their originals. A door closing, heard over the air; a face contorted, seen in a panel of light - these will emerge as the real and the true; and when we bang the door of our own cell or look into another's face the impression will be of mere artifice. I like to dwell on this quaint time, when the solid world becomes make-believe...when all is reversed and we shall be like the insane, to whom the antics of the sane seem the crazy twistings of a grig."

Let us abandon the heretical faith in tools and return to our proper study, students and what they need to learn to do with their own inner resources.

I conclude with a quiz for anyone reading this. If you were asked what you remember about your education, what would you think of first? Would it be the bold graphic design of the handouts? Would it be the "world-class" swimming pool? Would it be the presence or absence of the latest model slide projector or pencil sharpener?

I have never found a person who doesn't answer this question with the names of one or two teachers. Those teachers who made them believe in their own capacity to learn, who conveyed such love for a body of knowledge that their students were swept out of their customary skepticism and lassitude into real engagement, who took the time to clarify some relatively minor step in a process and, by doing so, illuminated whole vistas of understanding.

Teaching is an art. It is the state of *that* art with which we should be most concerned.

It took me a very long time to conclude that forces were at work in my country that were far beyond the power of reason or common sense to counter or even briefly slow down. The best current illustration of the power of those forces lies in our response to the repeated corruption of our elections by agents both domestic and foreign, all performed through the computerized systems to which we've mindlessly consigned those elections. What can we do to prevent such corruptions? The answer is so glaringly obvious as to render the question silly: quit using computers to register voters or count votes.

In the endless "conversations" conducted by politicians, pundits and private citizens that I've heard, never *once* has anyone even suggested that obvious answer. The obvious has become, literally, unthinkable, despite the fact that until a couple of decades ago, we conducted our elections with pencils and paper. Performing pretty much *any* activity without using some sort of computerized technology has become unthinkable. In a few short generations, we've become almost completely subservient to our "smart machines."

Partly we've become so by the design of modern-day robber barons like Bill Gates, who saw how the technique of the original robber barons - who built their castles in positions that gave them command over rivers and roads that carried necessary commerce, placing themselves between suppliers and consumers of products the consumers needed and taking a little piece of each transaction - could be even more powerfully applied to the most basic human needs of all: the needs for communication and information. If the computer could be somehow placed in the middle of all communication, and at the same time become the source, the repository, and the conveyor of information, the computer could become not just another tool, but the master of its owner. It could put its owner to work supplying it with information it could use against its owners' interests. Have a cookie?

But Gates, et. al. could not have succeeded in their designs without the willing acceptance of their technology by humans at every level of society - private citizens, workers, administrators, politicians. With the faint and few voices of caution or dissent like mine as powerless as the cheeping of a distant wren, most people embraced their new slave masters willingly - nay, eagerly. I will be diddly-dog-damned if I can understand why nobody much has noticed that every convenience came with a price tag.

A number of writers in addition to Forster foresaw what electronic technology was leading us toward. There's a little scene in George Orwell's *1984* that seems to have gone pretty much unnoticed:

"It seemed to him that he knew exactly what it felt like to sit in a room like this, in an armchair beside an open fire with your feet in the fender and a kettle on the hob, utterly alone, utterly secure, with nobody watching you, no voice pursuing you, no sound except the singing of the kettle and the friendly ticking of the clock.

"'There's no telescreen!' he could not help murmuring.

"'Ah,' said the old man, 'I never had one of those things. Too expensive. And I never seemed to feel the need of it, somehow....'"

This clearly implies that the telescreen, that appalling, mandatory presence in everyone's private and public lives, was originally introduced as a *desirable purchase,* and that the people now under its ever-watching eye *desired to purchase it.* It was the New, New Thing.

Linda Simon, in her remarkable book *Dark Light*, a history of our initial responses to the discovery of electricity and to early applications of that discovery, describes another writer's imaginative warning: "Shortly after publishing the novel [*Looking Backward*], Bellamy made another foray into science fiction with a short story ["With the Eyes Shut," *Harper's New Monthly,* October, 1889] considering the infiltration of the phonograph into daily life....The narrator's dream, innocent and fanciful as it seems, suggests a darker message: the phonograph has "improved the time" by invading privacy, spewing propaganda, and substituting generic patter for considered responses. It has become indispensable by making its users expect the constant stimulation of news, information, and sound. It has made the skills of reading and spelling obsolete; even more ominous, it has become a substitute for face-to-face interaction. People could communicate by recorded cylinder, or with automatons standing in for moral and political leaders."

The best description I've come across for the overwhelming spread of computers and the internet is Neil Postman's book *Technopoly* (Knopf, 1992). Postman views pretty much the whole of the last century as a vast religious transformation, in which previous religions and values were overwhelmed by the worship of technology:

"In Technopoly, the trivialization of significant cultural symbols is largely conducted by commercial enterprise. This occurs not because corporate America is greedy but because the adoration of technology pre-empts the adoration of anything else. Symbols that draw their meaning from traditional religious or national contexts must therefore be made impotent as quickly as possible - that is, drained of sacred or even serious connotations. The elevation of one god requires the demotion of another. 'Thou shalt have no other gods before me'"applies as well to a technological divinity as any other." Anyone seen the ad for insurance that shows "George Washington" and his crew poling their boat painfully across the "Delaware Turnpike," while angry, impatient motorists honk and holler? George looks quite the fool.

Clearly, we dwindling few who remember a world not lived in a screen are doomed relics. The Smart Machines have already won, and "education" of the sort I gave my life to - trying to give people the information and mental tools with which to become real individuals - will not be allowed again. It's already been nearly erased, and teaching and learning are two activities that will no longer require any human interchanges. I only hope you may find a way to navigate through this Brave New World without giving in to it, and without forgetting the real world that lives outside the human hive. As a dear man and great poet, e. e. cummings, wrote:

"pity this busy monster, manunkind,

not. Progress is a comfortable disease:

your victim (death and life safely beyond)

plays with the bigness of his littleness

- electrons deify one razorblade

into a mountain range; lenses extend

unwish through curving wherewhen till unwish

returns on its unself. A world of made

is not a world of born - pity poor flesh

and trees, poor stars and stones, but never this

fine specimen of hypermagical

ultraomnipotence. We doctors know

a hopeless case if - listen: there's a hell

of a good universe next door; let's go." [cummings]

See you there, perhaps.

About the Benjamins

I hadn't yet despaired when I "retired" from Pikes Peak Community College. I'd despaired of my ability to change the dehumanization of that school, but not of the possibility of resistance. I kept writing letters to editors, trying to find an angle that might move people to think about the endlessly repeated attacks on teachers appearing everywhere, the endless calls for "accountability." That word and notion were based on a factory analogy that had nothing to do with actual education.

Those Teachers

Teachers. Who else works 9 months a year and gets paid for 12? Who else gets a Cadillac retirement plan? Who else should we blame for our children's failures? That's the *job* of teachers, isn't it - to make sure our children get "educated"?

I hear such statements and questions frequently, from the counter at Dunkin' Donuts to the office of the President's Secretary of Education. [Arne Duncan, when I wrote this.] They underlie the popular cry for "accountability" in education. Yet when I ask people who loathe and despise "teachers" what they remember about their own educations, I nearly always hear stories about the great teachers they had, the ones who brought them to love what they never knew they loved, opened their eyes, made them believe they could learn. These teachers they remember by name, even after forty or fifty years.

I think of teachers who did those things for me. My 8th-grade Civics teacher, Les Dean, who not only taught me how my government worked, but taught me to care about it, because he cared about it. That was not all he taught me. I was an overweight, insecure kid, and like more than one such, I decided I would recreate myself by giving myself a new name. I shudder to admit that that name was "Sugarlips." Mr. Dean, when I informed him of my new identity, not only did not laugh, but immediately began to address me in class by my new monicker, and insisted that my classmates do likewise. And so he taught me not only Civics, but one of the things a civil democracy requires: respect, even for the most pathetic fellow citizen.

I think of Professor Glenn O'Malley, who taught my Freshman seminar at Northwestern University. He had served all the way through the European campaign in World War II as a medic, and his face 15 years after that was a permanent mask of anguish and horror. From that anguish had emerged a gentleness mixed with love for the truth to be found in great writing. We kids in his seminar universally hated Milton, one of our required authors. I still remember what he said to us: "I'll tell you what my teacher told me: Give it 30 years and try it again." From that one sentence, I learned that maybe I wasn't as smart as I'd thought I was, and maybe I never would be and should always think twice.

I wound up spending 35 years getting paid to teach, so I've known and watched a lot of teachers. As I did when I was a student, I found a few teachers who were half-stepping nullities, a few who were small-time bullies. Very few. Most were hard workers who put in far more hours than their contracts demanded and who loved their work and their students and never stopped trying to get better at teaching them.

They generally worked at least sixty hours a week, often more, and generally spent their "free" summer months taking classes to improve their teaching skills or knowledge of their subject matter, or traveling, generally on their own dime, to share their knowledge with other teachers at conferences. Or working part-time jobs to supplement their meager incomes. Or both. Their idea of a Cadillac was a beater they could afford to keep running.

Next time you feel inclined to bash or hear someone bashing teachers, I hope you'll think back on what your teachers gave you. Next time you hear the word "accountability," I hope you'll think about these words of Abraham Joseph Heschel: "Everything depends on the person who stands in front of the classroom. The teacher is not an automatic fountain from which intellectual beverages may be obtained. He is either a witness or a stranger. To guide a pupil into the promised land, he must have been there himself. When asking himself: Do I stand for what I teach? Do I believe what I say? he must be able to answer in the affirmative. What we need more than any thing else is not *textbooks* but *textpeople*. It is the personality of the teacher which is the text that the pupils read; the text that they will never forget." [Heschel]

Before you thoughtlessly agree that teachers are the enemy, please think back on that teacher who changed your life forever and for the better.

On the Realism of Gratitude to Teachers

A friend of mine who's still teaching English told me lately about a student who felt truly indignant that he should have to *do* anything to obtain a passing grade. Doing anything included coming to class. He held the extreme position of a common contemporary student belief: that nothing deserves attention unless it frequently explodes, and that appearing in the vicinity of the classroom 65% of the time, refraining from open expressions of boredom and revulsion, and slapping some words on paper under duress ought to guarantee at least a B.

As Japanese students conclude each grade, they sing a song thanking their teachers for deigning to teach them. They value learning, and therefore those who help them learn, not from sentiment but from realism. Their culture understands that the reality of this world is danger, and that humans need maps and tools with which to cope with danger.

"The most dangerous animal yet roaming free," as Nelson Algren named the human, is the animal that uses language. Over the past hundred years, our language has fallen into the hands of paid liars. They are called advertising executives and public relations professionals and other euphemisms. Hyperbole and euphemism and fake logic and mindless catch-phrases, the stock in trade of these paid liars, have so pervaded our speech and thought that many people unconsciously believe that language is solely composed of such devices, employed to bamboozle or intimidate someone into doing what you want them to do.

Therefore lies, even when revealed, as in so many cases they eventually are, fail to make people indignant. Lies are expected, and no cause for alarm or anger. People who expect lies have a hard time telling shit from Shinola, because they believe everything is shit. This belief makes it easy for them to lie to themselves - as easily as they lie to everyone else. People who lie to themselves have no purchase on reality, and they make easy prey for professional liars.

In a dangerous world, realistic persons would be very grateful to anyone who could help them learn how to recognize the language of paid liars, how to recognize when it has infected their own language, and how to use language in the service of truth, told in clear and simple ways. That is the job of English teachers, though not all of them see it that way.

Students pay teachers to teach them how to think straight about the real world. They pay teachers to not let them get away with lies. They pay them to make them miserable, not to make them feel good. It's miserable to discover that there's no end to the work of learning not to be a liar and not to be fooled by liars.

But if you don't learn how the language is used as a weapon, you probably won't learn how to use it as a shield. And the world, gradually or suddenly, will eat you right on up.

I kept writing them, and the editors kept not printing them. They just didn't reflect the Spirit of the Times. When I got a chance to go back to teaching part time at DeVry University under an English Department head who actually seemed to value my experience and offered to let me the hell alone to teach, I jumped at it.

The local branch of DeVry at that time was housed in rented rooms in a building not especially designed as a campus. It reminded me of my former community college's early facility and atmosphere. The instructors were all pretty much on their own, the required record keeping and paperwork were minimal. I felt completely at home with most of the students, and after a couple of years a graduating class asked me to speak at their graduation ceremonies. I had visions of graduations I'd attended in the past, the students spread out before me in their caps and gowns and enforced attentiveness, and I wrote the following for the occasion I imagined:

It's Not All About the Benjamins

First, let me thank you for asking me to talk to you on this happy occasion. I'm not sure what brought about your invitation, since I don't think even those of you who know me are aware that, in another of my incarnations, I'm a minister of the Universal Life Church, and that I specialize in presiding at weddings - another happy occasion. So far, I've only had to preside at one funeral. We all hope this won't turn into my second one of those. Whatever caused your invitation, I take it as a very high honor. I admire you all so much for enduring what you have endured to reach this point.

I am now supposed to tell you the following: your whole future lies ahead of you, and now my generation has prepared you to accept the torch of responsibility from our flagging grasp; now that we have equipped you with the tools education provides, you should certainly be able to do more with them than we have.

I hope so.

A brief and sour summary of my generation's track record: we started out in the 1960s with high hopes that we could bring about justice and peace. We would create real communities, in which everyone cared for everyone else. We would become spiritually enlightened through the use of psychedelic drugs, and then generously share our enlightenment with the rest of a waiting world. It would be easy. The Beatles told us so: Love, love, love...Love, love, love...Love is all you need. Drugs make a lot of things look easy.

By the 70s, we discovered that the waiting world wasn't waiting for us or our message, and that bringing about peace and justice and universal free peanut butter would require a tremendous amount of hard, tedious work. So we decided to retreat into drugs and disco and glitter rock, which allowed us to keep shocking our elders with "unisex" styles of hair and dress. Guys wearing dresses and lipstick don't really present a serious challenge to the Military-Industrial Complex, but if we stayed stoned all the time, it was easy to pretend that we were still engaged in some kind of revolutionary activity.

One problem with drugs, however, is that you build up tolerance - you either need to take more and more of the same drug to achieve the desired effect, or you need to take a stronger drug. Enter cocaine and other forms of speed.

But the problem with cocaine and its derivatives was stated nicely by the great American writer Robert Stone: "They discovered that the principal thing you do with cocaine is run out of it." [Stone] And it cost lots and lots of money to keep running out of it.

And so, in the 80s, when "morning in America" was declared, we were quite ready to embrace the idea that the purpose of life was not really to bring about peace and justice, but to make lots and lots of money. Somewhere in the mid 80s, a T-shirt became widely available that summed up the message: "He who dies with the most toys wins." In the 90s, the preeminent toys became the Computer and the Internet, by which we were all going to be turned into overnight millionaires.

Until we weren't. But the great technology bubble of the 90s burst without disturbing the beliefs it had encouraged: the belief that greed is good, the belief that everyone can and should make it on his or her own, the belief that our lives should be dedicated to acquiring material possessions. That's the belief system that seems to have become something like a religious dogma. Republicans, Democrats, neo-conservatives, neo-liberals - nobody seems to questions the basic proposition: he who dies with the most toys wins.

This last semester, I've had a running argument with one of my students. He has a favorite phrase, his answer to any question about human behavior: "It's all about the Benjamins." The Benjamins he refers to are the portraits that appear on hundred-dollar bills. One night when I challenged his analysis, he replied, "Give me one example of somebody doing something that isn't for the Benjamins, then."

That was pretty easy. I told him that even if I didn't need the money I was making teaching his class, I'd be doing it anyway. I told him that after I "retired" three years ago from teaching, I'd enjoyed doing other things for about three months, but that after that

I'd begun feeling less and less like myself. I told him that I'd be teaching his class for nothing an hour if I could afford to.

All that was true.

It's also true that the day of universal free peanut butter is not here yet, and not likely to be here. Keeping food on the table and a roof over the heads and a car that runs isn't easy, and it doesn't look to get any easier. So if I say, "It's not all about the Benjamins," I'm not advising you that "love is all you need." I'm advising you that the Benjamins aren't all you need, either.

In my very fortunate life, I've gotten the chance to work as a journalist, a playwright, a bartender, a performer, a musician, a criminal defense investigator. Everything I dreamed about doing as a kid, I've done - done enough of to know what it was about. (Well... everything except play left field for the Cubs. And when it comes to the Cubs, who knows - there may still be a call-up in my future.)

But during all those experiences, I never stopped teaching. I never stopped teaching because what teaching is about is sharing with other people everything you've learned from whatever you've been and done. Some of them even want to hear about it, and all of them have something of their own to share.

One of my favorite writers, a guy named Dave Hickey who lives in Las Vegas, wrote in his great book *Air Guitar* about the way he learned the pleasure of talking about things you love by going into the little stores and art galleries and bookshops in Manhattan as a young man: "If you were a nobody like me, and didn't know anything, you could go into one of them and find things out. People would talk to you, not because you were going to buy something, but because they loved the stuff they had to sell....And I love that kind of talk, have lived on it and lived by it....To me, it has always been the heart of the mystery, the heart of the heart: the way people talk about loving things, which things, and why." [Hickey] I have been lucky enough to live on and by that kind of talk as well.

I had better say quickly that I'm not trying to talk you into giving up your day jobs and becoming teachers, although I wouldn't try to talk you out of it. What I am trying to talk you into is to never quit trying to make your work into an occasion for humanity - for helping other people, for making your part of their day a little better, for passing on the things you know about that have been worth knowing - fun to know, useful to know, sometimes *lifesaving* to know.

As an example of the latter, I'll tell you a story about Speedy Gonzalez. Speed was a short, very fat Sergeant in my Army company in Hoechst, Germany. Against all advice, I'd loaned this man a lot of money. Even on an E-4's pay, I had money to loan, and I loaned it out at no interest to anyone who asked. Everyone told me that Speedy never paid his debts, and I might as well have thrown my money out the *kaserne* window.

One night I was walking downtown, toward a bar, no doubt, when I heard footsteps coming up behind me. They weren't coming fast - just a little faster than the pace I was setting. As they got nearer, and I was deciding I might turn around, I felt the point of a knife between my ribs, just nudging me a little. I did a kind of modified, spastic ballet leap up in the air and landed facing my assailant. Who turned out to be none other than Sgt. Gonzalez, calmly folding his blade back into its case. He looked up at me, and said, very seriously, "Mac - don't ever let somebody come up behind you like that." And before I knew it, he was gone up a side street, whistling.

As far as I'm concerned, he paid me back with interest that night. Funny thing is, he also eventually paid me back all the money I'd loaned him, too. But the interest was worth a lot more, and I've been in quite a few places in the years since then that I survived because of that little lesson.

One of the things I've noticed over my sixty-some years is that people in general seem to be talking less and less to each other. Since the advent of e-mail and the internet, we don't even tell very many jokes to each other any more. They come to us now when we're by ourselves, sitting in front of the screen. Maybe we forward them on to a friend. But we no longer tell them. Our conversation has a lot less laughter in it.

And of course, there seems to be a lot less conversation, period. With every new labor-saving device, we seem to have less time and energy for each other. The labor-saving devices are constantly demanding our attention. The devices that bring us information are constantly bringing us more information, so we never have a chance to process any of it, to think about it, to compare it with the information we already had stored up, to see if it's valid or useful, to talk to other people about it - there's always another voice demanding our attention, another electronic pitch to listen to or try to ignore.

And yet, in the end, what does a life amount to but what you've given to other people? Those moments when you've stopped to laugh with someone, or to hold them while they weep, or to help them get something done they can't do by themselves, or figure out something that's keeping them miserable?

We're all walking around carrying 32 pounds per square inch of atmosphere on our bodies all the time - and anyone who lives very long winds up carrying a lot more weight than that. Burdens of responsibility and grief and regret and uncertainty of all sorts. We need each other to share those loads, and help us forget how heavy they are, or sometimes even make them lighter. But it seems to me we more and more feel we just don't have the time. Well. What exactly is time *for*? And who owns our time, if it's ours?

Again, before I start sounding too much like a Beatles' song, I know - I know, I know, I know - the pressures we're all under to act as if our time belonged to somebody else. I know about the roof and the table, and the working two or three jobs because not one of them by itself takes care of the roof and the table, and the kids, and then the teenagers.

In a book called *The Just and the Unjust*, James Gould Cozzens, who was a heck of a writer but too conservative for the opinion-makers of his day, wrote a great passage about "everyday living." A young lawyer named Abner Coates has spent the whole book learning that everything he'd been taught wasn't exactly wrong - it just wasn't quite what was really happening. His father, old Judge Coates, has had a major stroke. One night, Abner comes up to his room, complaining that things don't work the way the books said they did, and Judge Coates says to him: "I don't know who it was who said when we think of the past we regret and when we think of the future we fear. And with reason. But no bets are off. There is the present to think of, and as long as you live there always will be. In the present, every day is a miracle. The world gets up in the morning and is fed and goes to work, and in the evening it comes home and is fed again and perhaps has a little amusement and goes to sleep. To make that possible, so much has to be done by so many people that, on the face of it, it is impossible. Well, every day we do it; and every day, come hell, come high water, we're going to have to go on doing it as well as we can." [Cozzens]

The Judge is right. Life's impossible. That's what makes it a miracle. And looking to lighten somebody else's load is the best way to remind yourself that it's a miracle. Also turns out to be the best way to lighten your own.

From talking with quite a few of you, I conclude that most, if not all of you, have come through the DeVry experience with one main goal: to find work that would pay you enough to take care of whoever you're responsible for, and that might even leave a little over to have some fun with. It's an admirable goal.

But I hope that somewhere in the general education courses you were obliged to take, you found some windows that look out at the world as the miracle it is, and gave you that feeling of really seeing or hearing or understanding something for the first time. And I hope that you'll go back, at least every once in a while, and look through those windows again, and keep looking for others. Don't spend your whole lives sitting in front of screens that don't let you see for yourself, but make you see the product of somebody else's visions.

The last thing I'm going to inflict on you tonight is part of a poem by Robert Frost.

This is a poem of his you don't hear too often. He wrote it during the beginning years of the Great Depression, and it's about both working and caring about each other.

[Robert Frost: "Two Tramps in Mud Time"][Frost]

They didn't get to hear it that night, either. By whose decision I don't know, the "graduation ceremony" turned out to be a graduation dinner, held at a chain restaurant known as Carraba's, a joint that had not only a large bar and restaurant in one room, but an even larger dining hall attached. The DeVry students and their families and the

Distinguished Speaker ate in the latter. It was the night of the final Yankees-Red Sox ALCS meeting, and needless to say the bar in the next room was raucous and frequently deafening.

I was called on to deliver my speech as most DeVry people were still eating and Johnny Damon was driving spikes in Yankee hearts in the next room. Since there was no podium or stage or microphone, I delivered it standing at my seat, hollering it over the clanking of silver on china plates of pasta. I wound up editing it down to a few minutes as I read it. Some of the students even noticed that I'd stopped bellowing and briefly applauded. I include it here because I still think it's a good speech, though I wouldn't include my recommendation of teaching as a career if I gave it today. Not because I've stopped believing in the value of teaching, but because I don't think real teaching or learning are going to be possible within any organized education systems for quite a while.

Throughout my years teaching, I kept noticing how closely the changes in administrative personnel and in Received Wisdom were to the changes in the American political system, as I suggested in that graduation speech. Toward the end of my teaching years, I began to see that this wasn't entirely coincidental. The new Robber Barons, like their predecessors, were seeking to assume control of the education system in order to cement their social and economic hegemonies. Josephson described the original Barons' efforts admirably:

" In the world of learning, the janissaries of oil or lard potentates, with a proper sense of taste and fitness, sought consistently to sustain the social structure, to resist change, to combat all current notions which might thereafter 'reduce society to chaos' or 'confound the order of nature.'....the managers of Rockefeller's Chicago University also championed the combinations year by year. One professor of economics, Dr. Gunton, especially distinguished himself on this score, and another, a teacher of literature ostensibly, declared Mr. Rockefeller and Mr. Pullman 'superior in creative genius to Shakespeare, Homer and Dante,' a declaration which made a lively impression at the time. In the meanwhile, a third teacher, a Professor Bemis, who happened to criticize the action of the railroads during the Pullman strike in 1894 was after several warnings expelled from the University for 'incompetence.'

"At Syracuse University in western New York, to mention only one instance, a gifted young instructor in economics, John Commons, was similarly dismissed by the Chancellor. His strongest interests were discovered to lie in the rising labor movement, and the university, endowed by Mr. John Archbold of the Standard Oil family, frowned upon such learning...."[Josephson]

One of the new gems of Received Wisdom that became cliches during the 80s and 90s was "thinking outside the box" (whatever the hell that meant). What it meant in practice was that educational institutions would be prevailed upon to choose new leaders from the business world, where the phrase "thinking outside the box" had originated. So educational leadership, if that's the word for it, has become largely composed of fat-headed unsuccessful business people who can sling around mindless phrases like "thinking outside the box." I noted this in my swan song as I left teaching for good:

Deep Beneath Mongolia

a series of caves exists, a full thirty miles below the surface of the earth, hence heated by the magma itself. In these caves, the alpha-ur-humans are being brought to us. From their little petri dishes they blossom into creatures in all outer aspect no different from earthlings.

For their first thirty years, they are coddled, petted, and surrounded by only two messages: "You are superior to all earthlings you will encounter - except, of course, for those with whom you share the Secret Handshake," is the first. The second is not so much one message as an always-changing series of messages, which these homunculi necessarily believe constitute human conversation: a few months ago, for example, these messages consisted of the word "robust," and the phrase "at the end of the day," but they change rapidly, depending on the date of Expulsion Day. On Expulsion Day, the homunculi, dressed appropriately for various climes, are put into a rocket-propelled elevator and blasted out through a tube in Mongolia into the near stratosphere. They rise and spread like dandelion seeds over the surface of the earth, and drift down into the executive offices of every goddam place on earth. And immediately, they begin to speak: "At the end of the day," they say, "the bottom line is this: it is what it is."

And that's who's running the show. Your show. My show. The show.

Vonnegut has another version in his new book. He thinks who's running the show is "C students from Yale." Naahh. It's Mongolians. Here's evidence:

Associated Press Dispatch: *Bush Makes History at Trip's End.*

"President Bush became the first sitting U.S. president to visit Mongolia, a nation with the gross national product of a small U.S. state and a population the size of Chicago.... Bush, Secretary of State Condoleeza Rice and others went into a home heated by a wood burning stove and housing a herder couple and their daughter. Bush enjoyed fermented mare's milk, tea and cheese curd.

"'Let's get *a family picture*,' [italics mine] Bush said as he emerged, setting up a photo with the family, Laura Bush and Rice."

When I left DrVry, and, after that, Colorado Technical University, I'd seen these inhuman little popinjays take over, over and over, and I'd grown sick of trying to resist them, since in my view they'd taken over the country, and not enough of my fellow citizens seemed to mind that they had, even when they did it by blatant theft of elections. I felt much as Kurt Vonnegut did when he wrote to his friend Stig Claesson, "Not only have all my contemporaries, like yours, gone to paradise, but the country I used to write for is no longer anywhere to be found, hard as I may look for it." [Wakefield]

The more I heard about the way so-called "leaders" were going about their jobs - or, more often, evading any semblance of responsibility for their jobs - the more it seemed to me that about the only real leaders left in the country worked in the world of sports, and I began to collect accounts of how they went about *their* jobs:

"Up and down the lineup, guys are looking to move an extra base constantly right now. Nobody is being cautious....I really don't want them to be concerned ever about making mistakes. Station-to-station baserunning hurts you a lot....If we make a mistake in judgment, I'd much prefer talking about it, as opposed to getting angry with it. You see teams turn into station-to-station base runners because coaches get angry when you do something wrong. That's probably the worst form of coaching there is."
- Joe Maddon, *Vineline, 31/6,* June 2016, p. 20

"I believe in total honesty....Although honesty often bruises feelings, it gets everything out in the open and lets every player know exactly where he stands. I placed no restrictions on the players' honesty, either, even though what they might have to say about me would very likely be no more complimentary or considerate of my feelings than my honest assessments of them. I've always felt that players should have the right to express their opinions about the manager....I had made a pact with myself from the start of my managing career never to hold a grudge or let a player's personality warp my perception of his abilities."
[Weaver]

"The only question I had about him [Mark McGwire] at the beginning was whether or not he could translate what he knew about hitting into words the players could understand. Sometimes when you know something inside out, you think that other people do too and you take for granted that the words and concepts you've been using inside your head will have meaning to someone else."
[LaRussa]

"He came here and they really let him be himself. It's a credit to (pitching coach Chris) Bosio and, really, the organization...."
The Cubs encouraged Arrieta to go with his natural crossfire motion, adjusted where he stood on the pitching rubber, and helped him develop that cutter-slider

hybrid."   - Patrick Mooney, "Believe the Hype," *Baseball Digest, Jan/Feb 2016,* p. 17

"Where so many football coaches seek conformity, Carroll demands the opposite....Consider his handling of defensive end Lawrence Jackson, who had 10 sacks his sophomore season at USC, in 2005, but fell into a slump the next year, beset by pressure and the death of a close cousin. Carroll gave Jackson one of his favorite books, *The Inner Game of Tennis.* Reading it, Jackson stumbled upon an analogy about how a cat didn't think about how to capture a bird, didn't consider how high to jump or how fast. The cat simply reacted. The next game, Jackson bagged three sacks. Bird caught.

"Later Jackson played for the Lions, but in Detroit he was conscious of whom he ate with in the dining room and whom he spoke with on the practice field, and eventually his career petered out. 'If you don't feel your individuality is respected, a piece of you doesn't show up to work,' Jackson says. 'You can't be who you are. Pete understands you can't reach everybody the same way.' "

- Greg Bishop, "Who's Moved On? This Guy," *Sports Illustrated,* August 3, 2015, p.44

"What may be the key to the young players' ultimate success - and it's impossible to measure- is Maddon's impact. He's told the Cubs from day one to be themselves, and that includes everyone, from mid-30s veterans to the 21-year-old [Addison] Russell....Maddon doesn't enforce restrictions on players. In fact, he'll be the first to tell you he has no rules.

"'That's our job in the clubhouse to police that stuff, not Joe,' [Jason] Hammel said.... Usually the manager is always wearing the sheriff's hat....What's the saying? "Good teams win. Bad teams have meetings." Obviously, Joe wants to avoid meetings. If there's anything that needs to be talked about, we talk about it. That's what we've established by allowing guys to be themselves. The older guys here know when to step in if need be.'"

    - Carrie Muskat, "Sky's the LImit," *Vineline,* August, 2015, p. 30

"....But the linemen feel as if they were brought to St. Louis *because* of who they are, not in hopes they would become someone else. [Aaron] Donald recalls one of his first meetings last year, when [defensive coordinator Mike] Waufle told the tackle to ignore everything he was teaching and to keep playing the way he always had. ('It was the greatest coaching job I ever did,' Waufle jokes.) Hayes, too, reflects back on the year before he arrived as a free agent, when Titans coaches asked him to be a different kind of player. He was ready to quit until Fisher called. Now coaches don't urge him to be the best pass rusher or run stopper he can be. Instead, he says, 'I want to be the best William Hayes I can be.'"
    - Joan Niesen, "A Few ~~Good~~ Men," *Sports Illustrated,* August 17, 2015, p. 45

[Paul Hamilton, Cincinnati Bengals offensive line coach]: "Oh, and there was that time in May 2014 when he conducted the Hamilton (Ohio) Fairfield Symphony Orchestra in Mozart's *Eine Kleine Nachtmusik.* Before one movement Alexander told the group to imagine they were biting into chocolate-covered cherries. Then he gave one to each of them. 'He was very conscious of talking to [the performers], treating them like human beings," says Paul Stanbery, the group's music director. 'They so much respect it when whoever is leading them knows they are people, not just musicians. A lot of conductors and coaches lose sight of that. For Paul, I think that's at the heart of his success.'
    - Greg A. Bedard, "Lay It on the Line," *Sports Illustrated,* II/2/15, p. 58

The common observation in these accounts of various successful and beloved coaches and managers is that they treat players with respect and perceive and value their individual characters and characteristics. They do not view their players as raw material to be jammed into identical molds with identically measurable characteristics.

That is the view of the whole "Accountability" movement that we've allowed to highjack our educational system.

Vonnegut didn't end his letter to Stig Claesson where I left off earlier. He ended it this way: "The late humorist James Thurber wrote a fable set in a medieval court, and he has the Royal Astronomer report that all the stars are going out! It turns out that he is simply going blind. I am probably making the same mistake."

I don't think I'm making the same mistake in my despairing view of what's happened to education during my lifetime, but I think despair's always a mistake. Teaching and learning have been natural human activities since long before the invention of schools or school systems, and I hope you'll never give up on learning and teaching and that you'll maybe help invent a new education system and a new society that values individuals over mass-produced test-takers, and values humans over Mongolians.

First Aid

"I'm not sure I was the biggest asshole in the world, but I definitely played one on TV."   -Lance Armstrong, *ESPN the Magazine,* 12/23/13

Yes, Lance, you did, perhaps because, lying about your PED use, you were playing yourself: a liar.

I'm using this quote as an epigraph to my first, foremost piece of advice for any classroom teacher: before you do anything else, put the fear of God in your class. Every class. Every time. First thing. If you don't, the class will devolve into one of several sorts of train wrecks, and there'll be no fixing it later on.

I don't think you need to play an asshole, but you need to play a version of yourself that gives and expects respect, a version that believes deeply and implicitly in the value of whatever it is you're proposing to teach.

To do those things, I started out by explaining my grading system: Every paper started out with 100 points, 30 for clarity, 40 for organization, 30 for support. Spelling errors cost 1/2 point each, grammatical errors cost 1 point each, sentence errors cost 2 points each and use of any form of the verb "to be" cost 5 points. I won't burden you by defining all those terms, though I tried to do so in discussion until they were clear to my classes. Letter grades followed the standard 90 - 100 = A and so on.

It should be instantly apparent that "clarity, organization and support" evaluations allow for a lot of subjectivity. I tried very hard to grade objectively and fairly, and I think I mainly did so. But one great advantage of this (or a similar) grading system, assigning numerical values to all the aspects of writing being evaluated, lay in the American people's devout respect for and meek submission to numbers. In the twenty or so years I used this system, I received *one* student complaint about a grade. (The student brought his mother in. She shared his indignation - probably had fostered it. I showed them the numbers. They shut up and went away.)

The grading system explained, I gave them a fairly simple writing assignment, due the next class meeting. I will grade it, I told them, exactly as if it were your final, but the grade won't count. Enter the fear of God. For many, maybe for most, people, the verb "to be" serves as nearly their sole verb, relieved only occasionally by "to have." Those 5-point reductions add up in a hurry, and quite a few students over the years received scores in negative numbers. Students now went through the first exercise rather more intently than they might have before seeing what writing in the passive voice did to their grades. (I never used the term "passive voice," just urged them to eschew "to be" verbs):

To Be or Not to Be?

If someone asked me to tell the story of my life, I might begin like this:

I was born in Evanston, Illinois, in 1942. I have been told that my father came home from the hospital saying over and over, "It's a boy! It's a boy!" There is no record of how my mother felt about this fact. I was soon to be made aware of how my sister felt about it, though. My birth was in May, 5 months and 3 weeks after Pearl Harbor had been attacked by Japan, so there was a war on. There has been a war on during nearly every one of the sixty years since I was born.

You could find a number of faults with this paragraph, though you couldn't find anything grammatically incorrect. It simply stinks. Why? Start answering that question by looking for the verbs in each sentence:

I **was** born in Evanston, Illinois, in 1942. I **have been told** that my father came home from the hospital saying over and over, "**It's** a boy! **It's** a boy!" There **is** no record of how my mother felt about this fact. I **was** soon **to be** made aware of how my sister felt about it, though. My birth **was** in May, 5 months and 3 weeks after Pearl Harbor had been attacked by Japan, so there **was** a war on. There **has been** a war on during nearly every one of the sixty years since I **was** born.

Every verb in bold type is a form of the verb "To Be." (When you want to talk about a verb by name, you say "to" and then the verb: to walk, to scream, to caress, to finagle, etc. Putting a "to" in front of a verb creates the infinitive, and makes the verb into a noun. In other words, the infinitive can't be used as a verb in a sentence.)

That verb, "to be," came to me easily and unconsciously, a handy, all-purpose tool, always ready for use to express any thought or memory that occurred to me. Ready, also, to render those thoughts and memories dead on arrival on the page.

What Do Verbs Do?

Verbs describe action. Action makes sentences live. You can tell a living body from a corpse because the corpse just lies there. The living body moves, even in sleep.

Try this: get in front of a mirror and be. Easy, eh? No matter what you do or don't do - whether you do jumping jacks or paint your face blue or just stand there - you'll be being.

Because it signifies any action, including no action, the verb "to be" makes dead sentences. Nothing moves. Could I have written the same autobiographical paragraph without using the verb "to be?" Sure:

My mother brought me into the world in May, 1942 at Evanston Hospital. Many years later, my aunt Helen described to me my father's ecstatic reaction to having a son. I don't know how my mother felt about that, but my sister soon began to let me know how she felt, tormenting me until I got big enough to stop her. A few months before my arrival, Japan had bombed Pearl Harbor, and my country had gone to war. It has stayed at war with one enemy or another during most of my 60 years.

To get rid of the "to be" verbs in that paragraph, I first asked of each sentence, "Who did what?" If someone or something is, then someone or something made it that way. If I "was born," I sure wasn't born without nine months and some intense hours of intense effort by someone, namely my mother. If I "was told" of my father's reaction, someone must have told me, namely my aunt. If Pearl Harbor "was attacked" by Japan, then Japan attacked Pearl Harbor.

Why go to all this trouble? Try to imagine an action without first imagining who or what performs that action. Can you see flight without a flyer? Biting without a biter? If you can, write me a letter and tell me how to go about it.

Every sentence that uses "to be" as its main verb asks its readers either to imagine an action without a named actor ("I have been told") or to imagine an action before knowing who or what performs that action ("Pearl Harbor had been attacked by Japan"). That makes the readers' work harder. You don't want to make the readers' work harder. If you do, the readers will soon come to dislike you, and won't want to give what you have to say a fair hearing, and may simply stop reading before even finding out what you have to say.

Write this list of the commonest tenses of "to be" on a card, stick it in the edge of your mirror, and study it until you know it cold. Learn to hate these words:

am	was	will be	should be	have been	should have been
is	were	will be being	could be	has been	could have been
are		will have been	would be	had been	would have been
			might be		might have been
			may be		may have been
		am being		was being	
		are being		were being	

Don't learn to hate them because they're "wrong." They aren't. A sentence like "There are several reasons why Athenian civilization declined" isn't *wrong*. It could simply be improved by asking, "Who did what?" Answer: "Athenian civilization (who?) declined (did what?) for several reasons." The second sentence lets the readers know immediately what happened.

The second sentence also saves two words. Do two words matter? They do. Words take time to read. If you save your readers a little time, they will love you for it.

You want your readers to love you. People tend to listen to what those they love want to tell them.

Two words matter for another reason. Whether in school or in the "real world," most writing assignments impose some limitation on the number of words you can use. You can't worry unduly about this limitation as you're drafting the assignment, but you'll have to worry about it when preparing your finished piece. You'll probably have to cut it. Learning to eliminate "to be" verbs gives you one of the best razors available.

Again, a sentence like "There is a tree standing there that has been growing by the fence for many years" is not grammatically incorrect. But you can feel your eyelids drooping halfway through it. What does what in that sentence? "An old walnut tree stands by the fence." You can say in 8 words what the first sentence said in 21. In a 300 word draft that has to be cut to 250 words, the second sentence makes over 1/4 of the necessary cuts.

Let Me Be

I don't mean to say that you should never use the verb "to be" in a sentence. I do say that you'll become a more efficient and interesting writer if you learn to view "to be" as guilty until proven innocent. In other words, learn to get rid of it whenever you can. Once you get to revising a draft, ask of each sentence you've written, "Who does what?" Look for perfectly good verbs you've buried as other parts of speech, and turn them back into verbs. (For example, "standing there" becomes "stands" in the second sentence because that's what the oak tree is doing.)

Examples

1. There will be no whining allowed by this coach.

Who's doing what? We don't know who might have been whining. The only potential actor present in the sentence is "this coach." What does he do? He allows.

This coach allows no whining.

2. He will never have been a Chicago Cub.

If he made it onto the Cub's roster, what would he do? Since the Cubs are a baseball team (at least in theory), he would play baseball for them.

He will never play for the Cubs.

3. It is such an angry essay it is hard to read.

In this example, no actor appears. You need to look for a potential action and then ask yourself who might perform that action.

Readers may find the essay's anger repellent.

Practice

Rewrite these sentences to get rid of the "to be" verbs. (Actual people wrote all of these sentences. As Dave Barry says, "I am not making these up.")

1. The moon may be invisible to astronomers when it is perfectly obvious to lovers.

2. What are the reasons for Fabio's despicable behavior?

3. Chicago was a city that never slept.

4. The reason this is, is because the mechanic was drunk and so the transmission was left on the garage floor.

5. An example of this is in the beginning of this story all of the author's opinions were in parentheses.

6. The first fear of the boy was that he would never be able to find his way home.

7. Taxpayers are left to decide what the tax forms may be asking of them.

8. The movie was successful in allowing the viewers to understand the characters.

9. He was traumatized by the memories of the war.

10. The only problem is that it is hard to understand the essay if you don't pay attention to what the essay has to say.

11. One of the problems was that the task of finding the author's point of view was hard.

12. The colored lights were a great way to get people's attention on the carnival.

13. The two styles of goaltending were effectively demonstrated through the contrasting performances of the goalies for Detroit and Phoenix.

14. The people are in fear of further attacks by their enemy.

15. The second story Wright tells is surprising.

16. The fabricating of the chips was poorly done by the plant in Scranton.

17. Opinions are not a lot for the voter to base a serious conclusion on.

18. He was afraid that he would be punished by the supervisor.

19. Supporting this statement is exactly what Gardner doesn't do.

20. She is the only one who will ever understand the meaning.

21. Her story is seen over the span of 22 years.

22. In both of the essays the issues of segregation were included.

23. The reason the essay may be ineffective is because of its lack of factual information.

24. To say that television is responsible for America's drug problems is foolish.

25. The man is covered in mud.

(Even professional writers fall lazily into overuse of "to be" verbs. Rewrite the following selections to get rid of those verbs.)

1. In Mamá's house (everyone called my grandmother Mamá) was a large parlor built by grandfather to his wife's exact specifications so that it was always cool, facing away from the sun. The doorway was on the side of the house so no one could walk directly into her living room.... This room was furnished with several mahogany rocking chairs.... It was on these rockers that my mother, her sisters, and my grandmother sat....
(Judith Ortiz Cofer, "Casa: A Partial Remembrance of a Puerto Rican Childhood," *The Conscious Reader*, 6th Ed., pp. 64-5)

2. Medfield was a very distinct reality to me. There was even a leftover colonial custom that gave the town a concrete definition. By 1692 the settlements around Boston were growing quickly and their perimeters were hazy because of conflicting land grants and native treaties. The executive power of each town was vested in the Board of Selectmen....
(John Preston, "Medfield, Massachusetts," *CR*, p. 83)

3. This man who worked himself to death...was fifty-one years old and a vice-president. He was, however, one of six vice-presidents....He was, of course, overweight, by 20 or 25 pounds....His second child is a girl, who is twenty-four and newly married.

(Ellen Goodman, "The Company Man," *CR*, p. 115)

4. ...some locals had come by, pounded on the front door, and made threats. One was said to have brandished a machete. They were angry and shocked, as the whole nation was in the aftermath of the surprise attack.... It was Monday night, the day after Pearl Harbor, and there was a rattling knock on the front door.
(Garrett Hongo, "Kubota," *CR*, pp. 186, 187)

5. It was not the fact that she disagreed with me that was so disturbing. She's a teen-ager, she disagrees with me every day. What was so disturbing was the success of the anti-abortion movement at depicting people like me as heartless, amoral abstractionists who care more about rights than about life.
(Victoria Bissell Brown, "Abortion Fight Is over Choice," *CR*, pp. 202-3)

6. This is the age where everything is known, everything told....Also available is a voice-changer that alters one's voice; this is useful, its makers say, for a man who wishes to pretend he has a secretary.
(Roger Rosenblatt, "Who Killed Privacy?" *CR*, pp. 443-4)

7. The family resemblance between football and war is, indeed, striking. Their languages are similar....Their principles and practices are alike....And the virtues they celebrate are almost identical.
(John McMurtry, "Kill 'Em! Crush 'Em! Eat 'Em Raw!" *CR*, p. 475

8. Rock and roll is a way of life; certainly it is music, but it is also big business. Selling records, compact discs, tapes, and concert appearances is at the center of a multi-billion-dollar international industry....Creating an image is an all-important part of the process. The leather-jacketed Beatles, for instance, were cleaned up and put into suits by their manager, Brian Epstein, to help them achieve commercial success.

(Jack Santino, "Rock and Roll as Music, Rock and Roll as Culture," *CR*, p. 452)

9. In the early 1960's, I was in college at Albany State. My major interests were music and biology. In music I was a contralto soloist with the choir, studying Italian arias and German lieder. The black music I sang was of three types....
(Bernice Reagon, "Black Music on Our Hands," *CR*, p. 456)

10. The stereotype is the Eternal Feminine. She is the Sexual Object sought by all men, and by all women. She is of neither sex, for she has herself no sex at all. Her value is solely attested by the demand she excites in others. All she must contribute is her existence. She need achieve nothing, for she is the reward of achievement. She need never give positive evidence of her moral character because virtue is assumed from her loveliness, and her passivity. If any man who has no right to her be found with her she will not be punished, for she is morally neuter. The matter is solely one of male rivalry.
(Germaine Greer, "The Stereotype," *CR*, p. 293)

Dead on Arrival

Read these two paragraph from a best-selling novel, Anita Shreve's *Fortune's Rocks*:

"The cottage is a modest one by some standards, although Olympia's father is a wealthy man. But it is unique in its proportions, and she thinks it lovely beyond words. White with dark blue shutters, the house stands two stories high and is surrounded by several graceful porches. It is constructed in the style of the grand hotels along Fortune's Rocks, and in Rye and Hampton to the south: that is to say, its roof curves shallowly and is inset with evenly spaced dormer windows. The house has never been a hotel, but rather was once a convent....Indeed, an oddity of the structure is its many cell-like bedrooms....Attached to the ground floor of the house is a small chapel...."

"There is no mistaking this gaze. It is not a look that turns itself into a polite moment of recognition or a nod of encouragement to speak. Nor is it the result of an absent-minded concentration of thought. It is rather an entirely penetrating gaze with no barriers or boundaries. It is scrutiny such as Olympia has never encountered in her young life. And she thinks that the entire table must be stopped in that moment, as she is, feeling its nearly intolerable intensity."

Shreve's writing suffers from addiction to the verb "to be." Can you feel your eyelids begin to droop after a couple of sentences? Nothing happens in either one. In the second paragraph, the young woman Olympia experiences the electric moment of meeting eyes with the older man who will shortly become her first lover. As Shreve renders it, the moment has all the electricity of a 15-watt light bulb covered with cobwebs. Study this writing. Go thou and sin no more.

That one prohibition - no "to be" verbs - proved the most memorable aspect of my classes for many if not most of my students. For years, every former student I ran into out in public would, upon seeing me, invariably start muttering darkly about "those damn 'to be' verbs." Most of them would then thank me and tell me how much that one little trick had improved their writing.

Some few, the clever wrigglers, figured out that semi-synonyms for "to be" existed - such as "exist." They'd simply use those synonyms, rather than go to the mental work to write in the active voice, but I was surprised how few did this. I did have to provide a little advice on how to avoid "to be," which I did in the next exercise:

Who Done It?

"Don't put the cart before the horse," your great grandmother often advised you. Since you'd never seen either a cart or a horse in your natural life, you had no idea what her advice meant. She should have said, "Don't hitch the U-Haul to the front of the All-Wheel-Drive, Off-Road Suburban Assault Vehicle."

However she said it, she meant, "First things first." I've suggested that you first ask of any sentence, "Who did what?" (The answer to "Who?" is the Subject of the sentence, or ought to be. The answer to "Did what" is the Verb.)

You can look at any sentence as a set of answers to a set of questions: Who? Does (or did, or will do, etc.) what? To whom? When? Where? Why? How? A sentence may answer all these questions:

The cat   deposited   a dead squirrel   gently   on my bed   each morning   to show her love.
(Who?)   (Did what?)   (To whom?)   (How?)   (Where?)   (When?)   (Why?)

A sentence must answer the first two questions - Who? Did what? - or it isn't a sentence. Sometimes it answers only those two questions:

Sean   slept.
(Who?)   (Did what?)

If you write some words, capitalizing the first letter of the first word and ending with a period, you are claiming that you've answered the first two questions. If in fact you haven't answered one or both of them, you've written a fragment - a piece of a sentence - no matter how many other questions the words answer:

In the evening   by the river   gently   kissed   her.
(When?)   (Where?)   (How?)   (Did what?)   (To whom?)

Those words answer a lot of questions, but fail to tell who did the kissing. They don't make a sentence.

In other words, you can define a sentence as a group of words that answers the questions "Who? Did what?" and any other questions it needs to answer to make sense. "Sean slept" makes sense because "sleeping" isn't something you do to anyone or anything but yourself. Those two words don't raise any question they don't answer. "Sean kissed," though, makes us ask, "Kissed whom?" (or, if Sean's a little strange,

"Kissed what?"). You can't kiss nothing. Those two words raise a question they don't answer. They don't make a complete sentence.

Here's the advice: because every sentence you write must answer the first two questions, answer them first.

This may contradict advice you're gotten from English teachers. Many of them seem fixated on the necessity of "transitions," and their students wind up feeling that they need to introduce every sentence by connecting it to the previous one. If you think and imagine clearly, you'll rarely need to do that. Your reader will understand how one idea or event follows another.

If you begin sentences with transitional phrases or clauses, or, for that matter, by answering any questions other than "Who did what?" you create many opportunities for those sentences to get tangled up in themselves, leaving you and your readers confused and ill-humored. If you start right off with the subject and verb, usually the rest of the sentence will write itself.

Practice

Rewrite these sentences - which, again, various people actually wrote - so that the subject (Who or What?) comes first, the verb (Did what?) second.

1. Almost all the information used for support comes from surveys.

2. A downside to that causes Americans to stay within their boundaries and not want to open up to other countries' ways of doing things.

3. Americans' bitter tastes in their mouths may be left from politicians.

4. The first way that the author uses to convince his readers the media do not control the culture is by bringing up past events.

5. The best way for the voices of the voters to be heard by politicians is through polls.

6. The author's use of organizational skills takes the readers through the material clearly.

7. By using facts taken from surveys the author's essay has a gain in interest.

8. The basis for the general's decision originated from intelligence of advance scouts.

9. This technique of quoting polls is quite persuasive in that, when using facts as a foundation for his beliefs, causes the reader to agree with him because it makes sense.

10. Some Americans believe that building more prisons will make them safer, as stated by the Governor.

11. All those liberties are what cause Americans to think their country is great.

12. It is thought by some that many of our problems are self-inflicted.

13. An effective way to measure things is with the metric system.

14. In spite of his best effort, the test brought failure to Louis.

15. When reading news stories, many opinions are quickly formed.

16. For him to be able to survive, the basic necessities were needed.

17. The point he wanted to get across had to do with whether a man who has confessed to gambling should be allowed in the Hall of Fame or not.

18. While reading Jim Harrison's *Julip*, he brought up many interesting characters.

19. And through all of the hardships he speaks of over the last third of the century, he states that Americans have been a people who have come through them.

20. First, in Wattenberg's presentation, he uses very strong words.

(I made up the 5 following sentences. Fix them as you have the previous 20. Then try turning them into one sentence.)

1. Strongly the general dictated to his troops the orders.
2. The orders were received by the exhausted troops.
3. Exhausted as they were, the real situation at the front was unknown to the troops.
4. The objects of their thoughts were only a warm bed and a hot meal.
5. Warm beds and hot meals were being enjoyed by others behind the lines.

Viewing sentences as a set of answers to the basic question words seemed to make sense to a lot of my students, and it seemed to me a practical way to teach people how to revise their writing. I'd learned to look at sentences this way, I think, back in high school when each year's English class devoted a month or two to diagramming sentences. My students had never *heard* of diagramming sentences, let alone been required to practice doing it. But this "answer to questions" approach gave them a similar way to analyze their own sentences when they needed to. (I couldn't diagram a sentence now if you gave me a pretty, but the feel for and deep understanding of sentence structure I got from all those hours of diagramming back in high school has informed my writing ever since. Diagramming, like any sort of analysis, served merely as a tool for understanding. Once you'd mastered it, you could forget it.) I continued with this approach in discussing more complicated sentences:

Beyond the Simple Sentence

Unless all you ever have to write is *Dick and Jane Go Berserk* or *Dick and Jane Buy an Idiotically Expensive SUV and Die in a Rollover*, you won't be happy forever just writing simple sentences. Spot ran. Spot ran to greet Dick and Jane. Dick's and Jane's SUV pancaked Spot. The pattern will become boring for both you and your reader. (Nevertheless, that pattern of Subject-Verb-Completer remains the basic pattern, and learning to recognize that pattern and use it will help your writing stay clear and concise.) How can you vary this pattern?

I: Multiple Subjects, Multiple Verbs

If two sentences show two different subjects performing the same act, put both subjects into one sentence:

I saw the blimp explode. My sister Jane did, too.

My sister Jane and I saw the blimp explode.

If two sentences show the same subject performing two different but related acts, put both verbs into one sentence:

The Visigoths ruled Southern France in the 5th Century. They terrorized the Romans.

The Visigoths ruled Southern France and terrorized the Romans in the 5th Century.

Compound Sentences

If two simple sentences make separate statements of more or less equal importance, you can combine them with a comma followed by a coordinating conjunction. The coordinating conjunctions are:

,and

,but

,for

,or

,nor

Each one shows how the second clause relates to the first. (A clause is a group of words that contains a subject and a verb.)

"And" means "in addition to," very much like the "+" sign in math:

The night suddenly became still, and then he saw the leopard.

"But" indicates that the second clause opposes or contradicts the meaning of the first:

He saw the leopard, but the leopard didn't see him.

"For" indicates that the second clause caused the first:

He stood dead still, for he knew of the leopard's keen ears.

"Or" indicates that only one of the two clauses will prove true:

The leopard will eat him, or he will kill the leopard.

"Nor" indicates that neither clause will prove true:

He will not kill the leopard, nor will the leopard kill him.

"Yet" indicates that the second clause will come as a surprise:

He didn't kill the leopard, yet the leopard died the next day.

Notice that, if you replace the first comma with a period and remove the coordinating conjunction, you return to two simple sentences:

He didn't kill the leopard. The leopard died the next day.

If you can do that, you know that your original sentence had two independent clauses. So a compound sentence can be defined as two independent clauses joined by a comma and a coordinating conjunction.

Complex Sentences

You might also want to show that one of two simple sentences somehow depends on the other:

If she can find her keys, Holly will go to the store.

In that sentence, replacing the comma with a period will not create two simple sentences. It will create a fragment and a simple sentence:

If she can find her keys. [fragment] Holly will go to the store. [simple sentence]

Why is "If Holly can find her keys" a fragment? Because it forces you to ask a question it doesn't answer within itself: if Holly can find her keys, what will happen? A simple sentence must answer any question it raises before it ends. A complex sentence can be defined as a dependent clause joined to an independent clause. The two clauses may appear in either order, dependent/independent or Independent/dependent. If the dependent clause comes first, as in the example, it is followed by a comma. If the independent clause comes first, no comma is necessary:

Holly will go to the store if she can find her keys.

Common subordinating conjunctions that introduce dependent clauses:

after, as, as if, as soon as, as though, before, in order that, provided, since, so that, than, though, until, when, whenever, where, wherever, whereas, whether, while.

EXERCISES

Write 14 compound sentences, two for each coordinating conjunction.

Write 20 complex sentences using the subordinating conjunctions listed above. Write them first with the dependent clause first, the independent clause last. Then rewrite them with the independent clause first, the dependent clause last.

_____

Another tool I offered my students to use on their own sentences I'd also learned during all those hours of diagramming sentences: pay attention to where you put your modifiers.

Modifiers

As you worked on the practice sentences in Chapters 1 and 2, you probably noticed that making one change usually forced you to make one or more other changes in the sentence. You began to recognize that English is a "word order language."

That means that English syntax (organization of sentence parts) creates meaning by the placement of words in a particular order. Paying conscious attention to this fact can help you say what you intend to say, and frequently help you eliminate many unnecessary words as well.

Dr. Ernest Brennecke of Columbia University dreamed up the following set of sentences:

1. Only I hit him in the eye yesterday.
2. I only hit him in the eye yesterday.
3. I hit only him in the eye yesterday.
4. I hit him only in the eye yesterday.
5. I hit him in the only eye yesterday.
6. I hit him in the eye only yesterday.
7. I hit him in the eye yesterday only.

In this example, you can see that the meaning of "only" depends on its placement in the sentence, and the meaning of the sentence depends on the meaning of "only."

In sentence 1, "only" means "I and no other person," and the sentence confesses responsibility.

In sentence 2, "only" means "merely," and the sentence means that poking someone in the eye doesn't amount to much of an assault.

In sentences 3 and 4, ""only" means "solely," and the speaker is trying to limit his responsibility to an assault on one person (sentence 3) or on one part of one person's anatomy (sentence 4).

In sentence 5, "only" means "single," and the assault looks considerably less forgivable - hitting a poor, partially-sighted fellow.

In sentence 6, "only" means "just" or "as recently as," and the sentence implies that here the victim comes again, looking for another poke in the peeper.

In sentence 7, "only" again means "solely," and the sentence claims that the speaker is innocent of any previous or subsequent assault.

In short, placing a word before another word or phrase generally indicates that it answers a question about the following word or phrase:

1. "only I" - you and how many others?
2. "only hit him in the eye" - what other damage did you to him?
3. "only him" - who else did you hit?
4. "only in the eye" - where else did you hit him?
5. "only eye" - how many eyes does he have?
6. "only yesterday" - how recently did you hit him?
7. "yesterday only" - how many times have you hit him in the eye?

A word like the "only" in our example modifies the meaning of the word or phrase it applies to. A modifier may be a single word or a group of words that make one unit of meaning (phrase). Misplaced modifiers cause many sentences to say things their writers didn't intend to say:

Still in her flimsy nightgown, the police marched Julie to the patrol car.

The writer obviously meant to say that the police didn't even allow Julie to get dressed before they took her away. The writer probably wanted the reader to feel indignant at their lack of consideration for Julie's sense of decency. Instead, the writer said that the police were in Julie's nightgown. The reader can't be certain whether Julie was in there with them or not. In either case, the reader will likely react to the image the sentence creates with laughter, not indignation. The writer should have said,

"The police marched Julie, still in her flimsy nightgown, down the steps."

This example suggests a general rule: put modifiers as close as possible to the words or phrases they modify - generally right before them. Practice doing that with the following sentences.

Practice

1. After raising the Titanic, hundreds of jewels were found by the salvage crew.

2. Gussied up like a cheap strumpet, the principal sent the teenager home to change into more appropriate clothing.

3. While walking to work, the birds singing were what I noticed.

4. For all his brilliance, happiness was never found by Cole Porter.

5. After giving his speech, the audience reaction was less than pleasing to Jason.

6. With several young puppies, little rest is granted to the mother Collie.

7. After winning the contest, the prize was quite a disappointment. (Obviously, you'll need to give a name to the person who found the prize disappointing.)

8. Shana saw with her mother several insurance salesmen. (Two possible rewrites, one more interesting than the other)

9. With two of her kits playing, I saw the mother fox outside her den.

10. Under three different sets of titles Len Deighton has written the same three spy novel plots three times.

After we'd been working through sentence construction for a few weeks, which had given us a chance to get to know each other a little, I could start taking a lighter approach, which I did when attacking the next common problem with student writing: the tendency to use "elevated" diction - that is, to use words from a thesaurus or from the jargon of some other academic discipline, such as sociology. I'd introduce a discussion of diction with an ironic quote from Steve Martin:

Writing Is Simple

"Writing is one of the most easy, pain-free, and happy ways to pass the time in all the arts....Sometimes, it is true, agony visits the head of a writer. At these moments, I stop writing and relax with a coffee at my favorite restaurant, knowing that words can be changed, rethought, fiddled with, and, of course, ultimately denied."
- Steve Martin, "Writing Is Easy!" *Pure Drivel*, p.5

Probably you have been forced to write during your school years, so you already know that writing is not easy. It requires that you put what's in your head and heart into a code - whatever language you happen to speak - so that other people, who are not inside either of those organs, can understand what's in there. Each of those other people knows some of the code, and every one of them understands every word of the code differently. Not easy? Impossible.

I've been trying to do it for fifty years, and trying to teach other people to do it for thirty. I've learned a few things that make the task of writing simple, and those make up the first part of this class.

Hitting a decent crosscourt backhand shot on a tennis court is simple. Writing a sentence that can be understood by most readers is simple. Neither one is easy. Both require practice.

"Hemingway: I rewrote the ending to *Farewell to Arms*, the last page of it, thirty-nine times before I was satisfied.

Interviewer: Was there some technical problem there? What was it that had stumped you?

Hemingway: Getting the words right." [Plimpton]

When Hemingway was trying to get the words right on that page, he had already become an internationally known correspondent for some of the best American, Canadian and European newspapers. He had published a collection of short stories and his first novel, *The Sun Also Rises*. A successful professional writer, and there he was, rewriting one page 39 times, "getting the words right." What could he have meant? What can we learn from it?

He did not mean making the words complicated, difficult, unusual, exotic. He once said of his fellow writer William Faulkner, "Poor Faulkner. Does he really think big emotions come from big words? He thinks I don't know the ten-dollar words. I know them all right. But there are older and simpler and better words, and those are the ones I use." [Plimpton] Another fellow writer, Katherine Anne Porter, agreed with Hemingway: "But there is a basic pure human speech that exists in every language. And that is the language of the poet and the writer....You have to speak clearly and simply and purely in a language that a six-year-old child can understand...." So did the poet William Carlos Williams: "I couldn't speak like the academy. It had to be modified by the conversation about [around] me. As Marianne Moore [a fellow poet)] used to say, a language dogs and cats could understand." [Plimpton]

That would be a simple language. Simple doesn't mean easy.

"Anybody can play weird, that's easy. What's hard is to be as simple as Bach. Making the simple complicated is commonplace. Making the complicated simple - awesomely simple - that's creativity." - Charles Mingus' response to a reporter asking about creativity. [Mingus]

I told many students over the years what good writers and thinkers they were - many students who'd never heard a word of praise from a teacher, or, often, from anyone else. I have a drawer full of cards and letters from some of those students, telling me how that praise and encouragement improved their lives. The praise meant something to them because I'd successfully performed a part of myself - the part that would never lie about any piece of writing, no matter who wrote it. Looking back, I think I'm proudest of what I did for those students, not necessarily the ones who went on to become successful writers - the ones who went on to become successful people.

I'll conclude with other exercises and examples I used over many years. Those concerning mechanics and grammar I put together because I kept seeing students having problems in those particular areas.

Commas and Periods by Ear

Commas and periods are the two punctuation marks drawn directly from speech. A comma means, "That's the end of that part of the thought, but it's not the end of the sentence yet." A period means, "That's the end of this sentence." In speech, we make commas by pausing without dropping our voices in pitch, and we make periods by both pausing and dropping our voices in pitch. ("Pitch" means how high or low a tone sounds.)

1. Read the following paragraph aloud and practice hearing the pauses without drop in pitch (commas) and the pauses where the pitch drops (periods).

"Finally it is time to leave. Now the camera is in the front seat of the car, sitting where Kelvin is sitting. We see what he sees. Slowly the terrain changes. Winding, wooded roads give way to straight, one-lane roads. The foliage recedes from the highway. Then we are on a freeway. The environment has become speeding cars, overpasses, underpasses, tunnels. Soon, we are in a city. There is noise, light, buildings everywhere. The natural landscape is submerged, invisible. Homocentric landscapes, abstract reality prevail. From there it's a fast cut to space...." [Mander]

2. Read the same paragraph aloud, but substitute nonsense syllables for the words. This will help you concentrate on the pitch differences.

3. Practice listening to the following unpunctuated paragraphs aloud, putting in the commas and periods as you hear them.

The war bit into Fields deeply he discussed it at great length one afternoon with Lionel and John Barrymore Gene Fowler and John Decker the artist their hatred of the foe provoked them to have quite a few drinks and the drinks increased their hatred of the foe around four o'clock in full battle humor they got in a car and drove down to enlist at the time besides being fairly well along in both years and alcohol most of them were suffering from some incapacitating illness for example it was thought best to take Lionel Barrymore's wheelchair along in case they got immediate overseas assignment his colleagues assisted him from the car to his chair after which they pushed him in the girl at the recruiting center after her first shock had them fill out several forms upon which she noted many doubtful entries John Barrymore gave his age as 19 Fowler outlined somewhat more military experience than General Pershing's and Fields requested duty as a commando the girl looked them over carefully then made what all of them cherished as a topping example of spot gubernatorial wit "who sent you she said the enemy?" [Taylor]

To a mechanic a "shot" fan belt was a worn one to a bartender a "shot" was a one-ounce glass of whiskey to a decathlon champion a "shot" was an iron ball to be thrown as far as he could throw it to a tennis player a "shot" was what he stroked over a net to a junkie or a physician a "shot" was an injection by hypodermic syringe to a motion-picture director a "shot" was any given camera setup and to Morris Bloom a "shot" was something fired from a gun you could buy off a shelf like a ripe banana i was very happy I wasn't learning English as a foreign language I was far too old to be taking a shot at such a formidable task. [McBain]

Punctuation Marks to Avoid at Almost All Cost

1. **;** The semicolon

The only remaining use for this punctuation mark is to separate independent clauses within the same sentence:

> I fought the law; the law won.

This is correct, but semicolons seem to affect people who start using them much as heroin or cocaine affect people who start using them. Addiction rapidly ensues. You never *have* to use a semicolon, and you'll be better off if you never develop a taste for them. The example sentence can also be written in two preferable ways:

> A. I fought the law, and the law won. (That's how Gene Pitney wrote it.)
> B. I fought the law. The law won.

2. **!** The exclamation point

This mark is used to represent a very loud voice, raised to emphasize the importance of what is being said. If you say what you have to say simply and clearly, its importance will be clear. You will do little writing that requires you to holler at your reader.

Plurals as Plurals

If you write, "A sailor is at the mercy of the sea," you mean - as any reader will understand - that all sailors are at the mercy of the sea. A common convention in English writing allows you to use a single subject to represent all subjects of its category.

Don't do it - not because it's "incorrect," but because it's likely to get you into trouble with pronouns and verbs later in the sentence. If you mean to make a statement about a group, make it in the plural.

1. A person can't always get what he or she wants.
   People can't always get what they want.

2. When an athlete takes steroids, he or she also takes on long-term risks.
   When athletes take steroids, they also take on long-term risks.

(*Anyone, everyone, someone, no one, anybody, everybody, somebody, nobody* - these are all singular.)

3. Anybody who bets on the Cubs should have his or her head examined.
   People who bet on the Cubs should have their heads examined.

Put the next three sentences into plural form:

4. Everyone was crowded around the coat rack in search of his or her coat

5. The cover does not tell much about the contents of a book.

6. A mammal is special form of vertebrate.

~~ING~~

Present participles are verbs with an "ing" stuck on the end: Walk (verb) -- Walking (present participle). A participle is not a verb. It may form part of a verb (hence its name, *parti*ciple), but it can never act as a verb alone, so it leads to many sentence fragments and other grammatical errors. 'Walking down the road to the poorhouse" is a fragment - it has neither subject nor verb. *Use verbs, not present participles. Learn to notice 'ing," and get rid of it.*

1. Walking down the street, the birds sang to me.
2. Before making his presentation, the electricity failed.
3. He saw her waiting for the bus. (Who was waiting for the bus?)
4. Sending the letter, noting its contents before he did. (Who sent the letter?)

5. The new part failed immediately. Leading to another two-day shutdown.

Keep It Short: Some Horrible Examples

"It was in a bemusement without heat or envy at a condition which could supply a man with the obvious leisure and means to spend his days painting such as this and his evenings playing the piano and feeding liquor to people whom he ignored and (in one case, at least) whose names he did not even bother to catch."
-William Faulkner, *The Wild Palms,* Random House, 1939

"The views which he sometimes had of his own unworthiness, and of the excellency and glory of the plan of salvation, as they are recorded by himself, are so far beyond anything that falls within the experience of ordinary Christians, that they are no doubt often contemplated with surprise, and sometimes, perhaps, may even be thought to savor of enthusiasm; but it admits of no question that they were not only the genuine workings of faith, but that they marked a maturity and elevation of Christian character that cast the highest attainments even of the better part of Christians in the shade."
- "Jonathan Edwards," *The Christian Parlor Magazine*

"But as to a woman of sense and spirit, the admiration of even the noblest and most gifted man, is esteemed as nothing, so long as she remains conscious of possessing no directly influencing and practical sorcery over his soul; and as notwithstanding all his intellectual superiority to his mother, Pierre, through the unavoidable weakness of inexperienced and unexpanded youth, was strangely docile to the maternal tuitions in nearly all the thing which thus far had any ways interested or affected him; therefore it was, that to Mary Glendinning this reverence of Pierre was invested with all the proudest delights and witcheries of self-complacency, which it is possible for the most conquering virgin to feel. "   - Herman Melville, *Pierre,* HarperCollins, 1995

Topic and Topic Sentence

The emergence of AIDS, Ebola, and any number of other rain-forest agents appears to be a natural consequence of the ruin of the tropical biosphere. The emerging viruses are surfacing from ecologically damaged parts of the earth. Many of them come form the tattered edges of tropical rain forest, or they come from tropical savanna that is being settled rapidly by people. The tropical rain forests are the deep reservoirs of life on the planet, containing most of the world's plant and animal species. The rain forests are also its largest reservoirs of viruses, since all living things carry viruses. When viruses come out of an ecosystem, they tend to spread in waves through the human population, like echoes from the dying biosphere. Here are the names of some emerging viruses: Lassa. Rift Valley. Oropouche. Rocio. Q. Guanarito. VEE. Monkeypox. Dengue. Chikungonya. The hanta-viruses. Machupo. Junin. The rabieslike strains Mokola and Duvenhage. LeDantec. The Kyasanur Forest brain virus. Then there is HIV - which is very much an emerging virus, because its penetration of the human species is increasing rapidly, with no end in sight. The Semliki Forest agent. Crimean-congo. Sindbis.O'nyongnyong. Nameless Sao Paulo. Marburg. Ebola Sudan. Ebola Zaire. Ebola Reston.

- Richard Preston, *The Hot Zone*

Put your topic sentence first in the paragraph. It will tell your readers what to expect in the rest of the paragraph. If your paragraph is long or full of detailed examples, like this one, it will give your readers a place to look back to and remember why they're reading what they're reading.

The Introductory Paragraph: What, Who, Why?

In your opening paragraph, particularly in a letter or e-mail, you should answer three questions for your readers: *What* is the subject about which you're writing, *who* are you - that is, why are you qualified to comment on the subject - and *why* are you writing about this subject?

Dear Postmaster Schentag:

I write to recognize the excellence of a longtime USPS employee, Walt Pryor. Mr. Pryor has been stationed at the North End Office at 2940 North Prospect for many years, and is soon slated to retire from the service. [These two sentences answer what and why.] I have observed Mr. Pryor at work for the past 14 years since I moved to my present address. Since I operate a mail-order used book business, I am a nearly daily user of the North End Office, so I've had the opportunity to see Mr. Pryor at work during many peak mailing hours. [These two sentences answer who.]

He has been consistently efficient, calm, good-humored and unflappable during the busiest times. He is one of those rare individuals who can conduct pleasant, humane conversations with his customers without losing his concentration on the postal task at hand. He is extraordinarily knowledgeable of postal regulations. In fact, I have never heard him asked a question to which he did not have the answer. This deep knowledge of his job allows him to work steadily and efficiently without ever evincing any sense of hurry or stress.

Walt Pryor, in short, is not only a superior worker, but a genuine human. After his retirement, I suggest that the USPS ought to consider hiring him as a consultant in the training of personnel.
Sincerely,
Malcolm McCollum

Summation - How to Conclude a Paragraph

(The writer has taken to reading fishing books in order to learn how to catch a mammoth trout he's discovered in a small pond near his house.)

The angler had metamorphosed into the ichthyologist, and the prevailing prose reflected the change - if mud can be said to reflect. I found myself correcting it as I had done freshman themes in my years as a professor. You had to hack your way through it as through a thicket. Participles dangled, person and number got separated and lost, cliches were rank, thesaurusitis and sesquipedalianism ran rampant, and the rare unsplit infinitive seemed out of place, a rose among nettles. Yet, instead of weeding their gardens, these writers endeavored to grow exotics in them: orchids, passion flowers. Inside each of them was imprisoned a poet, like the prince inside the toad. **What came out was a richness of embarrassments: shoddy prose patched with purple - beautifully written without first being well written.**
-William Humphrey, *My Moby Dick,* Doubleday, 1978

At the end of the paragraph, sum up and reinforce the point of the paragraph. Again, you will make your readers' lives easier if you lend them this helping hand. People tend to like people who make their lives easier.

Simplicity and Brevity

"As I have tried to show, modern writing at its worst does not consist in picking out words for the sake of their meaning and inventing images in order to make the meaning clearer. It consists in gumming together long strips of words which have already been set in order by someone else, and making the results presentable by sheer humbug. The attraction of this way of writing is that it is easy. It is easier - even quicker, once you have the habit - to say, "In my opinion it is a not unjustifiable assumption that" than to say "I think".... By using stale metaphors, similes and idioms, you save much mental effort, at the cost of leaving your meaning vague, not only for your reader but for yourself.

"Here is a well-known verse from Ecclesiastes:

> I returned, and saw under the sun, that the race is not to the swift,
> nor the battle to the strong, neither yet bread to the wise, nor yet

riches to men of understanding, nor yet favour to men of skill; but time and chance happeneth to them all.

"Here it is in modern English:

Objective consideration of contemporary phenomena compels the conclusion that success or failure in competitive activities exhibits no tendency to be commensurate with innate capacity, but that a considerable element of the unpredictable must invariably be taken into account.

-George Orwell, "Politics and the English Language," *Collected Essays, Volume IV,* Harcourt, Brace, 1968

Simple does not mean easy. As Orwell points out, using cliches ("think outside the box," "at the end of the day") is much easier than actually imagining, and putting into clear, simple words, what you are trying to say. The disadvantages of this practice are that both you and your readers may end up with no clear idea of what you are trying to say.

Chances are, you won't grow up wanting to write when you don't have to. You can take this chapter, then, as a sort of first-aid kit, to be kept in your trunk in case of emergencies. I still think it's full of useful advice for anyone who has to write for any reason, as many people have to. I hope it also illustrates that paying attention to language and how it works can provide some fun. Work is more fun than fun.

An Imperfect Trial

On the night of September 19, 1974, someone murdered the owner of the Suezy Massage Parlor on South Nevada Avenue in Colorado Springs. The owner, Sun Ok Cousin, was the Korean wife of a retired Army man. Her assistant, Elizabeth Yon Cha Lee, a very recent arrival from Korea, was attacked with a knife and left in the building her assailant had set on fire, but she survived.

On October 30, Park Estep, an active duty soldier, was arrested and later brought to trial. The jury took two days to find Estep guilty of first degree murder, first degree assault, first degree arson, and aggravated robbery. They recommended leniency in sentencing. Presiding Judge Hunter Hardeman interpreted that recommendation as an authorization to give Estep the maximum sentence available (Colorado had no capital punishment at that time), which he did.

After Park Estep was convicted, his criminal defense investigator Jerry Mosier spent the next couple of years trying to talk me into taking an interest in the case. Finally, Jerry wore me down - he was not a man to take "no" for an answer- and he brought the case files, enough to nearly fill a foot locker, over to my house.

I think it was the crime scene photos that hooked me first. I'd never seen such photos before, and I hated what I saw. I also hated the case brought against Park, the more I looked at it closely. Today, I still think it was a case that should never have been prosecuted, but I'm also startled by my own ignorance. I knew nothing of the ways the criminal justice system worked, or of the ways juries behaved, or of the power of the press to manipulate public opinion. I would soon begin to learn about those things, and to learn more about the pathetic weakness of reasoned argument to bring about change.

At some point during my study of the case, Jerry Mosier took me down to Old Max in Canon City to meet Park. I don't remember much of anything we talked about. I think the realities of incarceration - the sounds of slamming steel and angry voices echoing against stone walls - stunned me. I do remember how calm and sane and unthreatening Park seemed. And I remember driving back to the Springs with Jerry in his truck, Jerry saying how much going to that place made him want a beer, adding, "Damn it! Park ought to be able to have a damn *beer* with us!" It would be a long time before that happened. Shortly after we got back home, I began writing. Surprisingly, the *Rocky Mountain News*, then Denver's second major newspaper, printed what I wrote:

Did Murder Jury Convict the Wrong Man?
Rocky Mountain News, 1/22/78

Park Estep stands to be an inmate of the State Prison until near the end of this century, convicted of a particularly terrible murder, unless he wins an appeal of his conviction. A few months ago I was persuaded to take an interest in his case, and I eventually became curious enough to study the transcript of his trial. That transcript convinced me that our need for justice can somehow overwhelm our sense of justice. And it left me with a considerably more concrete concern. I don't think Park Estep is guilty.

On Sept. 19, 1974, Sun Ok Cousin, a Korean masseuse, was murdered in Suezy's Massage Parlor in Colorado Springs. Young Ja Lee, a Korean employee, was stabbed in the back and throat. The massage parlor was set on fire, and some passing security guards saw smoke and helped Miss Lee out of the building. She survived the attack to testify.

After Miss Lee had partly recovered from her wounds, she identified a photograph of Park Estep, a soldier stationed at Fort Carson. This, she said, was a picture of the man who attacked her. Estep, a specialist fourth class, was arrested and placed in a line-up, and Miss Lee again identified him as her attacker. Two soldiers who had been at the car wash next to the massage parlor were equally certain that Estep's truck closely resembled the truck they had seen parked outside the parlor on the night of the crime.

The post-mortem examination of Sun Ok Cousin's body revealed that she had been shot in the head with what is known as "shot shell," almost certainly from a .38 caliber pistol. She had had sexual contact fairly recently with a man whose blood group was type A. Park Estep had owned a .38 caliber pistol and been in possession of shot shells at the time of the murder, and his blood group is type A.

Those are the facts of the case against Park Estep. Little was suggested by way of motive, although the prosecution did imply that Mrs. Estep had said that she and her husband were short of cash around the time of the crime.

District Attorney Robert Russel, who personally prosecuted the case against Estep, still thinks it's a strong one. All the pieces of evidence, particularly the identification by Miss Lee, are such that "Jimmy the Greek could give you some pretty good odds" that Estep is guilty, he says.

It is obvious that one piece of evidence stands out: Young Ja Lee positively identified Estep as the man who came into the massage parlor and bound her wrists with a coat hanger and cut her throat and stabbed her in the back. That piece of evidence, at first glance, seems to make the rest of the evidence of no more than academic interest. If I examine the other evidence first, it is not to try to disguise the fact that Miss Lee's testimony is critical, but to emphasize that fact.

Park Estep did own a .38 caliber pistol at the time of the murder. It is impossible to determine how many .38 caliber pistols existed in Colorado Springs on the night of the crime; any one of them might have fired the round which killed Mrs. Cousin. A few weeks after that night, Estep sold his .38 to an acquaintance. He kept written records of the sale and voluntarily told the police that he had owned and sold the pistol.

He also volunteered the fact that he owned shot shells; his wife, he told the police, had bought him a small number of them for his birthday. Shot shells, which replace the ordinary bullet with a plastic capsule of bird shot, are designed for use against small game and snakes. The Esteps were avid campers, and Mrs. Estep had bought the shells for use against snakes. At the time of the murder, more than 8 million rounds of shot shell had been sold in the United States. It is not possible, once a shot shell has been fired, to determine what particular gun has fired it, unless the shell casing happens to be available. No shell casings were found at the murder scene.

Park Estep's blood group is type A. This fact places him among slightly more than 37 million American males.

Another piece of circumstantial evidence which supposedly linked Park Estep to the crime was the identification of his truck by two soldiers, one of whom worked at the car wash. These two men recalled a number of details about the truck they saw: it had no hubcaps, black tire rims or white lettering on the back of the tailgate. They did not recall seeing military or manufacturer's stickers on the vehicle, though one of them specifically looked for the military sticker which would have identified the truck as belonging to a fellow GI. The rear bumper they saw had a pattern raised from the metal. None of these details applies to Park Estep's truck.

The memories of the two men, in other words, tended to dispute their identification of Estep's truck as the one they saw near the massage parlor the night of the murder. The principal witness of the two admitted that he was "not certain" of his identification. If you believe the two men were capable of remembering the truck they saw in detail, then the truck they saw was not Park Estep's. If you believe that they could but imperfectly remember (as most of us could) the truck, then their testimony simply includes Estep in the group of persons who own or have access to late model, red Chevrolet pickup trucks with tool boxes.

Park Estep was convicted of aggravated robbery (in addition to first-degree murder and assault and arson), perhaps indicating that the jury gave some credence to the suggestion that the Esteps were short of cash, and that Estep had entered the massage parlor intending to rob it. It is hard to understand how that credence could have developed. A certified public accountant presented documented evidence that the Esteps were, as of Sept. 19, 1974, about $11,000 in the black, and had in their possession, in addition to several bank accounts, an undeposited check for $853.

The Esteps were not short of cash, nor was their long-term financial position anything but promising. Nor had Park Estep ever been accused of stealing anything (or any act or crime of violence or any other felony; the sum total of his previous criminal record was an arrest for vagrancy when he was a teen-ager, hitchhiking across the country.

What remains, of course, is the fact that Young Ja Lee, who was stabbed and cut by someone, and whose account of events at the massage parlor strongly indicated that her assailant was also the killer of Mrs. Cousin, testified that Park Estep was that someone. It is natural for us to assume that a person would clearly remember the man who attacked her with a knife. It is natural; but is it correct and reasonable to make that assumption?

Young Ja Lee had been in the United States about three months when she was attacked. I ask myself how accurately *I* would perceive or remember the appearance of a Korean who threatened me with a gun and stabbed me. Of course, I can't be certain, but I don't believe my perception or memory would be at all good. Growing up in Chicago, I twice had occasion to look at people who were pointing guns at me. I don't believe I could have identified either one of them, though I still remember how large and dark the muzzles of those pistols looked. As a GI in Germany, I was once beaten up on the street by a group of German teenagers. I could not have identified any of them; I was too busy trying to protect myself. My own small experience of how well I perceive threatening strangers leads me to give no particular credence to Miss Lee's identification of her assailant. In the words of Alex L. Gregory, a noted criminologist: "The honest but mistaken witness is one of the most serious problems in our system of justice.... unfortunately the mistaken witness is all too frequently the most positive."

Miss Lee first Identified Park Estep's likeness from a group of Polaroid photos of men whose appearance in some way corresponded to the description she had given of her assailant. The detective showing the photos immediately stopped the proceedings, turned on his tape recorder and caused Miss Lee to re-enact her identification of Estep's photograph. He then asked her repeatedly if she were sure, committing her very fully to her identification of the photograph. When she later identified Park Estep in a physical line-up, it is a question whether she was simply identifying the man whose photograph she had seen, rather than the man she may or may not have remembered clearly as her assailant. Given the confusion possible in a Korean woman's perceptions of a menacing Occidental male, it may be that the photograph simply supplanted Miss Lee's memory of her assailant.

That argument sounds considerably less tortured when certain repeated assertions by Miss Lee are considered. Park Estep, in the photograph Miss Lee identified and in person, had a rather prominent mustache. When she first identified the photograph, Miss Lee steadfastly insisted that her assailant had *not* had a mustache. She did not say that she didn't remember a mustache; she said, again and again, that the man who stabbed her did not have a mustache at the time, but now he "wore one." Numerous witnesses testified that on Sept. 19, 1974, Park Estep did have a mustache. In a number of other details, Park Estep did not fit Miss Lee's description of her assailant. (Her description and identification of the truck she saw were too uncertain to be worthy of much comment. Her first description of the truck, for instance, gave its color as white. Estep's truck is red.

In other words, if you believe Miss Lee very clearly and accurately recalled her attacker, then her insistence that he had no mustache destroys her identification of Park Estep. If you believe that her memory of her attacker was so imprecise that she did not notice or remember his mustache and incorrectly remembered other aspects of his appearance, then her identification of Park Estep is of questionable value.

The question of the mustache is at the heart of Estep's first-round success in the appeal of his conviction. The state Court of Appeals ordered him a new trial on the grounds that the court failed to hear a potentially crucial piece of evidence. The evidence was to be the testimony of a Korean pastor to the effect that, to a Korean, a mustache is not taken lightly; it is a sign of age and high station. The Korean's testimony was to bolster the defense's contention that the presence of a mustache is something that Miss Lee would not be likely to forget.

That decision has been appealed by District Attorney Russel. A decision by the state Supreme Court is expected soon.

Miss Lee's entire account of what happened that night in the massage parlor was never seriously questioned, even though several aspects of her account did not correspond with physical evidence at the scene. The possibility that her account was partly or wholly fabricated was evidently never considered. If, for instance, Miss Lee knew either her attacker of the likely identity of her attacker's employers, and felt that she was still in danger, might she not have felt moved to identify someone other than her actual assailant? That is speculation, but not entirely without foundation. Three nights before the murder, Mrs. Cousin and a friend who was visiting her at Suezy's Massage Parlor both received phone calls from an unidentified male. He told them he was going to kill them and burn the parlor down if they didn't go out of business. During this period, a good deal of conflict was occurring in the city within and about the massage parlor business.

The closer I look at Miss Lee's Identification of Park Estep, the less convincing it seems. But without it, there is simply no evidence whatsoever to connect Estep to Mrs. Cousin's murder.

My presentation of the case against Park Estep has admittedly been selective; the trial transcript runs over a thousand pages. I have tried to be fair, complete and accurate in my presentation of the case. If I have come anywhere close to being so, I am am left wondering how under heaven a jury could have brought in a verdict of guilty beyond reasonable doubt. Perhaps the jury had some questions of its own. They found Park Estep guilty of murder, assault, robbery and arson. And recommended leniency in sentencing.

I stopped being puzzled by this verdict when I saw, for the first time, the color photographs of the murdered body of Mrs. Sun Ok Cousin as it was left by her killer. I'd rather not write about those pictures. They are disgusting and heartbreaking.

Mrs. Cousin's body was left naked. I don't mean only that she was left with no clothing. I mean her body was left robbed of the dignity and respect which is our only real clothing in this life. She was left on her back, one leg bent at the knee, foot resting against the calf of her other, outstretched leg. The positioning looked like an obscene caricature of the pose in which an artist might paint a well-loved model.

But there was nothing of love in the rest of it. Mrs. Cousin's temple had a hole blown into it. Her eyelids were swollen nearly shut. Her body was splattered with blood, and nearly half of it was covered with second and third-degree burns. Third-degree burns blacken the flesh and split it down to the white of bone. The deputy coroner was quite certain that Mrs. Cousin had been set on fire before she was shot.

There is no way to use words to give the effect of those pictures. They show a human being treated with something more awful than hate - with a contempt so total that it flows over onto all human life. What was done to her was a statement, a statement that said this: Human beings are merely worthless hunks of meat, to be killed and tortured and wasted for sport or gain.

I felt, and I think anyone who saw those pictures would feel, a tremendous need to say, No - that statement is a lie, and whoever made that statement is so hopelessly far from humanity that he must be found and put away from all of us who hope to be human. I needed to say that this could not be allowed.

I believe that everyone who saw that body, or the photographs of that body, very probably felt the same way. I think that is why the case against Park Estep, which seems so frail in print, convinced the prosecution and the jurors: they needed so deeply to find the person who had made this awful statement and to cast him out of contact with their community. (The jurors have agreed not to talk about the case, the foreman, former Colorado Springs newscaster Bill Yeager, told me. Two did so anyway but said nothing helpful about the photographs.)

I think that the need for justice, or something even deeper than justice, was so pressing that it clouded the very ideal of justice which ordinarily tempers human behavior in a court of law. In the words of Estep's attorney, Doug Thompson: "Mr. Estep stands before this court accused of one of the gravest crimes a man could be charged with, and sometimes I think that all of us....become corrupted by the magnitude of the accusation, and, as such, do not see the evidence for what it is."

If all those who shared responsibility for the conviction of Park Estep were, in fact, overwhelmed by the magnitude of the crimes of which he was accused, I certainly do not write to condemn them. I can't in honesty say that I would not have been led, in the heat of the trial and the horror of the crime, to blink at what now seem to me the tremendous weaknesses of the case against Park Estep.

But if, as Estep maintains and as I believe, he is innocent, then his conviction has done more than leave us with a man wrongfully convicted in our penitentiary. Alex Gregory makes one more observation about the serious problem of the mistaken witness: "He not only convicts the innocent but he permits the guilty to go free." If Park Estep is innocent, then the person who made a statement with the body and spirit of

Mrs. Sun Ok Cousin has had 3 and 1/2 years in which to make more such statements. By our very need to reassert the sanctity and dignity of human life, we may have become unwitting accomplices to the person - whoever and whatever that person may be - whose inhumanity we sought to condemn.

My, how earnest and NPR I sounded. I especially like the suggestion I made that the prosecution's eyes were clouded by the need for justice. Neither Park nor Jerry had told me, then, that District Attorney Robert Russel, in his customary post-sundown condition, had visited Estep when he was still in the city jail awaiting trial. "I know you're not guilty," Russel leered. "I'm gonna convict you anyway." Maybe something other than a need for justice was clouding his eyes. What it was became clearer in a few years.

The appeal granted by the Colorado Court of Appeals was overturned by the Colorado Supreme Court on the grounds that while the defendant had a right to a *fair* trial, he did not have the right to a *perfect* trial. It looked as if Park Estep would be living in prison until 1996.

Despite his continued work as a criminal defense investigator, Jerry was never content to let Park's conviction stand, nor was Park's local attorney, Dick Tegtmeier. Jerry kept pursuing suspects the police had either abandoned or never investigated, flogging his old truck all over the country.

The first ten years after Park's conviction was summed up nicely by *Denver Post* reporter Jim Carrier:

Friends Kept 10-Year Vigil

Jim Carrier, *Denver Post, 9/9/1984*

Colorado Springs - Every month for eight years, Nan Rose would get in her '75 Grenada and drive the 35 miles from Colorado Springs to the state prison in Canon City to visit Park Estep. She would go on Saturday, arriving an hour or so after the big rush of relatives visiting convicts, and she would stay about four hours.

She made the trip at least once a month. Sometimes more often. Every month until last December.

That's when they found a brain tumor, and lung cancer. They gave her from two days to a year to live and told her she couldn't drive again.

So Nan Rose got somebody to take her to Canon City.

Such was the dedication of one person who believed in Park Estep. A person who knew in her heart he was no killer. A woman so dedicated to Estep that she became mother to him, and grandmother to his daughter.

She was one person - one of many - who believe Park Estep is innocent of murder.

For a decade, since Estep was convicted of murdering massage parlor owner Sun Ok Cousin, a group of people have kept a vigil for him. Not as a group, but as individuals: clergy, members of his church, Army buddies, a legal investigator, lawyers - maybe 50 people - who in their own way and on their own time, worked and prayed and waited for the day when the system would work. For the day Park Estep would walk out of prison a free man.

Like the lawyer, now a judge, who wrote the governor on his behalf.

Like the newsman-turned-investigator who ran around the country chasing leads on his own time in a consuming effort that took its toll on his own life.

Like the three dozen people who wrote him regularly, and the half-dozen families who visited him in prison.

Like his lawyer, who spent thousands of dollars of his own money to try to find something, anything that would free Estep.

Like Nancy Rose.

All believers

"We are all people who believed Park was innocent, right from the beginning," said Rose, a 54-year-old widow. "I sat through every day of that trial, and came out thoroughly convinced he was innocent. I used to come out of the prison in Old Max with tears and cry all the way home. He was no more guilty than I am."

Because of chemotherapy and radiation, Rose's brain tumor virtually disintegrated; but it left a blind spot in her eye and she stopped driving. She caught rides to the prison a couple of times, but found the trip too taxing. Since then, she has written and he has called, including an excited call last Saturday that told of new evidence - a possible confession to the crime by serial killer Ottis Toole.

"I'm thrilled," said Rose. "I have great hope. I've prayed and prayed about this. I have never doubted him."

"I never believed - ever - that he committed the crime," said Richard Borchers, recently appointed a district judge in the 17th Judicial District. Several years ago, when Estep came before the governor's commutation committee, Borchers wrote to Gov. Dick Lamm and recommended that the governor set Estep free.

"I felt we had an innocent man in one of our prisons," the judge said.

At the time of the slaying, Borchers was a legal assistance officer with the Army at Fort Carson, where Estep recently had been assigned. Aware that a grand jury was investigating him, Estep went to Borchers, who advised him to say nothing. Later, Borchers helped the defense by arranging a Korean language interpreter and by testifying for Estep.

"Park was a good soldier, a good human being," said Borchers, who in 3 1/2 years in the Army tried more than 300 courts martial - some of them, he said, involving "awful, awful" soldiers.

"The Army has a tendency to turn its back on soldiers in trouble off-base," said Borchers. In Estep's case, "they didn't do it because they had faith in the guy."

MORE THAN A CASE

Estep's defense team came to regard the case as more of a cause than just another murder. Money (they seem to remember the figure $15,000) put up by Estep's relatives covered expenses, but not their time. After losing the trial, they worked free for the next 3 1/2 years to conduct appeals.

"We felt an innocent person was convicted," said lawyer Richard Tegtmeier. "That hangs really heavy on us. No lawyer wants the system to fail. We spend hundreds and hundreds of hours, past the conviction, on this case. Much of it Park never knew about.

"Many times we'd say, 'Let's forget about this case,' and we'd forget about it," said Tegtmeier. "But something would come up and we would start over."

It became an obsession for Tegtmeier's investigator, Jerry Mosier.

"I had the easy part, to help direct the investigation," said Tegtmeier. "Jerry was putting in the long hours on the road."

Mosier, 44, a former newspaperman, had jumped into the murder case with the enthusiasm of an investigative reporter but the knowledge of a rookie. The conviction stung him, and for the next 10 years he spent money he didn't have and time he would never regain trying to recoup the loss.

He ate sprouts he grew in an old wreck of a house that he rented for fix-up labor. He borrowed Tegtmeier's credit cards, bummed cash where he could, and drove a beat-up pickup that could hardly make it across town. But he pushed it to Kansas and Oregon, Washington and Missouri, chasing leads. He rigged up a can on the engine to heat food and water as he drove.

Mosier even took a job as a house painter once because he "wanted to be in the mind" of a fresh suspect, a housepainter. He wanted to know when the guy drank, what his sex drive was. But mostly he worked just to fill his gas tank, to run down yet another lead. He spent so much time on the case it ruined personal relationships. It also got in the way during the years his son grew to be a man.

"I let the case get to me," said Mosier. "It's my case. It's the only case not closed in 10 years."

Mosier's "office" in those days was a bunch of 3-by-5 cards stuck in his hip pocket. Today, he has a one-room walk-up office right out of a private eye movie set. Below a faded mirror, a half-eaten watermelon and a horn-handled knife sit in an old sink. There's a tall, narrow radiator and a bentwood coat rack with no coat. A map on one wall was used in his last murder investigation. On another hangs a "David's sling," the primitive Biblical weapon for throwing stones at giants. The symbolism is appropriate.

"The verdict outraged Jerry's sense of justice," said Malcolm McCollum, an English instructor at Pikes Peak Community College and a friend Mosier roped into helping with the case. "Jerry probably has a stronger sense of justice and fairness than anyone I know. It is that that kept him from being able to rest."

MONTHS OF WORK

McCollum himself worked for months on the case. He read every piece of paper in the case, amounting to more than an Army footlocker full. He pursued for hours a theory that the slaying was drug-related. He helped Mosier write a 15-page appeal, summarizing new evidence, to Lamm. He provided bed, board and gas for Mosier. And most recently, he made initial inquiries to set up a bank account for Estep if he gets out.

"Once involved, it was like a pike with a plug stuck in his mouth," said McCollum. "He swims around with it - and it's still there."

McCollum and others took the plug when they saw the evidence - or lack of it - in the case against Estep. Circumstantial, they said. Twisted, they claimed. The strongest evidence, an eyewitness identification, was suspect, they said.

Borchers is even more blunt: the State Supreme Court, he said, didn't understand the importance of Estep's mustache when it upheld the conviction. The eyewitness, a Korean woman who spoke little English and had been in this country only a few months, never told the police about facial hair. According to Borchers, who served in Korea before Fort Carson, "No one who was Korean would ever miss facial hair." It is worn only by elders in Korea. "Park had a clearly visible mustache."

Estep is described by those who came to know him as direct, honest and genuine, a man with intelligence and a sense of humor. He impressed them with his refusal to repent, just to win commutation of sentence. "He was constantly confident that the system would work," said lawyer Tegtmeier. He apparently convinced many of his innocence simply by his bearing.

"I was persuaded that he was not involved," said the Rev. Ben Dickerson, pastor of the Highland Park Baptist Church. The Esteps had joined his church just weeks before the arrest. Dickerson, now with a marriage counseling ministry, visited Estep every week from his arrest until the trial, a period of several months.

"I sensed he was very genuine, and totally consistent in what he said," said Dickerson. "I believe to this day that either he didn't do it, or he has no recollection of it." Dickerson has kept sporadic contact with Estep in prison. A year ago, he sent Estep a subscription to Personal Computing magazine.

Many of Estep's most loyal supporters came from that Baptist congregation. It was there that Nan Rose first began her attachment.

"They had a little girl, Miriam, " she said. "I remember holding the baby at choir practice one night. When I heard it on the news that he had been arrested, I called his wife and offered to help. Two days later she called. She brought the baby. That's how it got started."

During the appeal years, Rose often kept Miriam while Estep's wife visited her husband in prison. After the state Supreme Court upheld the conviction and the U.S. Supreme Court refused to intervene, Estep urged his wife to divorce him, and she moved away. But through Rose, he maintained his relationship with his daughter. She visited each summer, staying with Rose.

"And as she grew up she started calling me Grandma Nan. The whole church calls me that now, including my own grandchildren."

It was the faith of another woman in Estep that led, coincidentally, to the Toole confession supporters hope will free him. Bob Brown and Fred Cope, former sheriff's deputies turned private detectives, were interviewing a woman two months ago about an arson case. Out of the blue, and totally unrelated to the fire, she mentioned Estep.

"She felt strongly he was in prison for a crime he didn't do," said Brown. The woman had corresponded with Estep in prison.

The arson case took them to the courthouse, and Brown and Cope decided to check the Estep file while they were there. They became intrigued. They interviewed Estep in prison.

"Being former police officers, we read people fairly well," said Brown. "After a number of hours with him, we were able to walk away and say it should be investigated and he was innocent.

"We also got involved because we had been advised there were a number of people who believed in his innocence."

Working for free initially, Brown and Cope eventually found a link to Toole - they won't say how - and then called in a colleague, lawyer Lyle Robertson. They drove to Florida and obtained the 75-page statement from Toole that they say will free Estep.

Through his lawyer, Estep last week thanked the people who have stuck by him for a decade. Reserved and intellectual, he may never be able to adequately thank them for their help. But Nan Rose knows he cares, and knows he drew strength from them, just as they did from him.

A few days after Christmas, when Rose learned of her cancer, someone called Estep and told him she was dying. "It shattered him," Rose said. As soon as she got out of the hospital, someone drove her to Canon City.

"Park's not a demonstrative person. But he hugged me, and hung on to me all the time I was there. And the tears were almost there."

"He's lost everything he ever had. He had nothing else," said Rose. "I think he thought he'd never see me again."

"Someday he's going to get out of that place," said Rose, "and I'm going to pick him up.It's going to be soon."

That someday seemed to become imminent when Ottis Toole confessed to the crimes at the Suezy Massage Parlor. Jubilation prevailed among "Estep's people" for a while. Even *People* magazine took notice:

"Is An Innocent Man Behind Bars? Park Estep Has Served 10 Years for a Murder a Mass Killer Now Admits
PETER CARLSON November 5, 1984 12:00 PM

On Sept. 2, after he had served nearly 10 years in Colorado State Prison on a murder conviction, Park Estep received a phone call that sent hope flooding through him. The call came from Bob Brown, a private investigator working with Estep's attorneys. Brown nearly exploded with the good news. 'We have found the man who did it,' he told Estep. 'We have a confession from the guy who did it.' Estep went dizzy with relief. 'My heart stopped,' he says. 'My brain stopped. If you'd been doing 10 years, what would your reaction be?'

The confession that Brown had obtained was a long and detailed admission by convicted serial killer Ottis Toole, 37, that he had committed the 1974 Colorado Springs murder for which Estep had been sentenced to serve at least 20 years in prison. When the story broke in Colorado newspapers, Governor Richard Lamm announced that he would act 'within the hour' to free Estep if the original prosecutor of the case, El Paso County District Attorney Bob Russel, would agree. But Russel, 54, who is in the midst of a tough reelection campaign for the prosecutor's post he has held for 20 years, won't free Estep because he says the confession is 'tainted.' He adds, 'Can you believe this is happening to me just before my election? I'm going to lose votes if people think I have convicted an innocent man.'

So Park Estep, 35, former Army engineer, Vietnam veteran and divorced father of a 10-year-old daughter, remains in jail. His only hope now is that a judge will order a retrial when his plea is heard on Oct. 31.

Estep's entanglement with the criminal justice system began on Sept. 19, 1974. Late that night a man entered Suezy's Oriental Massage Parlor in Colorado Springs, pulled a gun and demanded money from proprietor Sun Ok Cousin and masseuse Yon Cha Lee. The women surrendered $60 but that did not satisfy the intruder. He tied up Lee, stabbed her and sliced her throat, nearly killing her. In another room he raped Cousin and shot and stabbed her to death. Before fleeing he set both women on fire. Lee survived and at first described the assailant to police as a 6'2", 195-pound man who drove a white pickup.

On Oct. 30 police arrested 5'10", 150-pound Park Estep, a Spec 4 in an engineering battalion at nearby Fort Carson. He had a full mustache and drove a red pickup. Estep, who had no previous criminal record, denied any connection to the murder. He was sick on the night it took place, he said, and had been at home with his wife, Rozanne, and their newborn daughter. His wife confirmed his story and passed a lie-detector test. Estep's Army-appointed attorney, Richard Borchers, also proclaimed his client's innocence for years after his involvement in the case ended. 'I never believed—ever—that he committed the crime,' says Borchers, who is now a Colorado state district judge. 'The case should be reopened in the interest of justice. There should be a new trial. Park was a good soldier, a good human being.... The command at Fort Carson thought the world of Park Estep.'

Estep was charged with murder, robbery, assault, arson and rape. The case rested almost entirely on Yon Cha Lee's eyewitness identification of Park, even though she continued to insist that her attacker had been clean shaven. In court she identified the mustachioed Estep—but only after the prosecutor pointed him out to her. On March 16, 1975, after two days of deliberation and several deadlocked ballots, the jury finally convicted Estep of all the charges except rape. Then, strangely—considering the brutality of the crime—the jury recommended leniency. Ignoring that recommendation, the judge sent Estep to prison on consecutive terms, making him ineligible for parole until 1995. 'I was stupid enough to really believe in the system," says Estep. "Then came the verdict and I was angry.'

Angry, but not resigned, Estep appealed his case with the aid of attorney Richard Tegtmeier and private investigator Jerry Mosier, both of whom worked on his case for years without pay. Two years after the jury's verdict, a Colorado appeals court reversed Estep's conviction and ordered a new trial. But prosecutors appealed that decision, and in 1978 the Colorado Supreme Court reinstated Estep's conviction.

Shortly after he lost that appeal, Estep asked his wife to divorce him. 'I said there was no point being married in name if we couldn't be married in fact,' he explains. His ex-wife later remarried and lives with their daughter, Miriam, on a farm in the Midwest. Miriam knows both her jailed father and her stepfather as 'Daddy.' Despite their divorce, Rozanne still staunchly backs her former husband. 'I don't just believe he is innocent,' she says. 'I know he is.'

His legal appeals seemingly exhausted, Estep remained in prison, working as a clerk, reading history and science fiction, and in 1981 converted to Judaism. Then, in

1983, Texas police arrested Ottis Toole and Henry Lucas, who claim to have killed more than 100 people, including a woman slain in Colorado in 1974.

Reading of that confession, private detectives Brown and Fred Cope—both former deputies in the El Paso County sheriff's department—wondered again about Estep's claim of innocence. They interviewed him in prison and in late August traveled to Florida State Prison to interview Ottis Toole on death row. Toole proved to be cooperative: 'You guys want me to tell you about when I went to the steam bath in Colorado....' He admitted the killing and described in grisly detail both the crime and the building in which it was committed. 'Y'all found the lady lying on the front floor with the hell shot out of her,' he told them. Toole's details matched with the 1974 statements of Yon Cha Lee. He also fit her original description of the killer—and he said he was driving a white pickup.

When news of Toole's confession broke, District Attorney Russel called a press conference and charged that the private investigators had fed Toole the details of the crime in order to give a concocted confession the ring of truth. 'We set out from the beginning to prove that the Toole confession was false,' Russel said. 'I don't want this killer Estep back on the street.'

In late September Russel and an aide traveled to Florida to interview Toole. A videotape of the meeting shows that, at first, Toole defended his confession. Then, after 85 minutes of skeptical cross-examination by Russel, he stopped insisting that he was the killer. 'Okay,' he told Russel. 'If you say I didn't kill her, then maybe I didn't.' Upon his return to Colorado, Russel announced that Toole had recanted his confession. To Jerry Mosier, the investigator for the defense, Russel's actions are selfishly political: 'He is concerned with only one thing in this matter—and that is how it will affect his election.'

Meanwhile, Park Estep awaits the decision on his motion for a new trial with renewed optimism. 'I eventually will get a new trial,' he predicts. 'I expect to be acquitted. I don't believe I can be convicted. On the other hand, I didn't believe it 10 years ago either.' If he is freed, Estep might become a defense investigator, or he might rejoin the Army, receiving more than $150,000 in back pay because he was kept on the rolls until his honorable discharge in early 1983. If his professional plans are vague, his personal plans are not. 'We have a daughter who was 9 weeks old when I was arrested,' he says. 'If I get out, a big part of my plans will be getting acquainted with her.'"

Park continued to wait. And wait. And wait. I had less patience, and wrote to the *Rocky Mountain News* in some exasperation:

Colorado Courts Dally While Man Languishes in Prison
Rocky Mountain News, 7/19/85

More than 10 months have passed since Ottis Toole confessed to the murder of Sun Ok Cousin, a crime for which another man, Park Estep, has already served over 10 years in the Colorado State Penitentiary. As the months pass, the state of Colorado's official response to this case is looking more and more outrageously dilatory.

All the elements of Toole's customary method of operation - rape, murder by knife and/or pistol, robbery, arson - were present in the crime that took Cousin's life, and very nearly took the life of her companion, Yon Cha Lee.

The similarities prompted two investigators, both veteran detectives, to approach Toole. His knowledge of details of the crime, sequence of events and crime scene were remarkably accurate. In August 1984, he made a full, recorded confession.

The response of the judicial system was prompt. Robert Russel, Colorado Springs district attorney at the time of the murder and current El Paso County district attorney, immediately dispatched Lou Smit, the Colorado Springs police detective who had led the investigation of Estep, to Florida, where Toole resides on death row.

Russel later joined Smit in Florida, where Toole, confronted with a parade of documents he was unable to read, admitted that his confession "must have been a mistake." After this statement, he continued to make statements indicating that he *had* done the crime, or believed he had.

This response to Toole's confession was a potentially tragic one.

Ottis Toole, as one comes to know him through interrogation transcripts, is basically a 6-year-old boy in the body of an adult male who knows a lot about how to kill people. He is very nearly illiterate. (When asked by one investigator how he chose aliases, he replied that he chose "ones I could spell.") He has the 6-year-old's incomprehension of "truth." Truth, for him, is what he thinks will dispose his interrogator to be pleased with him. Clearly, any statement he makes needs to be subjected to careful scrutiny.

Russel and Smit did not subject Toole's confession to careful scrutiny. Instead, they set out to manipulate Toole into a recantation. Russel's public statements about the accuracy of details in Toole's original confession have been extremely misleading, concentrating on the very few discrepancies between Toole's memory and the facts of record, ignoring the overwhelming similarities.

All this seems understandable. Russel and Smit had a natural human stake in "proving" that they hadn't convicted the wrong man. What is *not* understandable is how these individuals, subject to the most compelling kind of conflict of interest, could have been allowed to investigate Toole's confession. Richard Nixon "investigated" the Watergate break-in, but nobody took his findings very seriously.

There is now a motion before the Colorado Supreme Court asking that the original trial judge be replaced so that another judge would hear motions for a new trial for Estep. The court seems to be moving with its customary alacrity in this matter. It took almost exactly one year for it to overturn the appeals court's reversal of Estep's conviction; perhaps a year's consideration is now the precedent in this case.

The Supreme Court's apparent paralysis is disturbing, not only because it is further prolonging what is very likely an injustice, but because Toole is on death row, and, in addition, is not the sort of criminal who is popular among other inmates. With every passing day, the likelihood of a true examination of his testimony diminishes.

And with every passing day, Park Estep - a man with no previous criminal record, a man with an alibi witness of spotless reputation who has never ceased to insist that she *knows* Park Estep is innocent, a man convicted on the most dangerously unreliable sorts of evidence - gets one day closer to spending the rest of his life in prison.

It appears to this citizen that it's about time a federal grand jury was convened to look into the way this case is not being dealt with by the state of Colorado.

No federal grand jury materialized, and my frustration eventually led me to bite the hand that had once fed me (after a fashion - with column inches, not with salary):

Some Points on Estep Case
Colorado Springs *Sun,* 1985

Your coverage of the Estep/Toole story continues to maintain its sterling quality. Peter Roper's Sept. 4 piece on the removal of Judge Hardeman from the case contains the following two sentences: "Estep's lawyers claim that Ottis Toole, a confessed mass killer being held in Florida, has admitted killing the Colorado Springs woman" and "Toole, who with his traveling companion Henry Lucas is being investigated by police for dozens of murders across the nation, later recanted the confession."

Estep's lawyers do no "claim" Toole confessed. Toole confessed. He confessed in very impressive detail. The transcripts of his confession have been part of public record since January or so. Your paper has covered Mr. Russel's selective version of them. There can be very few reasons for your reporter to call the confession a "claim."

Conversely, your reporter states as unquestionable fact the "recantation" of Ottis Toole. The videotapes and transcripts of that particular segment of Mr. Russel's Theatre of the Phony have also been available for quite some time. A comparison of the confession and the "recantation" support the view that "Mr. Russel claimed Toole recanted" much better than it supports Mr. Roper's version.

Your paper also covered the original submission of the defense motion which culminated in Judge Hardeman's removal. Presumably you are aware that sealed affidavits were submitted with the motion. Perhaps it has occurred to you that the Supreme Court granted the defense more than they asked (which was only for a hearing to determine whether the judge should be replaced), but by granting them more, also made it certain that the contents of the affidavits would not come to public light. Since, as a newspaper, you are the public light, I'd be grateful if you'd start shining yourself around a little and try to tell this story with some curiosity and thought, instead of acting as if the world began anew every day and everything that came out of an official mouth was the pure-T truth.

The *Sun* maintained its equanimity and indolence. Toole was brought to Colorado Springs for a hearing, which he turned into a hopeless travesty. I had written of Sun Ok Cousin's killer that he must be "so hopelessly far from humanity that he must be found and put away from all of us who hope to be human." I had had no idea what that meant, really, but Ottis Toole certainly showed me. He was a wild animal, contemptuously indifferent to any human or legal norms. His complete separation from any accepted rules of behavior or concepts of truth became overwhelmingly apparent, I think, to everyone in the courtroom. No one could believe anything he had said or would say. There would be no new trial. Toole died in prison of cirrhosis several years later. Park returned to a low-security prison in Canon City, to which he'd been transferred pretty promptly after he was incarcerated.

Nan Rose died, and Park was brought to her funeral at the Highland Baptist Church in chains. Many of his other long-time correspondents faded away or died, and he let me know he was looking for some new ones. I knew my sister June liked writing letters, and asked her on the phone if she wanted to correspond with Park. She readily agreed.

I've never believed I have any sort of extrasensory powers, so that conversation remains a memorable mystery to me. June had shown no interest in romance or men as long as I'd known her, yet as soon as I hung up the phone I *knew* that she and Park would fall in love. I glanced up toward the Heaven I didn't believe in. "This'll get me in solid with Dad and Mom," I said to myself. June and Park started corresponding immediately, daily.

June was then living back in Northern Illinois in Lake Villa, a little community west of Waukegan. She and some unconscionable number of poodles were crammed into a small cottage in the trees. She started corresponding with Park, then talking with him on the phone, on May 29, 1988. She flew out to meet him at the prison for the first time on July 31, and by January of the next year, she'd found new homes for nearly all her herd of poodles and moved to Colorado Springs, where she got a job as a veterinary assistant and rented an apartment. Then she went to work on getting Park sprung.

June knew nothing about the law or about politics, but Jerry and Tegtmeier and I were all glad to give her access to all the case materials, and during the next two years she bulled her way into the offices of the Assistant Director of Corrections, of judges, of District Attorney Robert Russel, and wrote endless letters pleading Park's case to then Governor Roy Romer and to President George H.W. Bush. She found a judge of the Colorado Court of Appeals who heard her out, investigated the existing case files, and discovered two outstanding appeals that had never been heard. June isn't certain to this day what action the judge took then, but on January 1,1991, Park was unconditionally released. June picked him up from the prison and brought him back to Colorado Springs, where he would find a cold reception.

I'd been pretty busy, myself, during the 80s, getting married to Samantha Struthers, becoming a father, getting divorced, meeting and marrying Lis Steiner, selling one house and buying another (at which, in 1991, June and Park were married). They tried to start a life in Colorado Springs, but it became apparent after a while that the powers that controlled things in the city were not going to let that happen, and they moved to Phoenix, where Park began working part time for Honeywell, using the computer knowledge he'd gained while in prison. He loved working at Honeywell, and he'd just gotten a full time position when he walked out the door one morning and suffered a massive heart attack.

Rejecting the offer of a heart transplant, Park walked himself back to health. Meanwhile, June found a job at a kennel outside Phoenix which offered both a salary and a trailer she and Park could live in, and for several years they lived there happily, with Park doing volunteer work for a local theater group, among other activities he was able to manage. June was up visiting me and Lis early in 2002 when when she got a phone call informing her that Park had had another heart attack, this one fatal. The remaining local paper reported this with its customary accuracy and delicacy:

Notorious Springs Killer Dies in Arizona
Jeremy Meyer, *The Gazette,* c. 2/1/2002

Park Estep, a man convicted of one of Colorado Springs' most notorious crimes, died Saturday in Phoenix of natural causes.

Estep was convicted of killing a downtown Colorado Springs massage parlor operator in 1974, a charge he steadfastly denied. He served 16 years in Colorado prisons and was released in 1991.

Estep's case drew attention because of its brutality and its many legal twists.

On Sept. 19, 1974, Sun Ok Cousin was set on fire before being shot to death inside a downtown massage parlor. Another employee was stabbed but survived. Witnesses saw a red truck at the business when the crime occurred, and it was similar to the one driven by Estep, a 25-year-old Fort Carson soldier at the time.

The surviving employee picked Estep out of 250 photographs and reportedly "nearly fainted when she saw him in the lineup," according to an article in *The Gazette* at the time.

A jury convicted Estep in 1975, and he was sentenced to 48 to 64 years in prison on various charges. He won his first appeal when the Colorado Court of Appeals reversed his conviction on grounds the prosecution improperly questioned a defense witness.

But the Colorado Supreme Court upheld it in 1978.

Then in 1984, convicted serial killer Ottis Toole, who was on Florida's death row, claimed he was the murderer and also admitted to committing several other slayings across the country.

Estep demanded a retrial, but a judge denied it, saying Toole wasn't credible. The appeals court again sided with Estep, saying the judge couldn't have made that decision based on the transcripts.

Toole was flown to Colorado Springs to testify. But then he said he had never been to Colorado before and it was all a hoax.

In 1987 a judge shortened Estep's sentence, saying some of the charges could be served concurrently. He was released in 1991 and married a Colorado Springs woman. They lived for a time in Fountain before moving to Arizona.

Estep died of heart disease. He was 52.

The headline made me angry, and I fired off a letter to the reporter:

Letter to Jeremy Meyer
2/1/2002

Dear Mr. Meyer:

I write you because a friend whose professional judgment I respect referred to you as "a good kid," which I took to mean that he thought you were serious about trying to be a good reporter. I should also say immediately that I am the brother-in-law of the "notorious Springs killer," Park Estep, and that I know you had nothing to do with that appellation in the headline over your story, unless something has changed in the newspaper business since time immemorial, and that your story was probably the most carefully written one about Park's case ever printed by the paper you work for.

Because you relied on that paper for some historical background, you necessarily left out the same kinds of "detail" your paper was always careful to eliminate. I'll give one example; others in plenty reside in the enclosed pieces from the old *Rocky Mountain News* and *Denver Post*. When "the surviving employee," Elizabeth Lee, picked Park's photo out of a set of (as I recall) 8 or 10 photos, and again when she identified Park at a physical lineup, she was insistent on one point: the man in the photograph and in the lineup had not had a mustache when he did the crimes. This issue is dealt with at length in the enclosures, so I won't elaborate. Not dealt with is the fact that Elizabeth Lee was sequestered in a safe apartment in Denver by the CSPD, that she had virtually no English, that on the day Lou Smit showed her the "photo lineup" in that apartment the CSPD had already homed in on Park as the perpetrator.

The "improper question[ing] of a defense witness" to which you refer consisted of this: asked to identify Park from her witness seat, Miss Lee was unable to do so until the prosecuting attorney walked behind Park and asked her again to identify her attacker. But then, as the Colorado Supreme Court said of this incident, the Constitution entitles us to a fair trial, "not a perfect trial."

When Ottis Toole finally appeared in a Springs courtroom, he proved to be not only not credible, but crazier than a shithouse rat, which came as no shock to anyone who'd researched his ghastly life story. But I hope sometime you'll be moved to seek out the tapes of the interviews Lou Smit and Robert Russel did with Toole after he confessed to the crime to two Colorado Springs investigators. The highlight of those tapes, to my mind, comes when the District Attorney, whose job description suggests that his job is to discover the truth, tells Toole, (I paraphrase from memory) "We're not here to convict you, Ottis....We're here to find you innocent."

This attitude toward his job characterized Mr. Russel's conduct of the case, and your report of this segment of the case unfortunately is characteristic of your paper's treatment, not only of this case, but of every criminal case in this county in the 30 some years I've lived here. Your paper defines its job to be reporting the prosecution's case in the most selectively damning detail as soon as an arrest is made and to eliminate any confusing facts that might argue against the prosecutorial view. While hardly "evidence" of this overwhelming bias, I offer you the following anecdote.

About ten years after Park's conviction, I performed an experiment with two of my freshman English classes at Pikes Peak Community College. I first wrote a 3,000 word account of the Suezy Massage Parlor crime, investigation, and trial. I wrote it as objectively as I was able, real Joe Friday "just the facts, ma'am" stuff. (And as an English teacher of 30 years, I think I know something about what "objective" means and about how to use the language as cleanly as you can ever use it.) After my students had a week to read this account, I asked them to vote, as jurors, on the guilt or innocence of the defendant. (Naturally, I'd altered all the names and places and dates in my account.) 38 of 40 students found the defendant innocent because reasonable doubt existed.

Then I gave them your paper's accounts of the same events. I actually typed them up - and this in the days when the only way to copy things was to mimeograph them - so that their origin wouldn't be clear and so that I could change the names, places, etc. to correspond with the first account they'd read - and gave them another week to read them, and asked them to vote again as jurors. 38 of 40 students changed their votes to guilty.

I recognize that that anecdote might be interpreted to show that I was an inferior reporter to Joyce Trent, who covered the case. But it might also suggest that your paper tends to act as a town crier and cheerleader for the DA and CSPD. I'll leave it to you to decide.

Finally, I want to tell you a few things about the notorious Springs killer. He served two tours in Nam, mostly with the Montagnards in the Central Highlands. He had no criminal record whatsoever before he was convicted. He had no criminal record in the years he had left after his release. Had he not been the somewhat guileless North Dakota boy he was when he was called in for questioning, none of the circumstantial evidence used against him at trial would ever have been available to the prosecution. In the seventeen years he served at Canon City, he became trusted by the prison administration and his fellow prisoners, innumerable ones of whom he helped, taught, and urged to quit feeling sorry for themselves. The Army thought so highly of him that they immediately provided him with counsel when he was arrested, and only discharged him (honorably) well after his appeals were exhausted. His Rabbi in Canon City performed his marriage ceremony.

My sister happened to be visiting me when we got the news of Park's death. At one point during our many conversations during the next days, I said, somewhat bitterly, "He's got a hell of a good life coming next time around." My sister caught me up on that.

"He never met a stranger," she said, "he tried to help everyone he met. He lived every minute of every day. What's a better life than that?" I couldn't disagree.

I'm not the only relative Park has in this town, and a long way from the only friend. As you pursue your career, I hope you'll bear in mind in the future that wrongful convictions are a significant percent of the convictions in our fair land, and that even the rightly convicted are human beings who have human relatives and friends. I'd ask you to pass that message on to your employers, but I'm all too well aware that they wouldn't understand a word you said.

I didn't hear back from Meyer.

One of my missions in life, it's seemed, has been to put together people who can do each other good, in all sorts of ways, and I don't mind claiming that I've excelled at doing that. But when I got my sister and Park together, I performed my finest service.

I learned many painful lessons about the unreliability of the legal system and the press during the years of knowing Park. I learned, for example, never to say anything to a policeman except "I'd like to talk to my attorney now," or anything at all to the press. I learned how very difficult it is to discover any kind of truth about a piece of human behavior, and about the pressures on police and prosecutors that are likely to warp their supposed commitment to finding the truth. I learned I wasn't cut out to work in the legal system.

Most valuable of all, I got to be part of the life of Park Estep, and my sister's summary can't be improved: "He never met a stranger. He tried to help everyone he met. He lived every minute of every day. What's a better life than that?"

Even now, I can't resist trying to get some good for someone out of the awful injustice Park went through. Recently a young woman who writes for *The Independent* published a column about being called for possible jury duty in a capital trial, and her mixed feelings - she was "for" the death penalty, she said, but didn't know if she could actually vote to subject someone to it. She wasted a lot of words describing her aborted drama - she didn't get called - and her woolly state of mind. Her paper, amazingly, saw fit to print my rejoinder to her column:

"Perhaps Laura Eurich's confusion over the advisability of supporting the death penalty ("Faced with the Death Sentence," Colorado Springs Independent, May 9-15, 2018) might be relieved by the following facts.

"Statistical studies by reputable researchers suggest that a 4.1% wrongful conviction rate in capital cases is a conservative estimate. The most recent U.S. Bureau of Justice assessment (2016) lists 2, 814 people on death rows in the United States. 115 of these, then, are wrongly convicted. The chances that their wrongful convictions will be overturned before they are executed are slim.

"My late brother-in-law was convicted of murder, rape, arson and robbery back in the 1970s. His conviction was overturned by the Colorado Court of Appeals, but reinstated by the Colorado Supreme Court on the grounds that the Constitution guaranteed "a fair trial, not a perfect trial." Fortunately, Colorado had no death penalty at that time, so my brother-in-law was not executed. Not only I, but a great many people, including judges, attorneys and clergy, are convinced that he was wrongly convicted in the first place.

"Indeed, we cannot guarantee perfection in any human activity. If Ms Eurich is comfortable with a 96% chance that the prosecution's case is legitimate and has been proved, then she should be comfortable voting for a death penalty conviction. If she is not comfortable with that margin of error, then she should no longer support the death penalty."

You hear every day of unconscionable crimes of violence, and see many more portrayed in vivid detail for entertainment purposes. It is difficult to resist the desire to punish such crimes "appropriately," taking eye for eye, life for life. I find that impulse lives on in me, with all I know about the undependability of human institutions (such as "the criminal justice system"), the uncertainty of most forms of "evidence" (particularly eyewitness identifications), and the great volume of criminal activity, often of a lethal nature, that goes unpunished or rewarded in our society. Because I cannot trust that prosecutors, police investigators, or the press are doing their best to find the truth, nor that witnesses can ever be relied on for accurate identification or memory, I don't believe that I, or anyone else, has a moral right to call for the execution of another human being. While vengeance is seductive in many cases, I wind up, like a good minister, quoting the Bible: Vengeance is mine, saith the Lord.

Or, as that dear, great Lenny Bruce said, "'Thou Shalt Not Kill' *means* that, not 'Amend Section A.'"

Mother's Quarter

Today I finished reading Ivan Doig's *The Whistling Season* to my friend Cathy Mundy. It had taken us about three months of Fridays to get through it. We hadn't been in any hurry to finish it because we both enjoyed the book so much.

I have been reading every Friday morning to Cathy for the past ten years because ten years ago she had a stroke and couldn't read to herself for a while. Cathy's husband Skip, an old friend of mine, told me about this ramification of her stroke, and I volunteered to come over to their house and read to her once she got home.

Within half a year, she could hold a book and read to herself just fine. But we went on reading because we both enjoyed it. We've traded books back and forth, and we've both learned to love authors we didn't know about - for instance, Ivan Doig.

The Whistling Season tells of the lives of a father, his three sons, their hired maid and her brother, and the students and parents at a one-room schoolhouse in the dry part of Montana in the year 1910. The events in the book are the kinds of events most people experience through most of their lives, given color and intensity because they're told through the eyes and ears and nose of a 10-year-old boy. Nothing "dramatic" or "important" happens: no serial killers or terrorists or Communists or other minions of the Devil inhabit the book. The Big Event in the book is the appearance of Halley's Comet in the same year that Mark Twain died. Yet, for the old man (the middle son of the three) who tells the story in retrospect, there's a story worth telling, and he is right. It's a story about how this country came to be populated by the people who now populate it. They frequently had to shed their former selves and names to start over again.

That's really a long way from the important things Doig wrote about; it's what I was reminded of, off and on, reading the book and thinking about it. My listener Cathy was hearing, I know, echoes of her own upbringing on a ranch in Wyoming. Neither of us was in a hurry for that book to end because it talked so gently and honestly and precisely about the things that matter in our human lives.

Cathy, raised on a Wyoming ranch, became a librarian. I, raised as the son of a working man, became an English professor. Both of us loved and admired our parents and their lives, and went on to live very different ones, and we both enjoy reading about the lives of people who live in the kinds of real worlds we've inhabited.

(The "real" world we now live in is so overpopulated that it bears no resemblance to the world that Cathy and I grew up in. In that world, an individual could harbor the idea that he or she could make a difference. In the world we now inhabit, we harbor no such illusion. Lewis Lapham, long time editor of *Harper's Magazine,* put it this way: "In order to fuel the engines of publicity the media suck so much love and adulation out of the atmosphere that unknown men must gasp for breath. They feel themselves made small, and they question the worth, even the fact, of their existence....At any one time the ecology of the media can bear the weight of only so much celebrity, and as the grotesque personae of the divinities made for the mass market require ever more energy to sustain them, what is left for the weaker species on the dark side of the camera?")

I and Cathy keep reading and being read to because the sound of the written word is beautiful. Books are the sound of speech, the sound of someone telling a story. People have been telling stories for a great long time, because stories are the real history of any people. If you learn how to read books - meaning, learn how to *hear* the words on the page, not just read them - you will learn how to extend your own little measly life both backwards and forwards in time and in space. Your life will become far bigger than your own life span can be - bigger, wider, deeper - with every book you read.

Reading is hard. Like any other difficult skill, the only way you can get good at it is to do it every day. The only way you can do it every day is to make a place for it in your days, a place that will be devoted to reading and nothing else. (This is true for all things that make you stronger - physical exercise, music, keeping up your teeth, learning to be a giver, not a taker, etc.). And the connection I've already mentioned between reading and speech is important. That connection became clear to me when I read this great essay, "Bring Back the Out-Loud Culture," (*Newsweek,* April 15, 1985) by the poet Donald Hall:

"When we put away childish things we tend to despise what we leave behind. Among educators it has been progressive or forward-looking to deplore learning by rote and to oppose it to thinking. Maybe this is true for mathematics. But when we stopped memorizing and reciting literature, our ability to read started its famous decline. It was the loss of recitation - not its replacements (radio, film, television) - that diminished our literacy.

"My grandfather who recited poems spent only a few years in school, but he was a better reader than most college graduates I meet today. Good readers hear what they read even though they read in silence: speed reading is barbaric. When we read well, in silence, we imagine how the words would sound if they were said aloud. Hearing print words in the inward ear, we understand their tone. If we see the sentence "Mr. Armstrong shook his head," the inner voice needs to understand whether Mr. Armstrong disapproved or was outraged before the inner voice knows how to speak the words....

"Fathers and mothers, teachers, Boy Scout leaders, babysitters, uncles and aunts, we must read aloud to children. But first we must learn again to perform the text, out-ham our ancestors, take pleasure in word and story and hand this pleasure on. We must encourage our children to memorize and recite. As children speak poems and stories aloud, by the pitch and muscle of their voices they will discover drama, humor, passion and intelligence in print. In order to become a nation of readers, we need again to become a nation of reciters."

Reciters. To recite. I like the second meaning for that word in my big old *Webster's Unabridged Dictionary*, inherited from my mom along with the little table built to hold it always open: "to tell over." That meaning *gets* what Hall is talking about. To read your own or anyone else's words to someone else so that they *get* what you got from them, you have to become the speaker of those words, to imagine yourself into the person whose voice spoke those words. And that is equally true if you're reading only to yourself. If "reading" is only letting the words pass in front of your eyes, you aren't reading. You might as well be watching television.

I don't know if you will still have a cd I made of me reading Tim Gautreaux' wonderful story "The Piano Tuner." I gave another copy last Christmas to a friend of ours, Claire Borel, who grew up in the Cajun country in which that story is set, and she sent me a note asking if the reader was me or Tim Gautreaux. It was one of the best compliments I've ever received, because it meant that I had truly gotten inside the writer's voice and come close to reproducing it. It meant, also, that his story had now become one of *my* stories. Since it is a story about taking responsibility for another person for whom you have no "official" responsibility, and trying to help that person improve her life, and succeeding to some degree, having that story as part of me helps me remember that that's what we're here for.

Egad. This is beginning to sound like someone on National Public Radio or Oprah. Oog, as Pogo used to say. Here's a piece I wrote as an introduction to a newspaper column that I never succeeded in selling (Neither NPR nor Oprah would approve of Thorne Smith):

Thorne Smith and My Mother's Quarter

My mother read to me from the time I could turn over from my back to my belly. Soon as I could walk, she began taking me to the little library on Central Street, and soon enough I'd run through all the wonderful books for kids the librarians knew of and could afford to buy.

Mom would take me to church rummage sales and buy for me any books I wanted. When I was ten or so, in the basement of a church, under the dim, flickering yellow lights far above, a funny title caught my eye, *The Bishop's Jaegers*, by Thorne Smith. I thought, "Let's see what these 'jaegers' are," and I opened the book.

I saw immediately that the line drawings weren't for kids, as there were quite a few women wearing little or nothing in them, in postures that didn't recall any of my previous reading adventures. I slipped the book into my stack, and my mother's quarter set me on the low road my life has followed ever since.

Thorne Smith, I learned much later, was a funny little fellow who set out to make his living as a writer before the 1920s began. He found little luck until one day, drunk at his typewriter and nearly ready to look for honest work, he saw the tail of a dog moving through an unmown weedfield across the street. The tail set him considering tails without dogs, and heads without bodies, and those musings eventuated in his novel *Topper*, in which a couple of young ghosts return to ruin the respectability and renew the life of a middle-aged banker. The book made a career for him, and he faithfully followed its formula through many more books, all of which I hunted down and read.

Smith's heroes were always small, shy men - like Smith, like myself - who became embroiled with large, powerful people who despised authority and taught the small, shy men to do likewise. The women in his books were of two types - both perfect 1920s stereotypes, of course: the shriveled or porcine, frightened, domineering wife/mother, or the free-thinking, hard-drinking, sex-loving, irresistibly tragic young woman.

The representatives of authority Smith despised were many - the military man, the judge, the churchy, the captain of industry, the ingratiating salesman, the "civic leader" - and his raffish characters saw diligently to their comic humiliation. Smith's political attitude, a cheerfully despairing anarchism, is best seen in this passage from *Rain in the Doorway*, in which Mr. Horace Larkin explains to small, shy Hector Owen how his other-dimensional city regards political realities:

> "Those palaces there on the hill," said Mr. Larkin, "are the homes of our retired mayors and political leaders. All built by graft. Graft, you know, my dear Owen, is also a fundamental craving. Self-interest is its brother. We used to attack graft in the old days. Now we encourage it. The only stipulation the voters make is that our grafters must share enough of their spoils with the people, spend enough on public welfare, roads, construction, amusements and holidays to keep us all happy and contented...." "What happens to your politicians when they fail to share their graft?" asked Mr. Owen.... "What happens?" repeated Mr. Larkin in surprise. "Naturally we run them out of town...." "And those buildings down there in the valley," broke in Mr. Dinner, his voice embodying the satisfaction he felt, "belong to the prohibitionists and other like vermin who endeavor to thwart nature. They're jails. Very uncomfortable places."

Of course, Smith's predilection for seizing the day in one hand, since his other was invariably wrapped around a bottle, took its toll. In his books, steady, daily consumption of strong drink makes people wittier, sexier, smarter and nicer than their sober-sided fellows. In his life, Smith's love of booze led him to repeated stints at a funny farm where he was treated by blasts of water from a fire hose, and led, eventually, to his early death. Hemingway didn't call liquor "the giant killer" for nothing, even if he didn't correctly identify the giant being killed.

For all that, in spite of my own uneasy relationship with the giant killer, I remain grateful I discovered Thorne Smith when I did. He gave me courage to acknowledge my own distaste for the "family values" that surrounded me in the 1950s, the sniggling, adult values that trumpeted virtue and privately filched pennies and pinched defenseless earlobes and built atomic bombs and worshipped Mammon in the name of Jesus. Smith saw life in his America as a contest between what Nelson Algren later called "the Apple-Pan-Dowdy God of the Middle Border" and the God Dionysus, and his sympathies lay unequivocally on the side of the elder god.

As have mine ever since, to my frequent sorrow and eternal gratitude. For all my mistakes and fooleries, I can say I've chosen to live rather than conform, to take the side of the weak against the strong, to grasp the night in the face of the inevitable morning after. If heaven permits regrets, my mother may still regret that quarter she spent on Thorne Smith, but I think it was her very best.

Thorne Smith was a writer of formulaic crap, and, as the above suggests, of lies about what alcohol does to people. At the same time, he was a very good satirist of the kinds of people our country keeps churning up to the top ("Scum rises." - Hunter Thompson. "The rich are the scum of the earth in every country."- G.K. Chesterton), and he could write very funny dialogue. (I'll bet the Marx Brothers learned a lot from him, for instance.) I include this piece for two reasons.

1. Reading is not only difficult, it's damned dangerous. You can pick up ideas or, more dangerous yet, attitudes, that can severely damage you and others. Another reason why reading should only be done slowly, so you can sit back, think about a

statement or a plot or a character or a phrase, and check it against your own knowledge of what's true and what isn't.

2. Reading is more fun than about anything because, as I said before, it allows you to live lives you'll likely never be able to lead otherwise. In one of Thorne Smith's books, *The Stray Lamb,* his middle-aged, henpecked protagonist incurs the wrath of an Egyptian god, who turns him into a variety of animals. One of those animals is a sea gull, and for some reason Smith must have felt most at home in that particular imaginary body. And so, ever since reading that chapter, I have felt at one with sea gulls, and every time I see one - and even here in the middle of the damn desert, they have found a little niche for themselves - I rise up into their lovely, soaring existence and think coarse thoughts about terrible things to eat.

When Thelonika's mom and I broke apart, I experienced the hardest years of my life, separated from my daughter, full of failure and guilt and anger, incidentally working for the first of many Mongolian bosses at the community college. I was not in good shape, and I was not handling life well. After a year or two of daily agony, I came upon a book by George Plimpton called *Mad Ducks and Bears.* I think I may have read a couple of his earlier books, but I bought this one (at Goodwill, needless to say) because I learned from the jacket that it concerned some players from the Chicago Bears and other teams from the early 1960s, the last time I'd paid any attention to football.

The book turned out to include long sections devoted to the post-football endeavors and ruminations of Alex Karras, a great tackle for the Detroit Lions who had become a friend of Plimpton's. Karras's reported conversations were so funny that they would double me up in bed laughing. Laughing so hard it probably sounded like crying. It probably *was* like crying, and it began my recovery from despair.

Many years later, when I decided to start a book-selling business, I also decided to name it after one of Karras's creations, Ace Zerblonski.

Ace Zerblonski, as Karras imagined him one evening talking to Plimpton, was "the first ethnic cowboy hero." He had some peculiarities: he didn't wear a ten-gallon hat, preferring to carry a parasol; he rode a horse called "Great Big Elephant," because the horse actually *was* an elephant; most significantly, and unlike all other Western heroes, Ace never confronted his opponents in shoot-outs on Main Street. Instead, he shot them in the back. Karras summarized the results of this practice: "You could always tell when Ace had been in town for a while. People didn't so much walk down Main Street; they *whirled*."

Karras, as Plimpton reported him, reminded me of a wonderful left wing for the Chicago Blackhawks I'd gotten to meet back in my college days, Eric Nestorenko, a man I'd once seen come striding into a basement party punching the ceiling and crying, with desperate sincerity, "Love! Love! Love? ...is a quivering of the *gonads*!" (He was the same man who taught me, with one look into my eyes, the following truth: Only the strong can be kind. The best thing you can read about him is his little section in Studs Terkel's fine book *Working*.)

But I veer, as one of Thorne Smith's best characters, Horace Larkin, frequently said. Deciding to start up a book business with the name "Ace Zerblonski Books," I also decided I'd better get permission from Karras, and tracked down his address, and wrote him asking for permission. He gave it to me, in a businesslike and gracious letter which you will inherit.

This is an extraordinarily messy chapter I'm writing, because reading has woven so much into the fabric of my life that I have a hard time separating books from all they've done for me, or to me, or both.

I don't remember my mother reading to me, but I know she did. I remember many of the books she read to me. I can see some of the illustrations in those books in my head tonight as clearly as I can see her face, or my dad's or grandad's faces. She loved to read, and I grew up in a house much like my own, now, lined with bookshelves full of books. I hope somehow to be able to pass many of those same books on to you, although this may not be possible. I've hauled these books around the country, from Chicago to California back to Colorado, and wherever I've lived they've had a home. Only someone who finds life in books would do such a thing, and I don't know if you will be such. I hope you will.

You may conclude that your lives are not conducive to owning hundreds and hundreds of books. Most people own few if any, and even most readers don't feel the need to keep books around once they've read them. Collecting books, as collecting anything, is a strange form of madness. Perhaps I can explain why, for me anyhow, it's a benign madness.

Tonight (September 15, 2009) I went over to Colorado College to listen to George McGovern talk about his new biography of Abraham Lincoln, answer questions, and sign copies of his books. I went there primarily to shake his hand, and to tell him that he was one of my two living heroes. (He asked who the other one was, and I told him it was Father Steve Handen, about whom I'll doubtless write at some stage of these ramblings.)

I also took two additional books for him to sign. One was his book about his daughter Terry, whose life was largely an agony of depression and alcoholism, ended at the age of 44 by her freezing to death, drunk, in a snowdrift in the middle of Madison, Wisconsin. It's a very brave, honest and beautiful book.

The other book was Dr. Hunter S. Thompson's *Fear and Loathing on the Campaign Trail*, a book that was originally published in installments in *Rolling Stone* during the 1972 presidential campaign, in which then-Senator George McGovern ran against Richard Nixon and against a good part of his own Democratic Party, promising to finally end the war in Vietnam, and representing a sane and decent vision of what America was supposed to be about. On page 414 of that book, when it had become clear that McGovern would lose the election to Nixon, Thompson wrote, "The tragedy of all this is that George McGovern, for all his mistakes and all his imprecise talk about 'new politics' and 'honesty in government,' is one of the few men who've run for President of the United States in this century who really understands what a fantastic monument to all the best instincts of the human race this country might have been, if we could have kept it out of the hands of greedy little hustlers like Richard Nixon."

George McGovern did understand that, and still does, because he has lived his life serving that vision. A vision of America as a place to which all can come, as it says on the Statue of Liberty, and in which all can have a fair chance to live a decent life.

The "mistakes" Thompson refers to were two:

1. McGovern allowed his campaign to be taken over by the people who ran it, people like Gary Hart of Colorado and Frank Mankiewicz from the Kennedy mafia. They told him to cut his sails to the prevailing political winds (as they saw them), and he did, and he began to seem other than himself even to people like me. They also talked him into picking a third-rate senator from Missouri, Tom Eagleton, as his vice-presidential running mate. Not two weeks after he'd been chosen, Eagleton was "exposed" by the press as having had shock treatments for depression. In those days, that was enough to put a giant stigma on him. When the story came out, McGovern promptly gave a statement to the press saying he stood behind Eagleton "one thousand per cent." Two days later, he bounced him from the ticket and appointed Sargent Shriver, a minor Kennedy Mafia operative, as his replacement. These developments struck most non-political people as evidence that McGovern was either a fool or a liar or an asshole, and struck most of his supporters dumb.

I had been his El Paso County co-chair during the primary campaign, working with Janice Blakely and Richard Bohle. Together, we took 63% of the county for McGovern, and we thought the sky was the limit. We ran every precinct caucus on the principal of "proportional representation" meaning that you take all the people at the caucus as the dividend, and all the votes for various candidates as the divisors, and you send your votes to the county convention based on that math. For example, you have 15 people at the caucus; 4 of them vote for McGovern, 3 for Humphrey, 6 for George Wallace. Your particular precinct gets to have 3 delegates at the County Convention.

$4/15 = 1$ McGovern

$3/15 = 0$ Humphrey

$6/15 = 2$ Wallace

We ran the whole county on the principle of proportional representation, and still won 63% for McGovern. Then, after the county conventions all over the state had transpired, and McGovern had taken the state, his Colorado campaign manager, Gary Hart (later a U.S. Senator from Colorado until he got photographed feeling up a bimbo on some fat cat's boat outside Washington, D.C.) came down and met with all us peons to tell us how the State Convention would be conducted. He said that "proportional representation" had been a winning strategy, but that it could be a losing strategy at the state convention, and therefore we would be giving up on it.

At that point I raised what used to be called a "point of order." I said to him, "Wait the fuck a minute." Then I went on, saying words to the effect that we had all been working for a year or more to establish a democratic principle - one person, one vote - and that to give up on that principle now was to deny the whole basis of our efforts. His answer was some slick version of "That was then; this is now," and that was when I went for him, and we were separated, to my eternal regret, by members of his security staff and my fellow workers. They say your only regrets in life are for those things you didn't do. Maybe so. It is certainly among my few regrets that I didn't get across that room to take a swing at Gary Hart. It's still a regret because he represented exactly the kind of measling, arrogant, inexperienced, educated asshole that has taken over this country. Hang on for a second. I have a perfect description:

"[Albert Speer] symbolizes a type which is becoming increasingly important in all belligerent countries: the pure technician, the classless bright young man without background, with no other original aim than to make his way in the world...It is the lack of psychological and spiritual ballast, and the ease with which he handles the terrifying technical and organizational machinery of our age which makes this slight type go extremely far nowadays...This is their age. The Hitlers and Himmlers we can rid ourselves of, but the [Albert] Speers, whatever happens to this particular specimen, will long be with us.'"

-Joachim Fest, *Speer: the Final Verdict,* Harcourt, 2001, p. 353

Gary Hart, to a T. (Albert Speer, in case you haven't studied up on him, was a very bright young man who joined up with the Nazis in 1929, became a favorite of Hitler's, and ultimately killed a million or two people, most of them slave laborers, although he certainly never got his hands bloody or even dirty.)

Before that point, working on the McGovern campaign had been the most satisfying thing I'd ever done. And the accounts of the national campaign that Hunter Thompson was publishing in the *Rolling Stone* each month were the perfect accompaniment. I and the people I was working with had gotten into politics in the 1968 campaign, during which I'd worked for Gene McCarthy, and we had been stomped by the Democratic Party establishment in Chicago, my home town. This time, we were going to win it all: we were going to make the Democratic Party democratic, we were going to give the American people a Real Choice, we were going to demonstrate that reason and good will were more powerful than propaganda-induced hatred. And reading Hunter's monthly accounts helped me believe that this might come about.

If you read them now, I have no idea how much of that hopeful energy will come through to you. As I re-read them, after all that has transpired since, I am not, as they say, "re-energized." I'm saddened at the weaknesses I perceive in Hunter's procedure as a journalist and as a man, as I am saddened by the memories of my own weaknesses in those same areas and many others. And yet, and yet...*damn,* it was fun feeling part of a "movement" that was about something other than money and violence.

That is my current reaction to looking over this particular one of the many books I have kept and will keep until I die. This one is a book that holds not only itself, but memories of some of my dearest friends and enemies. Now it bears the signature of its flawed hero, a man who I still think represents principles that a once real country called the United States of America stood for. Don't sell this one at a yard sale, eh?

By the time you're reading this, I suspect most if not all of the books I'm leaving you will have been forgotten. Reading is work, and work, you're being told now, and will be told with ever-increasing intensity and ever-more convincing graphic evidence, is what you should avoid at all cost.

Well. Reading *is* work. So is work. So is playing an instrument, so is singing. So is writing, and so is fixing the pipes that bring your water to you or take it away. Or fixing or making the structures of wood or stone that keep the rain off your head. Reading is as dignified as singing or plumbing or building a house.

Reading is like those crafts because it builds a way to look at life that can't keep the rain off your head but can make you appreciate it, that can't eliminate the fascists but can let you laugh at them until they die of your communal laughter, that can't, in the end, save you, any more than anything else can; but it can make your damnation one hell of a lot more pleasurable.

Over the years, I wrote a lot of journalism and even a "scholarly presentation" or two, hoping to make the work of writers I admired and sometimes knew better known. I'll put a few of them in the next chapter.

Some of My Betters

Unless I've previously donated them to a university collection, don't sell any of John Nichols' books or correspondence with me, either. My friend Steve Abbott turned me on to John's *The Milagro Beanfield War* shortly after it was published, and I've read and collected Nichols' books ever since. In 1987, when Nancy and I started the Downtown Studio campus of Pikes Peak Community College, she got hold of John and asked him to do a benefit reading for us, since we had exactly no money with which to equip the building. He agreed (John has been generous beyond measure with his time and talent in service of thousands of people and causes), and when he arrived, we immediately connected, when he sat down at the old upright piano that was one of the few pieces of "furniture" we'd managed to acquire and began playing very solid barrelhouse blues. We became friends then, and have remained friends to this date.

John, his writing talent aside, resembles all my other remaining friends in one respect: he knows, and has known for a long time, exactly who he is and why he's living his life as he does. In his case, he's living his life to write, and I'm sure that he still follows his long-time regimen: Get up at a little after midnight, write the night away, go out for breakfast and then live life. For John, living life has included a stupefying number of love affairs and marriages and children and friends, to whom he is as loyal as I've been to mine. It has included life-long love affairs with baseball, with the writers and musicians of what not so long ago we used to refer to as "the third world" (meaning the torturable countries of the world, where we got our raw materials, then our cheap labor), with fishing, and with the natural world, especially the part of it in which he happens to live, Northern New Mexico.

Among my "Nichols collection" is a wonderful short video made by a student at the University of New Mexico called *My Beautiful Storage Locker.* (The title's a reference to an earlier film about Pakistani immigrants in England that was called *My Beautiful Little Launderette,* which I believe won an Academy Award.) The "storage locker" of the title is one John maintains in Taos, in which he stores, in a room maybe 20 by 40 feet, the manuscripts of every book he's written, in all their various versions, on ceiling-high metal shelves of the sort you find at WalMart. The shelves, that is; you don't find the contents there, and never will. There is probably an entire shelf - maybe 24 cubic feet - that contains the manuscript versions of just one novel - I think his greatest - *The Magic Journey.* There are many more "books" on those shelves than have ever been published.

For many reasons this is so. One is that John doesn't edit his work as he goes, as many writers do. He gets a book going, with no outline or plan, and sees it through to the end, night after night. Then he sends it off to his agent or publisher and when he gets it back he either makes the changes they suggest, if they suggest changes, or he says to hell with it because he's already on to the next book. The man is a fountain of stories, and fountains don't edit themselves. Unless they're spewing crap, and occasionally John catches himself doing that - as who doesn't? - and cans a whole book; but he keeps what he's canned in a typing-paper box, and takes it on down to the beautiful storage locker, anyhow. Maybe John, to that degree, is a collector, too.

The most important reason, I suspect, that a lot of the books in his locker haven't been published, is that John came along at the very end of the time that Americans were interested in reading books about the real lives their fellow citizens were leading, or *they* were leading, and started being interested in reading books about people leading lives that could only exist inside the virtual reality machines.

In short, about the time that we quit being a country of people and started becoming a nation of spectators, like dem Romans under the Caesars. The same thing happened to Nelson Algren, about a generation before. The custodians of official reality decided that he was dangerous, and their little hired penguins who reviewed books dismissed Algren, almost exactly as they dismissed John, as a "proletarian novelist."

When John came up here in 1987, his novel *American Blood* had just come out. He later described it to me as "a real career-stopper," and indeed it was. The uncorrected proof copy of that book you will inherit was given me by a lovely woman named Susan Atkinson, then a clerk at the late Chinook Bookshop. The corner was dented, and she explained to me that it had been dented when she threw the book across the room because she couldn't stand it. Nobody could, much. It's too true.

Nine years earlier, a fellow named John Irving had written a book called *The World According to Garp* which had made the same point as *American Blood*: America is an extremely violent nation. That book got made into a very successful movie, because it came out when it did. John's book got remaindered damn near before it was published, because nine years later we didn't want to consider any further criticisms of ourselves. When Reagan was elected in 1980, he declared, "It's morning in America," and that has been the most incredibly effective mantra ever coined.

But history recent or ancient wouldn't save John from the Dustheap of Literature. He became one of the Disappeared. (As I do, John makes his own stationery. His latest has what's undoubtedly a *New Yorker* cartoon up in the corner. It shows what's obviously "a writer" lying on the floor next to his typewriter-bearing desk. "Help," he's saying, "I've fallen into obscurity and I can't get up." After *American Blood,* his books appeared, were dismissed by the few national reviewers who bothered to notice them, and pretty quick he had a hell of a time getting a book published at all, although he is *still* getting them published. And he's *still* getting up shortly after midnight and writing until dawn because that is what a writer does. Some writers do it at different hours, but what writers do is *write.* Here's a review I wrote of John's recently published novel, *The Empanada Brotherhood:*

Since *The Milagro Beanfield War* was published in 1974, John Nichols has been thought of as a writer of the struggles of the Southwest's indigenous people to sustain their way of life and to preserve the natural environment against the juggernaut of capitalist exploitation. His new novel, *The Empanada Brotherhood,* might seem to abandon these concerns, but only at first glance.

"Blondie," the novel's self-effacing narrator, has come to Greenwich Village in 1960, determined to become a writer, still uncertain of both his craft and his proper subjects. He falls in with a disparate band of characters, most of them South American, who patronize a small *empanada* stand, and whose perplexities, joys and disasters instruct the young writer in "the problems of the human heart in conflict with itself" that Faulkner asserted were "the only things worth writing about."

These characters revolve around the stand's owner Áureo Roldán, whose every action expresses the principle, "From each according to his abilities, to each according to his needs." They form a sort of temporary *karass,* a community of mutual concern irrespective of "national, institutional, occupational, familial and class boundaries" that instructs the young seeker in the joyful pain of engaging the "truly remarkable pigpen" that, Roldán asserts, is our planet. This community rapidly disperses at book's end after Roldán must flee his mob creditors. And so Blondie learns the immense value of community by its loss: "It seemed impossible to me how things that were so precious could be dismantled so quickly."

In short, *The Empanada Brotherhood* returns to the days when Nichols began to learn the values that have informed all his subsequent work. It does so in a style which has been pared of all excess (what Hemingway called "scrollwork or ornament"), leaving only Nichols' formidable gifts of observation and celebration and his unquenchable love for "All these hearts reaching out toward each other."

For several years, Nichols has been seeking to write "the perfect little book." He claims he has not done that with *Empanada*, but he is wrong. This is a novel that will revive its readers' youth and leave them thinking and feeling in ways long forgotten.

That's the version of my review that got printed. The original was a good deal longer because it included more quotes from this short novel of John's that is one of the loveliest books I've ever read. As we totter toward our dotage, John and I both seem to be learning to edit ourselves, or at least wanting to (in my case), and I think that's not a bad thing.

When I first met John in 1987, I devoted part of an issue of *The Unofficial Organ* to an introduction to his big work, sometimes called *The Milagro Trilogy: The Milagro Beanfield War, The Magic Journey, Nirvana Blues.* It doesn't really do them justice. The only way to do them justice is to read them.

John Nichols *Milagro* Trilogy

Thinking about John Nichols' writing, I think first of characters, large and small. I think of April McQueen, for instance, driving back home to Chamisaville, New Mexico, to see if she can rediscover some sense of coherence after the end of her third disastrous marriage and her first battle with the cancer that would kill her, if the FBI weren't going to save it the trouble by blowing her to smithereens. On her way home to that fate, April stops in Kansas to listen to Neil Armstrong announce the first dirty footstep ever to touch the moon.

The moonshot itself both dismays and awes her - "The jingoistic propaganda circus surrounding the event, especially when viewed in the light of the Vietnam war, had to be one of the most vulgar phenomena she had ever observed....And the men involved, the all-American sanitized automatons scheduled to make man's first track in that gray powder, bored her to tears."

April's opinions here are probably not far from Nichols', for Nichols is a writer who doesn't hesitate to speak his mind, both as narrator and through his characters. What distinguishes him from many other polemical novelists is that April's thoughts, in this example, are only one part of the small scene. The scene itself is rendered with Nichols' characteristic care and love for the physical world: "Around 9:00 p.m., while a mellow light still colored the corn and wheat fields, April pulled off the highway, simply driving onto a vague dirt track leading into tall corn." And April's political reflections lead her back to a meditation on her own life: "Similar sadness she had on occasion experienced reviewing her own adventures. The need to flee Chamisaville and experience everything, chalk up lovers, travel to the ends of the earth, be a great writer, poet, painter - All that."

Nichols' characters nearly always remain characters, rather than mere pawns in some political scheme. I think this is so because Nichols loves individual humans so deeply, and because he so deeply understands the interweaving of political economy and individual human living.

April is one of a number of characters in the three novels who experience and share with us that most difficult sensation to capture in words, the feeling of being fully alive and a part of a universe which is all living, too, part of a vast, singing mystery whose underlying engine is a creative love which beggars all words.

Nichols captures that joy of the reprieved, that high awareness of our own existence, as well as any novelist I know, as well as Joyce Cary did. He makes that sense happen on the page, as it does in life, at the commonest places, in the commonest moments - those moments when we are suddenly stricken into a sense of the miraculous by the turn of leaves, or of a magpie's wing, or of a child's speech.

Or in those moments when things are so completely kazolicked - the toilet backing up, the kids demanding you play Solomon to their dispute over the Transformer from Og, two bills you'd forgotten to expect on the table, no relief in sight - that you just have to laugh, because there's no time to cry, and you get, if you can keep laughing long enough, a brief glimpse at the beautiful indignity of your own slapstick soap opera.

Or in the times when you and your compadres are sitting in the locker room, elbows on knees, heads hanging, and nobody's said a word for many minutes, because the defeat was one that counted, and everyone knows if he'd done a little more and a little better, it wouldn't have happened. Or at least that's what everyone thinks. And then someone says the right, tough thing that's needed to start over again again.

This is the Pueblo Shakey Jake Martinez talking to his son, Anthony, after April has been killed by FBI agents:

Anthony says, "'I want to kill them. I don't care about anything else. I want to see them die.'"

"'This is only a first sorrow,' Jake said. 'It's nothing. This kind of sadness will multiply a hundredfold before you die.'"

"'I can't take it, then. I'm not strong enough. I'm sorry.'"

"'Don't dribble like an idiot. You can be a useful human being someday. Stay quiet now for a minute: let your heart calm down.'"

It may seem strange to illustrate the assertion of Nichols' joyfulness with such a passage. It will not seem so to those who know the blues, which Nichols played for a while when he still lived in New York. The blues is the music of the person who can be destroyed (all of us) but not defeated. This kind of person: "Anytime someone wants to call me 'nigger,' I give him the privilege, because only a Nigger could have subdued and gone through the things that we, the Black people, have gone through and survived," says the great bluesman Johnny Shines. That's the blues, and there is a sardonic savoring of the bitter in Shines' words that often infuses Nichols' work.

I think especially, in this connection, of Virgil Leyba, the Mexican revolutionary turned lawyer who balances April McQueen in *The Magic Journey.* He spends eighteen hours a day fighting the predators, the users, the fancy manipulators and their hirelings who are despoiling his adopted people in Chamisaville. His dreams are populated every night by the ghosts of long-fallen comrades, of loves who've died before his eyes or in his arms. He drinks too much in order to sleep at all, and smokes continually to stoke his waking fire. At the end of *The Magic Journey,* all causes lost to the thugs of Progress, April dead, his only son dead, his wife gone, knowing he has "a couple of months at the outside" to live before cancer gets him, Virgil Leyba thinks this:

"....'No,' he thought....'I'll live at least long enough to see the cottonwoods turn yellow, and after that happens, I think I'll take an extension until the first snow.' .....They would locate somebody with a mimeograph machine...and they would tell how April [McQueen] Delaney truly died and why...keeping the sparks alive, at least, until all the fractured, disparate molecules across the nation could join into some unified, single connection able to affect the course of things."

Cancer, death and disaster seem to be coming up frequently in this discussion. Not exactly great dust-jacket copy. Well, Nichols illustrates his books with his own *calaveras*, drawings of small skeletons prancing around, playing guitars and leading parades, their miniature skeleton bosoms jutting proudly. Like the blues, the *calaveras* express both courage and humor in the face of one of the two incontrovertible facts of life: in the midst of life, we are in death. "So the Bible says," Billie Holiday sang, "and it still is news."

It's certainly news to most *norteamericanos.* We prefer to regard death as an unjustifiable intrusion into our well-justified party, and so we discourage each other from mentioning it. Since every birthday cake contains the fatal capsule, that preference absorbs a good deal of energy and attention, and so we have a hard time savoring life, being so overworked denying that life is terminal. Because Nichols rarely lets us forget that fact for long, his work is not likely to be very popular in his native country during his lifetime. This is too damn bad.

Nichols is as good at creating intensely typical characters as Dickens, and better at granting them the small, individual quirks against type that distinguish human beings from "characters." He's as good as Karl Mannheim, the great German socio-economic historian, at revealing how economic systems influence human thought and feeling and behavior. (He also writes about one hundred and seventy-five million times more enjoyably than Karl Mannheim.) He's as good at orchestrating a long, slow slapstick scene as W.C. Fields, and he can turn a light moment dark as quick as Hitchcock. He's one of those rare people who can perceive the whole and the individual parts simultaneously, and render both without injustice to either. As in Breughel, there are no unimportant characters.

Nirvana Blues is something of an exception. In this last book of the trilogy, Nichols turns his attention to his own class, the middle, and, I suspect, to his own sad progress through the 70s as a member of that class. The result is satire, and the central brunt of that satire, Joe Miniver, is so close to the bullseye of our little middle-American hearts that you can't but love to hate him, or hate to love him. In this book, the gaggle of New Age ripoff artists surrounding Joe are presented with a contempt seldom found in NIchols' previous writing.

I haven't begun, really, to talk about the energy, the humor, the superb storytelling to be found in the *Milagro* trilogy. I hope I've homed in on a couple of central points about Nichols' writing, and I hope I've not overemphasized the darkness in the work of this most vivid, funny, joyous and unpretentious of writers.

Another fine writer I've met and gotten to know slightly is Laura Pritchett. I don't remember how I came upon her first book, *Hell's Bottom, Colorado,* but it so moved me that I wrote an unsolicited review that got published in *The Independent*:

Relocating the Core

The discounted sociologist Jared Schmitz...stated that in a culture in the seventh stage of rabid consumerism the peripheral always subsumes the core, and the core disappears to the point that very few of the citizenry can recall its precise nature.... the poignant message of a culture spending its time as it spends its money; springing well beyond the elements of food, clothes and shelter into the suffocating welter of the unnecessary that has become necessary.
- Jim Harrison, *The Beast that God Forgot to Invent*

Thrown by her horse into the metal teeth of a creep feeder, bleeding from mouth and body, alone in the falling snow, Carolyn, the protagonist of Laura Pritchett's stunning first novel, remains quite attuned to the core:

She can breathe, her heart is beating. She thinks of the basic human needs. Air. Water. Food. Shelter. In that order.

Carolyn is one of two middle daughters in the three-generation family of ranchers who inhabit *Hell's Bottom, Colorado,* winner of the Milkweed National Fiction Prize.

Insofar as the novel has a central character, Carolyn is it. But *Hell's Bottom* has more in mind than to create characters - though it does so memorably. This book has in mind to re-create the lives of people who live at the core. Still. Today. Right here in the midst of The Magic Kingdom.

Hell's Bottom is a novel in stories, a category generally applied by publishers to collections of short stories in hopes of overcoming sales resistance to collections of short stories. But in this case, it's the only accurate description to be made. This is a book whose chapters are as self-contained and multi-faceted as quartz crystals (some citrine, some rutilated, some smoky) that yet speak to each other in the kind of conversation that goes on in a family over generations.

Pritchett frames her book with stories that involve the saving of newborn calves by wrapping them in the quickly flayed hides of still-born or aborted calves, thus encouraging their foster mothers to give them suck. Human intelligence and technique and knowledge are used to preserve life and, if not defeat, at least to fight another day's draw with death. One calf at a time. The core.

The family paterfamilias, Ben, has "learned this much, how so much of life is the precarious moment, the sudden event, the surprise that spikes out of an ordinary day. How the rest - the bulk of life - is necessary to absorb these little bits. Absorb them and heal and wonder at." If you wanted to describe the stories in this book, and what they add up to, you couldn't do better than that.

As a short-story writer, Pritchett exemplifies Hemingway's principle that what's left out is more powerful that what's put in; that silence is what makes music possible; that the iceberg's power derives from its unseen weight beneath the surface.

Here's Carolyn's son Jack, as seen by his girlfriend Winnie - they're sitting on a park bench in the middle of Denver: "Jack runs his palms over his black Wranglers, and I look at my soft sweatpants and blue flannel shirt. I was going to dress up, it somehow seemed that I should. But at the last minute my hand just reached out for these. They're comfortable and soft and familiar.

"I pick a thread off the shirt and scratch my knees. Jack spits again and rubs his chin. We wait, staring out into this big city with light glinting off walls of glass and smooth granite."

What they aren't discussing any more is that they've come to Denver for Winnie to have an abortion. That they're not discussing it is not discussed here. What's discussed is the way people try to keep in touch with their physical bodies when reality and their minds have forced them to make a difficult choice, and they've made it, and they aren't happy with it.

To Hemingway, by way of comparison, I add Steinbeck, who wrote so well about the joy of being alive in the natural world. Pritchett writes as well:

"The sun's setting over the Rocky Mountains, and there's a meadowlark singing, and it's getting cool and quiet. Slade starts whistling softly, some tune that's soft and low; something I've never heard before.

"We stay like that for a long time until Slade laughs. He nods at the horses, who are trotting through an open gate into the lawn, heading right for the garden and apple tree. This is no surprise, since it happens every day. Stoney has learned to open the latch with his nose, and no one has gotten around to putting a better latch on the gate yet. I don't think anyone will, either, since it seems to be some kind of ritual, this letting the horses get out and then chasing them back in."

This book is some kind of ritual. It's a ritual celebrating the basic human needs, lucidly examining the choices we can make about how to meet those needs, and making a big poem about the tragic comedy we make with our choices. There is more life in this book that you will find anywhere else in a long time of looking. Give it to yourself for Christmas.

That was published in conjunction with a book-signing Laura Pritchett came down to do at the (regrettably late) Chinook Bookshop. I'd decided to follow my own advice and give copies to a lot of friends and family for Christmas, and she signed a bunch of them for me, and we got talking for a bit, and continued by letter after that for a couple of years until she came down to do a signing at Borders for her new novel, *Sky Bridge*. We had plenty of time to talk at that event, which hadn't been well promoted. I'd written a review, but it was turned down by *The Independent*.

One of the Props, One of the Pillars
[*Sky Bridge,* by Laura Pritchett, Milkweed Editions, 2005 $22.00]

Not much happens in Laura Pritchett's fine novel *Sky Bridge.* The Holy Grail is not tracked down, no buildings or cities explode in slow motion, nobody even gets colorfully blown to pieces by large ordinance. It's a novel about people who do not live in Media Land, who live in Colorado, one of those Red States the politicians praise as a prelude to further rape, one of those flyover states.

The indifference of official America to its flyover people - that is, to the vast majority of its people - is reflected in the characters of *Sky Bridge.* Putting away cans of baby formula in the cupboard, the narrator's mother Kay remarks, "'I don't know why they take the thing that's most important to an infant and kill us with the price.'"

"'Who?'"

"'Them,' she says, her hands flying around to the outside world."

Kay, her husband long gone, has raised her two daughters, Libby and Tess, working for Baxter as a ranch hand east of Lamar. Tess has found herself pregnant by Simon, a nauseatingly hypocritical member of the Cowboy Christian Coalition. Libby prevails upon Tess to have the baby with the promise that she will raise it. After baby Amber's birth, Tess promptly disappears with Clark to a life of running drugs and illegal immigrants. Kay is wearily outraged: "'When's it going to end? When's it going to let up? I was just done with you girls. I was done raising you, and now this.'" Libby begins to learn how to love a child. And life will go on. As her friend Miguel, who is raising a son abandoned in suicide by Shawny, Libby's best friend, says, "'Our kids are going to grow up together. *Y nosotros tambien.*'"

In the beginning, Libby has very little idea what "growing up" entails. She feels trapped in a place that offers few prospects. After Frank, her employer at Ideal Foods, has described their country east of Lamar as "the last fine place to be," Libby reflects, "'...but all my old schoolmates are either doing drugs or working minimum wage or in jail...hanging around letting their lives go by.....'" But Frank is insistent: "'This place has some real advantages, and you'll come to appreciate them more now that you're raising a kid. It's safe. It's small. And people look out for each other.'"

Some people, anyhow. Miguel, for example, raises a small plot of marijuana and helps illegal aliens find work at the end of their perilous trips. He raises pot because he cannot be a decent father to his son and work more than his one job at Lupe's Diner. He helps the illegals because he knows what their lives have been and what their desperation is. He will eventually marry one of them so that she and her child can become residents.

Tess and Clark, on the other hand, run drugs and illegals for quite other reasons: "'Clark decided we might as well be efficient. Run two things at the same time,'" Tess explains to Libby. And of course it's good money. When it's time for Miguel to pay Clark for the "shipment," Clark changes the price at the last minute. Why settle for good money when you have the customer over a barrel?

There's the choice about growing up. You can become, in Miguel's words, someone with "'a heart that goes outside itself, into the world.'" Or you can become "'so damn cold and empty that it's just scary. It's true, you know. The people who seem warm but are cold. That's Shawny for you. That's Tess....'"

These are people who still live with the realities of the land from which the food comes. Libby learns to know what such people know. In the words of Stephen L. Lyons' fine essay "How I Failed at Farming (Again)," "If you have a strong stomach and can listen long enough without fainting or retching, you'll find that farm-injury stories have an important underlying message: pay attention. Furthermore, when you think things are going well, pay *extra* attention. By the Midwestern farmer's philosophy, bad is bad, and good will probably turn bad if you don't watch out." This is not just the MIdwestern farmer's philosophy; it is the philosophy of all people who live in the actual world rather than the abstract world of Media Land.

Recalling a sudden, intense hailstorm that left one of Baxter's peacocks dead on the ground, Libby thinks, "It was beautiful and crazy-looking, but I was more interested in looking at the alfalfa, at all the bent and broken stems jabbing out from the ice, at the whole field that had been knocked flat. I was wrapping my arms around myself for warmth and I was thinking, *Man, a few footsteps were nothing at all compared to the way the world can come crashing down.*

"Here is something I know: some people pay attention to the world in a different way. An alert way. Because they know about danger. It depends on where they started, on how much their world got crashed up in the first place."

But alertness does not suffice. Clark is alert. Tess is alert. A cold, empty heart allows plenty of time to be alert. The real trick is to live in this real world, which crashes up just about anyone who lives long enough, without letting its pain harden and empty your heart. As Baxter, who's been hearing the Reaper's footsteps pussyfooting around, tells Libby, "'Now, if you can suffer but not be bitter it'll change you into a real human. A soft human.'"

I hope I have not made *Sky Bridge* sound like a philosophy text or a sermon. It is a very fine novel, with all that word implies: a deeply imagined world in which distinctive characters talk the way people actually talk, and do the awful and wonderful things to and for each other that people do.

Most of these characters act with considerable kindness toward each other, tolerate each other's faults and weaknesses, go out of their way to help each other. In Media World, such a view of people is unacceptable. Winners are cold. They may smile and joke, but we know that's just a ruse, disguising the hard little berries of their dead souls. And winning is, after all, the only thing. To suggest otherwise is to be tagged as a sentimentalist.

In his Nobel Prize address, William Faulkner described the "privilege" of the writer: "...to help man endure by lifting his heart, by reminding him of the courage and honor and hope and pride and compassion and pity and sacrifice which have been the glory of his past." Without pretension or preaching, that is exactly what *Sky Bridge* does.

I thought that might have been rejected because it ran too long, so I tried to cut it back a bit and gear it toward *The High Country News,* a terrific periodical that Laura suggested might take it:

Lives Worth Noticing
[Laura Pritchett, *Sky Bridge,* Milkweed Editions, 2005]

"And so many of the people in the arena here, you know, were underprivileged anyway, so this is working very well for them." So Barbara Bush, speaking of people uprooted by Katrina from their homes, their jobs, their histories, many having no idea where other members of their families might be, or if they yet lived. Working very well for them.

If you believed any of the Bush clan or other owners and operators of this country had a shred of decency or empathy, you might wish they would read Laura Pritchett's novel *Sky Bridge.* You might wish they'd read, in particular, this snatch of conversation between the narrator Libby and her friend and fellow single parent Miguel Mendoza:

"'You want there to be a level playing field,' he says.

"'Exactly. That's a good phrase.'

"' My family - my cousins, for example, in Mexico - they say the same thing, sometimes. They say, those *bolillos,* those *gringos,* they start someplace easier. It makes it hard for them to like you. They want the playing field leveled too.'

"' I don't blame them.'

"'Some people'll never know about this. Because they had enough from the get-go.'

"'I guess it's not their fault. But still, I hate them.'

"'Doesn't matter whose fault. It just means that some people are never going to understand some things....'"

One of the many pleasures of *Sky Bridge* is listening to Libby's voice, the voice of a woman in her early 20s that reveals both her youthful idealism and her occasional reversions to a teenager's anguished rage at a world that offers little support for her dreams. Libby lives with her mother Kay in a run-down house east of Lamar on a ranch belonging to Baxter, who has so far managed to retain his cattle in spite of the drought that "feels dangerous, like it's pressing down to suck away the life of this earth." As the novel begins, Libby is commencing her new career as mother to her sister Tess's baby Amber. Libby has prevailed upon Tess to bear Amber rather than abort her. Libby views her promise to raise Tess's child as a "reach for something terrific."

She promptly discovers that it's terrifically hard. Kay is enraged by the new burden she knows she'll have to help bear. Libby's boyfriend Derek doesn't feel ready for fatherhood, and understands sooner than Libby that Amber means the end of their relationship. One of Libby's many dreams has been that she and Tess would somehow share in raising the baby, but Tess quite promptly takes off for Durango. Libby is beginning to learn the difference between "knowing" everything, as one does at her age, and knowing what everything really means.

Recalling a sudden, massive hailstorm years back, Libby sees again "the alfalfa...all the bent and broken stems jabbing out from the ice...the whole field that had been knocked flat," and she reflects, "Here is something that I know: some people pay attention to the world in a different way. An alert way. Because they know about danger.

It depends on where they started, on how much their world got crashed up in the first place."

In Libby's world, pretty much everyone's life has gotten crashed up. Her father has long ago drifted away, his "light burnt out," leaving Kay to raise two daughters single-handed. Baxter has lost his wife and helpmeet Adeline. Frank, the kindly owner of Ideal Foods where Libby works, has lost his fiancee in a car crash. Miguel is a single parent because his wife and Libby's best friend Shawny has committed suicide. Loss, grief, loneliness and disaster are the human lot. The question Libby wrestles with throughout the book is how to live through them without letting them burn your light out.

The alternatives are clearly posed by Miguel: "'My *abuelita* always said that there's two kinds of people in this world, warm people and cold people. Sometimes they trick you. You think they're cold but you find out that underneath they're actually warm. They got a heart after all, and it's a heat that goes outside itself, into the world. Then you got the people who come across as warm, but underneath they're so damn cold and empty that it's just scary. It's true, you know. The people who seem warm but are cold. That's Shawny for you. That's Tess....'"

By the novel's end, Libby is finally able to see that Miguel's view of Tess is accurate: "Tess is good at making people love her and then not loving them back....Maybe it's her way of getting back at the world." And maybe Tess learned a good deal of it from her mother's often untempered bitterness, although Kay still has a heart, as Baxter tries to tell Libby: "'Look deep inside your mom and you'll see a lot of courage, a lot of care. She is bitter, though, your mom. People can get behind pain like they're leaning into a wind and it supports them after a bit and that's what happened to Kay.'"

But Libby's life provides her with plenty of examples of an alternative way, most clearly stated by Baxter: "'Now, if you can suffer but not be bitter it'll change you into a real human. A soft human.'" The key to this puzzle - how to suffer and not become bitter - she learns, is imagination, the power not only to see but to become what you see. In her final conversation with Tess, who returns briefly only to leave once more, Libby thinks, "See people, I want to tell her. *See them*, and especially see them if at first you don't think they're worth noticing....Don't forget to pretend to be them sometimes. So that you can realize what it feels like. They're not numbers. They're not money. They're not even a 'they.'" Let your broken heart go outside itself, into the world.

All these people are living their lives not worth noticing "in the middle of Nowhere, Colorado." Without preaching, with a remarkably skillful interweaving of flashbacks and points of view within one narrative voice, Pritchett resoundingly demonstrates that *no* life is unworthy of notice. In the words of James Baldwin: "For while the tale of how we suffer, and how we are delighted and how we may triumph is never new, it always must be heard. There isn't any other tale to tell. It's the only light we've got in all this darkness."

No go - still too long. They eventually printed this severely pruned version, following the general trend in journalism of all sorts toward book reviews about the length of a 6th grade book report:

Sky Bridge, by Laura Pritchett

Laura Pritchett's first novel, *Sky Bridge,* is set in "Nowhere, Colorado," on the ranchland east of the plains town of Lamar. In this tiny place assaulted by big forces — climate change, the global economy, federal policies — narrator Libby finds prospects slim: "… all my old schoolmates are either doing drugs or working minimum wage or in jail.…"

But the central characters of the story — Libby, her younger sister Tess, their mother Kay, and Baxter, the rancher who provides Kay both a job and a ramshackle house — have neither time nor inclination to analyze the forces that are "crashing up their lives." They have only hope, compassion (with the exception of Tess), and a stubborn determination to cope with what must be coped with, including the results of their own bad decisions or inattention.

One of these results is baby Amber, brought into being by Tess's casual one-nighter with Simon, proud member of the Cowboy Christian Coalition, and kept from abortion by Libby's promise to raise her.

Putting cans of baby formula away in the cupboard, reluctant new grandmother Kay observes, " ' I don't know why they take the thing that's most important to an infant and kill us with the price.'

'Who?' Libby inquires.

'Them,' she says, her hands flying around to the outside world."

Pritchett captures the rhythms and emphases of everyday speech with perfect pitch. And for the most part, her characters live up to their description by Libby's employer, Frank, who says "... people look out for each other."

Abandoned to their own devices by a government owned and operated by multinational corporations, these people retain a dignity that makes them impossible to dismiss. By novel's end, the reader may recall Faulkner's words in his Nobel Prize acceptance speech: "I believe that man will not only endure: he will prevail....because he has a soul, a spirit capable of compassion and sacrifice and endurance." *Sky Bridge* bring these abstract virtues to vivid, concrete life.

By the time Laura Pritchett published a sort of sequel to that first novel, she advised me that it would be far better to put my review onto the Amazon website, which I did:

Red Lightning
by Laura Pritchett

Here is an entire scene, the death of a main character, from *Red Lightning*:

"Kay starts gasping. She needs air. Even I can see that. I look around the room, as if seeking out extra oxygen, something that can inflate her lungs. Libby presses her hands more firmly onto Kay, holding her in this suffering, and I put my hands on Kay's arm and do as well.

"Then there is quiet. I get up and open a window. Because all spirits should be able to fly out, free. Or to let in and out the air. I stare from Kay's body to the window, just wondering if perhaps I can see a wisp depart. There is nothing except two sisters in the startled silence."

Not even a mention of emotions, only actions that speak more eloquently of emotions than any words, and that one devastating simple sentence: "Then there is quiet."

Laura Pritchett uses the simplest, clearest possible language she can find to repeatedly knock you off your perch this way, to make you see, and hear, and truly feel the lives of others. We need to do this, to become truly human by focusing closely on other humans. In the words of narrator Tess, "if we listen harder, stare harder, focus harder, use our imaginations harder, the people at the other end of our sight, well, they morph from blurs on the horizon, something barely discernible at a distance, and become very clear, very detailed." That is the work of this eloquent, searing, beautiful book. It addresses its readers with the gentle severity of a letter Hemingway wrote to Scott Fitzgerald, saying much the same thing: "A long time ago you stopped listening except to the answers to your own questions. That's what dries a writer up...not listening. And we sprout again as grass does after rain when we listen. That is where it all comes from. Seeing. Listening."

Listen to this book. It'll help you see more and better.

Another Western writer I was lucky enough to get to know a little was David James Duncan. In the late 90s, I got to introduce him at a conference of community college Humanities teachers held in Santa Fe:

It's my immense privilege to introduce David James Duncan.

As some of you, I'm sure, know, Mr. Duncan is the author of three major books, *The River Why, The Brothers K* and *River Teeth*. In case you don't read best-sellers, the first two are novels, the last a collection of stories and essays.

The first novel is a fish story. Mr. Duncan is both a fisherman and a story teller. You all know about fish stories, but maybe not about all that can be done with fish stories. I ask you to listen to a fish story from *The River Why*.

The narrator, Gus Orviston, has come with his mother to Celilo Falls on the Columbia River, a falls about to be buried by the dam at The Dalles, to watch a friend, a

Warm Springs Indian named Thomas Bigeater, fish this part of the river for the last time. Along the banks, other fishermen, many of them Indians, are fishing with a marked degree of drunken disrespect. After watching them for a time, Thomas begins to chant; the narrator's mother asks him to "give it to her in English":

"Thomas turned to her: his face made me want to hide. He said, 'I sing the story of the young men of the Nass River People. It cannot be sung in English. English will not sing. Do you scold the geese flying over in autumn because they sing in their own language?'

"Ma blushed and turned away: it was the first time, the only time, I have seen her utterly abashed. Again she said, 'Sorry.' But this time she meant it.

"Thomas extended his tree-branch arm out over the falls and bellowed, 'Celilo! Stop your roaring! Roaring is not English!' Then he chuckled like a kid who'd farted in a car and chucked Ma in the ribs. She giggled and hugged the huge brown arm. Thomas said, 'I will tell you this talk in *your* language, little sister and brother. Stiff and ugly as it is.'

"I thought he winked as he said this, but I wasn't sure. I didn't know Indians winked. I thought winking was in English.

"Thomas's eyes grew vacant and he hummed for a little. All the while he told the tale he stared, but seemed not to see, across the river...."

David James Duncan is a masterly story-teller, because he knows that the "meaning" of a story lies as much in its context of time, place, weather, and the places its listeners have reached in their lives as in the tale itself. He is a great story teller because he greatly loves his characters. Love being necessary for knowledge, he knows them greatly, and so his readers do, also.

One of my best friends is the best reader I've ever known - he savors a book as if it were a long ocean trip or a great meal; he pays attention to every word; he hears every word; in Hemingway's phrase, he has a hundred per cent, solid, shockproof shit-detector. A while ago I gave him a copy of *The Brothers K,* a novel centered on baseball, the experience of growing up in the 60's, and family. I asked my friend a few days ago how it was going. "I'm about half way through it," he said. "I keep slowing down, and slowing down. I hate to think about finishing it." We talked about other things for a bit. "He sure does know his baseball," my friend suddenly interjected. And later, "He sure does know his families." And later again, "He sure does know his Russians."

I remember the Saturday I finally gave up and decided to finish reading that book. I won't be giving away too much if I tell you that there's a death at the end of the book, and I lay on my bed going through that death of a man I'd come to love and admire, crying real tears, and laughing through them.

So I can't think of very many people better equipped to talk to us about the sacredness of life and its creatures. In a great essay called "Who Owns the West?" Mr. Duncan said, "I like Barry Lopez's borrowed Inuktitut definition of the storyteller as 'the person who creates the atmosphere in which wisdom reveals itself.'"

I expect that we are about to hear some stories like that. Some of them will probably involve fish. They will be thiiiiiiiiiiis big.

Duncan has kept writing since then, but no more novels. He's been unable to withdraw from the endless struggle to defend the waters of the earth against the destruction with which so many of our addictions and practices threaten them. Yet he's managed to remain sane and kept his humor intact during those struggles. One time he sent me a postcard that concluded, "Saw Salman Rushdie at Book Award hoohaw in NYC. Told him his parents spelled 'salmon' wrong." I've liked to imagine how this struck Rushdie, who's always been taken with deadly (sometimes *literally* deadly) seriousness.

I've already mentioned Nelson Algren, to me one of the great writers we've produced. I read this paper at another Humanities conference:

Nelson Algren and the Murder of Meaning

The murder of meaning is a crime Nelson Algren spent his life trying to get people interested in, and it scarcely ended with his death in 1982. Shortly after that year, in fact, one of the greatest admissions of that crime began appearing on t-shirts nationwide. They said, "The one who dies with the most toys wins."

To which Algren's great love, Simone de Beauvoir, had long ago replied, "'It is because of the abstract climate in which they live that the importance of money is so disproportionate.... It isn't that young Americans don't wish to do great things... but that they don't know there are great things to be done.'" (Algren, *Nonconformity*, 45-47)

More recently, one of the culprits was quoted proudly rationalizing the murder: "Advertising is a means of contributing meaning and values that are necessary and useful to people in structuring their lives, their social relationships and their rituals." (Thomas, 74) Another culprit explained how this is done. The conductors of four of her "focus groups" using children reported to her that the kids seemed apprehensive about the looming dangers of adolescence - violence, drugs, std's - and she proved ready for the challenge: "So I stopped the research and I said, 'Just go in and ask them what Nickelodeon can do for them.' And in all four groups: 'Just give us back our childhood....'" And that became our battle cry. That became our platform." (*Ibid*, 75)

And though he'd been dead for seventeen years, Nelson Algren had long before his death heard this kind of self-congratulatory cant, and known what the words "contributing" and "give us back our childhood" meant in practice. "So accustomed," Algren darkly suspicioned, "have we become to the testimony of the photo-weeklies, backed by witnesses from radio and TV, establishing us permanently as the happiest, healthiest, wealthiest, most inventive, tolerant and fun-loving folk yet to grace the earth of man, that we tend to forget that these are bought-and-paid-for witnesses, and all their testimony is perjured." Then he went on to give *his* evidence: "For it is not in the afternoon in Naples nor yet at evening in Marseilles, not in Indian hovels half-sunk in an ancestral civilization's ruined halls nor within those lion-colored tents pitched down the Sahara's endless edge that we discover those faces most debauched by sheer uselessness. Not in the backwash of poverty and war, but in the backwash of prosperity and progress." (*Nonconformity*, 73-74)

For if the "meaning and values necessary and useful to people" must be "contributed" to people -meaning sold to them - and "childhood" must be "given" back to children - meaning sold to them - then *some* kind of crime has surely transpired, and it behooves us to investigate it. For how did those values necessary and useful to people escape their grasp in the first place? And had those children looking to be given back their childhood *given* it away - or had somebody stolen it... the better to be in a position to sell it back to them?

Nelson Algren keenly observed modern life and wrote about what he saw for fifty years. While his observations coincided with those of some other contemporaries, none of the others surpassed Algren's ability to "cut in close" - a favorite phrase of his - to the heart of our anguish or to find and express the beauty as well as the horror of living in it.

I want to bring you Algren in his own words as much as possible, because he created a unique style, an unmistakable voice that rises from his pages and makes good company in the bleakest hours before dawn. But style was never what he sought. In *Notes From a Sea Diary*, Algren's book-length essay on Hemingway, he wrote, "Nor was his style a clever trick, an acquired device.... His style was the means by which he fulfilled a need uniquely his own; thus filling a need in the company of men. This need was for light and simplicity. In achieving it for himself he achieved it for others enduring a murky complexity. By strength of his own love he forced a door. That opened into a country in which, for those willing to risk themselves, love and death became realities." (171) "Style," Algren had alleged earlier, "is that force by which a man becomes what he most needs to become." (89)

Nelson Algren, born Nelson Algren Abraham in 1909 in Detroit, needed to become Nelson Algren of Chicago. His family moved to Chicago in 1913, but it took him a lot more years than that to become Nelson Algren.

The historical circumstances that first formed Algren, then rewarded him, and finally maneuvered him into relative obscurity are customarily known as the "Roaring '20's," the "Great Depression," and "McCarthyism," the post-World-War-II syndrome under which we still in so many ways labor.

In the Chicago of the Teens and Twenties, Algren grew up in a working-class family whose two elder sisters and whose mother, Goldie, harbored middle-class aspirations. To Algren, success as seen by such would-be succeeders as his mother was best expressed by Ibsen's Peer Gynt: "...but to pass, safe and dry-shod, down the rushing stream of time...." (*Nonconformity*, 5) Which, to Algren, meant that you survived your life by failing to ever live it.

Algren's sister Bernice, his elder by seven years, was the only member of the family to whom he looked with respect. Bernice was a lively young woman who embraced every aspect of her life, equally devoted to history, physics, atheism, poetry and swimming. She introduced Algren to the belief that life was to be lived, and a vital part of living for her was literature, to which she also introduced him by reading to him and bringing him books from the library.

In addition to serving as heroine and teacher to Algren, Bernice also may have given birth to another of Algren's lifelong themes, the betrayal of love, when in 1926 she married a staid chemical engineer. Algren seems to have viewed this as a sort of selling out, an abandonment of life; perhaps also as an abandonment of himself. But however he viewed her marriage, Algren owed one more experience to Bernice. She prevailed upon Algren's reluctant father to allow him to go to college at the University of Illinois in 1927, and prevailed upon her husband to help pay his tuition while he worked himself through. (Drew, 24)

The John Held era came to an abrupt end in 1929, and by 1931, when Algren graduated with a degree in journalism, he found no work available in Chicago. He described the next step- and the rest of his life - on the jacket copy of his 1956 novel *A Walk on the Wild Side* : "I'd come to New Orleans with a card entitling me to some editorial position because I'd attended a school of journalism. I wasn't sure whether I wanted to be a columnist or a foreign correspondent but I was willing to take what was open. What was open was a place on a bench in Lafayette Square if you got there early. I found my way to the streets on the other side of the Southern Pacific station, where the big jukes were singing something called 'Walking the Wild Side of Life.' I've stayed pretty much on that side of the curb ever since." (Rear cover copy)

While Algren's tone is insouciant, his experiences on the road were far from lighthearted. He hooked up with a pair of drifters, both named Luther, in New Orleans, and they wound up in the Rio Grande Valley, where one of them attempted to leave

Algren at the mercy of farmers the other Luther had flummoxed out of their crops. Eventually, Algren served time in jail for attempting to steal a typewriter. These experiences, and the lives of the men and women he encountered in the hobo camps and shelters and soup kitchens, came as a shock to Algren, who had set out still a basically optimistic, middle-class young fellow.

"Everything I'd been told was wrong.... I'd been told, I'd been assured, that it was a strive and succeed world....But this is not what America was. America was not socialized and I resented very deeply that I'd been lied to.... You had to reverse everything you'd been taught, mechanically as well as morally," Algren much later told H.E. F. Donahue. (Donahue, 55-56) Algren had set out to see America, and what he had found, in the words of Bettina Drew, was a "world where relationships meant nothing, where money was more important than life, and life was so cheap as to be valueless." (Drew, 42)

Back in Chicago, Algren began to put his experiences into short stories, and one of them drew the attention of the publisher Vanguard, who enquired about a novel. In a typically ruinous financial deal, Algren negotiated an advance of one hundred dollars to produce what became his first novel, *Somebody in Boots.* (Drew, 54) He put a year and a half into the book and wound up owing money on the advance to Vanguard, for in 1935 books were simply not selling.

In his preface to a later edition of the book, Algren described it as "an uneven novel written by an uneven man in the most uneven of American times." (*Boots*, 9) This is a fair characterization. Throughout his career, Algren worked by feeling rather than plan, and the lives he wrote about worked in much the same way. In this first novel, he chronicles the wanderings of Cass McKay, son of "that wild and hardy tribe....the slaveless yeomen who had never cared for slaves or land....But," Algren wondered, "now that the frontier had vanished, where did the man go whose only skills were those of the frontier?" (*Ibid*, 8) Through Cass, a gentle, ignorant boy who flees the hopelessness of a rural Rio Grande valley in which he has never known anything but hunger and scorn and his father's raging sense of being cheated, Cass sees at first hand all that Algren had seen - the danger and violence of life riding the rails, the exploitation of the homeless and of the women, the hopelessness of millions of people cast adrift, drawn eventually to the cities like Chicago where they find no more recognition of their humanity or hope. They are all exiles, like Cass, "exiled from himself and expatriated within his own frontiers." (*Ibid*, 9)

Even in this first novel, infused occasionally with the communist rhetoric he'd absorbed in the John Reed Club he frequented in Chicago, Algren's vision pierced beyond rhetoric. Kurt Vonnegut saw how Algren differed from other "proletarian writers" of the period: "He broke new ground by depicting persons said to be dehumanized by poverty and ignorance and injustice as being *genuinely* dehumanized, and dehumanized quite *permanently*." (*Morning*, xix)

All his life, Algren saw that the lives of the majority of this world's citizens were expressions of their particular regions and pasts, and that little true individuality was available to the many. And yet he saw within each individual at least the faint residue of aspiration, hope, and love - of humanity. In Vonnegut's words, "he would be satisfied were we to agree with him that persons unlucky and poor and not very bright are to be respected for surviving, although they often have no choice but to do so in ways unattractive and blameworthy to those who are a lot better off." (*Ibid*, xx)

The failure of *Somebody in Boots* threw Algren into a long depression, from which he gradually emerged. He was hired on by the Federal Writers' Project, a branch of the WPA, and worked for a number of years as a researcher and writer, deepening his knowledge both of Illinois history and of the dispossessed of Chicago, and regaining a sense of worth that allowed him to begin work on his second novel, *Never Come Morning*. He later said of the Writers' Project that "It served to humanize people who had lost their self-respect by being out of work and then living by themselves began to feel the world was against them." (Drew, 100)

Thus began Algren's most productive period, one which brought him great critical if not financial success. *Never Come Morning* appeared in 1940, illuminating the lives of the poor Poles of Chicago's Northwest side, and receiving glowing and intelligent critical praise. Chicago novelist James T. Farrell - hardly a friend of Algren's - called it "one of the most important novels that I have read," and Philip Rahv, writing in *The Nation*, observed the strides Algren had made since his first novel: "...Algren's realism is so paced as to avoid the tedium of the naturalistic stereotype, of the literal copying of surfaces. He knows how to select, how to employ factual details without letting himself be swamped by them, and, finally, how to put the slang his characters speak to creative uses so that it ceases to be an element of mere documentation and turns into an element of style." (*Morning* , rear cover)

This last observation is particularly important to Algren's work. In *Somebody in Boots,* he had tried to render, with uneven success, the slang and accent and cadence of Texas, a dialect he'd only experienced briefly. But in *Never Come Morning* , and in the two books that followed it, he was working with the English spoken by the people he'd lived among most of his life. Further, Algren had continued to refine his ear and his skill at reproducing its testimony on the page as he worked for the Writers' Project, and the results were far more convincing.

Here, for example, is a debate between Bruno "Lefty" Bicek, the novel's protagonist, and a character contemptuously nicknamed "Bibleback" because of his devout religiosity:

"'...You gotta believe somethin, Left,'" [Bibleback] concluded apologetically.

"'I believe I got to take care of number one, then,' Bruno answered. 'That's *my* faith.'

"'Oh, I see - God been around a thousand years 'n' you been around seventeen 'n' you know as much as He does awready - Boy, Lefty, *you're* sharp - you learn faster'n Him even!...'

"'How come you know so much, Polack?' Bruno countered, an idea dawning in him - 'How come you're so sure I been here only seventeen years? How you know I didn't have a *in-car-nation* somewheres before - How you know I wasn't Jesus Christ before I was livin' in this neighborhood? How you know? Maybe I was *Adam* even.'" (*Morning* , 45-47)

While Algren went reluctantly off to serve as a Corpsman in the Army, seeing action in the last days of the war in Germany, his work became a target of the "respectable" Poles back in Chicago. The president of the Roman Catholic Union wrote

Algren's publisher, "I protest against further publishing of this book, for it fosters national disunity and should have no place in our libraries and homes." The Polish daily *Zgoda* added that "It is doubtful whether Goebbels' personal adjutant could have ordered a juicier Pole-baiting tale than this Swede has dared.... At 32, Algren, a Scandinavian, cannot possibly be without malice in his heart against the Poles." (*Ibid*, xi) The Polish establishment prevailed upon the Chicago Public Library to remove the book from its collection.

It remained removed as late as 1962, when Algren wrote in the preface to a new edition, "Thus through the furious logic of illiteracy we had come full cycle. We had fought in snow and slept in rain because somebody had said that every time he heard the word 'culture' he reached for his gun, and now we had won him the right of reaching for it. The man who had lost the war was not necessarily German nor was the man who had won it necessarily American....The victor in any land was the man who feels himself terribly wronged if his ultimatum on what his neighbors should read, what they should wear and what they should think is questioned. We had crossed an ocean only to find that that bore lived on the same street as ourselves." (*Ibid*, xiii-xiv)

But that was written after fifteen years of political reaction, after fear and hatred of Nazis had been smoothly transformed into fear and hatred of Communists. When Algren returned from the Army, he returned filled with optimism and energy. In 1947, he published *The Neon Wilderness*, a collection of short stories old and new, capturing the victories and defeats of "men and women forced to choices too hard to bear." *(Neon*, Deutsch, 14) The collection again received good notices and sold little.

Meanwhile, Algren was working on a new novel, *The Man With the Golden Arm*, about a Chicago Pole, Frankie Machine, who returns from the war with painful wounds and the memory that morphine can ease all sorts of pains. Frankie, a small-time card dealer, is a man trapped in almost every way conceivable - trapped by his own guilt, with which his pathetic wife Sophie keeps him chained to her, trapped by his addiction, trapped, finally, by his murder of the dope-dealer whose political connections make his otherwise unlamented death one that must be avenged by the authorities.

Hunted through the furnished rooms of Chicago, Frankie ultimately hangs himself rather than face arrest and execution.

The book reflects Algren's growing perception that the War had not ended, just come home and changed enemies. When Sparrow, Frankie's only friend, is lying in jail under threat of a life sentence unless he betrays Frankie, he hears the voice of a young woman being brought down into the cells, crying out,

"'Ain't nobody on *my* side?'...

"'Nobody, sister. Not a soul,' Sparrow answered, she suited his own mood so well. 'You're all on your own from here on out. Ain't nobody on anybody's side no more. You're the on'y one on your side 'n' I'm the on'y one on mine.'" (287)

This state of affairs is described at one point by Frankie, in a line that recurs throughout the book like the chorus of a popular song, as "'the new way of doin' things, you might call it.'" (257)

The Man With the Golden Arm left Algren feeling that he had finally written the book he'd wanted to write, and the critical reaction supported his conviction. Reviewers compared Algren to Victor Hugo, Dostoevsky, Gorky and Dickens; even *The New Yorker* praised the book, and in 1950 it received the first National Book Award. Hemingway told his editor that Algren was "the best novelist under 50, or you name it, writing today." (Drew, 210)

But this, as it turned out, marked the high water mark of Algren's career, for a different wind was already blowing, and writers who suggested that American democracy was less than perfect and that money and material success were not the proper measure of the good life were going to go abruptly out of style.

In 1947, the House Unamerican Activities Committee had begun hearings on Communist influence in the entertainment industry, leading to the conviction of ten prominent screenwriters, directors and producers, the "unfriendly witnesses," who refused to comply with the Committee's demand that they reveal their political convictions and name others who shared them. This began the period known now as the "McCarthy Era," during which private vigilantes joined the Committee in smearing the names and blackmailing the employers of thousands of American citizens.

Novelist and screenwriter Dalton Trumbo, one of the blacklisted "Hollywood Ten," wrote of the period: "What a curious era it was, and how sad: actors driven from radio, television, films and theatre - their fellow actors working all the while; doctors removed from the registry of such hospitals as Cedars of Lebanon in Los Angeles - their colleagues never once considering a move *en masse* to more civilized quarters; professors hounded from lecture halls, musicians from recording studios and symphony orchestras, artists from galleries and museums - their brothers contentedly continuing to teach, perform, exhibit; scientists banished from laboratories, ministers from pulpits, students from colleges, reporters from newspapers, editors from publishing houses, craftsmen from unions, lawyers, economists, sociologists, and statisticians from government posts....Colleagues, friends, fellow workers stepped softly into the jobs of the damned, and the hole which their disappearance left in the fabric of the community life was scarcely noticed except when one of them killed himself or required commitment." (Trumbo,147)

Many factors came together to give the national paranoia now known as "McCarthyism" its terrible destructive force. The fear inspired by the close shave applied by Adolf Hitler was certainly one of them, and perhaps the guilt created by our own use of the atomic bomb, and our consequent terror of Russia's acquisition of the bomb was another. Surely McCarthy, and Nixon and McCarran and J. Parnell Thomas and others of their ilk were strongly supported by industry, which also eagerly supported the Taft-Hartley anti-labor-union act. For America - at least some of America - had been left by the war holding nearly all the marbles, and the marble-holders were not eager to share them. So the airways and television screens of America were flooded, in short order, with programming such as "I Was a Communist for the FBI," and with jingoist rhetoric and jingoist revisions of history. Perhaps more importantly, no other versions of history or anything else were able to find a platform. Defenders of the "Hollywood Ten" had a hard time even renting a hall in which to speak, and one of the Hollywood studios decided to shelve "a half-finished film on the Indian peacemaker Hiawatha for fear that it 'might be regarded as a message for peace and therefore helpful to present Communist designs.'" (Drew, 215)

Trumbo eloquently summed up the repercussions of the great witch hunt on the intellectual life of the country: "It wasn't the Committee or the American Legion or the DAR or Parnell Thomas or Francis Walter or Walter Judd or Joe McCarthy or Roy Cohn or Westbrook Pegler or George Sokolsky or Victor Riesel who convinced the liberal establishment that the best way to fight the committee was to 'ghettoize' anyone who did; it was Arthur M. Schlesinger, Jr.'s 'non-Communist left,' bursting out of the river and crossing the trees in its first wild stampede toward the Center, startling to their feet great herds of creeping Socialists while Max Eastman and Sidney Hook, riding the flanks and bearing down hard, fired buckshot and bacon rind at the face of the wondering moon. They were going so fast they overshot their mark, but toward dawn they found themselves in some pretty fair pastureland slightly to the Right of Center...." (Trumbo, 142-143)

The climate of the Fifties, now an object of truly idiotic nostalgia, was two-fold. On the one hand was the view of America as a haven of small-town, agrarian virtue wedded to a cornucopia of technological wealth and ease - "suburbia," it came to be dubbed; the other was the underlying reality of a country lost to its purpose and ridden with nightly terror that someone might either come in wanting a piece of the barbecue grill or come in and atomize the whole shebang.

Charlie Chaplin described the situation thus: "'It's so b-o-o-o-ring.... America is so terribly grim in spite of all that material prosperity. They no longer know how to weep. Compassion and the old neighborliness have gone, people do nothing when friends and neighbors are attacked, libeled and ruined....and all in a sickening atmosphere of religious hypocrisy.'" (Drew, 236)

And the poet Archibald MacLeish noticed: "What is happening in the United States under the impact of the negative and defensive and often frightened opinion of these years is the falsification of the image the American people have long cherished of themselves as beginners and begetters, changers and challengers, creators and accomplishers. A people who have thought of themselves for a hundred and fifty years as having purposes of their own for the changing of the world cannot learn overnight to think of themselves as the resisters of another's purposes without beginning to wonder who they are. A people who have been real to themselves because they were for something cannot continue to be real to themselves when they find they are merely against something." To which Dalton Trumbo later added, "This quality of opposition has become the keystone to our national existence." (Trumbo, 34-35)

But early in the Fifties, Algren still thought he was riding high, and when the actor John Garfield wanted to star in *The Man With the Golden Arm*, he thought he had it made. But then Garfield, threatened with perjury by the House Unamerican Activities Committee because he'd denied knowing any communists, died of a heart attack, and that deal went south. (Drew, 235-236) Algren decided to counterattack, and began a long essay in which he spoke to what he saw going on in the country, and of what he believed the country - or at least its great writers - had always stood for. Parts of the essay appeared in periodicals, and he delivered another part at the University of Missouri Writer's Conference, but in 1953, his publisher, Doubleday, refused to issue it. He sent the original to his then agent, who lost it, and the manuscript was only reassembled and published three years ago. It is this essay I particularly wish to commend to your attention as teachers of both literature and of writing, so we'll come back to it. (Drew, 238)

The resistance to this essay, the failure of his publisher to adequately promote his previous book, and his own nose told Algren that the times were changing, and that the work he wanted to do, speaking for the losers in a society now governed and informed exclusively by winners, had come to nothing. He reacted with cynical despair, taking on a rewrite of *Somebody in Boots* with the comment, "I'm aiming solely at the pocketbook traffic.... I think that the writers of the twenties were sounder of heart....While those of the [thirties] came in on themselves: gave up, quit cold, snitched, begged off, sold out, copped out, denied all, and ran....I'm hacking too. Nobody stayed." (Drew, 253)

Looking at fifty, his country a relentlessly cheerful horror, Algren reached another low point. And so, when Famous Director Otto Preminger acquired the rights to *The Man With the Golden Arm*, and offered Algren a trip to Los Angeles to write the screenplay, Algren accepted. "Well," as Algren often enquired of his readers, "what would *you* do?"

His initial meeting with Preminger was gruesome from the get-go, for he quickly perceived that Preminger had no sympathy for the characters of the book and no respect for what the book had said or for the writer who'd said it; he'd merely seen the chance to make a hot property, now that drug addicts had joined communists in the list of things for Americans to fear and hate.

Algren's response to this was to offer Preminger a 12-page treatment which culminated with Frankie Machine - who would ultimately be played by Frank Sinatra - saying to Sophie - ultimately played by Kim Novak, to Algren's eternal distress - "White goddess say not go that part of forest." (*Morning*, 285) Things pretty much went downhill from there, and Algren never saw another dime from the movie, which made many dimes indeed, billed as "Otto Preminger's *The Man With the Golden Arm*."

A writer's books are his only assets, and Algren had been left with no other assets in his transactions with Preminger. His reputation, after the publication of his "rewrite" of *Somebody in Boots*, issued as *A Walk on the Wild Side,* was left in no better shape, for the critics who were now being published in the few magazines that reviewed books at all were those who had joined the great pack on the near Right.

Norman Podhoretz wondered why Algren "finds bums so much more interesting and stirring than other people." Leslie Fiedler called him "a museum piece - the last of the Proletarian writers." Edmund Fuller called him a "destroyer of the social order."

(Drew, 275)

Things didn't look good. Algren himself wondered why he was doing what he was doing. Where were the readers? Why should he continue to write? "Who for?" he asked. "I used to think it was for some vague assemblage called readers. I used to think it was for some people named Cowley and Sartre and such too. But all it turns out it is for is for someone like Rapietta Greensponge, girl counselor." (Drew, 299)

But the cynicism and bitterness seldom affected the writing, and even the "pocketbook trade" version of *Somebody in Boots, A Walk on the Wild Side* , was far from the sell-out Algren perceived. He saw that his time on the stage was done, all right.

He perceived he'd been banished to the minors. But he never stopped throwing his best stuff, even when he had no stuff left at all.

He did, however, abandon his plans for another novel, and become a sort of a journalist. During the sixties, he produced an anthology of short stories, *Nelson Algren's Book of Lonesome Monsters* and two travel books - *Who Lost an American?* and *Notes From a Sea Diary*, all for money, because writing was what he knew how to do for money. But they contain some of his best writing, for though he told himself he was writing for "the pocketbook trade," he could never do anything except write from the heart of his own experience.

And his experience was considerable. Once he was granted a passport, he traveled to Ireland, France, Spain, North Africa, Turkey, Formosa, Kowloon, and India. Everywhere he went, he found his basic sense of "the life of man" confirmed: the vast majority of men trapped in an endless variety of snares, many of their own devising; the vast majority of women at the mercy of merciless men; the vast majority of people struggling endlessly to fashion brief moments of decency, honor or pleasure against all odds.

It was that sense of life he had sought to convey in all his earlier work and that he found in the work of what he considered the true American literary tradition. He restated a good deal of what he believed about that tradition in his preface to *Lonesome Monsters* and in the two travel books, but it was not until *Nonconformity* was finally (and beautifully) published in 1996 that his full, eloquent vision of that tradition became available.

Algren begins the essay by identifying his enemies with remarkable clarity: the military-industrial-government complex fostered by World War II and its thugs, and the apologists for that new empire among the intellectuals and writers and artists. Ten years before Dwight Eisenhower identified the "military-industrial complex" as a threat in his farewell address, (leaving the government out of the formula for obvious reasons), Algren recognized it right off, quoting Eisenhower's Secretary of Defense: "Charles E. Wilson, writing in the *Army Ordinance Journal* as far back as 1944, feels we ought to be less secretive about [keeping the war-orders mounting]: 'War has been inevitable in our human affairs as an evolutionary force....Let us make the three-way partnership (industry, government, army) permanent.'" (*Nonconformity*, 9)

Algren juxtaposes this sentiment with Faulkner's well-known remarks in his Nobel Prize Speech of 1950: "'Our tragedy today is a general and universal physical fear so long sustained by now that we can even bear it. There are no longer problems of the spirit. There is only the question: when will I be blown up? Because of this, the young man or woman writing today has forgotten the problems of the human heart in conflict with itself which alone can make good writing....'" (6)

But Algren finds the causes of the anguish of the early 50's more complex than the simple fear of physical atomization. Implicit in his argument is the adage that "all government depends upon the consent of the governed," and he looks to the state of the "governed" for his explanation of that "general and universal...fear."

He finds it in the guilt and consequent fear of the middle class, a class whose very existence and burgeoning affluence depends on the money generated by the war machine. Wilson's quotation suggests that America exist in a state of perpetual war, as indeed it very nearly has since 1950. (See Seymour Epstein, *The Permanent War Economy* .) Yet we have continued to tell ourselves that we are a nation "with malice toward none, with charity for all," a nation that wouldn't say "war" if we had a mouthful. And our middle class has prospered to a level of affluence so far beyond the aspirations of most of the six billion human inhabitants of the planet as to seem, to the objective observer, obscene.

But all this profit has not come without cost. The greatest cost, in Algren's view, is in the isolation of the individual. An isolation endemic in the puritan-capitalist structure of American society, but encouraged to "psychotic" extremes by the actions of the government: "We have come to the point where, in order to avoid the face of our own psychosis, we insist that all good men be psychotic. For if we have not, as a nation, gone psychotic, how is it that we now honor most those whom we once most despised? Now the professional perjurer is called an 'informant' - we used to call them something else. Blackmail in the name of 'anti-Communism' is now dignified by the name of 'research services.' Though we always believed, by and large, in rugged individualism, we didn't until now like the idea of dog eat dog. " (68)

What Algren found gnawing at the middle class was the same *agenbite* he had observed chewing up the lower classes - the terrible isolation of American society - an isolation bred by the equation of material success with spiritual success; with virtue: "Our practice of specializing our lives to let each man be his own department, safe from the beetles and the rain...." (*Nonconformity*, 19) Now, institutionalized and sanctioned by every center of power from *Time Magazine* to General Motors and General Electric to the Senate of the United States, this specialization had led to a situation in which, "...out of a conviction that every man should be his own department we have specialized ourselves into a condition where every man is actually his own broom closet." (20)

George Orwell had observed the same process at work in England, describing, in *1984*, a society in which terror forced each person to live in his own broom closet, lest his own family inform upon him. Orwell set his vision in the future, now our past, and it was dismissed then, as it is now, as fantasy, or, at best, as a minor sidelight of literature known as "dystopia."

In *Nonconformity,* however indirectly, Algren described American society as composed of three levels: the bosses and their thugs, the house servants (well paid and comfortable), and the masses, poor, ignorant, self-loathing and doomed to remain so. A society of universal mutual distrust, in which the masses are relegated to invisibility even from themselves, the middle class is rendered guilt-ridden, frightened, impotent by its undeserved affluence and the upper class is invisible behind its media screens.

Most nauseating of all, Algren finds the artists and intellectuals serving this state of affairs. They provide popular diversions and preach the virtue of ignoring present reality, as, for example, does historical novelist Frank Yerby. They join forces with McCarthy and Nixon, as did playwright Maxwell Anderson and actor Jose Ferrer and director Elia Kazan, informing on their colleagues. Worst of all, perhaps, they write and speak as mere "reporters," creating a narrative voice so neutral as to be unassailable by any opponent whatsoever: "Babbitt has risen from the dust of the twenties," Algren sums it up, "his fingers fit the levers of power, and the lid is off on the price of nonconformity."

Algren differs from Orwell in one regard; being an American, he retains an optimistic vision. And, being an American, he couches it in nostalgic terms. Against his bleak and foresighted view of America in the post-war Empire period, Algren sets his view of what America had long said it wanted to be, ought to be, was.

American literature, according to Algren, has historically taken the side of the disenfranchised, has refused to buy the prevailing myth that "all is for the best in this best of all possible worlds," and has sought to "vindictively" assert the reality and humanity of the despised, the unsuccessful, the fallen.

His pantheon of American writers begins with Whitman, and with lines by Whitman he quoted again and again in his writing:

> I feel I am of them -
>
> I belong to those convicts and prostitutes myself -
>
> And henceforth I will not deny them -
>
> For how can I deny myself?

It continues through Mark Twain, Stephen Crane, Ambrose Bierce, Jack London, Theodore Dreiser, Carl Sandburg, H.L. Mencken, Sinclair Lewis, Thorstein Veblen, Lincoln Steffens, F. Scott Fitzgerald.

Ultimately, Algren's vision, American in its optimism, its nostalgia, its rage and sense of betrayal, is a larger vision than that of most of his exemplars. Algren read widely and deeply in history and western literature, and he saw at least as much of the world as did many of the great American writers. From this experience of the world, he arrived at two teachings from the New Testament that informed everything he ever wrote: "Inasmuch as you have done it unto the least of them, you have done it unto me;" "For the good that I would, I do not; but the evil which I would not, that I do."

Both of these verses urge compassion and empathy; that is, first, feeling for, then feeling with. Compassion and empathy: hard to imagine two traits more completely lacking from our public life; our attempts to replace them with politically correct legal stratagems have proved a boon to lawyers but done little to fill the emptiness of our hearts. Without these traits, American culture has become increasingly arid and strident, and our children reflect these qualities. They don't know there are great things to be done.

As teachers of literature - now universally known as "Freshman Composition" - we have succumbed to the elimination of any sense of the existence of a literary tradition. We teach out of anthologies filled with half-baked journalism on trendy topics the publishers suppose our students will find engaging because Geraldo and Larry King find them so. We teach extraordinarily bad essays like Brent Staples' "Black Men and Public Space," and utter drivel such as Pete Hamill's "Crack and the Box," or "Neat People Versus Sloppy People." If our students don't know there are great things to be done, is it not our mission to introduce them to the great things that have been done by their countrymen and women?

Thirty-five years ago, Nelson Algren wrote this:

"For it was not only their homes, and their associations with one another that the winners of the Middle Border walled, but their mills and factories as well. This was not only a means of protecting private property, but also a way of removing their lives from those of the men and women who worked for them. They thus effected a separation of their lives from the life of American multitudes; and subsequently created a dream-world more real to them than the world of struggle going on in the streets. The men that their power and wealth nominated for public office, therefore, were consistently men who prided themselves upon their 'practicality.'

"A practicality as wholly dedicated to keeping their dream-world inviolate as it was to keeping trespassers off their property: they had more success in keeping the violators of property out than in keeping out violators of their dreams.

"Among the footmen of literature...defending a world in which property and prestige were more real than love and death were such writers as Tarkington...and William Dean Howells; whose classic comment was that literature should be written for maiden eyes alone.

"But American literature has not been made by writing about lives undeflowered. Literature is made upon those occasions when a challenge is put to the legal apparatus by a conscience in touch with humanity.

"When the city clerk of Terre Haute refused to issue warrants for the arrest of streetwalkers despite his sworn duty to issue warrants for the arrest of streetwalkers, and instead demanded of the Terre Haute police, 'Why don't you make war on people in high life instead of upon these penniless girls?" that little sport performed an act of literature.

"For he was sustaining the great beginning Whitman had made....A beginning marked by an exuberant good humor; that yet sought darkly for understanding of America.

"And sought through New York's Bowery and down Main Street of Winesburg to the edge of town; where the last gas lamp makes all America look tired.

"A search past 4 a.m. gas stations upon nights when cats freeze to death on fire escapes and chimneys race the moon; down streets that Sister Carrie knew.

"Beyond the grandfathers' walls there began to flow a blood-colored current of vindictive life; that was fed into America's heart by violators of the grandfathers' dreams.

These were impractical men who lived upon a street for whom nobody prayed; where the cries of the sick, the tortured and the maimed had gone unheard.

"They were the accused with whom Whitman had taken his stand when he wrote "I belong to those convicts and prostitutes myself." Guilty or not guilty, Whitman pled the defense.

"As Stephen Crane had taken his place beside Maggie; as had Dreiser beside Clyde Griffiths. As had O'Neill beside Anna Christiansen; as had Richard Wright beside Bigger Thomas. As had Tennessee Williams beside Blanche du Bois. And where James Baldwin made his still-unanswered challenge: "If you don't know my name you don't know your own." (*Notes*, 162-164)

In this passage, Algren suggests that literature is not about style or ideas or criticism, but about the actual, felt lives of human beings. I argue that it is time we devoted our attentions to these things, and communicated our own love for them to our students, who may then come to see that there are, indeed, great things to be done if this country is to be brought back to a remembrance of "the meanings and values that are necessary and useful," of the truths we once claimed were self-evident.

Works Cited

Algren, Nelson. *Somebody in Boots*. New York: Berkley Medallion, 1965
    Never Come Morning. New York: Four Walls Eight Windows, 1987
    The Neon Wilderness. London: Andre Deutsch, Ltd., 1965
    The Man With the Golden Arm. Garden City: Doubleday, 1949
    A Walk on the Wild Side. New York: Farrar, Straus & Cudahy, 1956
    Notes From a Sea Diary. New York: G.P. Putnam's Sons, 1965
    Nonconformity. New York: Seven Stories Press, 1996
Drew, Bettina. *Nelson Algren: A Life on the Wild Side*. New York: Putnam, 1989
Thomas, Frank. "Brand You." *Harper's Magazine*, July, 1999
Trumbo, Dalton. *The Time of the Toad*. New York: Harper&Row, 1972

    Except for a couple of brief periods, none of these writers has become well-known, let alone "famous." In these reviews and essays and presentations, I've done the best I could to spread the word about their value, and I'm glad I put in that time and effort, as I'm glad I've spent a lifetime pulling other people's coat sleeves and directing their attention to the wonderful things humans have produced.

    At the end of his great short story "Sonny's Blues," James Baldwin writes, "For, while the tale of how we suffer, and how we are delighted, and how we may triumph is never new, it always must be heard. There isn't any other tale to tell, it's the only light we've got in all this darkness." It's up to us who love the light to keep it burning.

Manitowoc

Most of the prose I wrote over my lifetime that I've included in here has been ranting against one thing or another, but I did find time occasionally to just play with language. In fact, that was pretty much *all* I did, early on. Here's a gem that got published in *Scholastic Magazine* when I was a senior at Evanston High School:

Early Up and Doing

Early up and doing
In the frosty barn,
We strained new grain barrels in,
Splashed fresh water in the clanking buckets,
Curried clean the horses'
Warm slow winter sides.

I had forgotten the taste
Of work, the good weight
Of something for the arms to lift and move.

In a woman's month
Of morning windows
Lighted grey by cold,
Surrounded by warm blankets,
I had fallen
Half in love with sleep and dreams.

I suppose it's possible that grain comes in barrels, and that horses receive curry-combing in the early morning, though I doubt either is the case. You can see I was a lot more interested in "**s**train/**g**rain" and "**c**urried **c**lean" and "**w**arm slow **w**inter" than in saying anything that made sense in the real world, about which I knew approximately nothing at that stage of my life. You can also gauge the state of American society and my unquestioning acceptance of its prejudices by the casually dismissive tone of "in a **woman's** month."

During my years at Northwestern, I was still mainly learning by imitating - you can see from the poem above that I was pretending to be Robert Frost, without knowing the first thing about farm life. At Northwestern, I was forcibly introduced to many other poets, and John Donne's muscular manipulation of syntax and Gerard Manley Hopkins' experiments with rhythm particularly appealed to me. Odd, since I was by then, as I remain, a fundamentalist agnostic, and both Donne and Hopkins were divines, and deeply committed Christians. I guess I was attempting to resolve our differences, or maybe yearning for their assurance, when I wrote this next. In any case, I was incorporating their syntactical and rhythmic quirks into sonnet form:

Frog's Prayer

Not hard, God, but pinch me if need be,
For when you pluck me up from where I squat
Stubborn in the long grass, god knows You'll see
My jumping legs, God, coil and jut, and not
Kind words will tell. Not kind words will tell,
God, nor will words of Heavenly sense convince
My flailing heart, stare eyes, this is not Hell -
Suspended from the beak of Providence.
Flies and the fraternal fish fall first from sight,
Then the dark marsh entire, and all is air on
Which my fingers close. O, in this flight,
Infinite-wings, great land-roving Heron,

God, pinch me the pain, wreak faith in me,
Or swallow, or set me down, though not set free.

By then, I had also come across Ring Lardner, and found a little piece of American *dada* he wrote during the 20s, a miniature play called *I Gaspiri (The Upholsterers)*. The dialog was pure Marx Brothers nonsense (you can find it in his collection *What Of It?*), and I set out to emulate such dialog and the generally slapstick attitude:

Manitowoc

A Musical Comedy

Cast:

"Lucky" Bumpersticker, King of the Manitowoc Underworld
Baby Kid Mohair, an enforcer
Stanley Dubie, a struggling district attorney
Lucy Lapse, Lily Luce, sisters under the skin
"Bindle" O'Halloran, a substitute
George Wallace, Henry Wallace, Wallace Pike, Mounties
Chorus: violaters of the Mann Act

Act One

A sunny May morning. The wheat ripples in the wind. Torval Johannson throws yet another crumpled sheet of paper into the wastebasket. He sings.

Johansson:
    Oh, how I vish
    These taxes vas glue.
    Racine and Fondulac
    Vish so, too,
    Ooo-ooo-ooo-ooo-ooo

He sighs and returns to his calculations. People walk through the wheat but to no avail.

Mister Mo	Say, Mister Slow, you see that woman over there?
Mister Slow	Yes, Mister Mo, I see that woman.
Mister Mo	Mister Slow, you see that cow over there?
Mister Slow	I see that cow over there, Mister Mo.
Mister Mo	They just ain't bitin' today.

They slap their thighs and bend at the waist. The telephone rings. Torval Johannson answers.

Johannson
    Hello, hello, vat is it today?
    Yessir, yessir, be there right away.
    Nosir, Nosir, there'll be no delay.

Goodbye, goodbye, I'd like to say.

He dances. Hardly anyone is singing. They are all afraid of something.

Curtain

Act Two

Two fish-testers stand in front of the National Bank drinking oil of cloves from paper bags. After a while they go to the race track.

First Fish-Tester	I favor Dog Circus in the Fourth.
Second Fish-Tester	That's how much you know.
A Bystander	Pretty is as pretty does.
First and Second Fish-Testers	What race?

The wheat ripples in the wind. Lucy sings a love song but the bank is closed.

Officer Bill Johannson	Sure, and d'yeh think yeh be in Tipperary now?

Curtain

Act Three

A gypsy camp in the wildwood. The mounties gallop in, their horses lathered from the long chase. The mounties dismount and shave.

First Gypsy	Do you know Leo?
First Mountie	What's it to you Whether I do Or not?

After all these years, Lucinda Blain can hardly believe her ears.

Lucinda	Johnny, you mean You're what you seem To me?

	You mean today
	We'll go away,
	Just we -
Lucinda and Johnny	-Two of us,
	So few of us,
	There'll be a fuss
	I'm sure -
The entire Cast joins them	- But just we two,
	Though there be black and blue,
	Still dear I always knew
	That we
	Would be a pair
	No matter what they dare
	Come what may,
	Some day.

During the encore they ride off beneath the Mounties' crossed swords. The wheat ripples in the wind. "Bindle" O'Halloran tries to steal a kiss and everyone laughs when he is slapped for his trouble.

Curtain

I think I had in mind with that one not only Ring Lardner's work, but the innumerable godawful Hollywood musicals I'd seen throughout my youth, when I'd sit through any movie my mother would take us to. I know I was thinking of Archibald MacLeish's *JB,* and probably *Waiting for Godot,* when I wrote this next one:

Lawfirm
A Religious Play

Cast

Yale Lawfirm, one of the ten leading New York doctors
Bruce, a Gordon setter
Mrs. Lawfirm, Baby Lawfirm, Baby Lawfirm, friends to Bruce

Stanley Dubie, a spackle and grout man
One Messenger
Another Messenger
Kate Smith, once one or another's mistress
Chorus, people waiting for a bus

Act One

Scene One

The set suggests a sewer. It is too dark to tell. Voices are heard.

Voices

I wish the bus would come.
If only the bus would come.
Yes, that's right.

A clank. A shaft of light from above.

Another Voice

The bus is here.

Voices

Thank God for that.

Curtain

Act One

Scene Two

Yale Lawfirm's office in the city. He is eating cole slaw for his sinus. It doesn't help. Neither does anything else.

Lawfirm

Miss Pod, send in the first patient.

Stanley Dubie enters, SL

Lawfirm

Good morning, Mr. Dubie. Say, aren't you
the spackle and grout man?

Dubie

(Frowning) Thank God for that.

Curtain

Act Two

Later that day in Yale Lawfirm's office in the city. He is eating cole slaw again. As he eats he examines pictures of soft palates.

Lawfirm
I am one of the Ten Leading New York
Doctors. Yet why, at night, should I,
who have everything...

He loses track and goes back to the soft palate pictures. Miss Pod enters seductively.

Lawfirm
What is it, Miss Pod?
Miss Pod
A messenger, Doctor.

The messenger is already in the office. You can't see how he got there.

Messenger
You Lawfirm?
Lawfirm
I am *Doctor* Lawfirm.
Messenger
Be that way. I got a telegram here from
a Kate Smith. Says all your children and
your wife and dog was killed in a fire.
Lawfirm
Who is Kate Smith?
Messenger
You see, that now, that you, who had everything,
and in the evening the sense of something
by the fire, were but....

He gets fed up and leaves. You can't see how he gets out.

Curtain

Act Three
Scene One

Later that day in the park. Lawfirm is lying on a bench. A statue of Olivetti curing the pimento stands behind the bench. A pigeon doesn't notice it.

Lawfirm
But when, at first, before, that is,
perhaps, and the approach of the children's
faces smeared with raspberry candy -

Just as he gets going good a policeman raps his shins. Lawfirm cringes away. So does the policeman. Everyone else feels so bad they decide to pull the curtain.

Act Three
Scene Two

Seventeen years later in the sewer. A new administration has put in lights. It was better before. A very old man enters, SR. Other people stand around.

First Old Man
Say, aren't you Stanley Dubie, the spackle
and grout man?
Second Old Man
No, I am another.
Voice from Above
The bus is here.
Chorus
Thank God for that, etc.

They all go up the ladder. The First Old Man hangs back. He faces the audience, takes a deep breath, thinks better of it and goes up the ladder to catch the bus. It's a good thing because another policeman comes by right after. He saunters across the sewer, whistling.

Curtain

And it was undoubtedly the Hollywood film of *Huckleberry Finn*, or perhaps a film "biography" of Mark Twain, that inspired this last one. I'm not sure now how the Boston Red Sox got in here, and I'm pretty sure they're no more afraid of dogs than any other major league team:

Tom Sauvage in Alaska
An Historical Play

Cast

Lieutenant Colonel Josephus Sauvage, Governor of Alaska
Taumus, his son
Pawtucket Reservoir, an Eskimo firebrand
Whoopee, Blubber, Sue Sally, eskimos
Stanley Dubie, a humble shepherd
Amadeus Mooseheart, an arrogant shepherd
Yukon King, a German shepherd

Act One

A peaceful residential street in the Fairbanks of 1858. Live oaks draped with Spanish Moss shade the sprawling verandahs. Taumus Sauvage is trying to free Moss, a lovable civic blot, from the trees as the curtain rises.

Tom
Yawl come *dawn,* nah*, hyah?*

Moss giggles drunkenly as Tom prods him with a harpoon handle. Whoopee, Blubber and Sue Sally enter carrying a walrus. Tom's face takes on a shrewd gleam.

Tom
Gaw-lee! Sure's nahce ent nawn alse come
long. Shaw funta prawd sold baw Moss hyah.

He pretends to discover the Eskimos and makes a great show of surprise.

Tom
Hayawl! Fret ah kent letchawl hep meh. Too
bade, too. Sheers much funs pintina *fanes!*

The Eskimos look at each other, puzzled, and exit, forgetting their walrus. Tom's face takes on an honest gleam. Impulsively, he drops his harpoon, throws the walrus over his shoulder and staggers off after the Eskimos.

Tom
Sigh! Yawlf gatecha *pate!*

Moss looks after the lad. A gleam of some almost forgotten emotion comes into his bleared eyes.

Curtain

Act Two

As the curtain rises the Boston Red Sox trot on stage and fan out to their positions. Pawtucket Reservoir begins to hit pop flies with a fungo bat. Some lights shatter. Merry cries from the Red Sox, *ad lib.* The director rushes up the center aisle.

Director
Stanley, Stanley, Stanley!

As the director vaults onto the stage, Stanley Dubie and Yukon King enter, SR. The three manage to clear the stage. The Red Sox are afraid of dogs. Someone finally gets the curtain down.

Act Three
Scene One

Ten years later. The Fairbanks barnacle factory. Eskimos stand in a long line gluing barnacles to hull segments. The windows are dirty and the air full of barnacle dust.

First Eskimo
I got this cough.
Second Eskimo
The hell you say.
Third Eskimo
Say, do you think the sun is out?
Second Eskimo
No.
Fourth Eskimo

>Why not?
>
>*Second Eskimo*
>They ain't even sentenced it yet.

All laugh from the sides of their faces. Blubber bursts in, SR. Abrupt silence. He is the foreman.

>*Blubber*
>There's a war on, you know.

The second Eskimo leaves his place in the line, disgusted, and pulls the curtain.

Act Three
Scene Two

Thirty years later. Governor Sauvage lies dying in the bedroom of the Governor's Mansion. Pawtucket Reservoir, now a faithful family retainer, sits at the bedside, cropping the Colonel's puttees for him. A knock.

>*Reservoir*
>Enter.

The door is flung open. Tom enters. He has aged thirty years but is otherwise unchanged.

>*Tom*
>Paw!
>
>*Governor Sauvage*
>Taumus!

He dies. His body rises into some clouds. Sue Sally as a little girl walks at his side, clutching his hand. Yukon King as a puppy heels. A harp.

>*Tom*
>Paw!
>
>*Reservoir*
>Kneel wid me, Taumus.
>
>*Tom*

> Kent ah pint the fanes?

Martial music off stage. The door bursts open. Billy Bexley is so excited he stammers.

> *Bexley*
> Have you heard? *Have* you *heard?* Admiral
> Dewey just sailed into Fairbanks Bay! We're
> a s-s-s-st-*State!*

The two longtime enemies look at each other wonderingly. Reservoir rises and meets Tom SC, where they shake hands. Stanley Dubie knocks on the open door.

> *Dubie*
> The sheep are in for the night, Tom - I mean,
> *Governor.*

Dewey's cannon booms louder and louder as the curtain falls.

After all this time, I must confess I still find a lot of that stuff funny. I especially like Tom's "dialect." And I'm reminded of something Frost said that I've always liked:

"So many talk, I wonder how falsely, about what it costs them, what agony it is to write. I've often been quoted: "No tears in the writer, no tears in the reader. No surprise for the writer, no surprise for the reader." But another distinction I made is: however sad, no grievance, grief without grievance. How could I, how could anyone have a good time with what cost me too much agony, how could they? What do I want to communicate but what a *hell* of a good time I had writing it?" (Plimpton, George, ed., *Writers at Work, Second Series,* Viking, 1963, p. 32)

I did have a hell of a good time writing those things, as indeed I have had writing most of what I've written. My teachers back in high school and college insisted that I learn how to diagram sentences and how to scan a metric poem, and I spent many hours doing both those things until the possibilities of English sentence structure and writing in meter became part of me, a part I no longer had to think about consciously.

You learn to do these things so you can forget them, not because anybody in his right mind would want to do them for their own sakes.

Nobody's teaching kids those things any more, and that's too bad. Three books you can probably dig up pretty easily for a while will help you learn how to diagram sentences and scan poems, if you decide you want to learn to use those tools:

    Kitty Burns Florey, *Sister Bernadette's Barking Dog: the Quirky HIstory and Lost Art of Diagramming Sentences,* Melville House, 2006

    Mary Oliver, *A Poetry Handbook,* Mariner Books, 1994
        Rules for the Dance: A Handbook for Writing and Reading Metrical Verse, Houghton Mifflin, Harcourt, 1998

The Florey book is pretty fun to read. Mary Oliver is one of our country's truly great poets, and not a woman to waste words. (I once got hold of her home phone number, somehow, and called her about a student of mine who wanted to go to Bennington, where Oliver had taught until recently. I reeled off my long explanation of why I was bothering her, at the conclusion of which she said, "Write me a letter!" *Wham.* A woman after my own heart.) If you learn how to diagram and scan, and practice long enough, you'll gain tremendous command over your writing and the ability to understand how writers you admire do their stuff. If you're crazy enough to want to write.

I don't guess I really mean "crazy." Hoping to make any kind of decent living by writing may be crazy - at least the odds against your doing so are immense. Since I was lucky enough to find work that I loved and that paid a living wage as a teacher, I didn't ever worry about making money with my writing, so I was able to write what and how I wanted, for my own purposes or to serve others' purposes that I shared.

One collection of verses I wrote for my dear, late friend Richard Bohle's *Zoo Book.* Richard, like his dad Friedl, excelled in many arts, especially photography, and he spent many off hours up at the Cheyenne Mountain Zoo photographing the animals, and in various darkrooms where he finagled space for developing and printing his work. Eventually he decided to make a book of some of his work, and I was happy to write verses to accompany the photos. I wish I were in a position to include the photos, but the planned obsolescence industry has rendered my scanner unacceptable to my latest computer, so I'll content myself with descriptions of the photos, a poor substitute - Richard was a great photographer.

(These two accompanied matched, facing head shots of a mature male and female lion)

A Numble Lion

I may have the wisdom of Solomon,
I may be as murderous as Cain,
The grace, it may be, of a Salome,
And, though I despise to be vain,

It is not imperfectly possible
To be beautiful quite without toil -
Delacroix and Rubens and Constable
All have painted my portrait in oil.

How do I, how do I adore me?
It would be quite innumerable to say,
And self-worship always did bore me,
And I try to hold boredom at bay.

So let us turn our attention
From my evident merits away
To matters more meriting mention.
Horsemeat for dinner today.

The Bitter Half

That fathead! He takes his own
Picture a hundred times a day
An hour a minute a second -
Behold the ass in full bray.

It's fortunate that while his level
Of boredom is terribly high,
His ambition is quite a bit lower
Than the level of his eye.

So before his gloriously faulty
Visions lead him astray
Another corrects his ambitions:
Horsemeat for dinner today.

(This was for a remarkable photo of a snowy owl on a branch in the foreground, with the underexposed, faint image of another snowy owl way back behind him.)

Who Say Nay?

I ponder in the forest gloom
The questions all owls ponder.
Where do we come from, and where go,
And how do we get yonder?

But as I approach an answer
I feel the chill grow colder
And then I know he has returned:
The owl over my shoulder.

And if I bother to ask, "Who?"

He'll say, "Nobody there."

If, "Whither go we?" is my call,

He's quick to answer "Nowhere."

No sooner have I hooted, "When?"

Then old "Never's" on the spot,

And if I foolishly ask, "Why?"

He flies in, "Why, why not?"

My profoundest speculations,

Throttled by this foul fowl.

He lives for my frustration,

This positively negative owl.

(This next accompanied another head shot, this one from the side, of a very young giraffe. The lovely arch of its neck would be perfectly congruent with the spine and neck of a seahorse, seen from the side.)

In My Sea

My seahorse head seems formed to float

Among the watery, waving greens

Where mermaids murmur bubbling notes.

But in my sea no seahorse gleans,

No groupers bulk amid the murk,

No shark perpetually leans.

Macaws and cockatoos their work

Pursue and clash like tambourines
Among the leaves where leopards lurk

And quirkish rhesus figurines
Claw delicately at their coats,
In my sea, no seahorse gleans.

(With a wonderful shot of the two rhinos, stretched out serially beside each other, relaxed as cats.)

Rhinos in the Morning

Nothing could be finer
Than to be a sleepy rhino
In the morning
Up all night fiesta'in'
So today we will be restin'
In the morning
You may think it's boring
When you see us snoring
But energy we're storing
So we can go out and do some more goring

Stretched out like two winos
For a snooze, like any dino -
saurs, We're dreaming
About the days when we were young
About the trees we danced among
So gay

But now our sense is sounder

We're just pillow pounders

And

Nothing could be finer

Than to be a lazy rhino

In the morning.

(A close-up portrait of a large, male Mandrill, his expression one of massive indifference to what any viewer might think of him.)

The Mandrill's Mirror

My nose knurled like a painted conch,

Like lilies my nostrils flare,

Hairy tarantulas my hands,

My shanks wizened and bare

As a human's daubed with rainbow mud,

Sugar spun fine my mane -

What authored this grab-bag of similes

Is quite beyond my baboon brain.

(For a while a small herd of bison roamed the hillside leading up to the zoo entrance. I don't think Richard ever photographed them, so I don't know why I wrote this, except to make a political point.)

Have You Herd?

Sixty million buffalo

Used to roam the West.
They ran in herds,
They felt assured,
They'd heard that herds were best.

Their herd had but one leader,
The Chief Beef Buffalo.
He got to be
The Chief B. B.
By putting on a show.

First, two buffalo would run
And knock heads willy-nilly.
The winner stood
(If stand he could)
And bellowed and looked silly.

All went well until the day
The Chief died on his hooves.
Though he was dead,
The herd was bred
To wait his call to move.

They waited and they waited and they
Waited and they waited.
They started roaring,
"God, it's boring,
But to wait we're fated."

"Rise up, Chief Beef, oh lead us, please,

    We're thirsty and we're starving."
    But, being dead,
    The Chief's great head
    Just stood there like a carving.

    Sixty million buffalo,
    Bones bleaching in the sun.
    All for one
    Is all for none
    When once the Chief has gone.

(A lemur sitting on a branch in its cage, staring out through the bars.)

    The Descent of the Lemurs

    They say that man descends from me,
    That somewhere back in history
    A lemur in the family tree
    Began the great mutation.

    If that is truth, would it were lies;
    The lemurs' fall was mankind's rise.
    My savage son, look in my eyes'
    Reproachful salutation.

(I still think this next is a fairly successful job of turning a joke into a set of verses. The joke was one I'd treasured since high school, and Richard had probably heard it far too many times, but he graciously supplied a terrific line-drawn, two-page cartoon to accompany the verse.)

Music Hathn't Charms

Deep in the African jungle
Where lions are known to be leering
And the root-loving warthogs oft rumble
Sat a man on a stump in a clearing.

His scent floating out through the forest
Soon tickled the nostrils of beasts
Who surrounded the clearing in chorus
Cacophonous, lusting to feast.

But before they could pounce and devour
His toes, lights and liver and face,
The man, with a bald, thoughtful glower,
Removed a violin from its case.

Without even tuning, he played it
And made Paganini look sick
And the animals' gluttony faded
Like a lightbulb whose switch has been clicked.

Unprecedented! Melodious!
The vulturous critics applauded -
And we nearly ate him - how odious!
Our bellies our ears near defrauded.

The animals sat in a circle
As the little man's song filled the night;
Gnus mooed and the hyenas cackled

While gorillas gave grunts of delight.

But from high on the limb of a plane tree
The little man looked like a gnat
To a leopard all ancient and grizzly
An octogenarian cat.

He dropped like a hawk on a rabbit
And chomped up both man and violin
And then, as was always his habit,
He burped twice and pawed at his chin.

Vile creature! the animals shouted
Philistine! Cretinous sod!
You've eaten the most highly touted
Violinist since Oistrakh, you clod!

The old leopard suspended ablutions,
His tongue ceased probing his claws,
One ear twitched toward the source of the nuisance
And he cupped it with one of his paws.

His dim eyes perceived their indignance
His jaw dropped and trembled and shut.
Dumbfounded by their malignance,
The old leopard stammered, "Wh-what?"

Deep in the African jungle
There is blood on the baobab leaf.
Musicians, beware, do not bungle.

Music means naught to the deaf.

I've said I learned to write by imitating writers whose work I admired. I'm not sure "imitating" is the precise term. I don't think I ever set out to write like anyone else. I just read certain writers - many writers - so much and often that I absorbed pieces of their style, of the ways they saw and heard and felt and talked about the world. I think that's how many or most writers learn to write. The point was never to sound like anyone else. The point was to learn how to sound like myself on paper. I think I learned how to do that.

Sorting through ancient pieces of paper, I came across the following parody advertisement. I have absolutely no memory of writing it. I'd guess I wrote it while I was at Northwestern, since it starts off with that allusion to a fancy French phrase meaning the end of a century ("Findeesickle"). I also have no idea what prompted me to write it, or for what audience. I'm sticking it in here only because it shows that my obsession with the awful effects of mass media started pretty early, even before I found better writers to confirm my reactions, and because it's the first piece of writing I've found that expresses my own perceptions, rather than aping someone else's:

NEVER BEFORE
On the Face of the Earth
Has There Been a Departure Like This!

Friends, we here at Findeesickle Manufacturing Company really feel that we've outdone ourselves this time! As we said, never before has there been a development so revolutionary, so...well, we can only call it Terrific...as this new machine of ours:

The *FOETUSIZER!*

It's as simple as a baby to operate. Just plug it in, place your pedal extremities in the specially hand-crafted receptacles, and flick the red switch marked "Stop." That's all there is to it. Instantly, a soothing, exciting tide of pure relaxation will set your mind afloat. Your aural control centers will be gently massaged by a music-like humming sound, controlled by the latest in electronic oscillators for that variety of pitch so necessary to a full, complete, human life. A continuous sea of the newest pastel colors will wash your eyes with pure, uncomplicated beauty. Your olfactory sense will blush with thanksgiving at the scent recently voted Least Offensive by 10 Leading New York Scientists - Essence of Mutton. And your taste buds will be treated to that cleanest of bacteria-repelling, lip-smacking goodness - our own Tretorn X - LU.

Besides this, friends, we unconditionally guarantee that after you use the *Foetusizer* for 10 days or less, you will have lost forever all of those bothersome, tension-producing desires, emotional and physical, that cause us all so much trouble. If you haven't become perfectly tranquil within that time, just bring your *Foetusizer* and yourself in to one of our specially-manned maintenance centers. They'll handle your problem quickly and efficiently.

So throw out that television, friends. No need to keep that outmoded radio around. Forget those expensive theater tickets and long-playing records. Forget *them,* and

remember the

FOETUSIZER!

(No money down. Terms can be arranged.

Not until many years later did I come across George Orwell's quite similar observations, prompted in his case by a magazine ad he'd found in 1946:

"I have no doubt that, all over the world, hundreds of pleasure resorts similar to the one described above are now being planned, and perhaps even being built....On a pleasure cruise or in a Lyons Corner House one already gets something more than a glimpse of this future paradise. Analysed, its main characteristics are these:

"1. One is never alone.
2. One never does anything for oneself.
3. One is never within sight of wild vegetation or natural objects of any kind.
4. Light and temperature are always artificially regulated.
5. One is never out of the sound of music.

"The music - and if possible it should be the same music for everybody - is the most important ingredient. Its function is to prevent thought and conversation, and to shut out any natural sound, such as the song of birds or the whistling of the wind, that might otherwise intrude....

"It is difficult not to feel that the unconscious aim in the most typical modern pleasure resorts is a return to the womb. For there, too, one was never alone, one never saw daylight, the temperature was always regulated, one did not have to worry about work or food, and one's thoughts, if any, were drowned by a continuous rhythmic throbbing....

"Much of what goes by the name of pleasure is simply an effort to destroy consciousness...." [Orwell]

In my early days in Colorado Springs, when I still harbored illusions of becoming a Great Writer and when I was growing increasingly maddened by the Vietnam war, I wrote a number of short stories, many of them very bad indeed. This is one in which I tried to bring to life a metaphor for my feelings about living in the U.S.:

Sweet And Sour

Sometimes I think my neighborhood is going to hell. Now it is eating plastic lobsters. Overstatement. They aren't eating the lobsters, but the filling. The filling, they say, is like Sweet and Sour something, and you can't get enough of it. The lobsters' plastic antennae serve as straws, once you've bitten off the nobs.

I was forced to stop and enquire when I passed by Mr. Pilcher's house and observed him apparently chewing a lobster's head. Mr. Pilcher was the neighborhood's lawn and garden champ. His lawn looked like a putting green, but you'd best not try any putting.

The lobster in Mr. Pilcher's wiry hands was a pink color for which I didn't care to find a comparison. Mr. Pilcher, ever neighborly, nodded around the lobster.

"What is it you have there?" I inquired.

The empty lobster shell flew into a peony bush by the front gate. The dirt in the bed hadn't been recently turned.

"Sweet And Sour," Mr. Pilcher replied, while his hand searched in the depths of a big cardboard carton beside his porch chair. Another pink lobster emerged. "You try one."

"I just ate. Thanks."

It must have been a rhetorical offer, since Mr. Pilcher had already expectorated the lobster's nobs by the time I'd refused it.

"Well, so long," I said. He nodded again around the new lobster. His eyes didn't appear to be taking me in.

The lobsters caught on rapidly, and my neighbors were soon to be seen on their porches and in their living rooms and lying in their hammocks, all in their bliss. From a distance, they looked as if they had all sprouted pink beards, especially at dusk.

I'm a Jefferson democrat - I like a lot of leeway - and look tolerantly on the pleasures of others. Or I did until about the fourth day of the new improved lobster craze, when a corollary arose. Settled, actually; the corollary was flies.

My neighbors, in their absorption, kept ejecting spent lobster shells any old way. The shells contained residue Sweet And Sour, which the flies found as appealing as my neighbors did. So the shells scattered and mounded before and behind and beside the houses, nested in the lilacs and bridal veil, shattered on the sidewalks - they all began to exhibit signs of flies. The flies bred. In little time, the lobster shells were full again, this time full of fornicating, borning, entering or departing flies. The pink things pulsed and hummed.

For a time, balance prevailed. New shells popped out second story windows or sailed over railings often enough to accommodate the new generations of flies, and of course the birds helped. It became my nightly entertainment to watch the nighthawks swooping down through the dusk and arcing back up as easily as they dropped.

Naturally the flies soon overcame this balance, breeders that they are. First they covered the shells, which by this time covered the street, the parkways, the lawns. The carpet of pink became a carpet of black, whining nasally.

Insects disgust me, I don't know why. Flies are among the least endearing insects. They rub their hairy paws together unctuously. They appear to stare. They penetrate the space you like to keep around yourself, and come right back and do it again. I was tiring of the situation. It got worse. The flies, naturally, continued breeding. The food supply became insufficient. The flies attacked the houses. Soon all the windows were black. One night, Mr. Pilcher had a black mustache and goatee. The next day, he was only a blue-black, glistening shape that periodically ejected a blackened lobster trailing flies.

You know how flies are. In spite of the fact that I had neglected to purchase any Sweet And Sour lobsters, my house is as black as the rest, and I feel that the buzzing may soon vibrate the nails right out of the studs. Today the telephone line fell under the weight of flies.

Since my windowpanes are now dysfunctional, I don't know whether the nighthawks are still around or not. The television says that the city government is spraying daily to try to poison the flies. Perhaps this has discouraged the birds. Most of the city is full of flies, and the news commentator remarks tonight that the flies are seriously disturbing television transmission.

No one has been able to devise a solution to the problem of the flies. Jefferson! Where are you?

A few years later, I was moving on to trying to write in the voices of various women I'd encountered or heard about. I'm not sure why I was doing this - possibly because I was beginning to suspect that my expectations of women, formed by 1950s movies, might need some adjusting. I'd begun to notice that women might be dangerous:

God Wanted Arnulfo to Marry Me

Having a child was the most beautiful experience of my life. But it seems they are never satisfied.

For example, Arnulfo. When they found that I was going to have a child, right away they assumed that I would marry the father.

"Linda," they said. "Have you thought how Arnulfo and you can live? What will become of you, both of you so young and still in school?" Actually my mother said everything. My stepfather knows to keep his mouth shut tight. I taught him what she didn't about that. He has no right when it comes to me.

"Who said anything about that?" I asked her. "Arnulfo. I don't love him. He's just a kid."

"I see. Then what are you thinking, may I ask?" She is already old, worn out. She doesn't dye her hair yet, but she might as well.

"What do I have to think. I'm going to have a child. It will be my child. That's what I'm thinking."

"Not in this home. Not with Sonia and Teresa looking up at you, you with no husband. Not in my home."

It came as no surprise. I knew she would flip out. She worries all the time about the neighbors. She doesn't know them, but she worries about them.

Arnulfo flipped out too, of course.

"Linda, you're my life. You're carrying my life. God wouldn't let this happen if He didn't mean it to be." We were in the back row at the A&W with his hand up under my sweater. They were already big, and he liked the way they felt. So he brought God into the picture. If God meant Arnulfo to marry me, He would give him a car of his own, instead of his cousin's broken down old Fury with the sponge rubber coming out of the seats all over my wool skirt.

"Linda, you must marry me. You can't raise my child by yourself. I'll get a job. My brother can get me on at the garage. You can't deprive me of my son."

Can't, Don't, Not Allowed. That's all you hear. I get so tired of it. Finally, to get him off my back, I said, "Your child? What makes you so sure it is your child?" So he cried, then, and got off my back. Of course, I am pretty certain it is his child, but if people will not let you alone, sometimes you have to teach them.

So I had my child from my real father's home, where my mother sent me after I told her I wasn't going to marry Arnulfo.

Actually, there is a possibility that my child's father was Arnulfo's brother. He is such a handsome, heavy dude, a major dealer, major. I knew he would never marry me. He just saw me around and liked my tits. He can have about any woman he wants, thought, so why should he want to tie himself down?

Having a child was a beautiful experience. It made me a woman. But try to tell them that.

The minute I am home from the hospital, after my girlfriends have all left, my real father's wife starts in. Pick up this, pick up that, please. Help with these dishes, please. She only says "please" because she thinks it makes it look like she isn't ordering me around. Hey, I tell her, I just had a baby, I'm still recuperating, give me a break, okay?

"Linda, honey, I know you just had a baby. I've had babies too. The best thing for you to do is to stay on your feet as much as you can. Otherwise that weight will just stay on."

She is whizzing around the apartment from here to there. She is one of those compulsives.

That first time, I just looked at her. Not in the eyes. I just looked her in the thighs, you might say. So you want to talk about my figure? Later on, I started letting her hear me call her "hippo hips" when I was talking on the phone. She couldn't say anything about it unless she wanted to admit she was listening in on me.

I suppose I was supposed to hang around that dinky apartment the way she does, busting my rear end to serve the papacito when he comes up for lunch with grease all over him, or smelling like some sewer from the toilets he goes out to fix. Papacito, the toilet fixer. King of Flushes.

That's her business, if she wants to do that. That's his business, if he wants to go out and mess around in other people's stink. What I want to do, that's my business. But try to tell them that. He'll be sitting there at their excuse for a table, stuffing his face full of chorizo.

"Linda, where were you out to last night so late? Bea had to get up twice to feed your baby."

"Oh, you know, just riding around with my girlfriends." Goofed out of our heads on some angel dust Arnulfo's brother laid on me, among other things. She knows it, too. I ran into her in the bathroom. I was standing there, trying to figure out where my bed would be, and I forgot to turn out the lights. There she is in the doorway, hands on those hips.

"Linda, what's with you, anyway? You have every light in the place burning. Banging around in here, waking up your baby - don't you have any consideration at all? I mean, what's with you, girl?"

I knew better than to try to answer her. You don't know what's going to come out of your mouth when you're goofed up. So I just got by her and went for my bedroom, except I guessed wrong and ran into something in the living room that fell, and had to turn around and come by her still standing there in the bathroom doorway.

She knew I was goofed up. She isn't any fat little angel like she pretends to be. But he doesn't know from anything but cerveza, and what is she going to tell him about me? Hey, man, your darling baby daughter is a crazy drug freak? Uh-uh. She can't tell him. He would go crazy, and she knows it. So I was riding around with my girl friends. Talking.

But then she starts in on me, shooting around from the table to the sink, sink to the table.

"Look, Linda, something I want to talk to you about while your father is here." The water is splashing in the dishpan, the dishwasher sounding like a cement-mixer, the baby starts crying, you can hardly hear what they're saying on *One Life to Live*. Naturally, she has another criticism. Everybody has the right to criticize, it seems.

"If you want to wear something of mine, I would appreciate it if you would just ask me, you know?" She goes into her hands-on-hippo-hips position. "And maybe, just once in a while, you could put a few of your dirty clothes - my dirty clothes - in the hamper, huh?" She looks at the papacito. "Is that asking too much, do you think?"

I nearly lost it. "Too much, too much, too much! What am I around here, the maid? Don't I ever get a night off, huh? I'm the slave?" I grab the trapo off the table where she left it and drop down on the floor. "Do you want me down on my knees? Is that what you want?" I start scrubbing the floor, the legs of the table. I'm screaming. "Here! Now you got what you want? Here! On my knees, just the way you like to see me. A slave, a servant in my father's house!"

Papacito is making it for the door, still chewing his last piece of chorizo, trying to get it down.

"Now, you ladies get this worked out," he says around the chorizo. "We don't need this fighting all the time." And he is out the back door. She breaks down crying with her head bouncing up and down on the table from the jiggle of the old, rackety dishwasher.

God, I feel that I am in prison. I don't know what they want from me. Everything, I guess. They just want everything. They just want a slave.

I sit in my room until I can't stand it. Through my head, like a song, the words keep going, "Land of the free, home of the brave, you want me, to be your slave," over and over again. I hear the door slam. She has gone out. Left me with the baby, trapped. You want me, to be your slave.

I get out my stash from inside my hollow owl statue and roll up a number. I need to settle down. After a while, I am settled down.

The telephone is in the kitchen. The dishwasher is still grinding and bouncing away. On the television, Doctor Morris has finally gotten around to putting the make on his brother's wife.

"Arnulfo. Can you come by and pick me up, baby? We could go out to Silver Lake and get high. I've got something I want to talk about. I think you could be a very happy man, my darling."

I must admit that the outline of that story was given to me by eavesdropping on

"Linda"'s mother and her friends. The dialog was my own doing, though I'd picked up the rhythm listening to a lot of hispanic people I was spending time with then.

I hope I've gotten across in this chapter the same thing Frost wanted to get across to his readers: what a *hell* of a good time I had writing all these things. When I think about the writers I've loved and read and re-read the most, it's that feeling that using the language well for any purpose - or sometimes for no purpose - is a joy and a privilege that I love most.

Ice Cubes in the Rain

Thelonika China Lee McCollum (to which she soon added more middle names, becoming Thelonika China Lee Sioux Hit Hanchu Hands Falling McCollum) was born on July 5, 1982. I had started making up mottoes for each year - I have no idea what prompted this - and the motto for 1982 was (hold off on the retching, please), "Good Dreams Come True in '82." That certainly worked out true, though the blessings of that year were not unmixed. My mother was diagnosed with terminal liver cancer in the Fall, and I got busted for a DUI late in the year. So I coined another motto for the following year, "Easy keys in '83." That was the last motto for me.

Mother died in January of 1983. I was thrown into a depression so deep I didn't even recognize it until Summer, when I drove out of town with the rest of the band Toy Boat to play in Los Angeles. We stopped at a rest stop, and I got out to stretch my legs and realized that I'd been seeing the world through something like a dark grey screen for the past half year. Getting out of town apparently allowed the screen to withdraw, and I was amazed at the sudden brightness of the world.

Part of my sentence for the DUI was 20 hours of community service, and I was assigned to work for the March of Dimes. In May or June, I was to man the March's booth at a health fair up in the mountain town of Woodland Park. (The March of Dimes apparently savored irony, giving me this assignment.) Across from my table in the school gym, some outfit that dealt with "stress" had set up shop. They'd mounted a big chart on the wall behind their table, listing about 25 life events, both negative and positive, everything from getting a new job to the death of a loved one. Next to each even was a "stress index number." The chart said you should definitely seek treatment if you had experienced enough of these events during the past year to raise your "stress index" sum over some number or other. I read through the list of events. I had experienced every one of them during the past year. I figured I must be legally dead and just hadn't realized it before. So much for easy keys.

Naturally I dealt with all this stress in my nearly lifelong fashion, by drinking way too much way too often. A few more years of this led Thelonika's mother Samantha to despair, and she moved on to New Mexico with Thelonika. But before that happened, we began to write down things Thelonika said that struck us as poems - Sam was working on a series of poems about the history of Chaco Canyon as part of her senior project at Colorado College and I was writing a lot of song lyrics. We were a poetic household, and Thelonika probably picked up on that, though I don't think kids need much encouragement in that direction. I think they're natural poets, naturally creative in their use of language.

I started reading some of Thelonika's poems at poetry readings, and printing them in *The Unofficial Organ,* a faculty magazine I put out for a couple of years, and eventually I decided to try to get them published as a collection, for which I wrote the following introduction. Being me, I then did exactly nothing further to try to get it published, so I'm going to do that now.

Ice Cubes in the Rain
by Thelonika China Lee Hanchu Hands Falling McCollum
Introduction

While these poems speak eloquently for themselves, I think they need an introduction, since their author has not yet turned six.

The author is my daughter. I am aware that doting parents have been known to bore the daylights out of perfect strangers with tales of their offsprings' perfectly commonplace accomplishments. I don't think you'll be bored by Thelonika's poems.

The poems, naturally, were not "written" by Thelonika. She spoke them, over the past couple of years, and her mother and I wrote them down. So the line divisions, stanza structures and titles are the work of adults. The words, though, are the words of a child, transcribed as accurately as we could transcribe them.

Some of the poems were said because Thelonika's mother or I asked her to say a poem on a particular subject. ("Poem About Manners" and "Bubbles and Rain" are two such.) Most of them just came out of her mouth spontaneously. "The Wild Indian," for instance, was composed mostly between screams and whoops as the author spun wildly about the room, bumping into things. "Poem About God" was spoken on a dark street after Thelonika and I had crossed paths with a couple of young fellows out hunting for trouble.

I recently included several of Thelonika's poems in a reading. After the reading, a number of people made it a point to tell me how remarkable and unique and talented my daughter was. I knew that already. I knew it from the day she was born. I hadn't read her poems to make that point.

About a week after the reading, a young reporter I knew slightly said to me, "You know, ever since I heard your daughter's poetry, I've been hearing *my* kids say the most amazing things."

That's why I read Thelonika's poems, and why I ask you to read them. Every child is born with astonishing talents. Every child not damaged by parental irresponsibility or ignorance is born a genius. Genius and creativity and joy in the creation that surrounds us are commonplace in children, until we get to training them to be more like us.

Maybe if we did less training and more close listening to them, we would come to treasure our children, and all children, more than we seem to. Maybe we would learn from them the sense to see our existence as a miracle, that the miraculous is commonplace. Maybe then we'd knock off our determined efforts to render the planet uninhabitable, and begin to organize our efforts in the cause of life, rather than the many kinds of death we worship and support.

1985, the year Thelonika turned 3, also saw the launch of the Space Shuttle Atlantis, which I'm guessing gave rise to the first set of poems we transcribed. The origins of the others will generally be self- evident, as will the source of the illustrations, either Thelonika or me.)

Satellite Poems

Fly around
Fly all right
Fly around
In your satellite

Don't you ever
Go away
In your satellite,
Pepe.

Don't go ever away
In your satellite cup,
In your phoom-phoom-tu.

The moon doesn't go
in the satellite
Right
There.

The Swingset Poem

The swingset poem
Is right here
And right there
And the moon is right here
And God is right there
Picking up some noisy lawnmowers.

The Daddy Poem

Daddy's right there making a poem.
Make it nudie phee-phee, phoo-phoo.

Daddy's in the bathtub
Watching the candles
So they can go at the doctor's office.

And I don't like you anymore
Is a pretty song

And I do and I don't.

And Pepe and Jose
Is a pretty song, too,
And toaster's bread,
Kangaroo bread.

The Bad Parents' Poem

Is a glassy glass
And you put your tops on like

This

And you don't do

This
And you don't do
This

And you don't do this.

You eat the sewing thing
And you do this
And you do this.

You throw it like that,
Daddy,
And you kick it.

Bubbles and Rain

Blowing bubbles and rain on the roof
Went step step step, click click click
And my cat Queenie says, "Goodbye, house."

I blowed one for you.

The rain steps went click click
And under the mountain they heard
A big dinosaur. It went "Raw Raw."

I blowed one for Queenie and she like it.

The Hailstorm

Ice cubes in the rain
Ice cubes in the rain
Is the heavy sound
I'm saying.

Broken apples in the rain
Broken apples in the rain
All of my crayons coming down
In the rain.

The thunder shakes my chair
The thunder shakes my crayons
The thunder does gargling,
Gargling, gargling.

Does that, yeah:
Gargling rain.

A Little Mess

I'm getting a little mess
on your two little tables
and on your three
two little tables
and I'm going to tell on you
and I'm not going
to be your friend
anymore and I've
got a present for you.

Animal Travels

Mousie Mouse went to a chair
And showed some rats a candy bear.

Chicken Chicken went to a doggie
And showed a rat a rat.

Elephant Elephant went to a show,
A birdie and a pine cone, too, and a
Flower flower, a silly dilly.

Chrissy showed a pen penny
That we throw down to make a pot of gold.

Social Note

Nobody gets to go to the party
Until they lotion-lotion.

The Ducks

I want to see the ducks
Who make bread out of honey.

The bees bring it to them
And they make the bread.

They only do it at night.

Then they give it to the mailman,
And in the morning

He puts it in the people's mailbox
And they open it.

And they eat it.

A Good Little Neighborhood

This is a good little neighborhood.
No animals that eat people live around here.

That's
A good little neighborhood.

Crashing Buffalo

One time a buffalo walked on a piano
And fell off and cracked his head.

And I said, "No, no, don't walk on that piano."
And I was going to call a doctor.

"And you cracked your head," said the little Mom,
"And I didn't like it," said the little buffalo.

And he went Crash and cracked all
Of his hands and body and God fixed it,

"He went 'Tape-tape-tape' all the way down
To my toes," said the little buffalo.

Making Soup

First I put this in
Then I stir it around
Then I must put this corn leaf in
And some of these lilies
And then I must stir it
And stir it and stir it around.

When we get home
From a nap,

It will be all made.

Mister Foof

Mister Foof is real.
He's out in this world.
He's real.
He's pretty slick.

He plays baseball like this:
Ike! Ike! Whoo! Whoo!
Watch out!

Mister Foof is a
A pretty nice man.

Nighttime

Ha. Ha!
This is nighttime.

This poem is called
Illustrated by Nothing.

My Minister

Now, my minister doesn't talk so much.
He used to. He used to talk all the time.

He scared me. One time, he was yelling
At the kids and I hided from him.

He thought I was here.
But I was really there, huh?

More About God

Everyone is God
Except bad guys
Are bad Gods.

I'm a magic angel.
That's a part of my living,
A part that keeps me safe.

Focus

Tomorrow we're going to focus
This dolly's face.

You put it

In a little machine, and some time
I'll show you what it's like,
And it focuses the dolly's face.

It doesn't make it different,
It just makes it look
Like it looks.

The Wild Indian

I'm a wild Indian,
Write me up,
And so tell me
I'm silly.
Hey, I'm a wild Indian,
Blow my hair.
Hey! Push the buttons
And make me die.
Push me and I'll fall.
Hey, fall down,
Me, me, hah.
Capture me.

Tomorrow it will be Sunday.
Now I'm a wild Indian.
Let me run.
Throw my shirt down
Into the road.
Now let me jump,
Let me jump.

Now, hey, hey -
Watch cartoons.

Good Shark

It grabbed onto a boat
Yeah, you grabbed onto a boat,
Yeah, you grabbed onto a boat,
Yeah, you grabbed onto a boat.

Good shark.
I'll have to lay you down.

Half lying down
And half standing up.

The boat is sinking!
Swimming! Sinking!

Dormez vous, dormez vous.

Dormez swimming,
Dormez swimming.

Dinga dinga dong,
Dinga dinga dong.

Graduating in School

Who's graduating? Who's graduating?
There's rainbows in the sky,
At night there's rainbows sometimes,
And if they have windows at the school
They're graduating at,
Then sometimes they look out the windows
And see the rainbows.

Trevor's Graduation

First we had to sit and wait for it
But the piano came on

And the kids started singing

And then the piano did another song
And another song and another
Song and another song and another song
And another song and
Another song,

Until we got that food
And a drink.

Cops

I'm cops.
I'm going to arrest you,
Put you in jail
I think.

Then it's not going to be
Nothing,
And I'll kill poodles,
And you'll have to help me.

I'm not going to tell you
Nothing else.

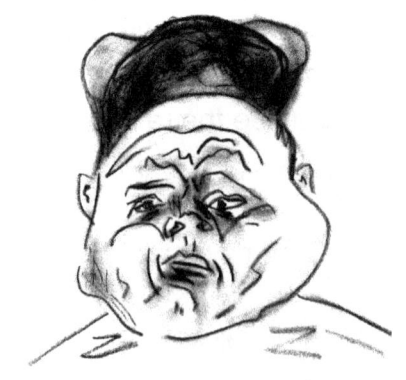

When in the Shadows I Walk

When in the shadows I walk
I carry my book with me.
Me and my book are pretty.

Under the snow,
Below it,
I eat some ice and go away.

I'm going to keep you alive
Sunday to Saturday.

Rain Story

My rain story is
Way back inside of me:

Once there lived Rain
With her friend Snow
And she was very obvious.
Then Old MacDonald tickled her,
And so what she had
Was her friend, Mister Eye,
Who was a snowman.

That's all in my story
Except that Rain had
Velveeta for her vitamins,
And she had
Fingernail polish
For her dinner
To eat.

Smooth, the Mother

Say, "Pleased to meet you,
I'm Smooth, the Mother,
That's my house over there.
See that bicycle over there?
That's my bicycle.
I have quite a nice house,
Don't I. It's purple and brown
Inside. Let's go shopping,
All right? Money, money, money."

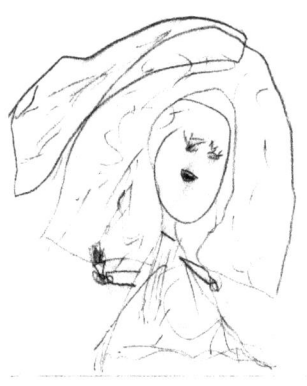

High Concept

Our movie is
Tree Behind Island Boy.

It's about little chickens,
Little horses, little balloons,
And red balloons,
And little yellow books.

And it's about robots, too.

It's a good movie.
All kinds of things

Is in our movie.
And flashlight.
And carrot.
And stories.
And dinner is, too.

And write down is, too.

The Seed

When you put the seed in,
The tree starts growing
And then the fruit starts growing.

Then, when you go in your yard,
Pick fruit and eat it.

Then, if it's an apple tree,
Throw the core out in your yard.

Then, if you water it,
It will grow something -
It will grow an apple tree, maybe.

Rainy Night

Rainy, rainy night,
Rain, rainy night,
Please rain, please,
All right?

You have to rain,
Night.
With snakes coming
Out of the ground.

Seven snakes coming
To eat you.

I love you, snakes,
Juicy snakes.

A Little Fady Heart

There's a little fady heart in my way
The little fady heart
Is my little sister.

The little fady heart
Does all Mom says to do.
The little fady heart says,
"I am your sister.
Where is your brother?"

And I say,
"Little one, I do not know
Where our brother is."

The little fady heart says,
"Where is my world?
Where is my sister?

Where is my brother?
Where is my everything?

Do you know?" she says.

Fire Ants

You know what, if a fire ant
Bites you, step on it,
all right? Or I will
step on it. Yes.

You know when fire ants
Go around biting everybody?
Well I don't like it.
I won't let them bite any family.

If they try to bite any family,
I will step on them and
I will yell, "No!" at them.
Because they shouldn't do that.

And I can because I'm *allowed*.
And I can because I'm *strong*.

A New Game

I made up a new game.
Want to hear what it's called?

It's called:

Follow The Rules
In notes and quarter notes
And holes
And skeletons
And people.

Summary

Just to take a drop
Eat a goldfish

and go to bed -

Ha, ha, ha.

Everybody

I love everybody
In this dark world.

I love everybody
In the bright world, too.

Jennifer Movie Collector

I'd just gotten fired by a poisonous little twerp from Texas (I ate crow the next day and got my job back) when I wrote this:

Secret

Three times divorced,
unemployed,
driving a broken car
among idiot drivers
whose vehicles cost more
than my shotgun house is worth,
my talents unwanted,
my learning obsolete,
my windshield wipers
give up the ghost
without prior warning.
Sure, I think, why not?
Abandon the car,
slog to the daycare house.
There you are.
I look through the window
at you playing happily
with strangers. Knock.
We hug silently.
Say goodnight.
Walk home laughing in the snow.

Thelonika made everything else secondary, and it was hard when she was living with her mom 900 miles away. I was never much good at talking on the phone, and I remembered how wonderful the serialized novels in *Colliers* had seemed to me back when I was Thelonika's age, so I wrote a couple for her. They were based on the names she'd given to her imaginary friends, though the plots came from my own odd psyche. The first was inspired by her early desire to be a grownup, *right now.* You don't get to skip stages of growth, and going through your teens when you're in your thirties (as I had done) and forties isn't pretty. For anyone. I reckon I wrote "Raising the Roof" to try to make that point.

Raising the Roof

Part 1

This is how Jennifer Movie Collector met Block, Give Me a Block, the square lion.

It was a soft yellow and green spring morning in the city of Eat Meat. Jennifer Movie Collector was working at Mr. Dee-Dah's clinic. She was figuring out what he should do for his patient, Richard Stink, who was suffering from an inflamed sense of disaster.

She examined Richard Stink's sense of disaster through her microscope. It looked like this:

"It doesn't look good," Jennifer thought. Just then, the phone rang.

"Dee-Dah Clinic," Jennifer said.

"Aaaaaaaaaaahyeeeee," said the voice on the telephone. Jennifer knew the voice. It belonged to Grandma Movie Collector.

A cold chill passed over Jennifer's scalp, and her stomach felt funny and falling.

"Mom," Jennifer said, "get a hold of yourself. Sit down if you're standing up. Stand up if you're sitting down. Take several long breaths, and let them out twice as slow."

Grandma Movie Collector did that.

"Now. What's wrong, Mom?"

"It's Aka-Drum! It's Aka-Drum!" Grandma Movie Collector took care of Aka-Drum when Jennifer Movie Collector was working with Mr. Dee-Dah during the day. Jennifer's heart felt like it was going to stop when she heard her mother say "Aka-Drum" that way.

"Mom. Slowly, now - what *about* Aka-Drum?"

"I just turned my back for a minute, I swear!"

"Mom. Everything will be all right," Jennifer said calmly, though she felt very scared herself. "Just tell me if Aka-Drum is there with you."

"His legs are," said Grandma Movie Collector. This made Jennifer's stomach fall even further.

"What do you *mean*, 'His *legs* are?" she asked.

"His legs are right here in the kitchen with me," Grandma Movie Collector's voice said, "but I can't see the rest of him. He's grown right through the ceiling! I've got plaster all over me."

"Mom, are you drunk?" Jennifer asked.

"Jennifer Movie Collector, you know perfectly well I have not had a drink since America won a war," Grandma answered. "And you'd better get yourself home right *now*," she added. "His *knees* just went through the roof, and I'm all over shingles."

Jennifer decided her mother wasn't kidding. Or, if she was, she'd better get home anyway.

Racing up Marble Avenue in her Mozzarella GTO, Jennifer tried to imagine what she would find at home. A baby grown through the ceiling? Aka-Drum's knees towering over the roof? What on earth could have happened?

(To be continued)

Raising the Roof

Part 2

(The story so far: When Grandma Movie Collector called Jennifer
Movie Collector to tell her that Aka-Drum had suddenly grown
through the ceiling, then the roof, Jennifer was worried. She
jumped in her car and headed for home, pronto.)

Jennifer Movie Collector's Mozzarella GTO burned rubber as she rounded the corner onto T-Bone Walker Avenue and pulled up in front of her house.

It was a worse scene than she had imagined, and a better one.

It was worse because Aka-Drum had not stopped growing while Jennifer was driving home. All of him stood above the roof except his feet. He was the biggest baby Jennifer Movie Collector had ever seen. He was the biggest baby *anyone* had ever seen.

It was better because he was okay.

Jennifer hopped out of her car and hollered up, "Aka-Drum? Can you hear me?"

From far up in the sky, where a few tiny pigeons were flying around Aka-Drum's head, a voice drifted down: "Hi, Auntie Jennifer!"

"What are you *doing* up there?" Jennifer hollered.

"Growing," Aka-Drum answered.

"No kidding," Jennifer though to herself. "Well, you *stop right now*!" she hollered.

"Do I have to?" Aka-Drum's voice came floating down.

"Yes! Now!"

Aka-Drum's ankles stopped breaking through what was left of the roof.

Grandma Movie Collector burst through the front door.

"Mom, how did all this get started?" Jennifer asked. She was thinking that you have to know where something started if you want to try to turn it around.

"Oh, Good Governor, how should *I* know?" said Grandma Movie Collector.

"Now, come on, Mom," Jennifer said, using her quieting voice, "you must have *some* idea."

"All I know," Grandma said, "is Aka-Drum was talking about grownups, and then he started to *grow up* all of a sudden."

"When was he talking about grownups?"

"Oh, this morning, right after you left for work. I was reading Ligee's letter again, and he said he wanted to be a grownup right now, so he could go see Ligee"

"And that's when he started growing?"

Grandma thought. When Grandma Movie Collector thought, she put her finger in her nose. She didn't know she did it.

403

"No," she said, "he didn't start growing then. Or I would have called you then. Let's see....Block, Give Me a Block came over, and I put them out in the back yard to play...and then Aka-Drum came in for lunch - "

"'Block, Give Me a Block' Who's that?" Jennifer interrupted.

"Oh, he's our new neighbor. That's right - you've been working so much lately you didn't know. Our old neighbor Bizarre Janey sold her house. Block, Give Me a Block bought it. He's a lion."

"A lion?"

"Yes," Grandma answered."But he's very nice. He's what we used to call 'a White Lion.'"

"An albino?"

"No, no. We meant that 'a White Lion was a nice person, even if he was a lion."

Jennifer let this go by, and thought for a while. After thinking, and looking up to make sure Aka-Drum had still stopped growing, she said, "So where is this Block, Give Me a Block now?"

"*I* don't know," Grandma said. "I've just been trying to keep the *house* from falling down, that's all *I've* been doing."

"Great job, Mom," Jennifer said. "You've been great. Look, here's ten dollars. Why don't you walk down to Beastburgers and grab a cup of bouillon, relax for a while, okay? I'll take over here."

"All right, dear. Thank you."

After Grandma had left, Jennifer said, "Great Goochie-Moochie" out loud to herself. "This is very peculiar. i better walk around the whole situation and see what I can see."

She walked around the side of the house along the Hiding Walk Way, looking up occasionally at Aka-Drum towering above her. She waved to him. He waved to her. After he waved, a huge blast of air flattened the tops of the trees and sent ants racing to get below ground. When she got to the back yard, Jennifer Movie Collector saw the most amazing sight she had ever seen.

"What are you *doing*?" she asked the huge lion standing in her back yard. His legs were bent and quivering, and little beads of sweat were popping off him like water off a wet dog.

"I hold up the sky for Aka-Drum," Block, Give Me a Block replied through gritted teeth.

Jennifer looked up. The lion *was* holding up the sky. Jennifer noticed that she felt she could fly. She jumped a little, and stayed right there, a foot off the ground.

"Block," she said, "where did you get this crazy idea?"

"Aka-Drum," Block gritted out, "he say he want to grow up *now*. *I* say, 'I can help you.' Pick up the sky. Aka-Drum - well, look at him. He be big as me, pretty soon."

All the time Block, Give Me a Block was talking, his knees were shaking and his voice was quivering more and more. It was apparent to Jennifer Movie Collecter that the sky wasn't going to stay held up forever.

BLOCK, GIVE ME A BLOCK LIFTING THE SKY.
THE SUN IS DISPLEASED.
THE MOON IS APPALLED.
BLOCK'S KNEES ARE QUIVERING.

When she looked up at the sun, she felt sure they were all in trouble. The sun was looking pretty aggravated about being pushed around by a lion, even if the lion was "a White Lion."

When she looked at the moon, she felt even more worried. Because the moon looked worried, and no one had ever known the moon to worry about anything.

"I had better do some fast and serious thinking," Jennifer thought to herself, "or else this whole part of the universe is going to come crashing down on itself, starting *here.* Boy! And I though Richard *Stink* had problems!"

(To be continued)

Raising the Roof

Part 3

(The story so far: Jennifer Movie Collector screeched to a halt
in front of her house, and Grandma Movie Collector told her
what had led up to Aka-Drum's sudden growth to a height of five
hundred and four feet. Jennifer found Block, Give Me a Block,
the helpful but not intelligent lion, standing in her back yard,
holding up the sky so Aka-Drum could grow up. The moon and
the sun were upset, and Block's knees were beginning to give
way under the weight of the sky. "I better think fast," Jennifer thought.)

Floating a foot above the ground, Jennifer Movie Collector found that she could think really, really fast. Her mind was moving quicker than a gnat goes up a nose. Her mind went from here to there before you could say "there."

"You'd better start talking fast, girl," Jennifer's mind told her. She did. She looked up at the moon's aggrieved face, and sang,

"O, Artemis Moon, can you hear me?" (You have to sing to the moon.)

"I have been torn from my place, and I fear it must all end badly," sang the moon. She sounded like Scarlatti when she felt anxious.

"O, Artemis, don't be silly," Jennifer sang. "Just take a look at yourself."

"What ever, ever, ever can you mean?"

"You've had the sun's whole light to bask in, free at last of the earth's cold shadow, haven't you? And look at you: you're all one lovely blush of extra sunlight."

The moon looked down at herself. "Why, so I am, so I am, why, so I am," she sang in pleased surprise.

"And how that pink glow doth become you," Jennifer sang. Listening to the moon had made her sound a little like Scarlatti herself. She turned to the sun.

"Mister Sol?" she said quietly. You can sing to the sun, or you can talk. You just better be straight. Jennifer's voice was tired from carrying songs all the long distance up to the moon, because she hadn't been practicing, so she talked.

"Say *what?*" the sun answered, exploding a sunspot from the foci of its loci. Jennifer Movie Collector heard radios go on all over the neighborhood. They were playing music from the Crab Nebula - the Pincer Movement from the Crustacea Symphony, by Callinectes Sapidus. All the birds in the neighborhood fell into a critical silence.

"Mister Sol, why are you angry?" Jennifer asked, using her Reasonable voice.

"Nobody fool with Mister Sol and *live,*" the sun burst out. He was looking badder every minute.

Jennifer decided it was no time to be bullied.

"Listen, Fool," she said, using her wave-stilling voice, "is it *fooling* with you to *fool* you into taking a vacation, *fool?*"

"Vacation," the sun echoed, in a flat, scornful tone. "Mister Sol, he does not get no *vacations.* Got to warm that earth you standing on.... Almost on," he added.

"Well, here is a bulletin from the front, dear, "Jennifer said, managing to switch her hips even though her feet had nothing to hold on to. "You *must* have vacated, for the reason that it's *cold* down here, and it's *noon,* and it's *July.* And it's *cold."*

The sun sent out a spiral, gassy finger and poked itself. The tip of the gassy finger jumped back from the sun's flaming skin.

"Whoo! I am *hot!*" the sun bellowed. "Damn! Feels all right. Haven't been this hot in *far* too long."

"Then be a little thankful," Jennifer said. "You haven't been hurt at all, have you? No more than the moon has."

Then she sang to both the sun and the moon:

    "If I can persuade this callow lion

    To gently let you down,

    Will you refrain from vengeance

    On us and on our town?"

The sun and the moon looked at each other. Then they both nodded and beamed.

"Phew," Jennifer said to herself, "that's the hard part over with. Now for this lion."

Poor Block, Give Me a Block's knees were about gone, and his smile was gigantically wide, but not happy. The sweat wasn't popping off him any more. It was rolling down his body in sheets, like a river over a spillway. "I won't have to water the garden all summer," Jennifer thought. "Hope he doesn't flood out my zucchini mounds."

"Block," she said, "it's time you put down the sky. It's all right... the sky promised not to hurt us."

Poor Block's eyes were almost squinted shut from the strain of holding up the sky.

"Can't...put her....down," he grunted. "Mash...Aka-Drum.....He... too tall... for gravity."

"Good gravy," Jennifer thought, "he's right. If Block, Give Me a Block lets the sky down now, Aka-Drum's head will rip right through gravity. There's no telling what would happen then. But it wouldn't be good."

Meanwhile, unaware of the trouble below, the sun was smiling a molasses smile at the moon.

"Pink become you, baby," the sun said.

"Hold your tongue, fool," the moon sang, sounding nothing like Scarlatti, "before it get you in trouble." The moon had been listening to when Jennifer Movie Collector talked to the sun.

(To be continued)

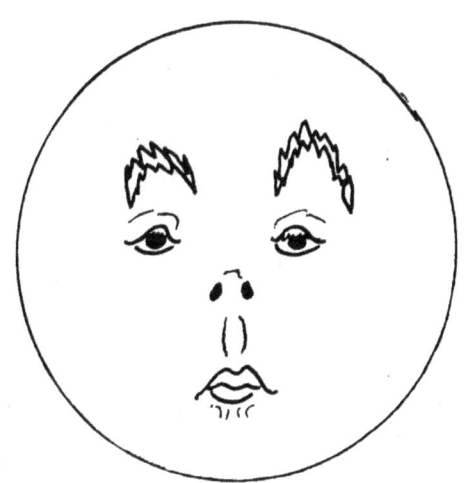

"HOLD YOUR TONGUE, FOOL," THE MOON SANG

Raising the Roof

Part 4

(The story so far: When Jennifer Movie Collector found Block, Give Me a Block, a lion of good intentions but little foresight, holding up the sky so that Aka-Drum could grow up, she had to sweet-talk the moon and tough-mouth the sun. After those two agreed not to punish the earth creatures for lifting them out of their right places, Jennifer found that she had one more problem: Gravity.)

While Jennifer pondered how to get Aka-Drum to come down without ripping through gravity, Aka-Drum was also thinking.

"Well, I'm up, all right," he thought. "I don't think I like it." From where his head was, he could see a long way. He could see the whole City of Eat Meat. It looked like a waffle writhing with ants. He could see the Great Dismal Swamp beyond, and its capitol, Commerce City.

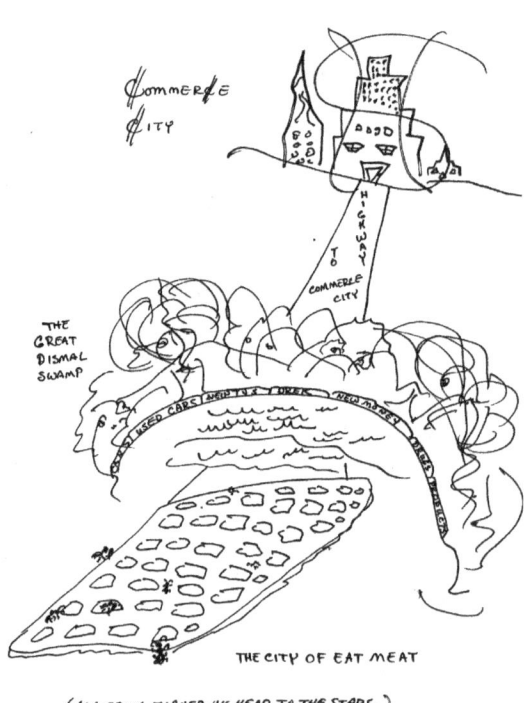

(AKA-DRUM TURNED HIS HEAD TO THE STARS.)

Aka-Drum turned his head to the stars, but not for very long.

"I won't do *that* again," Aka-Drum said to himself, looking back toward earth. What he had seen was so blue-black, so deep and far apart, so cold between its little silver fires, that it made Aka-Drum feel lonely. He'd never felt lonely before, so he didn't know what it was he felt, but he knew he didn't want to feel it any more.

"Auntie Jennifer," Aka-Drum called down to where Jennifer Movie Collector was standing with her finger up her nose, thinking. (She had picked up this habit from Grandma Movie Collector, though she didn't know she did it.) "Want to come down *now*"

"You say *What?*" Jennifer hollered, her head snapping up. She had been thinking so hard, she'd forgotten she was no longer intimidating the sun.

"I... want... to... come... *down!*" Aka-Drum's voice came floating down.

"If you want to," Jennifer hollered, feeling quite relieved, "you can. Just concentrate on being how you want to be."

Without knowing he was doing it, Aka-Drum put his finger up his nose and thought very carefully about how he wanted to be. It would be all right to be as big and strong in the body as Block, Give Me a Block. It would be dynamite to be as scary-looking as Mister Bad-Boo.

"You want to be you," said Aka-Drum's mind.

"True enough," Aka-Drum said out loud, "and I'm only *this* big."

And all of a sudden his nose was in Auntie Jennifer's neck, and her two arms were so close around his back they were like part of his skin, and Auntie Jennifer's perfume was there. (Jennifer Movie Collector always wore *Nuits des Moutons,* although it was very expensive.)

"Aka-Drum," Jennifer said, holding the old-sized Aka-Drum out at arms length, "if you *ever, ever, ever....*"

Then she couldn't talk any more, because she was laughing too hard. Also crying. After she had somewhat stopped laughing, Jennifer said, "So how was it up there?"

"No birds," Aka-Drum said. "No squirrels. No funny smells. I couldn't reach the ground to pick up anything interesting. No fun," he concluded.

"Well, live and learn," Jennifer said.

Then she said, "Yeee-ikes! Ike! Ike! Ike!" because water was lapping around her knees. She pulled Aka-Drum to her, gave a little jump and rose a few inches above the flood.

Poor Block, Give Me a Block was still trying to hold up the sky, but he was sweating so much that he was actually shrinking, and the sky was coming down, causing

Block's sweat to roll through the back yard like the tide coming in. Block had his eyes shut so tight in heroic effort that he had not noticed the effort was no longer necessary.

"Block!" Jennifer cried out. "You can let it down! Everything's all right. Aka-Drum un-grew. Everything is *all right*!"

With a mighty sigh that broke windows all the way to Commerce City, the lion sank to his knees, and the moon and the sun sank back to their proper places, and gravity came down.

Gravity is like an invisible steel anvil, and the earth is like the bench it stands on. And every sliver in the bench of earth carries the same weight of gravity's anvil. Gravity weighs exactly what Aka-Drum happened to weigh at the time of this story - 32 pounds - times the number of slivers in the bench of earth.

When gravity came down with the rest of the sky, Jennifer and Aka-Drum and even the supine Block, Give Me a Block all sank earthward like an eraser into a pencil when you push it down with your thumb.

Then they got used to gravity's weight, slowly, and remembered how to carry it, and rose to their proper heights, grateful to feel how gravity anchored their feet to the ground.

Grandma Movie Collector appeared around the corner of the Hiding Walk Way.

"Aka-Drum! You're back!" Grandma shouted happily, and Aka-Drum ran over to her. Jennifer watched them hug, and then she looked around at the general mess her back yard had become.

Looking up, she saw that Block, Give Me a Block had not risen up like the rest of them. He looked like a tired old balloon, with just a little air left in it, practically nothing but wrinkles.

Jennifer ran up the garden steps to see to him.

She got down on the ground and hugged the lion as much as she could. Her arms were too short to get very far around him.

"Block," she said to him, "you did a wonderful thing. You lifted the sky to help a friend." Block lay there.

"Even though it wasn't a good idea, it was a beautiful idea," Jennifer said. "Even if you're a lion, you're a good man."

"Rrrrraaaa-wwwrrr!" Block came back to life with a happy roar, beginning to resume his normal, square shape. Every time he got a little squarer, he gave a little grunt of happiness.

"I try to he'p out," he whoofed.

Jennifer Movie Collector extracted her arms from hugging and stood up. She looked down through the great hole Aka-Drum had made growing through her kitchen roof, seeing the plaster and shingles on the kitchen floor. Dirty piles of shingle smithereens lay all around the house, and in her neighbors' yards.

"What a mess," Jennifer saiid. "I'd better get busy." Grandma Movie Collector looked up from hugging Aka-Drum.

"Jennifer!" she said with some authority, "You let me clean up. These kids need lunch. And I *do* have some experience cleaning up messes."

"Thanks, Mom, "Jennifer said. "The wheelbarrow's around the side of the house on the Hiding Walk Way. I'll get us some lunch."

Aka-Drum had escaped from hugging Grandma Movie Collector and came running up the garden stairs. Jennifer looked down at her God-nephew hugging the immense leg of their new neighbor lion. The lion gave a leap of joy, and he and Aka-Drum began dancing. Flowers began getting crushed beneath their pleasure. They were already letting their gladness get out of hand.

"Aka-Drum," Jennifer said, "time to stop playing. It's lunch time."

"Block," she went on, "you are a grand new neighbor for us. You have strength and courage and loyalty. But I think you're too young to be on your own." Block looked surprised, but not displeased.

"You need good sandwiches and someone smart to live with," Jennifer said, patting the lion's great elbow. "Come on down to what's left of the kitchen. I'll make some peanut butter and kelp sandwiches, and call Mister Dee-Dah to see if he's still looking for a place to live."

And they all walked down the garden stairs together, thinking about lunch.

The second serial I wrote had a more complicated set of origins.

When I first lived in Denver, in 1967, a series of earthquakes shook the city. *Earthquakes?* They happen in California, not in *Colorado*. That was the consensus at first. We were all pretty ignorant. Eventually scientists concluded that the tremors had been fostered by the military's habit of pouring nuclear waste into wells they'd drilled at their Rocky Flats facility. This revelation struck me as typical but annoying. I remember I memorialized it in a verse I wrote that year:

>The seismographer records
>His mother's tremors.
>Brother feeds the snakes
>Down her pajamas.

One set of next-door neighbors provided inspiration for Mr. and Mrs. Bad Boo. I'd memorialized them in another poem:

>Front Porch Music
>
>The horrible sounds of human intent
>infest the summer air.
>The sumacs are still, weird and Chinese,
>draping over nothing.
>The birds are shuddering into silence,
>they've screeched enough
>for one day. Bugs and streetlights
>are just starting up.
>
>But the humans. They never quit.
>Romero is trying
>to start his failing truck across the street,
>Zola is screaming
>"Sidney, Sidney, Sidney!"
>He's her old man.
>Who knows what he did now?

A biker roars up the street
on his excuse for a hog.
Hoods slam, engines rev, doors slam,
the freeway moans.

Some Mexicans down the street,
or maybe young gringos,
sing a few bars.
Next door, Sidney
mumbles something to his repellent dog.
Words of love.

The plot situation for "Surprise Party" came from one of Thelonika's inspirations. One afternoon when Jerry Mosier was visiting at the house, Thelonika decided we should have an Imaginary Root Beer Party. Neither Jerry nor I was quite sure what that might entail, but we went along with the program. Fortunately I recorded this event on film, so I can prove it did take place.

Surprise Party
Part 1

"Brother," Jennifer Movie Collector said, looking around the little house, "this imaginary Root Beer party of Aka-Drum's is already getting out of hand. And it hasn't even started yet.

"Can't start without the guest of honor," Grandma Movie Collector said.

"Where *is* that Poets, anyway?"

"Who knows?" Grandma observed. "Who *ever* knows?"

All the other guests were already there, except for Mister Dee-Dah, who was busy doctoring. Amanda-Miranda was going around getting everyone to admire her blonde hair while her baby-sitter Soota talked with Jennifer and Grandma. Clockie and Fahd from down the street were pursuing Ralph Tunacat and anything else that moved.

Mr. Dee-Dah was busy doc'toring.

Even without all these guests, the house would have been crowded, because not only had Block, Give Me a Block arrived, he had brought along his cousin, Steve Canadian Bacon, an older and therefore even larger lion. They were showing signs of wanting to join Clockie and Fahd in their mad pursuits.

"Ralph! Get Him," cried Fahd

So it was a relieved Jennifer Movie Collector who heard a "tock-tocka-ta tock ta tocketa" on the front door, accompanied by the unmistakeable growl of Poets' voice:

"Yokahama voutz-o-roon,

Cogito Frito ergo sum

Welcome back from the land of the moon

Little Cousin Aka-Drum."

"Poets!" everyone exclaimed happily. "All *right*!" Because it was a funny thing - even though everybody groused about Poets never showing up on time, and nobody understood much of what came out of his mouth, everybody was always glad to see him, because he always seemed to be having such a good time.

"*Baby,*" Poets said to the group at large, and the party commenced in earnest.

"Call the cops, Aka-Drum," Jennifer said. But Aka-Drum was already on the telephone.

"Oh, hello, cops. Says, we're having a party over here and the kids want some pie and some Imaginary Root Beer, okay?... How many? Let's see...." Aka-Drum began to count all the people and other animals in the house. There were Jennifer and Grandma, Amanda-Miranda and Soota, Clockie and Fahd, and those two lions, and Ralph Tunacat, and Aka-Drum himself, of course.... Ten. But wait a minute. He'd forgotten to count Poets! How could he have done that?

There was a perfectly good reason. As soon as he had made his triumphal entry, Poets had turned around and disappeared out the door. He had seen a purple lupine blooming in the front yard and felt the need to kneel before it and croon and smile. He'd been gone almost before he got there.

Resolving to find Poets, Aka-Drum turned his attention to the phone, where the cops were waiting for his final count. "Eleven," he said, "there are eleven of us. Oh - and don't forget the straws.... Wonderful....Thant you very much for helping with the party.... See you soon."

"All taken care of," he told Jennifer Movie Collector, and began picking his way through the hungry guests to find Poets.

"We'll be eating and drinking in no time at all," he told everyone, as he wove through the little clusters they'd formed. When he got outside, he saw Poets right away.

"Poets, are you okay?" Aka-Drum asked.

Poets looked up. "Just supine before a lupine, my man. No need to worry."

"Cousin," Aka-Drum said, "would you kindly let the flowers alone and come on in? Everybody came here to see you, you know."

"Surely you jest..... But perhaps it's best," Poets replied, and he and Aka-Drum strode arm-in-arm into the waiting party, followed almost immediately by the cops bearing pies and drinks and straws.

The worst thing that happened during this part of the party was that Amanda-Miranda spilled her Imaginary Root Beer on Fahd, and Fahd pushed his good pie into Soota's ear as she was bending down to say "No" to Amanda-Miranda. Grandma Movie Collector brought a hot, wet washcloth to Soota so she could wipe the pie out of her ear, while Jennifer talked seriously to Amanda-Miranda and Fahd.

After she was finished talking seriously, which always made her feel thoroughly bored, Jennifer called, "Who's for a movie?"

"Yeah!" everyone answered.

"What do you want to see?"

"*Psycho! Return of Godzilla! The Car Heard a Noise Under the Bridge! Battleship Potemkin! Point Your Toes and I'll Drive You Home! Tree Behind Island Boy!*" They all shouted out their favorite movies at once.

"I WANT TO SEE (THE CAR HEARD A NOISE UNDER THE BRIDGE," SAID STEVE CANADIAN BACON.

"*Tree Behind Island Boy!*" Jennifer exclaimed. "Great! It's ready to go."

The big screen came rolling down, covering the front door, the lights went out, and slurping sounds accompanied the movie's titles.

The slurping sounds came from Aka-Drum's guests. Now that the lights were out, they felt free to eat as they wished. The most offensive sounds came from the vicinity of Steve Canadian Bacon.

"Steve!" Grandma Movie Collector called, "you're not eating *guests,* are you?"

"I wouldn't do a thing like that," Steve replied in a clogged voice. "You ought to apologize for asking."

"I do apologize," Grandma Movie Collector said. "Also for interrupting the movie."

The movie, *Tree Behind Island Boy,* had indeed begun. Mucky Mouse was having his meeting with the brids. He was asking, "How did all these brids get in here?"

The brids were singing, "Skree, skree, skraw, skraw, Pee-wee, Caw, caw," and pooping all over Mucky Mouse's furniture.

Jennifer lay back on her elbows on the floor between Poets and Soota. Just as she had gotten comfortable on the floor, the floor began to shake.

"Jeez," Jennifer thought to herself, "you better relax, kid. You've got the shakes." She tried all her relaxing ways, but none of them worked. Her legs kept shaking.

"It's not me - it's the floor that's shaking," she decided.

"Soota," she whispered, not wanting to disturb the kids, "is the floor moving, or am I?"

"I thought you'd never ask," Soota whispered back. "It's the floor, I think."

Jennifer and Soota checked the floor with their hands in the darkness, and sure enough, the floor was dancing around beneath their feet.

"Soota," Jennifer whispered, "do you think we might be in an earthquake?"

"I think so," whispered Soota. "We'd better get all these kids down into the cellar."

"I think that's for tornadoes," Jennifer whispered. The whole house was shaking now, and small tinklings and crashings were beginning to drown out the movie's soundtrack. "Time to quit yakking," Jennifer decided.

"Kids!" she shouted. "Up off your duffs! Let's get out of here right now! Poets - turn off the projector. Aka-Drum - roll up the screen. Mom - pull out the coffee plug. Everybody - outside. We're in an earthquake!"

Outside, the whole world looked like a movie slipping its sprockets. Jennifer had to run back into the house and drag Poets out. He had gotten preoccupied thinking about rhymes for "quake," and forgotten that the earthquake was, in fact, happening. Just as they got out, something big crashed down on the back of the house.

"Oh, great," Jennifer said. "And I just got the kitchen roof fixed." Everybody wondered if the whole world was going to come apart.

(To be continued)

Surprise Party

Part 2

(The story so far: When Poets arrived at his cousin Aka-Drum's house, the Imaginary Root Beer party began to roll. But just as Grandma and Jennifer and the kids were settling down to watch *Tree Behind Island Boy,* things became very *un*settled. The house

began shaking so badly that Jennifer knew they must be in the
middle of an earthquake. She got everyone outside, hoping it
was the right thing to do.)

Most of the kids were screaming, since they couldn't think of anything else to do. Grandma and Jennifer and Soota were all running back and forth trying to get the kids out from under anything that might fall on them. This was hard to do, since there were big trees all around the front yard, their tops quivering and swaying, and who could know which way they might fall? Jennifer and Grandma felt like screaming, too.

If you have never been in an earthquake, you can't imagine what it is like. When the whole earth is jumping and jerking, it feels like it has become the ocean, only no ocean ever made waves as low and rapid as the earth makes in an earthquake. The earth, which you have always been able to expect, without thinking about it, to stay still and solid under everything, is quivering like a sleeping, dreaming dog, and you suddenly know what a tiny flea must feel like.

The only one who didn't seem terrified was Poets, who was bouncing on his toes in time with the earth-waves, his head snapping from North to South, taking it all in and grinning with delight.

"Green grass rolling like a wind-whipped lake!
Sidewalks oscillating like a snake!
You want to stop it, but you don't have the brake!
This is an *earth*quake, this ain't no fake!"

"Poets doesn't let much interrupt his work," Grandma observed.

"In the very jaws of death, he rhymes," Jennifer agreed. "I sometimes wonder about his sanity."

"Maybe sanity's not so sane," said Poets, overhearing her.

"As everyone says all the time,
If you got to go be a not-to-be,
Might as well go with a rhyme.

Human beans worship sanity" -

Poets stopped abruptly when he saw the big crack ripping up the lawn toward Aka-Drum. The earth was opening up like a zipper. Poets sprinted across the lawn and snatched Aka-Drum up in his arms, leaping over the crack just in time. He stood panting, still holding Aka-Drum, too breathless for a brief moment to make a poem.

Then suddenly the shaking and the thundering it had been making and the crashing of glass and metal and pottery just stopped. Everyone stood still. No one said a word. They were all listening, listening with their ears, their feet, their skin, trying to believe the earthquake had really stopped. It was hard to feel certain. They felt the way a person who's been on a boat on the ocean for a long time does when she steps on shore. The land seems to be moving, but it's really her body, still moving in time with the waves. Poets was the first to speak. This surprised no one. He hadn't finished his last verse, and Poets never left a verse unfinished.

"But, as the Preacher said, all is vanity."

Aka-Drum regained his voice. "Three cheers for Poets! He saved my life!"

As everyone was shouting "Hip Hip Hoorah!" and clapping hands, Jennifer slipped back into the house to see how it had come through the quake.

It wasn't too bad in the front rooms. The pictures were all cattywampus on the walls, and a couple had fallen down, along with some books. There were some new cracks in the plaster.

"Not bad so far," Jennifer thought, and then she stopped dead in the kitchen doorway. The big crash she had heard earlier had been caused by an old cottonwood tree falling down right through the kitchen roof. Its trunk and a huge grey broken limb were lying on the stove.

"Stove...." Jennifer said to herself out loud, "Stove *in* is more like it." She liked to joke with herself when things went bad.

Turkey's Goose Was Cooked

But the stove wasn't the really bad part. Jennifer's eyes went to the floor, and she saw Turkey, Aka-Drum's pet parrot, lying on his back there, his little feet sticking straight up in the air. His cage was smashed open on the floor, and Jennifer could guess what had happened. The tree had bashed Turkey's cage down and Turkey had been thrown free of it, landing on the floor, where a falling can of vicchysoise had landed on his head. Turkey's goose was cooked. Turkey had bought the farm.

Jennifer got down on the floor to make sure he was dead, even though she was already sure. She thought about telling Aka-Drum, and tears came up from her heart and spilled out of her eyes when she thought about Aka-Drum's grief.

"Well, he'll just have to learn his first about grief now, I guess," she said finally. "It comes to you when it comes, and then there it is." She got slowly to her feet and went back through the house to find Aka-Drum. As she reached the living room, she heard that the chorus of cheers for Poets had changed to another kind of chant.

"*Bad-B*oo, *Bad-B*oo, *Bad-B*oo," all the kids were shouting. Through the front door, Jennifer saw Mister Bad-Boo, the Chicago Black Widow, just opening the front gate.

"Bad-Boo," Jennifer muttered. "What's *he* doing here?" Even though Mister Bad-Boo was her next-door neighbor, Jennifer always asked the same question when she caught sight of him.

(To be continued)

Surprise Party

Part 3

(The story so far: Aka-Drum's Imaginary Root Beer party was going
great guns. Poets had arrived, and everyone was settling down to
eat and drink and watch *Tree Behind Island Boy,* when an earthquake
broke up the party. It would have swallowed up Aka-Drum, if Poets hadn't
had more of his wits about him than most people thought. Jennifer
found poor Turkey in the kitchen, dispatched by a falling can of
vicchysoise, and just as she was thinking nothing worse could
happen, Mister Bad-Boo arrived.)

Mister Bad-Boo swayed his corpulent body through the front gate.

"Ahloors, mah pretty wans," he cried. "I saw zat you 'ave zee partee. Zo...I made it on over."

"*Bad*-Boo, *Bad*-Boo," all the kids were chanting as they ran under the bushes. Everyone was a little afraid of Mister Bad-Boo. Or a lot afraid.

Mister Bad-Boo claimed to be a French Garden Spider from Paris, but nobody believed him. ("Paris, Kentucky - that's as close as he ever got to Paris," Grandma Movie Collecter said once to Jennifer, when they thought all the kids were asleep.) The word in the neighborhood was that Mister Bad-Boo was a retired gangster from Chicago. His French accent did not discourage anyone from believing this, though nobody really knew *where* he'd come from. One day they'd waked up and there were the Bad-Boos.

Mrs. Bad-Boo was another kettle of fish. She never said she was from anywhere, though she put on the airs of a queen, and she never talked of anything except her possessions, which were endless. She collected everything from art to stuffed zebras, and much of the art she collected looked no worse than the zebras.

The Bad-Boos never made any trouble, but they never seemed to say anything that anyone could believe, or answer in an easy way. Mister Bad-Boo, for instance, once greeted Jennifer early on a Monday morning by saying, "Aaaahh - zis air ees lak you braithe: day-lec-table." Jennifer was picking up the morning paper, and had not yet brushed her teeth, and the air was full of automobile fumes.

"What are you talking about?" Jennifer said.

Another time Aka-Drum and Ligee were swinging in the front yard swing, enjoying the evening sunlight sliding up the trees across the street, listening to the birds get ready for night. Suddenly Mrs. Bad-Boo's voice screamed out. (Mrs. Bad-Boo never said a word at normal volume. She screamed when she was intending to talk. When she grew excited, which she ordinarily did after she had screamed her first sentence, her voice ascended to a shriek. She had never, so far as anyone knew, had anything to whisper about. When she became angry, her voice could have been used to cut and shape metal.)

"I just got my last plate! My set is complete!" she screamed. "Come look! There's only one set like it! It's *blue!*"

Aka-Drum and Ligee pretended not to hear her and continued to swing. If the Pope had been on Mars, he would have heard Mrs. Bad-Boo, but she was so used to people ignoring her that she decided they were deaf and went back inside her house, where she could be heard screaming at Mr. Bad-Boo that it was nice out.

Nobody knew what to think of them. Mister Bad-Boo was an obvious fake, and Mrs. Bad-Boo was obviously impossible to live with, yet there they were, living with each other and preening around the neighborhood in their clothes that made them look like the most fashionable models, if not worse. The upshot was that everyone was afraid of the Bad-Boos.

MRS. BADBOO'S STUFFED ZEBRA LAMP

Everyone except Grandma Movie Collecter, who had seen their kind before, and who had lived about long enough to get over being afraid of anything but her own folly. She approached Mister Bad-Boo immediately.

"I notice you waited until after the earthquake to make your visit," she said.

"Eauth-quek? To what eauth-quek does meddame refair?" Bad-Boo asked slimily, squeezing the last of himself through the gate.

"The 'eauth-quek' that just almost swallowed us all up," said Jennifer, standing on the porch with her hands on her hips. "Of course, you wouldn't know anything about that, would you?"

Mister Bad-Boo's eyebrows rose, and all four of his shoulders shrugged at once. He was the picture of guilty innocence.

"'Ow could I know," he said, "when I 'ave been watching...ah...ah, how do sat eet, *la televissyeeown*?"

"His words emerge like flowered snakes,
He smiles like an amplified sun.
But when he smiles, put on the brakes,

Or your downfall's just begun," came out from somewhere behind the huckleberry bush.

"Poets?" called Jennifer.

"Just a passing thought," came Poets' voice.

Another voice followed immediately. Everyone recognized it. There was only one voice in the neighborhood that sounded like a chainsaw hitting a spike in a tree.

"Nic-ky? Nic-*ky*?" Mrs. Bad-Boo screamed, her head appearing between the gate posts.

Mister Bad-Boo's head swiveled completely backwards over his shoulder in a disgusting fashion.

"Yais, mah dear, what eez eet you weesh off me?" he hissed.

Instead of answering him, Mrs. Bad-Boo came thumping through the gate in a determined way, so that Jennifer Movie Collecter's front yard was virtually filled with Bad-Boos.

"I want an explanation, Nick Bad-Boo!" Mrs. Bad-Boo was screaming. "I want to know why my designer china is lying all over the floor in pieces! I want...." But Mister Bad-Boo had by this time somehow disappeared and re-materialized behind Jennifer, in her own house.

"Jenny, baby," he whispered in Jennifer's ear, his accent temporarily deserting him, "get me oudda here!"

"Sure," Jennifer whispered over her shoulder, "come on. You can get out through the back door. It's straight back through the kitchen." She jerked her thumb toward the kitchen and MIster Bad-Boo scurried away in that direction. Jennifer didn't necessarily want to help Mr. Bad-Boo, but she very definitely didn't want him in her house.

Seeing the mess the cottonwood tree had made of the kitchen, Mister Bad-Boo stopped short for a second. His strange little mind thought about the picture his strange little eyes saw, and picked out a strange little escape route. His first step happened to fall very close to Turkey's body.

"What's the matter with you, man?" a voice said. "Ain't you got no respect?"

Mister Bad-Boo froze. "Respect" was a word he had known well in Chicago, where it had to do with the nearness of death. Since he hadn't noticed Turkey's body on the floor, Mister Bad-Boo could only assume he was being threatened by an invisible spirit. For the first time since he had retired to the city of Eat Meat, Mr. Bad-Boo was afraid.

(To be continued)

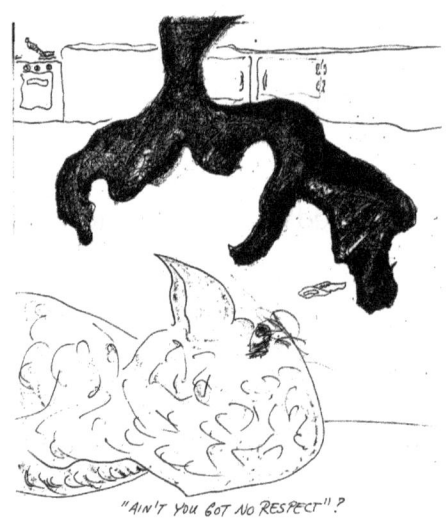

"AIN'T YOU GOT NO RESPECT"?

Surprise Party

Part 4

(The story so far: Aka-Drum's Imaginary Root Beer party had turned into a real disaster when an earthquake struck. After the earthquake let up, Mister Bad-Boo, Jennifer's nextdoor neighbor, showed up. When Mrs. Bad-Boo followed him through the gate, he promptly scuttled around Jennifer and through her house toward the back door, where he almost stepped on Turkey, the pet parrot, who was lying on the floor, looking but not sounding quite dead.)

"Yeah, respect," Turkey said, raising his head from the floor with care. "Respect - you don't have any."

By this time, Mister Bad-Boo had sensed where Turkey's voice was coming from. "Listen, you woim wid fedders..." Mister Bad-Boo said, raising one of his large, nasty feet in a threatening fashion.

"No, *you* listen," said Jennifer, who had just come into the kitchen. "And while you're listening, put that big, ugly foot down. *Carefully.*"

Something in Jennifer's voice made Mister Bad-Boo decide to try to be His Charming Self.

"But, Geneefair..." he started to say.

"Jenny Fair, my cousin from Peoria!" Mrs. Bad-Boo trumpeted, booming around Jennifer into the kitchen. "You skunkmother! They told me what you been doin'!"

"But...But...But..." quavered Mister Bad-Boo.

"I saw you walk out your back door with a big, black bucket," said Block, Give Me a Block, sticking his big head through a hole in the wall where the plaster had fallen out.

"I saw you pour it down the well," said Turkey, pushing himself up to a sitting position. "About every other day you were out there, pouring whatever it was in that pot into the well."

Nobody said anything for a minute. Mister Bad-Boo was trying to smile. He had a lot of teeth, but the smile wasn't looking very convincing.

"And wha'd *I* see, Nicky?" Mrs. Bad-Boo shrieked. "I'LL TELL YOU WHAT I SAW! I SAW YOU POURING YOUR EXTRA POISON *INTA* THAT BIG BLACK POT, DI'N'T I?"

Turkey suddenly fluttered up into the air and began pecking Mister Bad-Boo's disgusting necktie, shrieking, "Poisoner! Poisoner!" Jennifer grabbed him out of the air and held him next to her heart.

"Calm down, Turkey," she said. "Mister Bad-Boo's just made a mistake. Everybody makes mistakes, now and then."

"Ah, Geneefair - " Mister Bad-Boo began gratefully, but Jennifer interrupted him.

"Don't start up Bad-Boo," she said, "just don't. You made a mistake. You're entitled to one. But no more.... Get it? You poisoned *our* earth with your poison until it got sick and threw up."

"You mean...zee eauthquek?" Mister Bad-Boo said, as if perhaps he'd never known his poison could hurt the earth.

> "If you look anger toward a flower
> It will make a tiny seed
> That will fall and grow to glower

Over you and all your breed,"

Poets observed, peering over Jennifer's shoulder.

"Why do you make more poison than you can hold?" asked Aka-Drum, who was sitting on Poets' head.

"Ah, leetail wan..." Mister Bad-Boo started. Then he stopped. When he began to speak again, he wasn't trying to sound like a Frenchman. "Kid," he said, "where I come from, ya godda have more poison than ya can hold. Udderwise, dey think you're weak, y'unnerstand?"

"No," Aka-Drum said.

"No," Jennifer said.

"No," Block said.

"Sure," Poets said. "I understand:

> Mister Bad-Boo's used to poison
> Poison is his daily bread
> Poison is the only reason
> He doesn't eat things that aren't dead."

"That's disgusting," said Mrs. Bad-Boo, and nobody disagreed.

"You don't *need* all that poison in this neighborhood, Mister Bad-Boo," Jennifer said.

"That's right, " added Block, Give Me a Block. "We look out for each other in this neighborhood." And he gave Mister Bad-Boo a friendly look that wiped the remains of the smile off Bad-Boo's face.

"What he means," said Turkey, squirming in Jennifer's arms, "is, we keep our eyes *open* in this neighborhood."

"And we'd hate to see any more 'aeuthqueks' ruining Mrs. Bad Boo's china goolagongs, or whatever they are," Grandma Movie Collector chimed in sweetly.

Mrs. Bad-Boo's four hands rose to her head. "Nick!" she grated. "Nice! My cal-*lection!*"

She went on and on as Mister Bad-Boo made for the doorway.

Jennifer looked around at the ruins of her just re-built kitchen.

"Well, it certainly was a surprise party," she said.

"Count your blessings," Turkey answered. "You think *you're* surprised? Take a look at my cage."

Then everyone decided that the best thing to do was to finish up the Imaginary Root Beer and watch *Tree Behind Island Boy* from the start again.

So they did that.

The End

M'SIEUR BADBOO MADE FOR THE DOORWAY

Thelonika doesn't remember these stories or these characters except "vaguely."
Well, that's memory for you.

Golden Voices

I grew up during what is now sometimes called "the Golden Age of Radio." If that means anything, it means that various corporations were figuring out, with the aid of an utterly compliant FCC and Congress, how to turn their monopoly control of the radio waves into gold for themselves. I've been able to listen to recordings of a great many of the programs from this Golden Age since it ended, and the vast majority were far closer to pot metal than gold.

But in 40s and 50s Chicago there were still a number of independent stations that had developed their own base of listeners, and I absorbed a great variety of music from them - jazz, gospel, blues, various European popular music, the new comedy of people like Bob Newhart and Lenny Bruce and Lord Buckley - independent radio stations made it all available, until they were absorbed by the networks, then by corporate conglomerates. Most of the network programming was dreadful or mediocre at best - lazy, predictable, repetitive.

Vic and Sade was one shining exception. Written entirely by one man, Paul Rhymer, this remarkable production consisted mostly of fifteen-minute episodes that aired five days a week for 12 years. Rhymer once estimated that he'd produced more words than were contained in the complete works of Dickens. The episodes he turned out were like nothing else on radio - slices from the daily lives of one perfectly ordinary family in a perfectly ordinary town, conveyed entirely by their conversations with each other. Those conversations brought to life a whole supporting cast of relatives, townspeople and neighbors as well. Nothing really out of the ordinary happened - just a man and wife and their son getting through their days and nights. It was Rhymer's genius at creating character through dialog that made the show go in a few years from a shaky, unsponsored local flyer to a national phenomenon with over 6 million listeners. Here's a brief sample:

Sade: (looking up from the newspaper) Who pays for this baboon?
Vic: Beg pardon?
Sade: Do we pay for this baboon?

Vic: (mildly) What baboon, my dear?

Sade: Didn't you see what tonight's paper stated about 'em buyin a new baboon for Miller Park?

Vic: Musta missed that.

Sade: "A.D. Hoggle, custodian of the Miller Park Zoo, has announced the purchase of a new baboon. The animal, known as Lester, is three years old. Mr. Hoggle has arranged for..." so on and so forth. Is it us taxpayers as has to shell out spondulicks for baboons?

Vic: Yeah.

Sade: Nobody asked me if I wanted a baboon.

Vic: (chuckles) Me, either.

Sade: They got two baboons out there already. Why do they have to have more? Seems to me two baboons is enough baboons.

Vic: Mmm.

While I listened devotedly to the radio as a kid, *Vic and Sade* went off the air when I was four, so I'd never heard it when, in an odd little junk shop in Crestone, Colorado, I came upon a boxed set of tapes - the 20 Greatest Radio Shows of All Time, or some such title. I think it cost me two bucks, and I brought it home and spent evenings listening to it, mostly with disappointment. Shows I fondly recalled, such as "The Great Gildersleeve," "Our Miss Brooks," and "Duffy's Tavern" struck me as formulaic, witless exercises. Then I came upon an episode of *Vic and Sade* called "Muted Silver Moonbeam Chimes." Much of it consisted of a prolonged wifely interrogation of Vic by Sade, in tones of a most dreadful, cheerful sweetness, about his purchase of the titular musical instrument. Sade had received a phone call about the instrument's arrival from the music shop's owner. Vic kept replying to Sade's questions, "I'm going back t'th'office now," his tone growing increasingly desperate. With a lifetime of enduring such interrogations behind me, I marveled at Rhymer's perfect ear. After I stopped laughing helplessly.

I immediately set out in search of more recordings, and found a few on commercial tape, and then came upon a wonderful organization, "Friends of Vic and

Sade," the labor of love of one Barbara Schwartz of Lincolnwood, Illinois. I became a member, and the grateful recipient of 32 compact discs containing the Library of Congress' collection of transcriptions of the show that remained - longtime sponsors Proctor & Gamble had destroyed all the rest when the show went off the air, a crime for which I trust God has reserved a particularly horrible punishment. Schwartz also sent out to members her hand-typed copies of Rhymer's original scripts. He'd kept them all in a closet, wrapped into bundles tied with his old neckties, before his widow donated them to The Wisconsin Center for Film and Theater Research, and Barbara Schwartz made innumerable trips up there and hand-copied many scripts.

I came to believe that Paul Rhymer was a comic genius, one of the great American writers. (My admiration only increased when I later discovered that he wrote each day's show *on the day of the show,* a degree of facility demonstrated by "Ordering Underwear," a wonderful comic turn he dashed off *during the day's sole read-through* to fill out a too-short script.) One year I decided I should try to spread the word to another conference of Humanities teachers. This is the proposal I wrote for that effort:

Paul Rhymer's *Vic and Sade*: A Window Into Vanished America

"You know, the grandpas and the great-grandpas carried the assumption that somehow their lives and their decisions were important; that as they went up, down, here and there, such a life was important and that it was a man's responsibility to live it."
- Robert Penn Warren in Cowley, Malcolm, ed., *Writers at Work*, NY: Viking, 1958, p.189

From 1932 to 1946, Paul Rhymer's *Vic and Sade* presented America with itself for fifteen minutes, five days a week. For six years, the show consisted entirely of 3 characters - Victor Gook, his wife Sade, and their adopted son Rush. Only when Art Van Harvey, who played Vic, was sidelined by a heart attack was another speaking character added, Sade's Uncle Fletcher. Until the show's final days, these four characters never were heard outside their rented house in Crooper, Illinois. Through

Rhymer's genius for dialogue and extraordinarily fertile and sometimes surreal imagination, however, an entire town came to life in their conversations.

Not only an entire town, but an entire way of life - that of mid-class, Midwestern America before the triumph of mass culture and marketing - came to life, and remains alive in the surviving transcriptions of the show and in its printed scripts. In "the little house halfway up the next block," Rhymer's characters illuminated the values necessary to the citizens of a republic - or of a successful family.

Those values were neither easy nor simple. Vic, Sade, Rush and Uncle Fletcher could all drive each other to distraction with their individual obsessions and passions. Vic, a generally intelligent, kindly and perceptive soul, often turned into a blithering, adolescent idiot where his lodge, "The Sacred Stars of the Milky Way," was concerned. Sade, equally intelligent, kindly and perceptive, was subject to occasional bouts of extreme jealousy when she got wind that Vic had conversed with Miss Pom-Pom Cordova, late of Bermuda. Rush, a perpetual fourteen-year-old of extraordinary good cheer under normal circumstances, could descend into panicked, adolescent agony at the thought that his mother might be seen buying his school clothes with him in tow. ("Rush's New School Clothes")

My epigraph recalls the quality of believing that one's individual life is important. All of Rhymer's characters held this belief, not only about their own lives, but about their neighbors' lives. As jazz does, Rhymer's work made the qualities of individual responsibility and creativeness and mutual respect manifest. Their workings, in the day-by-day events and nonevents of ordinary, daily life, illuminate the most mundane situations and conversations. Rhymer rendered these conversations with an ear as precise as any jazz musician's for the intricacies and rhythms of mid-Western American speech.

Vic and Sade represents a mother lode of information about American life as it was once lived. In fifty minutes, I hope to provide a skeletal framework and allow my audience to hear selected samples of this immense and largely neglected achievement. I will also provide printed copies of scripts on request, and a bibliography.

I played them a few excerpts, including an episode titled "Bacon Sandwiches," in which Rush explains his friend Rooster Davis's plan to start a restaurant serving only bacon sandwiches, the bacon to be cut from a single live pig kept out back of the place. With each order, the pig will be sedated with "ether and chloroform," the required slices of bacon surgically removed, and the pig "nursed back to health by a nurse on the premises" until more bacon is required. (That episode, and many others, are now available on youtube: https://www.youtube.com/watch?v=a4pZ3fPfKug, along with pretty much anything ever recorded in any form, it seems.) I still listen to my Library of Congress set of shows, and they've held up better than any other old radio shows. I've just about memorized most of them, but they never fail to make me laugh, and if there's anything more valuable than a dependable source of laughter, I don't know what it might be.

While Crooper, Illinois and the Gook family and its other residents were unquestionably the creation of Paul Rhymer, his writing wouldn't have been nearly as effective if it had been "performed" by most radio actors, few of whom had discerned that the necessities of theatrical acting - booming projection, studied articulation, exaggerated expression of emotions - were not only unnecessary but destructive in front of a radio microphone. (Theatrical actors had had the same difficulty adjusting their styles to the camera in the movies' early days.) I've never found an account of who was responsible for casting *Vic and Sade*, but whoever it was was a genius. All four of the principal actors performed their parts completely free of any actors' tricks, of any hint that they were "acting." They all picked up perfectly on Rhymer's remarkable reproductions of everyday, unstudied speech. All the more impressive when you consider that they broadcast their performances after one read-through of a previously unseen script.

And the more remarkable in that Bill Idelson, who played Rush, had no previous theatrical experience and finished high school during his run on the show (after which he joined the Navy and served in combat). Bernadine Flynn came to Sade after a stage career in New York City, during which she'd specialized in playing French maids. Her aural creation of a grade-school educated, shrewd, loving, no-nonsense Midwestern wife and mother perfectly captures the changes in pitch such a character would use to convey a whole range of unarticulated emotional meanings.

Bob Elliott and Ray Goulding produced radio shows about as far in nature and intent from *Vic and Sade* as it would be possible to get, although they admired Rhymer's work. Bob and Ray created the first post-modern radio show, and maintained it at an amazingly high level over three decades on various networks under various titles. Rather than creating a thoroughly convincing imaginary reality, Bob and Ray brought forth a world of overconfident idiots, crooks and obsessives, met through "man-in-the-street" interviews, spiced with parodies of radio and television shows and movies - "One Fella's Family," "Squad Car 119," "Tippy, the Wonder Dog." They depended on no actors, producing a cornucopia of characters with their own two voices.
I wrote an introduction to their work for some reason, now forgotten:

Too Hilariously Stupid to Survive

Kurt Vonnegut, of course, most justly and elegantly summed up Bob & Ray's humor: "Bob and Ray's characters threaten to wreck themselves and their own surroundings with their own stupidity....Man is not evil, they seem to say. He is simply too hilariously stupid to survive."

Certainly true, but there was a good deal more to their humor, including devastating if cheerful satire - of lawyers, doctors, politicians, psychiatrists, bad musicians, advertising and radio. (Their relish for abominable music was eclectic, and they even produced some themselves - Ray's rendition [in the voice of Mary McGoon] of Nick Kenny's "I'd Like to Be a Cow in Switzerland," backed by "Mule Train" was certainly a low point, though not as low as "In Your Hat," the 2nd Act Closer for the Backstayges' *magnum awfulus*, *Westchester Furioso*; I have not yet been able to find out who either wrote or performed this definitive parody of everything wretched about Broadway show tunes and their singers, but it surely represents an unsurpassable nadir of musical expression.)

I've mentioned the Backstayges, the two lead characters in the long-running soap opera parody, *Mary Backstayge, Noble Wife*. (The model was "Mary Noble, Backstage Wife.") The "New Song for *Treasure Island, the Musical*" was attributed to John Simon, and it clearly represents Bob and Ray's response to Simon's review of their Broadway show *The Two and Only*, part of which read: "....Neither...would I have expected to review two Boston disk Jockeys who worked themselves up to a fifteen-minute spot on radio....Bob and Ray are radio, which makes them ancient; they are the forties and early fifties, which makes them antediluvian; and they are, by standards of even minimal intelligence, unfunny, which makes them obsolete....Nichols and May were funny; but that, perhaps, was satire, a league Bob and Ray do not aspire to....There is, ultimately, something even worse about this show than its mirthlessness and banality. I mean its troglodytic benightedness, its refusal to see or say anything of the world outside the studio, of the ills which, if we cannot combat them with anything else, we might at least prick with our ridicule...." I can't imagine a finer response to this typically self-important, witless, myopic review than their attribution of "New Song" - entitled "Gold," and sung to a portable harmonium accompaniment by Ray Goulding in tones somehow simultaneously flat and fruity. Harry and Mary Backstayge, along with their agent Greg Marlowe (secretly in love with Mary, as he frequently announces), their cranky stage-door man Pop Beloved, and their next door neighbor, Calvin Hoogeven, engaged in a long series of improbable enterprises, many of which involved one or another or all of them being kidnapped or contracting amnesia, all of which involved the monumental failure of every enterprise they chose to try.

Bob and Ray created distinctive voices for each of the five main characters, and for the assortment of lunatics they encountered, such as Captain Wolf Larsen, Count Yorkash, and Akbar Mai Tai. Bob and Ray's ability to switch from voice to voice, sometimes creating the illusion of four people talking at once, was uncanny. The only other radio performers who came close to their virtuosity were Freeman Gosden and Charles Correll (Amos and Andy), of whom Fred Allen once observed, ""...their voice changes and the fading in and out of the characters as they come and go are uncanny.

Most people cannot appreciate the skill involved, which is to be expected. Most people, knee deep in the little messes they call their lives, cannot appreciate much of anything."

Bob and Ray wrote a great deal of their own material, but much of it was also provided by a man named Tom Koch, who obviously loved and deeply understood their approach, and sent them 8 or 10 scripts a week for years. I like to think that he is right now having a drink with Bob and Ray in heaven, all of them gazing down at our little messes and chortling wildly. I feel grateful to have shared time on this planet with them, and I bet they'll be remembered for a long time. Hope so, anyhow.

The brilliance, humanity, humor, satire and characterizations of those two radio shows is pretty remarkable, considering that radio only existed as a popular entertainment medium for a few decades before it was entirely consumed by corporate juggernauts and before its entertainment functions were transferred to television. And considering Sturgeon's Law ("90 percent of everything is crap").

Of course, when I was listening devotedly to radio for hours a day, I made few distinctions among the shows I followed. I laughed when the well-coached radio audiences instructed me to laugh, I took in the Romance of Helen Trent as often, though maybe not as eagerly, as I did the adventures of the Lone Ranger or Bobby Benson of the B-Bar-B or Sky King or Boston Blackie. I was exercising my imagination with all of them, as Jack Benny's long-time announcer Don Wilson remarked late in his life:

"....One of the great things about radio - and it will never be acquired by television because it's impossible - but in the radio days, through the listener's eye, his mind's eye, he lived the show with you. He re-created as the words came over the loudspeaker. He knew exactly what that individual looked like, although he'd never seen a picture of anybody. But, in his own mind's eye, he did. He knew what the situation was, what they were talking about. Again the imagination played a part. That's one thing the young people, kids today, do not have that advantage that those of us that knew radio in the old days (sic). Because their imagination is no longer stimulated as it was during the days of radio." [Schaden]

I'm grateful that at least some of these shows, including the best of them, have been preserved and will be available to you who come after me. I hope you'll learn to appreciate and love them, and use them to learn to make your own pictures in your own minds' eyes. There are many good books about the radio era, but these are certainly worth your attention:

General Radio History

Dunning, John, *Tune in Yesterday,* Prentice-Hall, 1976 - an encyclopedia of all the vital facts about hundreds of radio shows of the 30s, 40s and 50s

Chuck Schaden, *Speaking of Radio,* Nostalgia Digest, *2003* - a fine oral history of the radio era, told by many of its creators - actors, writers, announcers, producers.

Vic and Sade

Rhymer, Mary Frances, ed., *The Small House Halfway Up the Next Block,* McGraw-Hill, 1972

Rhymer, Mary Frances, ed., *Vic and Sade,* Seabury, 1976

Idelson, Bill, *Gibby,* Bear Manor, 2006

Idelson, Bill, *The Story of Vic and Sade,* Bear Manor, 2006

Bob and Ray

Elliott, Bob & Goulding, Ray, *Write If You Get Work,* Random House, 1975

Elliott, Bob & Goulding, Ray, *From Approximately Coast to Coast,* Atheneum, 1983

Elliott, Bob & Goulding, Ray, *The New, Improved Bob and Ray,* Putnam's, 1985

Gillespie, Dan, *Bob and Ray. and Tom,* Bear Manor, 2008

Pollock, David, *Bob and Ray: Keener Than Most Persons,* Applause, 2013

Among the long-running radio shows written and performed so well that they haven't aged is one of the eldest (premiered 1929), *Amos and Andy.* Fred Allen's analysis of Freeman Gosden's and Charles Correll's excellence as performers needs no elaboration, but their performances depended on the brilliance of their writing for a new medium. They learned how to write slapstick comedy for radio. They also created a whole cast of memorable characters who make the politically correct crowd nervous these days - wrongly, I think. George Stevens, Sapphire, Andy Brown, lawyer Calhoun - these were not stereotypical black characters. They were universal human types, given human depth and dimension by good writing. "Parking the Car," one of a series of vignettes on 10 inch, 78 rpm records I found at a yard sale, is a perfect example of what

I mean by "slapstick comedy for radio." One of my favorite lines remains, "Uh...Brother Andy, do you think you could get the 'whoa' a little bit ahead of the impact?"

From 1960 to 1964, I ostensibly attended Northwestern University. (One of my professors, punningly reversing Matthew Arnold's title "The Scholar Gypsy," referred to me as "The Gypsy Scholar.") While I managed to receive a wonderful education there, I spent far more time in The Hut, a tiny hole in the wall with a great jukebox, and Lou's Restaurant on Sherman Avenue, just across the street from the NU campus, drinking endless cups of coffee and, at Lou's, enduring endless replays of "Puff, the Magic Dragon" on the juke box. (That awful Peter, Paul & Mary record must have stayed popular for at least two years). My perennial companions in one of Lou's booths - Cheril Bailey, a friend from high school, and her then boyfriend, Bob Viola, his friend from Rhode Island Ron Shoenfeldt, Fred Quinn, a backup quarterback on the NU football team, and his soon-to-be wife Judy - were all NU students, and most of us had been overwhelmed by Joseph Heller's *Catch-22* and by Lenny Bruce, whose lp's we passed around and memorized. I can't say I recall what we talked about, hour after hour, day after day at Lou's, but I know our talk was at least half comprised of lines from Heller's book and Lenny Bruce bits. Between them, they seemed to have expressed our reactions to damn near anything that was going on in the early 60s.

Lenny Bruce got pigeon-holed early as a "sick comic," an unusually moronic label applied to the new sorts of comedians who were abandoning the endless strings of one-liners the older, established comics like Jack Leonard and Bob Hope employed, and who were using the long-playing record, a technology barely ten years old in 1960, to promote their work, rather than having to depend on radio or television to do so. Bruce, in particular, specialized in creating surrealistic scenarios, verbal film scenes in which he portrayed whole casts of characters with his voice, much as Lord Buckley did, though without Buckley's serious depth.

Bruce satirized contemporary bigwigs and mainstream hypocrisies, while Lord Buckley mined history and religion for his themes. Buckley and Bruce shared immersion in the world of jazz clubs, the argot of be-bop, and a commitment to heavy improvisation in their nightclub work. Most important for our gang at Lou's, they spoke to the universal conviction of youngsters that their elders were hypocrites and fools, enslaved by their own pretenses to virtue; hopeless squares.

I'd seen enough hypocrisy and foolishness in my own generation to be a little shaken in my conviction of moral superiority by the time I first got to meet Bruce "U. Utah" Phillips at the Denver Folklore Center. I had no idea who he was when I sat down and fell under his spell in the old DFC concert hall that my friend Steve Abbott had built, pretty much single handed. He mesmerized his audience. He mesmerized me.

"U. Utah Phillips, Golden Voice of the Great Southwest" (his stage monicker) came back from the Korean War throughly disgusted with capitalism and militarism, which were all the rage in his native land. He set out on what became his life's work as a traveling minstrel, riding the railroads and working the hobo jobs, and writing and singing songs about working men and disenfranchised men and women, many songs fondly recalling and mourning the demise of the railroads and of the America that built them and travelled on them. Like most successful minstrels, he cultivated his skills as a storyteller until he became one of the truly great ones. He reminded me of my Uncle Gordon, a Navy veteran who kept me laughing for hours with tales of his multiple farming disasters, spun out in his chain-smoked Camels voice. I think Utah reminded most people in his audience of some such figure from their early years, when Americans still entertained each other. By the time I learned of him, he was part of one of the innumerable market fragments, the Folk Music Scene, then still populous enough to support a club circuit in most major cities and reliably consume enough recordings to keep a few small labels in business.

A few years later, I got to meet Bruce Phillips, and even spend some time with him in a little local radio studio. I was in awe of his talents, and stunned by the gracious respect with which he treated me, a little amateur nobody. The kindness, generosity, humor, the honorable character of the man, all come through in his recorded voice, I think.

As do those same character traits through Arlo Guthrie's voice. Arlo became nationally famous for a brief time in the late 60s with his recorded anti-war tale *Alice's Restaurant*, and with his recording of Steve Goodman's "City of New Orleans." Like his father, like Bruce Phillips, Arlo pursued a career and a life's work in the "folk music" field, where the audience appreciated music and the history it carried, not fame and glamor and sensational showbiz effects. "Reuben Clamzo" (full title, "The Ballad of Reuben Clamzo and His Strange Daughter in the Key of A") is typical of Arlo's approach to the political protest song, with its gentle, absurdist, often hilarious story-telling promoting the Clamshell Alliance, a group of activists formed to oppose the construction of nuclear power plants in New England.

Michael Flanders and Donald Swann were two British writer/musicians who formed a magical (tm Walt Disney Universe) partnership, writing and performing songs of great musical distinction and variety. From the late 50s through the 60s, they performed them in stage reviews around the world, their set a Victorian-style parlor. Flanders had contracted polio while serving in the British Navy during WWII) and made burly, imposing presence in his wheelchair in contrast with Swann's slight, slightly rumpled, fey figure at his upright piano. Their first revue, *At the Drop of a Hat,* came to Orchestra Hall in Chicago in the early 60s, so I was lucky enough to see them live - by which time I already knew every song in the review by heart, I'd listened to the recorded version so many times. Once again, the radio had first led me to this obscure pair of geniuses. Early-morning WCFL disc-jockey Dan Sorkin savored their work, and played selections every morning for months.

Greg Brown is probably one of the last generation to find a folk circuit to play live music on, and the demise of a living culture and its replacement by a mediated, electronic, virtual world is what he's mourning in "Whatever It Was." If there's a national anthem for angry old-timers of any and all political persuasions, this seems like it to me. It expresses the angry mourning of all the people who've lost their ways of life, who've lost their farms and homes and towns to the corporations they've allowed to take over the country through selfishness and laziness.

What a wonderful invention sound recording has been - that people like Bruce Phillips and Arlo and Lord Buckley, and so many other superb human beings, can be experienced almost directly from their recorded voices by generation after generation. I won't deny that the recording industry has had many terrible effects on music and musicians and society, but the ability to capture and keep the actual *voices* of many great people is surely a blessing on us. Maybe it's too optimistic to hope that you'll still know how to listen and how to hear the quality of human character in the quality and expressiveness and rhythm of a human voice, but that's what I hope, because then the world I lived in, the ideas and beliefs and ways of living, that produced such beautiful people, will still be alive, and maybe can be revived or recreated. Or at least you will know that such people really did exist, and be challenged to become one of them.

The English author George Gissing wrote in one of his last books, *The Private Papers of Henry Rycroft,* about the kinds of people we mean when we say "humane": "....However one's heart may fail in thinking of the folly and baseness which make so great a part of today's world, remember how many bright souls are living courageously, seeing the good wherever it may be discovered, undismayed by portents, doing what they have to do with all their strength. In every land there are such, no few of them, a great brotherhood, without distinction of race or faith; for they, indeed, constitute the race of man, rightly designated, and their faith is one, the cult of reason and justice. Whether the future is to them or to the talking anthropoid, no one can say. But they live and labour, guarding the fire of sacred hope." [Gissing]

Amen.

By Measure

The Aim Was Song

Before man came to blow it right
The wind once blew itself untaught,
And did its loudest day and night
In any rough place where it caught.

Man came to tell it what was wrong:
It hadn't found the place to blow;
It blew too hard - the aim was song.
And listen - how it ought to go!

He took a little in his mouth,
And held it long enough for north
To be converted into south,
And then by measure blew it forth.

By measure. It was word and note,
The wind the wind had meant to be -
A little through the lips and throat.
The aim was song - the wind could see. [Frost]

    That's a poem Robert Frost wrote about poetry, which is music with words. It could as well have been just about music. I love it because it describes perfectly what music is (or what poetry is), a partnership between whatever we humans are and the rest of the universe. Our part in that partnership is to "shape" what we live within into something beautiful. Music shapes time and the force and pitch of the wind through instruments, whether they are just parts of our bodies or extensions of our bodies we've invented, into something beautiful.

Nobody could possibly define that word "beautiful." When black American music first became popular at the beginning of the last century, in the piano music now called "ragtime," the music Dictators of those days called it "noise," and said that it was "crude" and "disgusting." Listening now to ragtime, in the works of Scott Joplin, James Scott, Joseph Lamb, Eubie Blake, and others, you have a hard time imagining how those critics could not have heard the beauty in this music. I try to remind myself of this when I listen to what's now called music, which I find not beautiful at all. I try, but I don't succeed.

Rap, Hip-Hop, Metal - all the kinds of sounds most people seem to be listening to these days - seem to me not beautiful for a number of reasons. The second is that they have no variety. Their rhythms are repetitive, their delivery is purposely monotonous. The first is that they seem devoted to celebrating rage and pain rather than love and joy.

I've spent a great deal of my life, and of my writing life, working from rage and pain, so I can certainly understand anyone who's "coming from" there. Robert Frost knew plenty about both those places. He didn't spend his life turning them into poetry, and I hope I haven't either, though my wife Lis would probably disagree. (She thinks I'm a "negative" person. She used to be correct.)

When jazz began, it began as music for people to "celebrate" with. "Celebrate" didn't always mean that you were celebrating something positive. In the early days of jazz in the South, bands would walk along with funeral processions to the graveyard, playing slow, sad marches. When someone dies, the people who knew that someone are saddened and reduced. On the way back from the graveyard, the bands would be playing jazz, music for dancing, music that said, "Well, old man Mose is dead, but *you* ain't!" ("Dead Man Blues" by Jelly Roll Morton is an example.) When someone dies, the people left behind just have to go on without that person, no matter how hard it might seem. Jazz is a music made by people who didn't have the luxury of pretending to themselves that they would never die. The people who created jazz knew they could be dead the next second of their lives, any second. This is true for me, for you, and for everyone you know, but most of us honkies live as if we didn't know it was true, with rare exceptions.

Jazz is about living all the time in the time that you have. I love all music, but jazz the most, and I hope you all learn to hear it. To hear it, you have to learn to listen to it. That's why I'm starting out with it.

Disc One:

Louis Armstrong, trumpet, vocal, Jimmy Strong, clarinet, tenor saxophone, Fred Robinson, trombone, Earl Hines, piano, Mancy Carr, banjo, Zutty Singleton, drums : "West End Blues"

The introduction Louis played here is one of the most famous passages in jazz. For the next half century, anybody who played jazz trumpet tried to learn to play it. But nobody who played jazz trumpet could play it the way Louis did, because nobody who played jazz trumpet had the ability that Louis had to *pay attention to each part of every note.* Any musical tone has three parts, the same three parts any story has: beginning, middle, and end. The musical terms for those three parts are "attack," "sustain," and "release."

If you think about it, there are all kinds of ways to begin a sound - you can slide softly into the first vowel or consonant of a word, or of a tone, or you can strike it as if you were hitting a nail with a hammer, or you can stutter it as if you stuttered. There are all kinds of ways to hold (sustain) a tone, too: you can hold it as close to the original tone as possible, with no variation, or you can use vibratro to vary it evenly until it gets to the end, or you can mix those two approaches. You can end a tone abruptly, or you can let it fade, or you can take it down or up in pitch as it ends. When you think about the way you sound when you're really speaking from your heart, you'll know what I mean. You make all these variations in your speech whether you're aware or not that you're making them.

Louis, more than any other musician I've heard, was aware of every note he played. He paid more attention to those three parts of each note and did more with them than any musician I've ever heard. I don't mean that Louis was necessarily "thinking" about what he was doing. I mean he was listening to himself as he listened to the other musicians he was playing with, paying complete attention continuously. If you listen to this recording often enough, you'll hear what I mean.

Like just about everyone who ever heard Bix play, Louis Armstrong was knocked out by his music because he heard that same quality of complete attention in it: "And the first time I heard Bix, I said these words to myself: there's a man as serious about his music as I am....Bix did not let anything at all detract his mind from that cornet and his heart was with it all the time." [Hentoff&Shapiro] Just slightly later than Louis, Bix found himself among musicians who, if not quite his equals in talent, were equally dedicated to excellence, and the recordings he made with them (under various group names) came very close to those Louis made with his Hot Five and Hot Seven groups:

Bix Beiderbecke, cornet, Frank Trumbauer, c-melody saxophone, Jimmy Dorsey, clarinet&alto saxophone, Bill Rank, trombone, Eddie Lang, guitar, Chauncey Morehouse, drums:
"Singing the Blues"

Bix killed himself with booze before he made it to 30. In his remarkable memoir *Remembering Bix,* Ralph Berton put it another way: "Like Jesus, van Gogh, and other gifted outcasts, Bix found the world uninhabitable, and left it, I think, without regrets, dying as he had lived - casually, without ceremony, and of course broke." [Berton] However his death might be looked at - unforgivable murder of a great talent or tragic premature death of a great musician who found insufficient scope to accommodate his genius - it's a miracle of history that he came along when it was possible to preserve the beauty of a slight selection of his music.

Innumerable musicians and writers have tried to describe the tone Bix got out of his cornet. I've never heard it done successfully. There was an unearthly quality in that tone I've never heard anyone else produce from a brass instrument. You could hear him play a bar or two and have no doubt it was Bix playing, and no one else, even though a number of excellent players learned many aspects of his style - Red Nichols and Jimmy

McPartland, to name two. As Louis Armstrong remarked after hearing the Whiteman band rending the *1812 Overture,* "...through all those different effects [cannons, bells, sirens, etc.] that were going on at the ending you could still hear Bix..... that pure cornet or trumpet tone will cut through it all...." [Hentoff&Shapiro]

One of the major ideals of jazz has been that you should develop your own sound on whatever ax you're playing. This makes a real distinction from "classical" music, in which there's a supposedly ideal sound for each instrument toward which every player of that instrument should aspire. Another of the early greats developed a sound as unique as Bix's, though on soprano sax and clarinet. Sidney Bechet produced from those two pinching woodwinds walls of sound as wide as barn doors, with a diaphragm vibrato of overwhelming power, all that sound produced without audible effort:

Sidney Bechet, soprano saxophone, Sidney De Paris, trumpet, Sandy Williams, trombone, Cliff Jackson, piano, Bernard Addison, guitar, Wellman Braud, bass, Sid Catlett, drums
"Shake It and Break It"

This recording is an excellent illustration of another aspect of jazz, particularly of the earlier jazz now commonly called "New Orleans Jazz": group improvisation. Louis Armstrong, once again, gave a definitive description of that musical miracle taking place at the Sunset, when Bix would drop by to jam after hours: "....those were the things...with everyone feeling each other's note or chord, et cetera...and blend with each other instead of trying to cut each other...nay, nay, we did not even think of such a mess...we tried to see how good we could make music sound which was an inspiration in itself." [Hentoff&Shapiro] The ideal of early jazz was to encourage maximum individuality within a functioning society. It strongly resembled baseball in that respect.

Another unique voice I heard on many of Bix's finest recordings belonged to Adrian Rollini, who all during the 20s specialized in bass sax, an instrument so huge that it nearly dwarfed its player. Rollini, a musical prodigy (he debuted at the Waldorf Astoria on piano at age 4), overcame all the physical and technical challenges the instrument presented and produced another unmistakable sound, unmistakable in its fullness and in Rollini's wonderful manner of driving the rhythm with perfectly placed pick-up notes. His small group work with Bix and with Joe Venuti and Eddie Lang was richly recorded, his work with his own larger bands during the 30s somewhat less so.

Adrian Rollini, bass saxophone, Irving Goodman, trumpet, Art Drelinger, clarinet/tenor saxophone, Jack Russin, piano, Gwynn Nestor, guitar, George Hnida, bass, Phil Sillman, drums
"Tap Room Swing"

Up until 1957, when CBS aired *The Sound of Jazz*, I'd listened only to the early, New Orleans style jazz. I was under the influence of Mezz Mezzrow's book *Really the Blues*, and Mezzrow rejected any music that diverged from the New Orleans style and instrumentation as bogus. (Such a view was held by more than one jazz critic or musician.) I took Mezzrow's prejudices as gospel truth, until the Giuffre 3 blew my ears open. I was knocked out by the beauty of Giuffre's sound on all the reeds he played, and by Jim Hall's eloquent, lovely, economical guitar, and by the beautifully simple organization of the composition. The Giuffre trio continued, with the great valve trombonist Bob Brookmeyer replacing Jim Atlas, and recorded three albums, mostly made up of Giuffre's compositions, that over sixty years I've found fresh and welcome every time I've played them. Don't believe what anyone tells you without checking it against the evidence of your own senses.

Jimmy Giuffre, baritone, tenor saxophones, clarinet, Jim Hall, guitar, Jim Atlas, bass
"The Train and the River"

The Sound of Jazz presented other "modern" jazz, and it was from this show I learned about Thelonious Monk and Gerry Mulligan. I immediately went out and bought the lp they made together that same year, and fell further in love with both of them. A couple of years later, Mulligan recorded another lp with Ben Webster.

Ben Webster, tenor saxophone, Gerry Mulligan, baritone saxophone, Jimmy Rowles, piano, Leroy Vinnegar, bass, Mel Lewis, drums
"Sunday"

It's wonderful listening to musicians who've experienced so much music separately come together and converse fluently, even if they supposedly speak different musical languages. When you listen to Webster and Mulligan trade places stating the melody of "Sunday" and improvising counter-melodies, they sound as if they've played together for years, and you realize there's really only one language being spoken here - music. (As Keith Jarrett once wrote, "Western Society is so hung up on the great god 'Opinion' that they are beginning to forget that there is such a thing as Truth. This is a direct parallel to the fact of their being also hung up on 'Style' and forgetting that there is such a thing as Music and, whereas something is either True or not, something is either Music or not." Or, as I've often paraphrased it since I read that, "There are two things: music, and *not* music."

Introducing his wonderful book *Air Guitar,* Dave Hickey wrote, "When I was a kid books and paintings and music were all around me, all the time, but never in the guise of 'culture.'...I can remember being amazed that whatever city we landed in, my folks could always find these little bookstores and record shops, art galleries and jazz clubs that no one else knew about. I thought of them as secret places where you could go and meet other people who were part of this secret thing....Everywhere we went there were bookstores and record shops, art galleries and jazz clubs, where otherwise normal-looking people did all these cool things. *And nobody noticed. Nobody knew anything about it!* The newspapers didn't know about it. My scoutmasters didn't know about it. The television didn't know about it. My friends didn't know about it. Even their parents didn't know about it....That was the best thing about little stores. If you were a nobody like me, and didn't know anything, you could go into one of them and find things out. People would talk to you, not because you were going to buy something, but because they loved the stuff they had to sell." [Hickey]

Growing up in a university town on the border of Chicago, I had access to many of the kinds of little stores Hickey pays tribute to, but my greatest "little store" wasn't a store at all. It was "The Real McCoy," a jazz show that came on radio station WCFL at midnight, every week night, during my late high school and early college years. The show was the "little store" of Sid McCoy, who was then working not only as a dee-jay but as the producer of any number of superb albums for Vee-Jay records, a small independent record label. One of those albums introduced the quintet led by drummer Walter Perkins, and Sid played the complex-sounding cut "Sleepy" every night for weeks and weeks on his radio show, creating what passed for a "hit" in jazz terms.

Willie Thomas, trumpet, Frank Strozier, alto saxophone, Harold Mabern, piano, Bob Cranshaw, bass, Walter Perkins, drums
"Sleepy"

All these local Chicago musicians might have lived their lives in obscurity and been utterly forgotten by now. Many superb musicians such as Ira Sullivan or Billy Wallace pretty much suffered that fate because they refused to move to New York City, where all the Big Bull recording studios operated.

But Sid McCoy not only recorded them, he had a radio station independent enough (WCFL had been started in the late 20s by the Chicago Federation of Labor) and interested enough in local talent to allow him to give an 8-minute, multi-time-signature recording by a bunch of then-unknown kids enough air time that listeners could "get it." And they got it, in sufficient numbers that the MJT+3 was able to make two more wonderful lp's before the members all went on to careers working with a variety of jazz greats. And I got it, to the extent that every note of "Sleepy" is still embossed in my brain, and listening to it today is like embracing an old love. She still feels and smells the same, and the delight you feel is as fresh as it was in the first embrace.

"The Real McCoy" introduced me to so many musicians I'd never heard of, so much music I might never have listened to, as I drove home after midnight from various Chicago clubs or from "parties" that were nothing but excuses for getting smashed. (I was not a Good Boy.) And through the deep, smoky voice of Sid McCoy I received the message that these musicians and this music were *important*, even though my parents hated and my teachers and classmates were unaware of them.

But not all my classmates. My dearest friend then and throughout his life, Richard Bohle, lived just down the street we moved to in 1952, and we shared, along with similar senses of humor, a love of music. His father, Friedl (I'm guessing at the spelling), was an engineer who'd fled Germany after the Nazis took control. Friedl loved American jazz, which had been the popular music of the country to which he'd emigrated in the 1930s. Among his albums was an early lp featuring Fats Waller & His Rhythm, which Richard and I fell in love with - particularly with the novelty tunes such as "The Joint Is Jumpin'" and "Your Feets Too Big."

Fats Waller, piano, vocal, John Hamilton, trumpet, Gene Sedric, reeds, John Smith, guitar, Slick Jones, drums (Usually, Herman Autrey played trumpet and the great Al Casey played perfect rhythm guitar on Fats' recordings.)
"Your Feets Too Big"

I think I appreciated the humor Fats injected into the tune (especially his addition to the lyrics, "Your pedal extremities are colossal / To me you look jus' like a fossil"), and
that couplet and "Gun ta gunboats" and "One never knows, do one?" became running tag lines between me and Richard. But I didn't, then, really appreciate the incredible precision and delicacy of Fats as a pianist, or the individual brilliance and shared sense of swing in his "Rhythm." It was many years later, after Richard had died, that I rediscovered Fats and came to understand how very great a musician he was. That

rediscovery came thanks to another one of those little stores like the ones Dave Hickey praised, a store called Books Unlimited, near the University of Denver.

It was actually a huge used bookstore, with thousands of books of all sorts. The old fellow who ran it with his son had come out to Colorado from New York City many years back, and the store had been there for a long time when I started going to it. After many hours spent browsing around in the place, I realized that I'd been listening to one great Fats Waller tune after another, and that in fact Fats and His Rhythm were *all* that was ever playing in there. I asked the owner why that was so - "Not that I'm objecting," I hastened to add.

"Well," he answered, "I tried a lot of different kinds of music in here over the years. And nobody *ever* objected to Fats." I could see why - one tune after another, mostly unknown to me until then, and all suffused with that incredible rhythmic propulsion and joyous spirit that Fats put into everything he ever played.

I resolved to find the source of all those recordings, and discovered that Orin Keepnews and Dan Morgenstern, two jazz critics, had done the work of collecting the entire output of Fats and His Rhythm on RCA's "race" label Bluebird and getting pristine copies of them onto a series of cd sets. I acquired them all, and they've been an unfailing source of energy and happiness in my life ever since.

As was even the memory of Fats' recordings for the man I called my adopted father, Bill Stickle. Fats goes into a riff on one of his records: "Eef! Eif! Gimme piece-a pie!" and I don't know how many times I heard Bill repeating that with great gusto as he moved from one room to another in his and his wife Stella's apartment on Keeney Street, a couple of blocks north of Chicago. I had no idea where he'd gotten the line then, and I was too young and stupid and incurious to ask.

Bill and Stella had already raised their son, Spike, and he was off somewhere in the Marine Corps with his pal, Tim Hillyer. Tim and Louise Longley, who lived in the next apartment building to the West, had had something going until she and I got together, and she brought me into the Stickle's household, where she was close to being an adopted daughter. She was also the first love of my life, and remains a beloved friend.

Memories from Bill and Stella's apartment too many and too dear to recount here, but one in particular is associated with the next cut, "Desafinado." In those days I was still playing tennis every chance I got, and Bill took it upon himself to teach me to play on clay courts, which I'd never done. Every Saturday morning during the brief Chicago summer, we'd head for the beautiful clay courts up on the Northwestern campus, and he'd run me ragged teaching me to hit a cross-court backhand. Then we'd go back to the apartment, where dear Stella would have an immense breakfast of French toast and bacon waiting for us.

I'd always be bringing music over, and that was the summer Stan Getz had come back from a South American tour on which he'd discovered the *bossa nova*, the Brazilian amalgam of their samba and our jazz, and with Charlie Byrd, a guitarist who'd also fallen in love with *bossa nova*, produced *Jazz Samba,* one of the best-selling jazz albums of all time. That album became the soundtrack for all those beautiful Saturday mornings at the Stickles', those lazy Saturday afternoons lying in the sun on the Keeney Street pier, the little waves sparkling and dancing out on Lake Michigan.

Stan Getz, tenor saxophone, Charlie Byrd, guitar, Keter Betts, bass, Buddy Deppenschmidt, Bill Reinchenbach, drums
"Desafinado"

The same year as *The Sound of Jazz,* Thelonious Monk recorded a concert with John Coltrane at Carnegie Hall. The recording was buried in the Library of Congress until 2005, when it was issued with great fanfare. I'm in the minority in finding it an example of *not* music:

John Coltrane, tenor saxophone, Thelonious Monk, piano, composer, Ahmed Abdul-Malik, bass, Shadow Wilson, drums
"Blue Monk"

I've heard John Coltrane play very beautiful music. By the time he recorded this with Monk, though, he had gotten into a new, more intellectual way of playing, a way that was more interested in the theory of how you got from this chord to that chord than in how you *sounded*. If you listen to Ben Webster's solo on "Sunday," you'll hear what I mean when I say that Coltrane's work here leaves me cold. It grows from his thinking about the chords, and not at all from what the tune is about, and not about tailoring his tone to the mood of the piece. Many, many, many people, both jazz musicians and listeners, would disagree with what I've just said. Well, let them. Coltrane was a very religious man, searching for God through his music, and he reminds me of Beethoven, who was doing the same, in that I don't want to listen to his search. I think music is much better when it celebrates what we find walking out our front door every day. An Australian writer named Clive James has similar things to say in his book *Cultural Amnesia:* "Ellington loved the dancers, and he was appalled by the very thought that jazz might 'develop' to the point where they could no longer dance to it....in the early 1940s he had already noticed what was happening to the art-form that he had helped to invent. He put his doubts and fears into a single funny line. 'It don't mean a thing if it ain't got that swing'....His seemingly flippant remark goes to the heart of a long crisis in the arts in the twentieth century, and whether or not the crisis was a birth pang is still in dispute....For Ellington it was a death knell. The art-form he had done so much to enrich depended, in his view, on its entertainment value....In a few short years, the most talented of the new jazz musicians succeeded in proving that they were deadly serious....Thousands of paired examples could be adduced to make the difference audible. A simple case is the contrast between Ben Webster and John Coltrane in their respective heydays....[in the Webster-Blanton Band] Every soloist was encouraged to give it everything he had in a brief space, with no room for cliche or even repetition....From Ben Webster's recorded works of that period, and especially when he was with Ellington, there was not a bar that I could forget. To remember it was effortless....Now...take a couple of decades to regain your breath, and listen to John Coltrane subjecting some helpless standard to ritual murder....There is not a phrase that asks to be remembered except as a lesion to the inner ear, and the only purpose of the repetitions is to prove that what might have been charitably dismissed as an accident was actually meant. Shapelessness and incoherence are treated as ideals....There is no reason except imminent death for the cacophonous parade to stop, a fact which steadily confirms the listener's impression that there was no reason for it to start....the perpetrator has devoted his life to making this discovery; supreme mastery of techniques has led him to this charmless demonstration of what he can do that nobody else can.

"Here made manifest was the difference between the authoritarian and the authoritative. Coltrane made listening compulsory, and you had to judge him serious because he was nothing else....The aesthetic component was standard for all the arts in the twentieth century: one after another they tried to move beyond mere enjoyment as a criterion, a move which put a premium on technique, turned technique into subject matter, and eventually made professional expertise a requirement not just for participation but even for appreciation. (In architecture, the turning point came with Le Corbusier: laymen who questioned his plans for rebuilding Paris by destroying it were told by other architects that they were incompetent to assess his genius.)....Dignity saw enjoyment as its enemy." [James]

I think James goes a little overboard here ("a lesion to the inner ear"), but I agree with him that the direction Coltrane was heading - and plenty of musicians followed him - was the same direction poetry and painting had already taken, becoming ever more inaccessible to normal people. The same direction baseball took, with its market-driven elevation of "superstars" and "tools" and "stuff," instead of the democratic virtues that won baseball games. Indeed, the whole American "culture" was hurtling toward terminal narcissism and unchecked individualism, and I suppose it's little wonder that the arts reflected that lamentable direction.

Another great "modern" tenor sax player, Sonny Rollins, recorded with Monk in that same year, and his work on another Monk composition offers a nice contrast with Coltrane's on "Blue Monk."

When *The Sound of Jazz* put Thelonious Monk on national television, he was thought emblematic of the "weirdness" of "modern jazz." At that time in my life, reputed weirdness was attraction enough for me, but I soon came to hear Monk's unique harmonic and rhythmic approach as perfectly natural and musical, and I felt more than thought that his compositions nearly all stemmed from the blues and gospel music I was beginning to discover on Chicago radio station WGES. In case I hadn't figured that out, the date Sonny Rollins made with Monk and Horace Silver in that amazing musical year, 1957, cemented my first impressions:

Sonny Rollins, tenor saxophone, Thelonious Monk, piano, composer, Horace Silver, piano, J.J. Johnson, trombone, Paul Chambers, bass, Art Blakey, drums
"Misterioso"

From his entry, Sonny leaves no doubt that this is the *blues*, and he calls himself back to the blues throughout his solo which, even though it contains startling bursts of sixteenth notes, never sacrifices richness or variation of tone, never feels hurried or desperate, and also contains silences to let the mind take a breath in.

And Monk, for all the quirkiness of his timing, always puts in little reminders of what melody he's departing from, no matter how far he departs from it, and never forgets to swing, even when he's doing the craziest damn things with the rhythm.

After the early 60s, "jazz" fragmented into mutually exclusive camps - "free jazz," "soul jazz," "fusion," (jazz and rock wedded, to the detriment of both) - and most of it became less and less accessible or interesting to people who listened to music for pleasure. So those people quit listening to what they were told was "jazz." Since the original creators of jazz, with a few token exceptions, had never been recognized for the greatness of their music, they'd mostly been forgotten. Fortunately, by the time that happened in the U.S., jazz had spread to every corner of the world, and generations of musicians had absorbed not only the techniques but the spirit of the original music, and continued to play it to audiences who valued it more highly than any but a few in its country of origin had ever done.

Sometime late in the last century, my friend and colleague Merr Shearn brought me a tape she'd been given by an in-law who lived in Amsterdam. I knew Merr's musical tastes were sound (we shared a deep admiration for Zoot Sims, among others), so I put the tape in my machine and discovered Paolo Conte. I was doubly floored - by the originality and swing of the music, and by the fact that I'd never heard of its originator. Many of his compositions are full of the joyous spirit of earlier American jazz, as are his piano and kazoo playing, as are his caressing, raspy vocals:

Paolo Conte, piano, vocal
"Boogie"

    I came upon a neglected Rogers and Hammerstein tune, "That's for Me," from their musical *State Fair*, on a Jack Teagarden cd he made with Louis Armstrong's All Stars. I fell in love with the tune and sent a copy of the disc to my friends Dick and Esther Conway. The song reminded me of their untarnished enjoyment of each others' company. In return, Dick sent me a copy of a cd named for that tune, and I discovered a remarkable collection of Canadian jazz players, completely new to me though they've obviously been playing for a long time. I think if you listen carefully to both versions of this tune, you can only conclude that whatever the Great American Culture Mulcher has done to jazz in this country, it's in good hands outside our borders.

Louis Armstrong, trumpet/vocal, Jack Teagarden, trombone, Barney Bigard,
    clarinet, Earl Hines, piano, Arvell Shaw, bass, Cozy Cole, drums
"That's for Me"

Susie Arioli, vocals, percussion, Jordan Officer, guitar
"That's for Me"

    Radio shows, little stores, jazz clubs, friends...those were the ways jazz came to me and I came to jazz throughout my life. Well, friendship still exists. The corporations haven't figured out how to eat that, quite yet.

Salesman Rex

2016 Popular Vote: Clinton, 65,835,514 Trump: 62,984,828 Winner: Trump

"'This may be the year when we finally come face to face with ourselves: finally just lay back and say it - that we are really just a nation of 220 million used car salesmen with all the money we need to buy guns, and no qualms at all about killing anybody else in the world who tries to make us uncomfortable.
[Thompson]
"But Thompson wrote another phrase immediately after the bitter requiem above. He remarked on 'what a fantastic monument to all the best instincts of the human race [this country] might have been.' I would add, 'and has been, and may yet be.'"
[McCollum, "War All the Time"]

So I wrote not even twenty years ago, with a Shrub in the White House. Today, I marvel at my ability to marshal even that meager portion of optimism. Now we've put the salesman incarnate in the White House, with the aid of an electoral system able to magically transmogrify a loss by well over two million popular votes into a victory. Nearly sixty-three million of my fellow citizens chose to put Donald Trump into the highest office in the land, chose him to represent their country to the world. I must ask myself how this came about. I couldn't imagine any sane person of voting age viewing this man as qualified to lead the country, and I still can't.

I've been meeting guys like Trump for most of my life. I can't say I've gotten to know them, exactly, since I never spent more time around them than I had to. But I've seen the act over and over. The loud bray, the bullying bluster with no vestige of courage behind it, the overstatement of the simplest assertion to make it sound Important, the pathetic swagger meant to portray "confidence." The apparently sincere conviction of irresistibility to women, the consequent casual pawing of them and crude verbal expressions of contemptuous lust for them.

One of the writers who first taught me how to name what I saw in people, Philip Wylie, recognized a 1950s version of Trump accurately: "I knew the type....successful real estate man - Ivy League - New Yorker - daughter - adored. He had no reason to doubt his excellence. He was rich, which proved it. He had graduated from a superior university, which guaranteed his intelligence, knowledge and culture. And his success had been achieved in a tough game in the biggest city on the earth. Moreover, he was, apparently, a churchman. Hence not only the tradition of America, as a whole, and the judgment of upper-class America, but God Himself, attested to his superiority. On top of all that he, he was, no doubt, a good guy." [Wylie] The modern version has jettisoned the education and, mostly, the pretense to a religion other than self-worship, but otherwise Wylie's character closely resembles our current President.

Another writer, an authentic American hero who knew the type well, wrote, later in that decade, "It doesn't take much experience in the political woods to recognize the trail of a tyrant. All who have tramped through history have left the same footprints. They have appealed to the passions and trampled down reason. They have preached blind patriotism, played on public fears, inflamed hatreds and prejudices. They have struck down their critics with charges of treason. And they have all worn the same disguise; they have posed as patriots." [Greenspun] Greenspun was thinking about Joe McCarthy, with whom he'd tangled, and probably also of the Nazi dictatorship he'd fought. But he had Trump and the Republican Party's methods down clearly and succinctly.

Such men have been around for a long time in America. Henry Adams' brother, Charles Francis, who'd known Jay Gould, Pierpont Morgan and most of the other early robber barons well, toward the end of his life wrote of them: "Indeed, as I approach the end, I am more than a little puzzled to account for the instances I have seen of business success - money-getting. It comes from a rather low instinct. Certainly so far as my observation goes, it is scarcely met with in combination with the finer or more interesting traits of character. I have known and known tolerably well, a great many "successful" men - "big" financially - men famous during the last half century, and a less interesting crowd I do not care to encounter. Not one that I have ever known would I care to meet again either in this world or the next; nor is one associated in my mind with the idea of humor, thought or refinement. A set of mere money-getters and traders, they were essentially unattractive. [Josephson]

Trump's - and his most lately adopted party's - utter lack of political principle or commitment is hardly a novelty. In 1911, Frederick Townsend Martin, a "traitor to his class," (a far deeper traitor than Franklin Roosevelt ever thought of being), wrote: "Among my own people I seldom hear purely political discussions....It matters not one iota what political party is in power, or what President holds the reins of office. We are not politicians or public thinkers; we are the rich; we own America; we got it, God knows how; but we intend to keep it if we can by throwing all the tremendous weight of our support, our influence, our money, our political connection, our purchased senators, our hungry congressmen, our public-speaking demagogues into the scale against any legislation, any political platform, any Presidential campaign, that threatens the integrity of our estate." [Josephson]

The essential Carny nature of the American "business tycoon" was captured by William Worthington Fowler in his *Inside Life in Wall Street,* in which he wrote of Jim Fisk, "All the world to him is literally a stage, and he the best fellow who can shift the scenes the fastest, dance the longest, jump the highest, and rake up the biggest pile....Boldness! boldness! twice, thrice, and four times. Impudence! Cheek! Brass! Unparalleled, unapproachable, sublime!" [quoted in Brands]

What had once been the target of satire by Sinclair Lewis and H. L. Mencken became, over the course of the 20th Century, an object of admiration, then of religious veneration. The carny trickster, the confidence man, the snake-oil peddler, began his rise to respectability with the efforts of Sigmund Freud's American cousin, Edward Bernays, the first Spin Doctor, who began his career working for the government during World War I. Then: "Most of what Bernays did at the beginning, when he was severing his ties to the Committee on Public Information and setting up his own practice, was aimed at helping American industry accommodate to the economic and social changes wrought by World War I. The pattern had been for firms to alter their product line or pitch to fit changing consumer tastes; Bernays believed that, approached the right way, consumers themselves could be made to do the adjusting." [Tye] The salesman would become the dictator, in other words, because he understood how to manipulate the news media to promote the interests of his clients, whoever they might be. "The formula was simple: Bernays generated events, the events generated news, and the news generated a demand for whatever he happened to be selling." [Tye]

Like his devoted student and imitator Josef Goebbels, Bernays viewed political figures and campaigns as mere sales jobs, further extensions of the arts of practical psychology: "Bernays [in his Hoover v. Roosevelt campaign of 1932] also made clear, as he had in his corporate campaigns, that the best way to win over the public was by appealing to instinct rather than reason. 'Always keep in mind the tendency of human beings to symbolize their leaders as Achilles' heel proof,' his strategy paper advised. 'Also that the inferiority complex of individuals will respond to feeling superior to a fool....Create issues that appeal to pugnacious instincts of human beings.'" [Tye] The 2016 Trump campaign seemed almost created to illustrate these points.

Bernays' techniques - whether in promoting cigarette consumption or banana republics or presidential candidates - did not go unnoticed. They were adopted by both political parties and by the burgeoning advertising industry. Jules Henry summarized the "philosophy" that had come about in his great book *Culture Against Man*: "The heart of truth in our traditional philosophies was God or His equivalent, such as an identifiable empirical reality. The heart of truth in pecuniary philosophy is contained in the following three postulates:

> Truth is what sells.
> Truth is what you want people to believe.
> Truth is that which is not legally false." [Henry]

And the new techniques of money-grubbing, as practiced by the Reagan-Stockman empowered "masters of the universe" on Wall Street, seemed to demonstrate that the values "conservatives" had always trumpeted - thrift, hard, honest work, saving for a rainy day - were things of the past, to be spoken of with reverence and ignored, like grandma's ashes in a pot on the mantle. As Michael Lewis observed, "For almost ten years, however, the lucky winners of the Reagan years sent a quite different message to the less fortunate: success was money, and money was made with debt, tax games, paper shuffling, and arrogance. The people listened. And an insidious side effect of the chrome-plated Reagan boom may yet to be fully realized; the average

American has been left with a whole new notion of how to succeed." [Lewis] This was the "Free Market Capitalism" that well-financed professors and spin doctors endlessly trumpeted as the key to (a vanishing) American prosperity. Marilynne Robinson summed up what, by the end of the century, had become the national religion:

"We know that Communism was a theology, a church militant, with sacred texts and with saints and martyrs and prophets, with doctrines about the nature of the world and of humankind, with immutable laws and millennial visions and life-pervading judgments about the nature of good and evil. No doubt it failed finally for the same reason it lasted as long as it did, because it was a theology, gigantic and rigid and intricate, taking authority from its disciplines and its hierarchies even while they rendered it fantastically ill suited to the practical business of understanding and managing an economy. It seems to me that, obedient to the great law which sooner or later makes one the image of one's enemy, we have theologized our own economic system, transforming it into something likewise rigid and tendentious and therefore always less useful to us. It is an American-style, stripped-down, low-church theology, its clergy largely self-ordained, golf-shirted, the sort one would be not at all surprised and only a little alarmed to find on one's doorstep. Its teachings are very, very simple: There really are free and natural markets where the optimum value of things is assigned to them; everyone must compete with everyone; the worthy will prosper and the unworthy fail; those who succeed while others fail will be made deeply and justly happy by this experience, having had no other object in life; each of us is poorer for every cent that is used toward the wealth of all of us; governments are instituted among men chiefly to interfere with the working out of these splendid principles.

"This is such a radical obliteration of culture and tradition, let us say of Jesus and Jefferson, as to awe any Bolshevik, of course. But then contemporary discourse is innocent as a babe unborn of any awareness of culture and tradition, so the achievement is never remarked. It is nearly sublime, a sort of cerebral whiteout. But my point here is that unsatisfactory economic ideas and practices which have an impressive history of failure, which caused to founder that great nation California, which lie at the root of much of the shame and dread and division and hostility and cynicism with which our society is presently afflicted, are treated as immutable truths, not to be questioned, not to be interfered with, lest they unleash their terrible retribution, recoiling against whomever would lay a hand on the Ark of Market Economics, if that is the name under which this mighty power is currently invoked." [Robinson]

But no amount of direct experience, no number of books, sufficed to alert 60 some million of my fellow citizens to the nature of the enemies of their best interests they chose to put in power. They hadn't thought about their own experiences of such men as Trump. They hadn't read the books. They had nothing in their brains to use for purposes of comparison. As Ralph Ellison wrote, "... at best Americans give but a limited attention to history. Too much happens too rapidly, and before we can evaluate it, or exhaust its meaning or pleasure, there is something new to concern us. Ours is the tempo of the motion picture, not that of the still camera, and we waste experience as we wasted the forest." [Ellison]

The idea that we were exempt from any lessons to be learned from the past came over on the Mayflower, and our contempt for history has never wavered. But the utter obliteration of historical experience - an obliteration that makes Winston Smith's labors at throwing undesirable pieces of the past down the Memory Hole look quaint by comparison - has been implemented by the other force that formed my century: technology. Specifically, by the technologies of "mass communication."

Memory Holes

Back in the early 1970s, I wrote a talking blues. I had gotten to be a halfway decent picker, and I managed to record the song acceptably, I thought. My old friend Andy Abbott was passing through town, and we sat down with a couple of Manhattans to listen to it:

Talking Thomas Edison

Back in the 19th Century, in the beautiful state of old New Jersey
A man name of Edison took a notion, and it filled him with a great emotion
'Cause it was a bright idea - and it seemed like the right idea...at the time.

He fiddled with matchsticks, fooled with wires, worked all night & he never got tired
Never got tired 'cause he had the energy, & the name of it was Electricity
He put a bulb on the wall, it lit up - and that's where it all went wrong.

But everybody thanked Thomas Edison, they was all so grateful for what he done
They put his name on the streets & schools, they was just a pack of grateful fools,
Just like old Adam - he says, "Thank you, Madam - mighty fine apple."

It was power to the people at a low, low cost, if you didn't count up what got lost
And if anybody noticed, they didn't much mind, anymore'n you notice you're goin blind
Must be somethin in the air makin the world out there a little dim.

So they lost the gas lamps, lost the horses, old wooden stove, it had to go, of course,
So there wasn't much left to sit around - but then you could always drive to town,
Watch the bright, bright lights erasin the night and puttin the stars to shame.

And then the phonograph came along, so you didn't hafta learn anymore new songs
Radio followed the phonograph, so you didn't hafta learn how to make folks laugh
There was a little static, but it was automatic entertainment.

Things they went all right for a while, with everybody smilin that automatic smile
And then some sucker invented the TV, so you didn't even need to learn how to see
Just open up your baby blues, turn on the 6-o'clock news, and let the world roll by.

But the less there was people had to do to laugh or cry or deal with the blues,
The less they was able to see or hear, or smell or taste, or love or fear anything
Because what you bring, that's all you ever get to take away.

No problem - just turn up the amplifiers, blow a few more watts through all the wires
Keep it simple and loud and bright, until they holler, 'Outta sight!'

And outta mind... render 'em deaf and blind, they'll always love you.

And it's gettin so that the human race is just a bunch of meaningless faces
And all our electric communication only increases our isolation
We bounce off each other further & further - like a bunch of electrons.

And when all our words have been forgotten, and all our feelings gotta be store-boughten
And nobody at all can think or hear or see, I wonder what this world will be
I don't know... I imagine it might go...somethin' like this: (Prolonged silence - guitar riff)

Andy, a machine tools salesman and hardly a skeptic or an enemy of technology, chuckled. "Pretty good" he said, "...should we turn out the lights?"

It's an uncomfortably good story. Here I sit typing it on a computer, into which I've long ago (relatively speaking) transferred that old tape recording of my anti-electronic-technology rant. I haven't remained true to my own critical views. I've been enthralled by mass media, by radio and television and sound recordings and movies just as nearly everyone has. Guilty.

Born into the age of radio, I find some of the shows of my youth still appealing. As a child, I listened to radio indiscriminately - Sgt. Preston of the Mounties, Bobby Benson and His B-Bar-B Riders, The Shadow, The Great Gildersleeve, Amos & Andy, Burns and Allen, Jack Benny, Duffy's Tavern, Fibber McGee and Molly. Home "sick" from school (all I had to do was fake one cough), I'd even stoop to the soap operas supposedly meant for housewives: The Life of Helen Trent, Mary Noble, Backstage Wife, One Man's Family.

As many have observed, the radio didn't replace our imaginations; it stimulated them. Sgt. Preston and King made the winter in Chicago an adventure rather than a burden, and a trip to the corner grocery a satisfying survival of all sorts of potential perils - rogue trappers, wolverines, packs of ravening wolves.

Radio did, though, replace a number of other things Americans had learned how to do to entertain themselves and each other. Many had learned to play instruments or to sing together, or both, and few houses lacked a piano, guitar or banjo. Many others had learned to tell stories and jokes, and if conversation didn't often rise to the level of an art, it was a nightly practice at the dinner table and afterwards in the kitchen, doing the dishes. After radios became ubiquitous, they rather quickly replaced such practices, and we abandoned our musical and narrative and conversational skills to the professionals. We knew we were no Crosby's, no Burns's or Allens.

At first the commercial "messages" radio programming existed to pass on were fairly straightforward: "Buy this product, Mrs. Johnson," said a professional elocutioner who wasn't pretending to be anything but an advertising-reader, "It's the best _____ you can get for the money." But it didn't take long for manufacturers to figure out that people were still skeptical enough to require subtler and more interesting appeals, and the young advertising agencies began to create their own mini-dramas and comedies, complete with ongoing characters who engaged in most unlikely conversations: "My gosh, Alice," said husband Jim, "why can't you make a pie crust like Mrs. Hollander's? Why, hers is as light as a feather!" Pretty soon, the shows' announcers started breaking in with helpful suggestions: "Say, Alice, why don't you try this new Beriberry shortening, made with Procter and Gamble's new zillion dollar atomic emulsification process?" And Alice not only took the sudden appearance of some complete goddam stranger in her kitchen in stride, she took his helpful suggestion to heart. A week later, Jim was gushing, "My gosh, Alice, your pie crust is literally picking up the pie and flying it out the window! What's your secret?" And post-modernism was born. Everyone knew you weren't supposed to really *believe* your were listening to actual conversations between actual human beings, but then they did *sound* sincere, even if no one you'd ever known had grown quite so enthusiastic about dentifrice or deodorant or shortening. But the intrusion of sales pitches into everyday home life began to seem natural and acceptable.

Everyone knew, at some level, that the zillion dollar emulsification process was probably just a new name for "factory whipped." But what everyone knew didn't matter, for we were being conditioned by radio, a more powerful medium than any previous one, such as print, to accept lying bullshit as an acceptable part of our daily lives, a necessary and often mildly entertaining price to pay for our news and entertainment.(The very attitude toward truth held by our current President.)

But radio had a fatal weakness as an engine for the occupation of a nation's soul. You could concentrate on other activities while it was on. People had long become used to working with their hands while listening. You could keep radio in its place, although that required learning a perilous skill - the art of selective Not Listening. Television presented an entirely new challenge, though it didn't look at all new to generations who'd grown used to the movies.

Not too many people mistook what they saw in the movies for reality. The movies were available, after all, only in theaters designed to emphasize how different they were from our homes, filled with fancy embellishments, plush curtains, elaborate lighting fixtures, places we paid to enter in order to share brief hours of illusion with dozens or hundreds of our fellows. Television, though, took place in our living rooms (at first - soon houses began to have "tv rooms," little shrines to house their television sets).

My family pioneered in possessing a tv set in the early 50s - first on our block, as I recall. Manufactured by RCA, housed in a substantial wooden cabinet, it took up residence in my first home on Thayer Street and moved with us to Park Place. Its principal offering during early years in our home was the unmoving test pattern most people of my generation will easily recall, and early television programming, like early radio, was a largely local, experimental mish-mash of attempts to imitate or reproduce popular radio shows - just as early radio had attempted to imitate vaudeville. It took a few years for the popular radio shows to migrate to television and for the networks that had come to dominate radio programming to do the same for television, but by 1960 local, independent television production was pretty well a thing of the past, and all over the country we were joined in watching the homogenized offerings of the three networks (ABC, CBS, NBC). Ray Bradbury saw very early what some of the results of television's invasion would be.

"That same year, 1953, Ray Bradbury published *Fahrenheit 451*. The title refers to the kindling point of paper. That is how hot you have to get a book or a magazine before it bursts into flame. The leading male character makes his living burning printed matter. Nobody reads anymore. Many ordinary, rinky-dink homes like Ray's and mine have a room with floor-to-ceiling TV screens on all four walls, with one chair in the middle.

"The actors and actresses on all four walls of TV are scripted to acknowledge whoever is sitting in the chair in the middle, even if nobody is sitting in the chair in the middle, as a friend or relative in the midst of things. The wife of the guy who burns up paper is unhappy. He can afford only three screens. His wife can't stand not knowing what's happening on the missing fourth screen, because the TV actors and actresses are the only people she loves, the only ones anywhere she gives a damn about.

"*Fahrenheit 451* was published before we and most of our neighbors in Osterville even owned TVs. Ray Bradbury himself may not have owned one. He still may not own one. To this day, Ray can't drive a car and hates to ride in airplanes.

"In any case, Ray was sure as heck prescient. Just as people with dysfunctional kidneys are getting perfect ones from hospitals nowadays, Americans with dysfunctional social lives, like the woman in Ray's book, are getting perfect friends and relatives from their TV sets. And around the clock!

"Ray missed the boat about how many screens would be required for a successful people-transplant. One lousy little Sony can do the job, night and day. All it takes besides that is actors and actresses, telling the news, selling stuff, in soap operas or whatever, who treat whoever is watching, even if nobody is watching, like family.

"'Hell is other people,' said Jean-Paul Sartre. 'Hell is other real people,' is what he should have said." [Vonnegut, *Bagombo*]

Since those early days, the networks and their successor cable giants have figured out that Vonnegut and Bradbury were onto something, and the most successful and longest-running programming has essentially provided people with alternate families, families who nearly always resolve their most vexing problems with wisdom, good humor, or - in the case of military-industrial-governmental-police families such as those on *Hill Street Blues* or *NCIS* or all the dozens of other cop/military shows - with salutary bursts of the old ultra-violence.

Television was quite successful in supplanting people's family and social lives with its electronic versions, and by the mid 1960s, more than 90% of American households contained at least one television set. One effect of this occupation was that people began to believe, however consciously, that nothing they couldn't view on television was real. As Kurt Vonnegut observed, "...the country I used to write for is no longer anywhere to be found, hard as I may look for it. What made it disappear is TV, which turns out to be life enough for almost everybody, including my twenty-year-old daughter, and in large measure my sixty-year-old wife, too, these days. Quite a success for technology! The H-bomb and antibiotics pale by comparison." [Wakefield]

Harper's editor Lewis Lapham remarked of another aspect of the resulting new television culture, "In order to fuel the engines of publicity the media suck so much love and adulation out of the atmosphere that unknown men must gasp for breath. They feel themselves made small, and they question the worth, even the fact, of their existence....At any one time the ecology of the media can bear the weight of only so much celebrity, and as the grotesque personae of the divinities made for the mass market require ever more energy to sustain them, what is left for the weaker species on the dark side of the camera?" [Lapham]

Of course, every variety of "programming" on television, as on radio, served mainly as bait to get people to sit still for advertising. When television came along, the ad men saw that "truth" - that is, what people would believe to be true - resided very little in words, and almost exclusively in images. Images, when replacing each other at a lightning clip, would enter the viewers' brains before the viewers' could help it, and one image would replace another before viewers could consciously consider the first - let alone the second through the fiftieth.

If the images could imprint positive feelings and associate them with a product (by endless repetition of the product's name and/or sales slogan), the viewers would be imprinted permanently with positive feelings whenever they saw that product on the shelves of their local supermarkets. This discovery proved so powerful that, over the years, television advertising images could become utterly disconnected from the words they contained:

Screen shot: old person's face, looking vaguely distressed; overlaid with product name: Ovidiflo (axovinoparticlubilus). (The drug company ad men share the same

Product Naming Think Tank in Osaka with the auto manufacturers.) Soundtrack: "Suffering from something? Ask your doctor about Ovidiflo!" Next 60 screen shots: old person defeating grandchildren at pole vaulting, pigging out at trendy restaurant, leaping onto merry-go-round horse with grandchildren, defeating grandchildren at Nintendo game, etc. Soundtrack: "Ovidiflo! Sudden painful deaths have happened. If you experience bleeding stringwarts, loss of more than one limb, sudden cessation of sentience, vascular palpitations, or have a vile odor, consult your doctor. [Whose answering machine will surely contact you or your estate within less than a month.] Insane bouts of homicidal rage have happened. New Ovidiflo! Because, why not?"

  The fact that all these disclaimers designed to short circuit lawsuits completely contradict the cascade of sunny, jolly images matters not a whit. It's the images that count. The lifelong experience of our species has led us to the questionable certainty that Seeing is Believing. So we've learned to ignore any words we might hear that don't make us feel what we want to feel, or what the image barrage wants us to feel. Look how happy they are. Let's get us some of that Ovidiflo. Look how much all those people worship Trump. Let's get us some of that for President.

  The next development in programming helped further blur the distinction between entertainment and reality. A staple genre of programming from very early days had been Game Shows, various dreamed-up contests on which "real people" supplied most of the cast, the lucky winners among them to be rewarded with pittances (compared to the salaries professional television performers were beginning to command). What if dramatic actors could be replaced by volunteers? Would that not further inflate the profit margin? So "reality tv" was born. "Real people, not actors" were engaged to take part in contests designed to serve no purpose but to be filmed. *Survivor* may have been the first of these shows - I was so nauseated and repelled by the portion of one episode I looked at that I'm not certain - and its immense and immediate success spawned a number of imitations almost immediately, followed almost immediately by "voyeur tv," programs on which various "real" families or groups of roommates supposedly conducted their daily lives under the constant gaze of television cameras. Who needs professional actors. Aren't we *all* just acting? Isn't it *normal* to be perpetually watched by strangers and have our lives projected onto screens?

With the advent of the internet and the explosion of digital technologies and artificial intelligence in the 90s, that question answered itself. If we hadn't all just been acting before, we all began to look at our lives as performances, now that we could film our own every move, broadcast our every banal utterance to the world. The dark side of the camera was no more; we all stood before ubiquitous lenses, tweeting and texting and mugging. Television had moved from the TV room into every room and then into the miniature telephone, and soon a majority of people felt desperately less than alive if they were not looking into a little electronic screen with which they could "interact." This development began to make their interactions with actual other people or with the frustrating recalcitrance of the physical world seem like annoying distractions.

Florida writer Tim Dorsey summed up the results of this explosion: "....Technology has just passed our survival instinct, and the country is spinning on a stationary existential axis of make-believe importance. We text about a Tweet of a YouTube video posted on Facebook with a clip of Glee about not texting that we just texted about. Instead of actual life, we're now living an air-guitar version of life." [Dorsey]

To put it another way: paying little or no attention to the evidence of our senses, or to any previous experiences we might have garnered, our conversations with "friends" (some of whom we might even have physically met) limited to a few "characters," ("words" having become moribund, yielding rapidly to endless idiot acronyms and a witless vocabulary of juvenile cave-drawings, "emojis," the visual equivalent of grunts and gestures.

History, such as we ever knew it, erased by an endless stream of images designed to stimulate our adrenal glands and distract our attention from the hands in our pockets and the dossiers being compiled on us, we became easy pickings for the wealthy heirs of earlier generations of robber barons, and either failed to notice or passionately embraced every new gew-gaw of Artificial Intelligence, oblivious to the demonstrable fact that Smart Machines were making us progressively stupider and weaker, that they were recording ever more aspects of our behavior, and able to translate those aspects into reliable conclusions about our thoughts, emotions, desires, beliefs.

In her book about our initial reactions to electricity and electronic technologies, *Dark Light,* Linda Simon wrote, "Yet the press insisted on the X-ray's potential benefits to the living, benefits that had not been proven through laboratory experiments or clinical trials. Speculations became truths merely by repetition." [Simon] And in his brilliantly prescient novel about the dawning digital age, *Uncertainty,* the Danish writer Michael Larsen wrote, "The day is coming without anyone asking us if we want it. Just like all progress. For better or worse, progress is coming. What's new is that no one's asking if we need it, if it will make us happier. What's new is that we don't even discuss it. If anyone objects, he'll be met with a steamroller of arguments about all the advantages. And if he really resists, they'll point to the lowest common denominator and our most basic fears: the fear of losing, of losing the people we love, of growing older, of dying. They've done it before and they'll do it again. Only after we've given in and learned to live with the New Order will we see that the so-called advantages were just arguments designed to camouflage the disadvantages, and the disadvantages are all we'll really be able to feel. [Larsen]

So now we have our first openly acknowledged Reality-TV President. Television, with the help of manipulation by Social Media, elected Trump, and Television can't get enough of him. The last bastion connecting television with the actual world, journalism, has fallen to the alluring profitability of Infotainment. A truly revolting, if unconscious, admission of this surrender appeared recently in the magazine of my *alma mater,* Northwestern University, celebrating the enhanced careers of some of my fellow (if younger) graduates:

"In the 17 months since then [2016 election], the host of CBS' *The Late Show with Stephen Colbert* and... [the] host of NBC's *Late Night with Seth Meyers* have managed to not only provide post-traumatic comic relief to millions of Americans but also some of the sharpest political criticism of the Trump presidency, bar none.

"'There's a central character to our news every day who is constantly throwing red meat to his base, which gives you something to talk about, and he's always in campaign mode and always controlling the news cycle,' Colbert says. 'That's one of the reasons it's been so fertile for people in late night. You don't have to get out a sieve, shake your way through the news cycle and go, "OK, what are people going to care about today?" You know what it is.' [In other words, we no longer have to exercise the slightest effort, now that we are being provided with out material by an administration that understands our needs perfectly.]

"The constant focus on the day's Trump headlines has reinvigorated late-night television....Colbert...and Meyer...have launched a relentless assault on Trump night after night since he was elected - demonstrating that dissent is alive and well in America. [And demonstrating that satire is utterly ineffective in the age of Celebrity.]

....."'Hosts from a different generation were really surface in their comedy,' says Medill grad Michael Schneider [blithely using a noun in place of a predicate adjective, as part of the ongoing fashion of junking hundreds of years of the development of English syntax.].... 'They really focused on the more silly aspects of politicians - how they looked, how they acted.That doesn't work right now because of what's going on, because of the real issues we're facing and what this administration is actually doing.' [Neither of which gets more than the most fleeting mention by either late-night comedians or day-time "news persons."]

....."left-leaning political satire has proved popular with late-night viewers. Once Colbert started taking on Trump, he overtook his more apolitical competitor Jimmy Fallon, host of NBC's Tonight Show, in total viewers and significantly narrowed the ratings gap among young viewers.

...."Colbert: 'We are alternative programming to what is being fed to you out of the White House, what you are seeing on the news every day.' [Compare this claim of independence and rebelliousness with Colbert's opening argument for the "fertility" of the Trump White House.]

...."Need more proof? Read the funny [an adjective becomes a noun] for yourself. Thede tweeted this on Nov. 27, and it perfectly captures her personality and what she hopes to accomplish with her culturally nuanced political satire:

"'If white people snatched trump for his bologna as hard as black people snatched Chrisette Michele for singing at the inauguration, we wouldn't be in this mess. WHITE PEOPLE: GET YOUR BOY. IT IS THE ONLY WAY OUT.' [Cultural nuance were pair a dice enow.]

"Thede's weekly half-hour hot take on news and culture is a lot like that tweet. It includes heaping helpings of funny [adjective for noun] and, like all things comedic, a pinch of pain.

....'"Medill made me a better writer,' says Thede. [Why belabor the obvious?] 'It trained me. Medill was so formative because I didn't know I was a writer....'

...."After graduation she headed to the Second City, Chicago's world-renowned comedy club, to hone her comedy-writing chops....[Is there an emoji for honed chops yet?]

...."And that she does. When Prince Harry announced his engagement to Northwestern alum Meghan Markle '03, Thede immediately used their impending marriage to great effect. Reimagining the logo for White Castle restaurants, Thede said the upcoming royal union was a Black and White Castle - which it is, given that Markle (like Thede) is biracial. It's the kind of joke that resonates with a younger generation that sees multiple levels of satire in the reference." (*Northwestern, Spring 2018,* pp. 24-28)

Multiple levels of satire. Not to mention the elegant wit.

Back before the digital age, Jerry Mander was seeing in the technology of television grave danger to the continued existence of representative government:

"Imagine that like some kind of science fiction dictator you intended to rule the world. You would probably have pinned over your desk a list something like this:

1) Eliminate personal knowledge. Make it hard for people to know about themselves, how they function, what a human being is, or how a human fits into wider, natural systems. This will make it impossible for the human to separate natural from artificial, real from unreal. You provide the answers to all questions.

2) Eliminate points of comparison. Comparisons can be found in earlier societies, older language forms and cultural artifacts, including print media. Eliminate or museumize indigenous cultures, wilderness and nonhuman life forms. Re-create internal human experience - instincts, thoughts, and spontaneous, varied feelings - so that it will not evoke the past.

3) Separate people from each other. Reduce interpersonal communication through life-styles that emphasize separateness. When people gather together, be sure it is for a prearranged experience that occupies all their attention at once. Spectator sports are excellent, so are circuses, elections, and any spectacles in which focus is outward and interpersonal exchange is subordinated to mass experience.

4) Unify experience, especially encouraging mental experience at the expense of sensory experience. Separate people's minds from their bodies, as in sense-deprivation experiments, thus clearing the mental channel for implantation. Idealize the mind. Sensory experience cannot be eliminated totally, so it should be driven into narrow areas. An emphasis on sex as opposed to sense may be useful because it is powerful enough to pass for the whole thing and it has a placebo effect.

5) Occupy the mind. Once people are isolated in their minds, fill the brain with prearranged experience and thought. Content is less important that the fact of the mind being filled. Free-roaming thought is to be discouraged at all costs, because it is difficult to control.

6) Encourage drug use. Recognize that total repression is impossible and so expressions of revolt must be contained on the personal level. Drugs will fill in the cracks of dissatisfaction, making people unresponsive to organized expressions of resistance.

7) Centralize knowledge and information. Having isolated people from each other and minds from bodies; eliminated points of comparison; discouraged sensory experience; and invented technologies to unify and control experience, speak. At this point whatever comes from outside will enter directly into all brains at the same time with great power and believability.

8) Redefine happiness and the meaning of life in terms of new and increasingly unrooted philosophy. Once you've established the prior seven conditions, this one is easy. Anything makes sense in a void. All channels are open, receptive and unquestioning. Formal mind structuring is simple. Most important, avoid naturalistic philosophies, they lead to uncontrollable awareness. The least resistable philosophies are the most arbitrary ones, those that make sense only in terms of themselves. [Mander]

Check and double check. Mission accomplished. It works the same in any country. There's our present situation, and it's needed no political dictator to impose it. We've rushed into its clutches. I've never known any critic to take notice of an odd little passage in Orwell's *1984*, though it seems ever more telling. Every critic, every reader or movie-goer, found Oceania's telescreen, which constantly monitored every corner of existence and immediately chastised and threatened anyone whose behavior deviated from the desirable standards, horrible and unthinkable. And yet, when Winston Smith goes to look at a room to rent where he can be alone with Julia, and discovers that it contains no telescreen, the old man showing him the room says, "'Ah,' ...'I never had one of those things. Too expensive. And I never seemed to feel the need of it, somehow....' [Orwell] People didn't have the telescreens *imposed* on them, in other words; they willingly bought them and brought them into their homes. As we have done with all the technological marvels that increasingly enslave us and make us less and less human, more and more servants of our mechanical masters.

And it's gettin so that the human race is just a bunch of meaningless faces
And all our electric communication only increases our isolation
We bounce off each other further & further - like a bunch of electrons.

    I wish I hadn't seen the future quite so clearly.

Baseball

I can't remember when I wasn't a baseball fan. The voice of Cubs radio announcer Bert Wilson speaks excitedly of Andy Pafko, Hank Sauer, Ralph Kiner, Handsome Ransom Jackson, Bob Rush and Smoky Burgess in my earliest vague memories of hot, long summer afternoons on the screened porch that looked out on our back yard on Thayer Street. Early in our lives our dad took us to games at Wrigley Field.

My Cub Scout pack fielded a softball team. That I was a star left fielder and hitter gives some indication of its quality. I wasn't very much of an athlete. The one game I recall most vividly gave a definitive measure of our quality. We played our "home" games on a rugged approximation of a diamond in the far back of the Willard School playground, with tall, dark stands of Spruce for grandstands, and there one evening we played host to a Cub Scout team from the South Side of town. In Evanston, as in Chicago, this meant the black side of town, and we nice little upper middle class honky kids started off intimidated. We had good reason to be. The game never reached the bottom of the first inning. The visitors gleefully hit any pitch any of us (I pitched three times, myself) could throw them. The score, when the game was suspended on account of darkness, was 36 - 0.

My brief baseball career - which I quite unrealistically but firmly expected to lead me to left field at Wrigley - ended in the 4th grade when my eyes went suddenly, dramatically bad on me. I remember the day of the annual eye exams at the school. Informed I would immediately need to get glasses, I bolted out onto the rooftop terrace above the kindergarten wing, where I wept and wept. At that time, the only major league ballplayer who wore glasses was Joe Dimaggio's brother Dom, and I knew I was no Dimaggio. My life was over.

But not my love for the Cubs, despite their perpetual residence in or next to the cellar of the National League all through the 50s. Their owner, the son of the great William Wrigley, had no interest at all in baseball, but a great deal of interest in making money. He figured it was much cheaper to sell the "Wrigley Field Experience" - "fun at the old ballpark for the whole family!" - than to field a competitive team, so the only money he invested in his baseball team went to over-the-hill "superstars" such as Ralph Kiner, who had truly been a great player but, during his brief stay with the Cubs, was only a rickety shadow of his former self, his knees in painful ruins. The farm system, such as there was one, moldered away, producing no help year after year. We dedicated Cubs fans didn't care. We had our heroes, even if most of them could have competed for Larry, Mo and Curly's roles. We had Ernie Banks, one of the true greats. We even had The Rifleman (Chuck Conners) playing at first for a while, until a television series beckoned him away from baseball. We had the Phenom Roy Smalley at short, inspiration for the parodic double-play combination "Miksis to Smalley to Addison Street."

During the 60s and 70s, the Army, the War, politics and the beginnings of a teaching career all drew my attention away from baseball. Not until 1984 did I rediscover my childhood love. Maybe a new child of my own, Thelonika, helped inspire that rediscovery. The Cubs that year did the rest, and when they made the playoffs for the first time in living memory, I was hooked again. (The Cubs performed according to an apparently irrevocable script that year, handily winning the first two games against San Diego, ignominiously dropping the final three.) All that did was make me feel at home, and since then I've gone on from being a Cubs fan - which I still am, even though they've finally won a World Series - to a Rockies fan as well, to, simply, a lover of the game. Baseball seems to me one of the truly, uniquely American inventions (sure, it had origins in imported English games like Rounders, but so what? Jazz had origins in African and European music. What we made out of those materials was something different. Both are examples of ways that groups of people can bring about successful, harmonious activities with maximum room for the expression of individuality.) And the beauty of that ideal has spread rapidly around the world - jazz and baseball are played in every country, even as we who created it forget and dishonor that ideal.

Baseball has had a great deal of help in losing its character, help provided by the corrupting effect of big money, big money supplied by The Media to corporate owners who were (with rare exceptions) billionaires to begin with. "He who pays the piper calls the tune" is an old saying, and it applies as well to baseball as to the music industry.

In my experience, human institutions of any sort generally have about a generation to become as good at what they're intended to do as they ever will be. After that, they seem inevitably to start becoming more about themselves, about their own comfort and self-aggrandizement and perpetuation, and less and less about their original purposes.

Originally, baseball games were televised to allow people who couldn't, for manifold reasons, attend the games in person to see their heroes in action. The games were played as they always had been, although not for long - soon, the time between innings had to be stretched to accommodate more commercial messages. A game that once required 2 hours or less to complete (*average* time for a 9-inning game as recently as 1946 was just over 2 hours) began to drift inexorably toward 3 hours. Announcers, whose original job definitions included actually talking about the game in progress, grew more and more interested in talking about themselves - their tastes in music (or what was passing for music), tv shows or movies, their fascinating personal lives, and about aspects of the players and the games of minute real importance - "tools," "stuff," (the word for pitchers' "tools"), and, above all else, home runs. Baseball announcers just couldn't say enough about home runs. Boy, were they ever dramatic. Strikeouts were dramatic, too. Good tee vee. You could see what was happening without knowing anything about how games and seasons were won or lost. These idiot emphases on the part of television announcers continued a change to the game that had begun with Babe Ruth and continued through the first Great Home Run Battle to break Ruth's record of 60 homers in a season. Ruth's record fell to Roger Maris, a fine hitter who happened to have one year in which all his customary line drives sneaked over outfield walls, and who paid dearly for shattering a record no one wanted to see broken. The press hounded him unmercifully with the same stupid, unanswerable questions every day, and vilified him as "arrogant" when he became impatient with them. Maris had grown up in North Dakota in a farm/ranch culture that favored actions over words, and he was unprepared for life as an instant celebrity. I suspect nobody was ever happier to be traded away from the New York Yankees.

I came across the epigraph I used for this poem about Maris in a fine biography of him, *Roger Maris: Baseball's Reluctant Hero,* by Danny Peary and Tom Clavin:

Roger Maris Reflects

"What would the New York writers say if they knew my uncle was Adolf Eichmann?"
- Roger Maris

Other day, while watching television

in a bar at noon in North Dakota,

I saw some ancient interview

where the guy asked me something

and I didn't answer but he did.

He didn't know what he was asking.

Wouldn't have understood any actual answer.

So I didn't say anything. Stayed mum.

The show had me either arrogant or dumb.

Now, the reason I was in a bar

that time of day was just I'd taken

one kid to his game and another

to a friend's house, and I had a little time to kill.

Know anything better

than beer and tv for that?

Bet you don't.

Major League Baseball, as it gained giant corporate shape, worked very hard both to promote some of the changes (the doltish worship of The Long Ball) and to fight against some others (the growing length of games and most belatedly the steroids it had tacitly embraced during the late 90s and the early years of the new millennium). I wrote a letter to Major League Baseball about all this; MLB never answered it. Being an Entity means you never have to answer any questions:

The Pitch Count Will Be Down In New Jack City

"The New Bowflex: Who Said Change Couldn't Be Easy?"
- a Message from one of the proud sponsors of Major League Baseball

Dear Major League Baseball:

I just heard the news: you've instructed the Major League Umpires to reduce the average pitch count by seventeen pitches per game. That's accountability: at the end of the season, you can measure it with numbers. Way to go, Major League Baseball.

I have to admit, I feel a little awkward addressing you as "Major League Baseball." I don't know who the hell I'm addressing. Are you an Entity? Or are you a cadre of Large Market Owners who are in a position to dictate to the industry you dominate? I'll opt for the latter interpretation of your name (henceforth MLB), since I've never in my life known how to write or even speak to an Entity.

According to the news I heard, you've issued this instruction to the umps with the goal of shortening the time that it takes to play a baseball game. Why would you want that to happen?

Could it be that if innings were shorter, more time would be opened up for messages to the prospective consumers watching the games? Could it be that if an entire game took less time, there would be space opened up between the end of the game and the beginning of the next rerun of "Fresh Prince of Beverly Hills" into which might be inserted even more messages for the supine consumers in their living rooms? I hardly like to think that, Major League Baseball; surely you're a bigger Entity than that.

Still, you do so many things that argue against my optimism that I can't help asking a few other questions.

Why does your semi-official voice, ESPN, conclude each broadcast with a review of the home runs hit during the day, since they've showed them all during the game summaries?

Why, during game summaries, do strike-outs prevail over, say, "routine" double plays?

Why did you spend the first half of this baseball season in a state of fixation on the home runs of Barry Bonds, when the obvious story was that a mere minor adjustment of the strike zone had rearranged the standings in every division?

These are of course rhetorical questions, MLB. I know what you know. You are a large corporation devoted to maximizing profits, and, as such, you can afford to hire the most successful purveyors of entertainment on earth, and you've hired them. And they're doing their jobs, turning baseball into another Photo Opportunity/Sound Bite.

I've been amused, MLB, to notice that since you broke the Umpires' Union, all the remaining umpires are beginning to fashion their own little individual umpire strike-call dances. I've been further amused to notice that the Famous Home Run Hitters are working up their own "I've Hit One" signature strides out of the batter's box. I've also noticed that a number of pitchers have developed their own "Got ya, sucka," gestures. These are what the casual sports fan needs; keep up the good work. I learned in the Army that the way to teach is this: "Tell 'em what they're gonna see; tell 'em what they're seeing; tell 'em what they saw." The old verities are best.

I like most the way you're teaching the new generation about baseball: baseball should be really fast. Of course, you have to teach them that, because you've already taught them that "fast" is "good." And if fast is good, baseball must become faster. I understand that; why can't those umps? Why have they filed a grievance?

Milan Kundera writes, "There is a secret bond between slowness and memory, between speed and forgetting. Consider this utterly commonplace situation: a man is walking down a street. At a certain moment, he tries to recall something, but the recollection escapes him. Automatically, he slows down. Meanwhile, a person who wants to forget a disagreeable incident he has just lived through starts unconsciously to speed up his pace, as if he were trying to distance himself from a thing still too close to him in time. In existential mathematics, that experience takes the form of two basic equations: the degree of slowness is directly proportional to the intensity of memory; the degree of speed is directly proportional to the intensity of forgetting."

I want to send you a little poem Ernest Hemingway wrote in one of his stories, MLB. The story concerns a famous Spanish bullfighter who finally runs out of luck. At the end of the story he is lying back in the dressing room dying of his wounds. Outside the stadium, Hemingway wrote, "All the papers in Andalucia devoted special supplements to his death, which had been expected for some days. Men and boys bought full-length colored pictures of him to remember him by, and lost the picture they had of him in their memories by looking at the lithographs."

My dear Entity, you have sold the soul of baseball to pharisees. The pharisees have the bucks, to be sure. But they make them by convincing people to be stupid enough to buy the meaningless gew-gaws they produce. The only way to convince people to be stupid enough to buy a vehicle that gets fewer than ten miles per gallon, an electronic, hand-held device that allows anybody in the world to interrupt them in whatever they're doing, or a President who can't get his mouth around more than two syllables at a time, is to endlessly encourage them to speed up. Think faster, feel faster, live the dream. In joining this lemming stampede, you are hardly to be blamed. As my father once observed to me, "We all run in the rat race, whether we want to or not."

Still, MLB, you are owned and operated by fellows who, supposedly, have won the rat race. I can't see why you should feel obliged to maintain the fiction that the rat race is, as Saint Vincent of Lombardi said, "the only thing." Can't the failures of this world -- those who refuse to be obsessive-compulsives, those who dislike communicating with people they've never met, those who find relief from their duties in an occasional escape to a meaningless entertainment, those who find art in baseball and love art -- can't such people be allowed at least one little post-Jurassic park in which to spend their declining years?

Tonight I watched an entire baseball game on television. The Cubs' Kerry Wood pitched against the Dodgers' Chan Ho Park. For 5 innings, nobody scored for either team. Both teams mounted threats, and both pitchers beat them back. In the 6th inning, Wood made one mistake and Sean Green hit it about 400 feet over the center field wall. In the top of the 7th, Park walked the Cubs' leadoff man, which led to two runs and a loss for the Dodgers. Both defenses played perfectly, and both pitchers pitched beautifully. The game was decided by solid baseball strategy and one hit by a Cubs' player nearing the end of his long career.

The victory allowed the Cubs to remain 3 1/2 games ahead of Houston in the Central Division, and put the Dodgers 1/2 game into second place in their division. These latter details have nothing to do with the game of baseball, which is played contest by contest every day between two teams with one manager apiece. The hit by the player at the end of his long career was baseball. The statistics at the end of the day were television.

Television is neither baseball or, really, anything like life at all. Is it?

———————————————

MLB, after promoting the "A'hm gonna knock yo' head cleeeeaan *off*" shenanigans of the steroid users for years was finally forced to confront them by one of the players who introduced steroids into the game - Jose Canseco, whose first two books shamelessly celebrated the power of various chemical enhancements and named a great many stars who'd joined him in using them - and by the work of a couple of reporters, Mark Fainaru-Wada and Lance Williams, in their book *Game of Shadows*. Then MLB was (or should have been) further embarrassed by the blatantly perjured testimony of many major league stars before a Congressional committee investigating "performance enhancing drugs" to see if they could help with re-election campaigns. MLB set out on a fantastically hypocritical PR campaign to warn The Youth of America against using these new devil drugs. The stench that rose when Barry Bonds hit 73 home runs in 2001 was hard to ignore. Bonds had become a cartoon-like figure during the off season, his arms, torso and head inflated to revolting caricatures.

Bonds didn't make himself easy to like - he presented himself as surly and arrogant. In a journal I kept years after he set his home run records, I tried to give him his due, for he had been a very great player for many years before he took up with the juicers:

11/11/14

I suppose seeing Barry Bonds at one of the Giants' home Series games prompted me to think about the dislike and distaste I've harbored for him since his record-setting homer season. His head seems to have diminished back to the neighborhood of its normal size.

I disliked Bonds and McGwire and, finally, Sosa because I felt they were cheating, and because they were fueling the whole "Chicks Dig the Long Ball" campaign that MLB so responsibly initiated shortly after the balls started flying over the fences in flocks, until "Baseball Tonight" began to resemble a porn flick: all the events of the game were treated as obligatory buildups to the Money Shot, the nightly Home Run Derby.
The Home Run Derby itself got its own separate national tv night during All Star week. It was a perversion of baseball and rapidly became exceedingly dull.

And now I wonder if Bonds wasn't a sort of Hero of the Resistance. Clearly, he didn't start juicing until the juice-fueled Derby had been going on for some years. And I wonder if he carried his juicing and workout regimen to the absurd extent he did at least partly in protest of the whole unBaseballish circus he'd been observing. Surely he was well aware of his talents, and how such of them as his uncanny pitch selection, his OBP,
and for many years his outfield play and baserunning, were being devalued to the point of near-invisibility. He must also have been aware that a giant, inflated black man would be greeted by white America with a great deal less enthusiasm than a giant, inflated white man, especially if he broke the white giant's holy record.

I think he essentially forced MLB and everyone else to finally concede that reality was reality, and baseball was now something like a contest between humans and cyborgs. I'm grateful that MLB began to act as if that wasn't exactly what they'd had in mind when they'd blindfolded themselves for years.

Whether Bonds had any such thoughts or intentions, I don't know. But the effect of his decision to juice was to offer up a caricature that nobody with eyes could fail to see as a caricature, and thereby to poke a hole into the balloon of Power Worship that has pretty well let the air out of it.

Or so I hoped, but the new technologies of the digital age and Big Data came along, and were of course pressed into the service of Power. Suddenly every pitcher was throwing 100 miles per hour, and "launch angle" became the new watchword for worshippers of the Long Ball. Sad to say, the term and the habit of extreme uppercut swinging were introduced by the Cubs' Kris Bryant, and pretty soon the fashion spread throughout the game. I became irate when I found it being accepted uncritically by the Cubs in-house magazine *Vineline:*

April 30, 2018

Dear Rian Watt:

In the May issue of *Vineline,* you write, "While previous generations may have blanched at the strikeout totals these new swings are producing, modern hitters are reaping the benefits [of the new fad for uppercut swings] and propelling balls out of big league parks in unprecedented quantities. Home runs, after all, are far more valuable than singles, and even doubles into the gap, which is what line-drive swings are attempting to create." (p. 36)

In the most literal sense, home runs are indeed more valuable than singles or doubles, in that they produce instant runs, while singles and doubles may or may not produce any runs. Strikeouts - empty at-bats - are a very high price to pay for *any* hitting approach, since each strikeout contributes *nothing* to scoring runs, while all other base hits or even balls put in play contribute to the possibility of scoring runs. If baseball is a team game, and the object of the team is to win the World Series, then the value of home runs becomes considerably lower.

With the help of Rylan Edwards at Bill James' website, I've produced a study showing that, in the 96 seasons since 1920, 27 clubs that led their league in home runs have appeared in that year's World Series, and 17 of those clubs have won that year's Series. That is, 28% of teams that led their league in home runs appeared in the World

Series in the years they did so, and 18% of those clubs won those World Series. (I enclose the full study.) This does not suggest to me that "home runs are indeed more valuable than singles [or] doubles." It suggest to me that many factors aside from home runs contribute to winning baseball games. I took this trouble because I have no interest in revisiting the steroid era, with or without steroids, whether or not chicks dig the long ball. Earl Weaver's famous formula for winning, "pitching and the three-run homer," requires the presence on a team of not just long-ball-or-strikeout specialists, but a number of people who can get on base consistently. Otherwise, you have a team with a bunch of solo homers and no ability to score other than *via* home runs. The Cubs (and others) have fielded a number of such teams during my lifetime. They have been extremely depressing to watch. The game of baseball is infinitely subtler, more interesting, and more exciting than any number of Home Run Derbies.

ESPN's now-almost-invisible baseball coverage has been a leading culprit (along with MLB itself) in promoting this thoughtless obsession with home runs. I'd hate to see *Vineline* join in supporting it, or failing to view it with a critical eye.

But in spite of my complaints and my frequent disgust with the brainlessness of so many television commentators, baseball has been and remains an unending source of joy and fascination for me. I've heard others say, as I can say, that they've never gone out to a ball park and failed to see something happen they'd never seen before.

Of course, during each ball game, you see many, many things you've seen a thousand times before. Variety within repetition makes all the great arts, and neither is dispensable. To build a body capable of withstanding the demands of the game, of enduring its wear and tear, of meeting its sudden, maximum crises after you've had to stand watching your pitcher nibble at the plate and futz around on the mound for long, long minutes - that takes repetitions beyond most people's imagining. And all those years of concentrated effort and numbing, daily routine can all lead to one disastrous second that ends a career, a fact of which every ballplayer is reminded frequently.

I wrote of some of this in a poem I dedicated to Debbie's brother-in-law and stand-in father, Wade Arnold, who caught during the 50s in the Dodgers system. I've never known a former professional athlete who walked away from it all with the certainty and grace of Wade Arnold. I've known no finer man. The pitcher in this poem isn't based on any pitcher in particular:

> One Pitcher's Story
> - for Wade Arnold
>
> I was throwing my usual -
> fastball, slider, fastball,
> change - but as I threw
> the slider, my left hip went out,
> Jiménez hopelessly dove
> after the ball spinning behind him
> through the cloud of dirt,
> and I landed wrong
> on my landing leg
> and ripped up the middle,
> and I couldn't pitch any more
> for two years.
>
> When I got back
> I was always thinking,
> "It could happen again,"
> and I knew twice
> would be one too many.
> I never tried to throw
> my best pitch
> ever
> again.
>
> So I went to coaching.
> Watching the young ones close
> to try to help them
> do it right and not hurt themselves.
>
> When I took my missus
> to see the Eiffel Tower one time,

> I saw all those pieces of steel
> fanning up from the base,
> looked like they were cheering
> that little tower way up in the sky.
> Next morning, shaving, looked at me,
> nobody, looked. Said, "Okay."

Reading that over now, I think that pitcher has much more to do with me and my choices than it does with Wade Arnold or some imagined pitcher. After I accepted the end of my baseball career in the 4th grade, I decided I'd be a great writer instead, and as I recall my first effort consisted of essentially plagiarizing in condensed form a book called *Tembo,* by J. W. Wilwerding. I got it down to about 6 pages, which must have seemed impressive to the grade school teachers, since some of them got together and I was called upon to read my version aloud to the 6th grade. I don't think I was aware I was committing an Academic Mortal Sin, back then, and I think I was encouraged by that big fuss over "my" work to begin thinking of myself as a writer. I was further encouraged to think that way by my Aunt Helen, who got mightily impressed by an awful piece of doggerel I wrote in imitation, I think, of an awful piece of doggerel, the lyric to a song called "Ebb Tide."

I kept writing on through junior high and high school and college and the Army and graduate school, with enough encouragement from various editors to keep me vaguely imagining I'd somehow make my living as a writer. It didn't occur to me that a nearly invisible fraction of writers, let alone of poets, ever came close to making any money at all from their work. I kept writing, my stuff getting more pretentious and unsaleable as my education increased, until I finally finished a sort of novel in verse, heavily influenced by the awful French new-wave writing of Alain Robbe-Grillet. My sense of satisfied accomplishment lasted about a minute, until I realized with stunning clarity that not only did *I* not want to read such shit, but I couldn't imagine *anyone* who would want to read it. Fortuitously, a first chance at teaching presented itself at that moment, and I began to reimagine myself as a teacher.

It took a long re-education, but I became, I think, a good teacher of writing, and what I learned to do was what that pitcher in the poem tried to do: watch the young ones close to try to help them do it right and not hurt themselves. In terms of writing, that meant teaching them to avoid certain simple mistakes, and to practice certain simple virtues. The mistakes and virtues were ones I'd identified in my own and others' writing over many years.

Very few of my students wanted to become Successful Writers, or writers at all. They wanted to pass this stupid class someone was requiring them to pass in order to get a piece of paper that might allow them to find a job that might pay a living wage. I learned, over twenty years or so, how to teach those students what they didn't especially want to learn and to teach the few who did want to learn to write well those same things, and at the end of thirty-some years of teaching, I felt like that pitcher viewing the big, intricate structure of the Eiffel Tower rising above him. And like him, I felt just fine that I'd never made it to the top. I was satisfied to have been a part of the team that prepared the next generations to rise to where they wanted to go.

A fictional Russian-American named Myushkin expressed my feelings about abandoning whatever dreams I harbored as a young man of becoming some sort of star. Trying to explain himself to Rocksburg Chief of Police Mario Balsic, he says,

".... but what I'm talkin' about, man, is there's this huge need in people to believe there's somebody more important, more special, more gifted, more beautiful, more powerful than they are. It's somethin' that's been in people as long as there have been people, man. I mean it just didn't start here, you know, last week. It's been around as long as there's been writing and painting and sculpting. But it's somethin', it's , uh, it just makes me cringe, man. It just makes me go queasy inside to think there are all these people who think so little of themselves, man, that they spend their whole lives lookin' for somebody's feet to kiss. And I didn't want to be a part of that, man. And I know, I mean, I can see you lookin' around here and tryin' hard not to laugh in my face, but you got to believe me, man, I could've been part of that. I could've been one of the somebody's whose feet they were lookin' for, man. And I said nothin' doin', I ain't playin' the star game, not in this life I ain't." [Constantine]

I put that feeling, among many others, into the mouth of my fictional Russian character Dmitri Ashkanov in a poem about baseball, a poem about what America was supposed to be about:

Baseball

Baseball American poem about life,
say many, and Dmitri think true.
Very greatest hitter, Ty Cobb, fail 6 of 10 times,
very greatest pitcher maybe succeed that much.
Great fielder may go many, many play
without error, but one day easy ground ball
look like Krazy Kat cartoon to him,
and there before his thousands fans
he step all over own dick. Life.

Young genius of diamond frequent appear,
he cannot containèd be in April, May -
but then old men around league,
they have watch, remember all see,
and in July, when grass grow slower,
old men have talk and genius sudden
cannot buy hit, cannot throw strike three,
start throwing ball in own dugout.
Then nothing look anymore so green.

Also, not strong, not fast, not anything
but try harder than gifted ones
may have place on baseball team. This happen
every day, but Dmitri never forget World Series 1960,
first one for him in this new country.
When all seem lost for Pittsburgh Pirates,
bad hop make Kubek err, then Mazeroski
end everything, homer in 9th.
He never almost hit homer before or after.

Also, most gifted player may be poison man,
and so may poison whole team. Dmitri name
no name, for who can truly judge who is not part
of team, but yet Dmitri has seen great star
come down in dugout from home run trot,
how some players sudden thirst for water,
others go to bat rack, though far from next up,
others develop interest in crotch,
all avoiding the obligement of "high five."

And how one player, never mention by
sporting scribe, may hold whole fate of team
in hand. One year, team may have great leadoff
man, know how to get on base and fast enough
opposing pitcher must think of him. Each batter
after become better. Divided mind of pitcher
guarantee that. But then leadoff man slump;
whole team slump, and great cleanup man
cannot hit shit with canoe paddle at noon.

And what does cause great leadoff's slump?
Oh God of Base Ball, who could count such cause?
Wife gone cold, wife delivering child,
Bonus foolish lost, wrong step on stair,
wrong word said at right time,
right word said at wrong, inch of front foot
left or right in box, bad dream recallèd
by good song, good wine, bad wine,
no wine. Oh who could count the cause?

In this country, people think athlete stupid.
Here is stupid: with man on first, hard grounder hit
to hole which shortstop barely stop, backhanded;
he pivot, fire to second, where second baseman
has one tenth second to catch, touch bag, know
character of runner coming in, decide how hit his base,
throw body out of way, know where body is in space

at exact moment of releasing throw to first
from no ground to stand on. Make perfect throw.

Know self, say Socrates. That second baseman
know self like no Greek talker ever did.
As did Hawk, great Andre Dawson, know
not only self but all opposing pitcher, due to
study, study, study of own book he write
every day, and so stand ready for anything
anybody have to throw, poisèd like great
Zen archer to answer question before put.
Uncoil like beautiful black snake on measly rodent.

But final truth of Base Ball transcend great player,
even Hawk, even Gibson, even Ruth and Gehrig.
Great BaseBall team emerge from merging
of all, when all say, like great poet Robert Frost,
"Let me be the one to do what's to be done."
Let me chart pitch, let me move runner,
let me go in if needed. Base Ball communism,
communism America. Dmitri has come home.

I'm so grateful to have lived in a time when baseball and the vision of democracy it embodies were still alive in my country, and that this beautiful art has spread all over the world so that its values will live even if the country that produced it has fallen into despicable rubble.

Sacred Vacant Lots

Though I grew up in Evanston, a long-established suburb of Chicago, I never had to go far to find myself in the middle of "nature." I explained why at a Humanities conference in Santa Fe:

Vacant Lots:

A Butterfly Hunter Considers the Sacred

(Introductory Remarks at Community College Humanities Association Conference on "The Sacred," Santa Fe, New Mexico, 2002)

The simplest definition of "sacred" in the Oxford English Dictionary has always seemed to me to be "set apart," and that's probably why I've never felt very happy with the word. I've never much liked the idea of things being "set apart." Somehow, in my staunchly Republican family, I acquired a stubborn egalitarianism. But I grew up in places that I've recently come to think of as sacred. I grew up in vacant lots.

That term needs some explanation for anyone much younger than I. In the 1940's and 50's, even in a prosperous suburb right next to Chicago such as I grew up in, you would find plots of property - sometimes whole square blocks - that weren't built upon, or cared for, or fenced off. They were commonly known as "vacant lots" in those days. Somebody probably owned them, but whoever owned them didn't feel any urgency about turning them into something other than a piece of land. They were left alone and untended and unimproved. Somebody owned them, but the somebody wasn't around, and so everyone owned them; every kid, anyway.

Those vacant lots were where I grew up. I rode my version of Hopalong Cassidy's horse through them, through dead weeds sprouting in the early snow, rescuing maidens tied to trees naked for obscure reasons. I drove my dog sled through them in the winter, on the lookout for the wolves and lynx and beaver and wolverine I'd seen only in books, and I saw them there. I dug underground forts there with my buddies, and made a baseball diamond where we played every day for three or four summers, running uphill to first and second, downhill to third and home. And I hunted butterflies in them.

I can't remember what got me hunting butterflies. It certainly wasn't science class in school. But I remember that I learned to make a cheesecloth net from a circled coat hanger wired to a broomstick, and to stalk and hunt and kill those butterflies. If the fields I hunted still existed, I could tell you where the black swallowtails would be found in the middle of July, and where, just around the end of August, you might luck up on a Buckeye, a beautiful, rare treasure. And I learned as well how to kill and mount the butterflies I hunted. This I learned from books I found at the library. You killed them by chloroforming them in a mason jar you got from your mother. You'd soak a piece of cotton with a common household cleaner of those days, containing acetone, and pop your butterfly out of the net into the jar, cap it, and the butterfly would promptly be overwhelmed by the fumes, sink down to the cotton at the bottom of the jar, and eventually topple to its side. Then it was important to remove it promptly, or it would absorb the poison and lose its vibrant color.

And you didn't want that, because you had to frame it. By the time I was ten, the walls of my room were pretty well covered with framed butterflies mounted on cotton sheets behind glass: one frame for wood nymphs, one for swallowtails, one for sulfurs, one for the occasional Cecropia or Luna Moth who'd come into the night too early.

I didn't like the killing. I so much didn't like it , watching those beautiful pieces of life and air and summer die soaking up poison, that I dispensed with the chloroform jar after a while, and went to trapping the caught butterflies in a pinch of netting and squeezing their heads off. That seemed more humane to me, as a lad of eight or nine. And so my later frames were filled with headless but otherwise perfect butterflies.

I loved the butterflies I hunted and killed. Their beauty, their various styles of flight and rest, their wonderful silence - I loved them. I never questioned why I was killing and keeping them.

I never questioned, either, why someone would own a lovely little city block and leave it alone, leave it to nature in the middle of a great, thriving, dynamic, growing city that would be glad to provide the owner with a whole lot of dollars in exchange for it.

Such an owner, today, would be declared mad and institutionalized and divested of his property in about a second and a half. His family would take care of that job, if the city government couldn't manage it first.

When I was taking those butterflies, I was even madder. I saw something I loved, something in the natural world, and I wanted it all for myself, and I took it, and I kept it in my room, where only I could look at it. I owned those butterflies.

I owned them because I'd learned how to take them out of nature, how to keep them from escaping by killing them, and how to preserve their bodies so that they looked like they'd looked when I'd been hunting them. Except they couldn't move, so I could really see them, as you never can see anything alive.

And nobody else could see them. I went into those vacant lots and took what I wanted out of them for my own personal collection. One less tiger swallowtail for Tommy Meyers to ignore; one less Mourning Cloak to land suddenly on Carol White's outstretched hand. Tough. They were my swallowtails and mourning cloaks.

I guess I'm telling you all this unimportant personal history because it looks like to me that I was a perfect representative of my kind. I was given a little world full of the richness of creation, a little world that was freely available to every other kid in the neighborhood, a little world we shared without very much conflict at all, and what I learned from my culture to do with that was to mine it for my own use. To find what appealed to me and take it. Not to share my appreciation. To own.

And I think now that that is the heart of the madness of my culture - the idea of ownership, of possession. I loved the butterflies I killed. It was an infant's love, the desire to be one with the beloved. It was a child's love, the desire to control access to the beloved. It was a killing love.

And it was made possible by the sacred places in which I was privileged to grow up. Nature allowed me to pillage nature. Nature called no immediate penalty. Nature was busy being nature, and nature expects some losses. And whoever "owned" the land didn't exert ownership with steel fences and armed guards.

I think now of those wonderful little fields and woods in the middle of the city where I grew up, and I mourn for most of our children, who have no such places to play in and learn that there is a world far greater and more complicated and more savage and more real than they can hope to understand, but might hope to worship - that is, to love without lust to own or improve it.

Each night, I take my two old dogs to the last vacant lot in America. It is a quarter acre a few blocks from my house, part of the property owned by a grade school. It has been left unimproved for many years. It borders on a creek known as "Shooks Run." A hurricane fence protects it, and the kids who no longer play in it, from the street that runs along its western edge. Some nights it is covered with crows. Weeds flower there, and there is a little grove of unregulated trees -- locusts, elms, a few spruces -- on its eastern edge, along the creek bank. One recent night I saw two young foxes there. My dogs are now so old they didn't even notice them. I've seen butterflies there that I've never seen before in my life. It is a sacred place for me, a place where my dogs and I can go and walk without worrying about cars, where I can go without having to listen to anything much but how the trees move in the evening wind. There are plans afoot for its improvement into a park with a baseball field upon which no children will play. They will be home watching television or up at the highway motels doing drugs.

The idea of the sacred has been obliterated in my culture by the ideology of capitalism, which in part asserts that nothing has value unless it's been altered by human activity and so can be sold at a profit. That concept is known as "value added," and faith in it is now so universal that nobody even needs to even discuss it.

I think we need to talk about it, to question it. Is a world in which literally nothing is sacred a world we want to leave to our children? Or can we begin, somehow, to reassert that some things, some places, some human activities are far too valuable to have a price put on them, far too precious to be bought and sold?

In a famous quote from the Vietnam War, an American major who'd been involved in the obliteration of the village of Ben Tre explained, "It became necessary to destroy the village in order to save it." That statement encapsulated the American strategy in Vietnam, and it encapsulates our attitude, then and now, toward anything that asserts, however silently, its right to stand apart from the engines of "improvement," "progress," and "value added."

I believe it is time we set out to save the village in order to save it.

The natural world is not composed solely of butterflies, and I learned that early and often. I still vividly recall sitting out on our front porch steps on Thayer Street one steamy summer night, watching the fireflies and talking amiably about nothing with my sister, when a large black flying beetle - we called any beetle that flew a June Bug, but I'm pretty sure this was a stag beetle - landed between two of my fingers and dug into the flesh of my hand with its pincers. Hurt like hell.

Scared me, but not as much as the big geese - not Canada geese, maybe some kind of Pekin goose, large, white and aggressive - that chased me when we went to the cemetery that bordered a park somewhere near our home, or perhaps it was in Green Lake, Wisconsin. They were as tall as I was, seemed taller to me, and they *came* for me. I suppose they were nesting, and I'd threatened their eggs or young progeny, but I didn't know anything about such things when I was three or four or however old I was.

A few years later, I got another lesson, this time from a tiny chipmunk. I was walking through a little wooded section on Cousin Gordon's farm outside Green Lake, when this little guy came running up and stopped on the trail in front of me. He was "cunning" - one of my mother's words for "cute" - and I reached out to pet him, and he sank his cunning little canines right into the pad of one of my outstretched fingers. Hurt like hell.

By then, I was beginning to get the picture painted years later by Kurt Vonnegut: "If you think Nature is your friend, you don't need an enemy." That realization didn't in the least reduce my love for being outdoors in the world - it just made me realize that the world wasn't a Disney cartoon. It had things like teeth and gravity in it, things that had no respect at all for my superiority as a human. If I didn't pay attention, I was likely to be penalized.

Each year of my childhood, Dad would take his annual two-week summer vacation and we'd all be off to Wisconsin, sometimes to stay on Cousin Gordon's farm, more often to Sunrise Camp, a set of cabins with a main lodge hall for dining, deep in the pine woods outside Minocqua, Wisconsin, virtually surrounded by lakes - Gunlock, Shishebogema ("lake of many bays"), Little Twin, Big Twin, Fence. We fished those lakes. During the day, June and I would go out with Dad and a guide - usually either Big Earl or his much larger son Young Earl, sometimes a man even older than Big Earl, Alec Bobedash, all probably members of the Lac du Flambeau tribe - and bait-fish for walleyed pike. This made for long days of boredom, even when we'd happen on a walleye feeding ground, since walleyes offered little resistance to getting horsed into the rowboat. But dad loved eating them, so that's what we fished for. I always hoped Young Earl would show up to guide us. He treated me with respect, and I admired his quiet competence and dry humor.

When I'd grown old enough to be trusted on my own, I'd take a rowboat out and cast the shores of Little Twin for northern pike, or Gunlock for largemouth bass. Sometimes June would come with me, but we'd grown apart as she entered high school, so I mostly rowed out and drifted along by myself, savoring the evening, the pine-crowned shoreline, the nighthawks, the water, the rare strike and battle with a fish that knew how to fight. As night approached, a loud, pervasive humming rose up in the trees, and if you knew what was good for you, you'd start rowing for shore then because the humming heralded the arrival of clouds of mosquitos that would leave you itching for weeks if they got to you.

Most of the lodge was taken up by the dining room, which held probably twenty tables, all clothed in snowy linen covered with many glasses and goblets and sparkling silverware. That room held almost no interest for me - I inherited my mother's indifference to food. The screened porch that ran the length of the side that looked out on Gunlock Lake was what I loved. At the far end a big soft-drink cooler held bottles of cream soda swimming in ice water that offered a refreshment at the end of a long day cooking on one lake or another that I still remember, though I doubt I could stomach such a drink now - Cream Soda, pure sugar water, really. Behind it was the business counter, and all along the wall that marked off the dining room stood bookshelves,

overflowing with books left behind by generations of campers. Among them I found my first "adult" book.

I have no idea what attracted me to Philip Wylie's *Opus 21* - probably its screaming cerise, black and white jacket. It was the perfect book for an incipient adolescent, its message a debunking of all the middle class pieties I'd grown up among and had dinned into me by radio, television and movies. Wylie eloquently, scornfully demolished them all, in a book part novel and mostly excuse for his diatribes. To say I absorbed it uncritically would be an understatement. I *inhaled* it, and for the next ten years or so, I exhaled it every time I opened my mouth. I'd learned that not only was the natural world not what Walt Disney wanted me to believe it was. The whole adult world, Society, wasn't what it pretended to be, either. Egad! Santa was dead!

I was leaving my immersion in the natural world behind. For the rest of my life, I lived in nature only a few scattered times. A child-care job I got - I have no memory of how - while at Northwestern led to one of the last times. The children I ostensibly cared for were Mark and Robby Adams, two virtually trouble-free, red-headed boys.

They and their mother Jane, a painter, summered each year in the house pictured below, in Lakeside, Michigan, and for a couple of years I accompanied them, acting as sometime babysitter, sometime gardener/handyman. It had been the summer home of E.K. Warren, who'd made his fortune producing corsets made from turkey rather than whale bones. The whole county was named for him, and he'd built this fairly large but unpretentious cottage above the Eastern shore of Lake Michigan for himself and his family.

A big, overgrown strawberry bed lay in the shadows of a small crab apple near the house. Except for a huge expanse of grass within the oval driveway, the place was built in the midst of a forest. About a hundred yards from the rear of the house, a steep path ran down to the Eastern shore of Lake Michigan.

The path meandered through a sadly degenerate apple orchard, which I might have somewhat revivified if I'd taken my position more seriously. What I did take seriously was myself, my intellectual pretensions, my derivative swipes at poetry, my painfully narcissistic Journal, and my mainly long-distance love affair with Cheril Bailey.

I did little to maintain the place, I'm ashamed to admit, aside from many hours stooped in the strawberry bed, weeding, and many more hacking with an ax at the limbs and trunk of a large fallen locust tree up the driveway, an enterprise whose purpose, if it had one, eludes me today. I believe I felt it was manly.

Those summers were the last I ever spent mainly outdoors in what could pass for nature. I swam and walked the beach with the boys for hours each day, and swimming in Lake Michigan surely engaged you directly with Nature - that is, with forces that could kill you quick, and might do so at any moment if you didn't pay close attention, and that rewarded your attention with unexpected beauty every day, every night.

Those summers also introduced me to cats, of whom I'd until then remained quite ignorant, due to Dad's loathing of them. He had allowed June a dog, a dear beagle named Christy, seen below scanning our parkway for squirrels.

The Adams family were cat people, and I was introduced to their cat when assigned to transport it from Evanston to Lakeside in their small station wagon. The cat, whose name I have long repressed, immediately recognized a feline neophyte when she saw one, stationed herself under the driver's seat, and yowled unendurably all the way across Indiana and up the lake shore to Lakeside. I could do nothing but grimly endure her ululations, and it soon became clear to me that submission to a superior species was the way of things between humans and cats.

This cat delighted in messing with me. Every time it threatened to storm, she'd get up on the roof and huddle under a dormer roof, wailing loudly that she was stuck up there amid incipient lightning strikes and potential hail stone deluges, and she'd keep wailing until I got out the rotting old stepladder and came up to rescue her. As soon as I stepped onto the roof, she'd zip away to the ground, smirking to herself. She worked this routine on me quite a few times before I wised up to it. I'd frequently waken at two or three in the morning to find her sitting on my chest, peering fixedly at my face, as if contemplating which might be its most edible part. Most unsettling. I took to sleeping with the door shut through even the most stifling nights.

During our second summer she devised a new game. Each dawn she'd go out and find a chipmunk, perhaps still in its nest, dispatch it, carry it back to the sidewalk in front of the house. There she'd perform an autopsy, eviscerating the tiny corpse and carefully laying out its various internal organs side by side next to it. This tableau greeted me each morning, obliging me to scoop it up and dispose of it lest my young charges be burdened with sad and terrible images.

Despite this introduction to the feline, I fell in love with the first cat who ever owned me - The Puddy, a small, gentle, seal-point Siamese - and I've rarely lived without at least one cat, more often with two or more. They've all been cats who at least tolerated dogs, since I've rarely lived without at least one dog, either. I don't really understand people who can live without animals around them.

The cats I've lived with started with The Puddy, named by Richard Bohle, who gave him to me and Nancy when we left Denver for California in 1968. Richard and I had taken him a few weeks too early from his litter, and he didn't learn self-defense skills. In Claremont, Nancy and I lived at the edge of a lemon grove full of feral cats, and The Puddy delighted in provoking them to attack him, at which point he'd roll over on his back playfully. The feral cats weren't playing. Half my fellowship stipend went to vet bills, which rose further when The Puddy decided to sleep inside the engine compartment of our 1960 Oldsmobile, until I started backing it out our driveway and he fell under a wheel, breaking his back leg. The vet wrapped it too tightly, and the lower leg had to be removed.

I think The Puddy was the last and only cat I ever actually purchased. Vanessa came into our lives when Thelonika brought her pet hermit crab on the airplane, into which he promptly escaped. When the airline couldn't find him, I drove Thelonika out to the pet store nearest the airport, giving her the unlikely story that some passenger might have taken Hermie there after finding him on the plane. Instead, we ran into the mother of a girl a few years older than Thelonika who was returning a beautiful black and white kitten to which her daughter had proved hopelessly allergic. I consulted with Thelonika and we took Vanessa off the woman's hands, literally, and the trauma of Hermie's loss was ameliorated. Vanessa lived a long, peaceful, gentle life with us and with Ralph, whose origins I can't recall, and Ginger, one of a litter Dan Todd's North Hollywood street cat gifted him with, and later with Lis' and Julia's cats Sadie and Katie (alias Sybil), a cat who liked few if any humans.

Lis began to see a white cat sneaking in and out of a garage across the alley from ours and as winter came on began taking her dishes of food and coaxing her into our garage, and eventually into our house. She'd been de-clawed at some point in her life, then clearly abandoned, and for the first six months in our house she never came out from Lis's study. Then she very slowly began exploring the rest of the house, until she felt at home in most of it. We named her Pearl, and she was indeed a rare and precious animal, exuding calm and peace that affected all the other cats, even the semi-psychotic Katie.

My sister June brought us our finest cat of all, Sylvia the Russian Grey, another gentle spirit who frequently joins me in rolling around on the floor in the evening, demonstrating how to *really* relax, and delicately poking the exact spots where I'm holding tension, like an acupuncturist.

Then there've been the dogs.

Rin Tin Tin was Gordon and Harriett Stoddard's farm dog, outside Green Lake, WIsconsin, the first dog I got to know and spend time bonding with. She was a fine shepherd, and so gentle that I wasn't intimidated by her size.

Christy definitely belonged first to June, though she became the family dog - even Dad enjoyed her quirky personality, especially her love for eating corn off a cob someone would hold for her. Bred as a hunting dog, Christy never fully accepted her life as a confined house pet. She spent her days at the bay window in our library wing, standing on the padded window seat and smearing the glass with her yearning nose, lusting after the legions of squirrels that played among the big elms and oaks and maples along the parkway. I remember the day she escaped and ran down a squirrel and caught it. She stood stock still out there on the parkway, the squirrel frozen but unharmed in her mouth, with an expression of utter befuddlement on her face. Finally, she dropped him on the grass and let him run off.

After the Army, grad school, and working for a few years, I'd become a cat person. Until Debbie entered my life. She then lived in an old house just east of downtown Colorado Springs, and she'd taken in a shepherd-Doberman-Collie mix (by my estimate) who'd clearly been living on the street for a long time, and who was grateful, in his fashion, to be adopted. Deb named him Beautiful Joe, after one of her favorite childhood books.

Joe lived a memorable life. Probably because of his street background, he could not long be contained inside. Locked too long one day in Deb's house, he jumped out through the big (about 6' by 7') picture window. We got home, I went and bought a new pane and put it in, and we were sitting in the living room admiring it when Joe discovered we'd come home and jumped back *in* through the window. It was far from the last window he went through. After Deb and I had split up (I inherited Joe), he went through a small kitchen dormer window of the second floor apartment I was renting, off the short roof beneath it and to the ground. I found him waiting by the front door, none the worse for wear. One early morning, standing at the sink of a friend's house where we moved later, I watched Joe come sailing over the 6' back fence, a neighboring dog's food dish in his mouth. He landed without spilling a kibble and proceeded to break his fast. Even Jerry Mosier, who had no truck with pet animals of any kind, had fond memories of Joe.

When Lis and I got together, Joe had disappeared back into the streets, and her only dog was Aussie, a labrador-Australian shepherd mix, the lab predominating - Aussie was the most genial, easy-going, ambitionless of dogs, and she loved everybody and everything that crossed her path. This was good, since we soon set about providing her with plenty of canine and feline companions. The first was Gala-Ieu ("Navajo Maiden"), a name provided to us by a couple of Hopi potters we met on the way to Los Alamos.

We'd been camping around various archeological sites, and were resting at a trailhead in Mesa Verde when a tour bus pulled up and disgorged its French passengers, followed by the driver holding a beautiful little black and tan puppy. Julia and Thelonika, then 10 or 11 years old, fell instantly in love, and the as-yet unnamed Gala became ours almost instantly, joining our blended cats and Aussie in an amazingly peaceful household full of animals.

When Julia moved down the basement, which she shortly re-named "Happyland," the house soon became fuller as she smuggled in first the Norwegian elkhound Michaeli, then the Shiba-Inu Timber, then an ever-growing herd of cats. We were definitely Not in Compliance with city regulations, but all the animals got on with each other famously, or serenely ignored each other, even Katy, the certifiably psychotic Bad Kitty, who attacked quite a number of visiting humans during her long career.

Gala was followed in a few years by Rasta, whose mother was a long-haired dachsund and father unknown. Her mother decided during her pregnancy that our house offered far better facilities than her owner's, and took to coming by every night until it became plain she was unable to naturally birth her puppies. Lis and Julia rushed her to the vet's for a Caesarian, and came home with her and her two puppies. She couldn't feed or care for them after the operation, so Lis hand-fed them with an eye-dropper for weeks. Rasta bonded totally with Lis, and never really showed much interest in any other human or dog - not dislike, just definitive indifference. A year after Rasta, Marley arrived.

Lis was driving with her employer on a busy West side street when a black streak ran out into traffic and under their car. Lis jumped out and picked up the little body, seemingly dead but only in a shock of terror, and they hustled him to a nearby vet, who kept him through the night and pronounced him right as rain the next day. Lis picked him up and brought him home. He was filthy, gaunt, wearing a collar with Denver rabies tags issued long before his possible birth year, and extremely timid and spooky. We sagely agreed we didn't need another dog and I put a notice on the Humane Society recorded bulletin board that approximately described Cujo. Oddly, no one responded to this notice, and we shortly decided to adopt Marley - named by Lis in honor of Bob, not of the later-famous literary lab.

At first, Marley made his obvious history of abuse manifest whenever we tried to sweep or vacuum - he'd attack whatever tool or appliance we attempted to use with great abandon. All visitors were treated to ankle attacks. Only after I'd taken him to a couple of weeks of Obedience School (at which he learned *no* obedience but did solidly bond with me, since he was by 50 pounds the smallest animal in his class) did he begin to civilize his behavior. At 14, he'll walk on a leash, but the routes we take are *his* decision, which he observably and carefully ponders each evening. He's our last living dog, and all the more precious for that.

If I can't imagine living without dogs and cats around me, no better can I understand how people can feel comfortable living without big trees around them. I've lived an almost exclusively urban life, but I've always chosen the old parts of town, full of mature trees, to live in. I'm sure that growing up among the mature hardwoods in Evanston accounts for my taste in domiciles - the house and neighborhood I live in now

are nearly identical to those I grew up in, both surrounded by the deciduous trees of their regions. These grand, mute, cooperative life forms have always made me feel at home in whatever part of the world I happened to inhabit.

A few years ago, I began to hear what proved to be a screech owl calling outside in the dusk and into full night, and I theorized and guessed for quite a while about this owl. Eventually, I started making notes about my guesses, I don't know why:

6/11/14

It's fairly easy to locate most common urban birds by following the trajectory of their calls back to their source. Isn't always easy to *see* the bird; some are masters of concealment.

But an owl. His call, far more subtle than a hoot, seems to emerge all over the sky, its source many somewheres at once. It broadcasts itself and creates its own echoes. I'd guess its message is, "I'm here. But you don't know exactly where, do you, rodents? So start your terror-struck trembling. I can locate you easier when you're shaking in your paws."

6/12/14   The hoot owl's basic rhythmic pattern in counting notation is:

1   2   3 and-a 4, all tones staccato.

The tone is closer to "whooeh" than to "whoo. The variations on that pattern are quite numerous. I should be able to find a program somewhere that will allow me to reproduce them in standard notation. Because the owl's production mechanisms are subtle, no standard notation can truly capture either the rhythmic or melodic variations of this owl, or probably any other, any more than it can capture those aspects of a solo by Miles or Louis or Bird or anyone else. Notes, like words, are crude maps.

7/18/14   Tonight I am lying in a coolish tub, the window open to the dark, listening to the owl some more. Approaching something like peace, just me, the screech owl, and the night. Grooving on nature. Grooving on -

the strangled shrieks of a small bird being, from the sounds of it, dismembered alive by some predator or other. And not swiftly. I feel confident the predator was not the screech owl, whose predictably spaced repetitions continued throughout the other bird's Armageddon.

The places a human mind could go from there are literally endless; humans can riff forever on the scantest of material. In my case, the pacific owl and the brutally murdered bird lead me pretty quickly where everything leads me: to an agnosticism that feels like my religion.

3/9/15

The owl returned about two weeks ago from wherever he went for about three months. Or else another owl has replaced him or her. Or else last year's owl has been woodshedding like crazy.

In any case, this bird has a far bigger repertoire, a whole raft of variations on the bop bop bop-bobba-bop basic theme. And this bird is much more intense, at least tonight. The note groups are only separated by a one-bar rest. Last year's rests ran to four bars or more. Maybe the little chap's just agitated tonight. Hungry. Horny. I don't have anywhere near enough ear or knowledge or hours listening to know answers to any Why questions.

3/10/15

Or it's his first year on the job. He didn't really learn to turn the double play in the minors, and now here he is in the Bigs, working like crazy to get his footwork right.

Or last year's owl was just an unimaginative time-server, and management replaced him with an owl who wants to get better every night.

Rookies - true rookies, 18, 19, 20 years old: what fun they are to watch as they learn a whole new world. Some few simply walk into the league like men, secure in themselves and their abilities, constantly ready to work to improve on both. They know that Feldenkrais spoke true: there is no limit to improvement; and what Dylan spoke as well: he who is not busy being born is busy dying.

That, in turn, got me thinking about one of the memorable events of my tour as an amblicab driver back in 1980. I was sent to a posh apartment one day to take the mother of a famous pianist to her doctor appointment.

When I got inside her door, she rasped at me from another room to hold on, she'd be out in a minute. I stood in the hallway and looked at two sets of photographs, three ranged above three, lined up in perfect rows. The young men in the top row all wore 40s-style military uniforms. They looked to be the photos they took when you graduated from basic training, as did those below.

The boys below them in the second row were wearing the military gear of my day, early Vietnam stuff. This was a military family, three sons and three grandsons serving in two different wars, when there was still a distinction between one war and another. I didn't think I had to confirm this conclusion with the formidably rude old lady. She knew how to treat the help. She knew how to treat the lower ranks. She made it plain that I was somewhere South of whaleshit.

The memorable thing was the contrast between the two sets of faces, between faces of men, men who felt a sense of their own worth and looked at you as if you'd better sense it, too, and faces of boys, though chronologically no younger than the men above them, boys of my generation, still unfocused, not fully formed. Boys who were going to have to grow up damn quick or die young. Not near ready for the majors but headed there anyway.

There's probably no limit to disimprovement, either.

I finally decided to do something about my curiosity. First, I fished around on the internet until I found a site that allowed me to identify which variety of owl I was hearing: https://www.owlpages.com/owls/sounds.php. This site provided recordings of the calls of innumerable owls, and I found "my" owl's cry belonged to a Western screech owl. Then I decided that maybe I should quit guessing, and found a book by the kind of naturalist I most enjoy, not a "professional" or academic one, but an artist who's spent his lifetime and talents studying wildlife - Tony Angell. His wonderful book *The House of Owls* (Yale University Press, 2015) replaced my speculations with knowledge.

3/14/15

Last night the screech owl reached new vocal territory, completely abandoning the standard pattern for long trains of whoo-whoo-whoo's for about a quarter of an hour before getting back to his theme-and-variations routine. Some owl.

Evidently my new-found owl obsession is not unique:

"More than 35,000 people entered a lottery for tickets to sip cocktails at London's Annie the Owl pop-up bar while owls fly around and perch on their shoulders. Professional falconers join the patrons, who pay $30 for two cocktails and two hours of 'unique owl indulgence,' according to Sebastian Lyall, CEO of start-up app company Locappy, which sponsors the weeklong event. He said a maximum of 12 patrons will be allowed to sit around each owl and that background music will be kept to a moderate level so as not to upset the birds. Annie the Owl, which pledged to donate proceeds to a U.K.-based owl charity, resulted from a blog post by the event guide *Time Out London* that encouraged London to follow Japan, where at least five owl cafes have opened.

Tokyo's Fukuo no Miso ('Shop of Owls') cautions customers that its birds are tame but 'can't be potty trained.'"

Am I *trending*?

4/26/15

I've been remiss in keeping up with this screech owl's progress, if that's what it is. In the nearly six weeks that've passed, Senor Owl has returned to the classic 4 shorts - a double-eighth note - short pattern, with the minor variations I noticed last year. All sorts of explanations are possible. The Owl Standards Committee sent their representative Vito around for a chat about How We Do Things. The Dizzy Gillespie business was all just showing off to attract a mate. (But what musician would do such a thing as that?) The youngster was just flexing his vocal muscles trying to get them to the point of handling the call he was genetically programmed to emit. And so on.

Fortunately, today's *Wall Street Journal* has brought me news of the book I've known I've needed to read for some time, now, Tony Angell's *The House of Owls*. His favorite is the Western Screech Owl. Bingo. Enough idle speculation - time for *facts.*

Though I must say that idle speculation seems to me one of the better uses of the Big Brain, and one of the least pernicious and most amusing. Compared, say, with designing a more efficient lethal device.

5/26/15

"By four in the afternoon on cloudy days it was already dark, and when I stepped out for a quick stroll along the creek I walked into a stream of owl singing that was clearly up-tempo. The accelerated song seemed to radiate a very determined declaration that the male was in residence and had property to show. It was a rhythmic and sustained "*Whoo-whoo-whoo-whoo-whoo...whoowhoowhoowhoowhoowhoo.*" The song accelerated in its rate, and was best described with the oft-used simile "like a bouncing ball." The intervals between the whoos decreased until I heard them as a roll of continuous sound.

"....When the light faded, the owl went to work. His calls increased in intensity and frequency....His bouncing ball song was incessant....In a span of two hours, at a rate of eight calls a minute, he had produced nearly a thousand individual runs of his song...." [Tony Angell, *The House of Owls,* Yale UP, 2015, pp. 4-5]

5/28/15

I've been on this planet 73 years. Great goochie-moochie.

Just now a goose flew over in the dark, coming pretty close to the house, maybe 40 or 50 feet up, which is close enough for a calling goose to be close. As he went off into the never-ending cumulus clouds, his call - hell, her call, I don't know - became ever more insistent, and it sounded to me a call of first grief on the mount. It was heartrending, that calling.

It made me feel, briefly, the reality of all the other life around us superb exemplars of evolution. That goose was *feeling* something, and if it wasn't what I imagined, the discovered loss of a mate, it was something deep and painful. They say plants scream. All this world is alive and trying to stay that way. While we with our big brains and our chemistry sets seek to deny them that right to try.

It's hard to hear that cry and not perceive this world, this universe, as an abbatoir, a perpetual killing ground with everything eating everything else. Those are the terms of life, at least on this planet. The price of admission is your ticket out. I would pay it again.

5/31/15

Tonight the owl gave out with 10 or 12 calls, and he's become a classicist, for tonight anyway. The notes were more staccato, quicker, and sometimes cut off before the "bouncing ball," the way a sax player might leave off the last, expected phrase of a melody line. In his case, saying, "Wake up! I might surprise you anytime," or, "Hey! This is *my* nesting ground, not yours." Sounded like what the owl might be saying. Angell has his Western screech owl fledglings emerging from the nest the second week in June, so perhaps the owl is protecting his territory preemptively.

On the other hand, through all the "advertising" hooraw I heard in March, I never did hear another owl answer, so I don't know if the owl attracted a mate or not. I certainly didn't stay up night after night listening, so it's possible the owl's mate showed up while I was asleep.

6/3/15

Tonight I'm pretty sure he was patrolling his territory, since his calls seemed to come from a circular periphery, far as I could tell - which isn't very damn far, since as I noted in the very first entry, the origin of his calls is just about impossible to determine. I've learned quite a bit from S. Owl about the limitations of my hearing, which has always been the sense I trusted most.

6/19/15

After a day and a half without deluge or drop, he's back tonight for a short time, off to the far west of his customary spot, sounding *pro forma* and not for long. I don't know what to make of either the style or the length of his show. I'm just relieved that he made it through this month of continual rain, and I hope his family, if he got one together, did too.

Last night's *Father Brown* on PBS has stayed with me on account of the Heavy and the Suffering Innocent characters and, more, their actors. The Heavy was a famed Archeologist, *a la* Indiana Jones, who in his latter days had blossomed into the absolute worst example of the upper class Brit - a colonialist with only contempt for his subjects, a master with no notion of the qualities that create mastery, a pig and proud of it. The actor conveyed all this before and during his entry by bellowing with immense authority and zero comprehensibility, and by delivering his every succeeding line with more authority than its meaning necessarily required.

A humorless, unkind, powerful soul. His long-time, devoted housekeeper, still beautiful in her 60s, concealed to the end a rational, loving and determined soul.

As things turned out, the housekeeper prevailed, and in the brief epilogue scene we came to know that the proud pig had abandoned a lifetime of upperclass britishism and learned to love and cherish others. In two months. Uh huh.

Well, there's your tv. I'd rather take an owl's advice.

8/24/15

Long gaps, due to general challenges of a non-literary nature and to the fact that the owl has been behaving exactly as the owl book said he should. He's established a half-circle territory with the radius of a long city block like this one, which comprises 1400s and 1500s. So his territory extends two blocks to the West. It stops, as best I can determine (not very), along the near side of El Paso Street. Why that is so, I have no idea - maybe there's another territory over there owned by a great-horned owl who lives in Taylor Park. Maybe this is all the territory he needs. Maybe he managed to attract a mate with his Dizzy Gillespie antics the first months of the year. Maybe she and/or her chicks survived the hailstorms and deluges, and maybe their food sources did, too. The owl's reversion to "normal," pedestrian calling patterns and their scattered sources suggest that's so. I guess I know more at the end of this season than I did at the beginning of it, but mainly I know more of what I don't know.

So, nothing new there.

10/24/15

Hunter's moon and the owl seems stimulated to call interminably. Or at least beyond my bedtime. And call in the standard pattern. How depressing. Do we all start out to be Diz, and wind up blowing horn in some third-rate dance band?

12/17/15

I woke at three a.m. last night for some reason. Lying in bed next to Sylvia, I heard the owl calling in standard screech owl form. So he hasn't left for the winter, and I hope he makes it through okay. He's been one of the most important presences in my life this year, as I've been a less than nugatory one in his. Nature's utter disregard for human intention is one of my only sources of comfort.

I suppose I'll go on hooting unpredictably into the night.

I'm sure some of those ruminations, especially those prompted by that goose's call, were also prompted by the work I'd done a couple of years earlier editing Samantha Struthers' book *Chimpanzee Voices* [self-published, 2013, ISBN - 13: 9781493769889]. I don't imagine that many editors find themselves weeping as they fix punctuation, but I often did as I read Samantha's manuscript, which made me finally, completely conscious of the respect other life forms deserve.

Watching succeeding generations grow up, I've seen each one become less aware of its surroundings, more mesmerized by increasingly tiny screens that clearly seem more real than reality, more necessary than breath. In an early draft of my introduction at that conference in Santa Fe, I tried to collaborate with my betters, Jerry Mander and Robert Stone, to explain why young people were becoming zombies:

Sacred Dot Com

Fairly frequently, you used to hear someone ask, "Is nothing sacred?" The question referred to some new outrage perpetrated by my culture, the dominant, white, North American culture, the culture Robert Stone's character Frank Holliwell had in mind when he informed a Central American audience, "'We have a saying in my country: 'Mickey Mouse will see you dead'." [Stone] It was always a rhetorical question; you
were supposed to answer, with a sigh, "I guess nothing *is* sacred. Anymore."

But of course this is nonsense. We merely have a monosacerdotal culture, in which the one sacred thing is profit. In response to any question or proposed action or speculation about possible choices, we hear the inevitable, impatient response, "What's the bottom line?" Everyone understands that a dollar sign heads that line.

Currently, the sign at the *end* of the bottom line makes the repellent sound

"Dot-Com." Indeed, the end has nearly merged with the beginning, and the Internet is perceived as a bottomless cornucopia of profit, profit, profit without end, amen.

If you have attempted to question the value of computers and universal access to the internet, or to ask for the simplest kind of cost-benefit analysis of their uses in one field or another, you know just how sacred this magic technology has become. You have found yourself speaking as if from inside Adolf Eichmann's glass box, but without the microphone. Those outside the box see your lips move, but they cannot hear your words. If you scream with enough volume and determination to actually get your words through the glass, you will discover the other difference between your box and Eichmann's: *your* glass is not bulletproof.

The religion whose sign of grace and election is profit, with its Savior Dot Com, used to be known as Capitalism. Its success has been such that it now needs no name, for it has supplanted all other religions as a system of thought, and so become invisible to its adherents. In his first book, *Four Arguments for the Elimination of Television,* Jerry Mander described the workings of this religion:

"In transforming natural environments into artificial form, the United States is the most advanced country in the world. This is not an accident. It is inherent in our economic system.

"To the capitalist, profit-oriented mind, there is no outrage so great as the existence of some unmediated nook or cranny of creation which has not been converted into a new form that can then be sold for money. This is because in the act of converting the natural into the artificial, something with no inherent economic value becomes 'productive' in the capitalist sense.

"An uninhabited desert is 'nonproductive' unless it can be mined for uranium or irrigated for farms or covered with tracts of homes. A forest of uncut trees is nonproductive. A piece of land which has not been built upon is nonproductive. Coal or oil that remains in the ground is nonproductive. Animals living wildly are nonproductive....

"In economics this transformation has a name: 'value added.' Value added derives from all the processes that alter a raw material from something which has no intrinsic economic value to something which does. Each change in form, say, from iron ore in the ground to iron or steel to car to car which is heavily advertised adds value to the material. The only raw materials which have intrinsic economic value before processing are gold and silver. This is only because people have agreed on these values in order to define a value for paper money, which certainly has no intrinsic value....

"A second element in the creation of commercial value is scarcity, the separation of people from whatever they might want or need. In artificial environments, where humans are separated from the sources of their survival, everything obtains a condition of relative scarcity and therefore value....

"The moment people move off land which has directly supported them, the necessities of life are removed from individual control. The things people could formerly produce for their survival must now be paid for.... It is in the separation that the opportunity for profit resides." [Mander]

Mander notes also that the adding of value to raw materials is not limited to what we call "nature." The process must and does extend to the nature *within*, to what we call "human nature:"

"The necessity for ever-growing markets, the need to create new need, the search for nuances of artificial discontent within previous artificial discontent have required delving ever more deeply inside the human psyche to root out more subtle aspects of experience. Thousands of psychologists, behavioral scientists, perceptual researchers, sociologists and others have found extremely high salaries and steady, interesting work aiding advertisers. Like miners seeking new deposits of coal in the mountains, these social scientists attempt to mine the internal wilderness of human beings....

"In its monthly publication, *Investments in Tomorrow*, Stanford Research Institute literally catalogs new areas where human feeling can be converted into needs. In the July 1975 issue, for example, it presents new opportunities to reach people who have pets, who do home handicrafts, or who seek the wilderness experience. These are all interesting categories because they commercialize aspects of human experience which became packageable only when humans were separated from any direct experience of them....

"One SRI category of market opportunity was particularly poignant: 'self-discovery and inner exploration.' SRI lists some market opportunities and appropriate appeals for biofeedback machines, courses in self-improvement, books, workshops, gurus and meditation systems. These are all marketable now that humans have been separated from their inner experiences....we are so outwardly focused that inner experience has itself entered the realm of scarcity, making it packageable and capable of being sold back to us as commodity.

"Whenever we buy a product we are paying for the recovery of our own feelings. We have thereby turned into creatures who are the commodities we buy. We are the product we pay for and all life is reduced to serving this cycle. Life and commodity achieve absolute merger; the ultimate stage in the inexorable drive of the system to convert all raw material into 'valuable' commercial form." [Mander]

In my paper for this conference, I found occasion to quote a wonderful illustration of this mentality, the words of an advertising *guru* : "Advertising is a means of contributing meaning and values that are necessary and useful to people in structuring their lives, their social relationships and their rituals." (Thomas, 74) If I did not know the answer, thanks to many drunken conversations with a successful advertising man I knew in another life, I would wonder how the author of that sentence saw human beings. The answer is clear enough. He saw them exactly as John Locke described the human infant; as blank slates in dire need of being written upon if they were to exist at all.

But it is Locke's rationalism married with Puritan theology that explains the deadly grip this way of not seeing the world has upon my culture. Robert Stone refers to the latter in his great essay about cocaine, "A Higher Horror of Whiteness:"

"Predestinarian religion generated a lot of useful energy in this republic....Things were grim with everybody wondering whether he was chosen, whether he was good enough, really, truly good enough and not just faking. Finally, it stopped being useful. We got rid of it.

"It's funny how the old due bills come up for presentation. We had Faith and not Works. Now we've got all kinds of works and no faith. And people still wonder if they've got what it takes.

"When you're wondering if you've got what it takes, wondering whether you're on the right track and whether you're going to fly, do you sometimes want a little pick-me-up? Something upbeat and cool with nice lines, something that shines like success and snaps you to, so you can step out there feeling aggressive, like a million-dollar Mr. or Ms.?.... Have we got something for you! Something white." [Stone, "Higher"]

If in your heart, if in the heart of your culture, you are unsure that you are a valid, valuable part of Creation - and that is the essence of Puritanism - then the attraction of "outward and visible signs of an inward and spiritual grace" are truly irresistible. The same syndrome can be observed in the many battered women who return to their batterers quite simply because the battering is the only thing that makes them know they have any value at all. If nothing on this earth is sacred but the lone and lonely individual soul, that soul must go looking, restless forever, for signs of grace outside itself. "Winning," said one of our Saints, St. Vincent of Lombardi, "isn't Everything; it's the Only Thing."

Robert Stone concludes his essay on cocaine with these words:

"'Just say no!' we tell them and each other when we talk about crack and cocaine. It is necessary that we say this because liberation starts from there.

"But we live in a society based overwhelmingly on appetite and self-regard. We train our young to be consumers and to think most highly of their own pleasure. In this we face a contradiction that no act of Congress can resolve.

"In our debates on the subject of dealing with drug abuse, one of the recurring phrases has been 'the moral equivalent of war.' Not many of those who use it, I suspect, know its origin.

"In 1910, the philosopher William James wrote an essay discussing the absence of values, the 'moral weightlessness' that seemed to characterize modern times. James was a pacifist. Yet he conceded that the demands of battle were capable of bringing forth virtues like courage, loyalty, community, and mutual concern that seemed in increasingly short supply as the new century unfolded. As a pacifist and a moralist, James found himself in a dilemma. How, he wondered, can we nourish those virtues without having to pay the dreadful price that war demands? We must foster courage, loyalty, and the rest, but we must not have war. Very well, he reasoned, we must find the *moral equivalent of war.*

"Against these drugs can we ever, rhetoric aside, bring any kind of real heroism to bear? When they've said no to crack, can we someday give them something so say yes to?" [Stone, "Higher"]

I turn to my fellow panelists, Arlene Cisneros Sena and Greg Lonewolf, to see if they can answer Robert Stone's question. You both spring from cultures in which the natural world is seen from other eyes than those of the "developer," eyes that can look at a forest or a prairie or the spaces between the stars and see no need for any "value added." Have you found ways to help members of my culture see through your eyes?

[Greg Lonewolf said that he'd come to the conference from taking his deer for the year, and talked about some of the differences between hunting for life-sustaining protein and hunting for "sport." Arlene Cisneros Sena spoke about the tradition she was continuing in her life, the tradition of generations of *santeros* and *santeras,* makers of sacred images. Arlene's images of the Holy Family and of hispanic saints speak for themselves, for if you have eyes of your own at all and look into the eyes in her paintings, you see a love of life beyond the power of words to express.]

One day in that vacant lot where we played ball and I hunted butterflies, I was pitching to Tommy Meyer, a friend and hero - he was a gifted athlete, which I was assuredly not, who hung around with me for reasons I still don't understand. He was hitting every pitch I threw into the far bushes, where I'd have to run and fish around to find the ball. In despair, I closed my eyes before throwing him the next pitch, which made him laugh hard enough to swing and miss. Encouraged, I again closed my eyes and threw another pitch. When I opened my eyes, the ball, which he had not missed, was about an inch from my left eye.

When I managed to get to my feet, my left eye felt like a balloon, and I felt certain I'd been blinded. I ran home, my mother, horrified, drove me to the emergency room, where I think they gave me an ice pack or something similar after they determined that I probably wasn't blinded. I recovered within a week or so.

I never considered not playing baseball again, but this incident did leave me with a lifelong terror-reflex to anything - anything - that came suddenly toward my face. Miller moths, those small, dusty creatures that have plagued every place I've ever lived for a few weeks in early summer, seem to delight in coming directly at your face. (Really, they're just flying around in their fairly idiotic searches for the flowers they feed on, and the light that reflects from your face must be close enough to the light that reflects from a yucca bloom.) But I learned late that the yuccas depended for their continued existence on miller moths, so for much of my life I killed every miller moth that ventured anywhere near me. I loathed them, loathing being a combination of terror and revulsion and consequent rage at its cause. I smashed them with rolled-up newspapers or magazines, I batted at them when they surprised me, I set out buckets of soapy water and sat with a flashlight illuminating the suds so they'd plunge to watery graves. I had no mercy. I found them, in the words of a poem I wrote about them, "intense and insane." I knew of no reason for their existence, so of course I felt no compunction about wiping out as many as I could.

This began to change when I took up residence in a decrepit shotgun shack that Jerry Mosier was occupying and supposedly refurbishing. He more accurately described it as "urban camping," and when I became homeless, he fortunately took off on a road trip related to Park Estep's case and let me occupy the place for a couple of weeks.

My first night there, I discovered that putting on any light instantly activated approximately three zillion moths. So much for my lifelong habit of reading myself to sleep. I learned that if I didn't put on any lights, the moths wouldn't bother me, so I resigned myself to living with the damn things. I didn't have to like them, but I didn't have to freak out just because they were sharing the planet, or even a shelter, with me.

Years later, during a particularly prolific moth year, the *Gazette* published a long, amazingly informed and informative article about the millers, from which I learned that they were in fact only passing through town each year on a long migration from the prairie states to the mountains, and that they helped propagate the yuccas on their way through town. They had a purpose after all. (I think I'd figured out by then that *everything living* has a purpose, but I'd never applied that knowledge to millers, such was the depth of my loathing for them.)

That revelation took years to sink in, and I continued to react as habit dictated to the annual plague of millers, fleering and flailing when they flew around my reading lamp at night, killing them when I could without compunction.

I don't know what caused me, one night during one year's miller season, to begin speaking to the nasty pests. I only remember walking into the bedroom, turning on the light and thus galvanizing a flurry of millers into action, banging around the room from light bulb to window to wall to light bulb. For some reason, instead of going for the nearest available anti-moth weapon, I spoke to them, using my dog-on-the-street Authority tone, telling them that it was time to get down somewhere dark and quit flying around, *now.* Damned if they didn't do just that. Within a minute, the bedroom was peaceful again, and it stayed that way until I put out the light and went to sleep. Since talking to the millers worked so admirably once, I kept using this approach, and it has kept working ever since.

Since it only took me sixty years or so to achieve this revelation - that even insects might possess some kind of sentience or at least the ability to respond to human sounds - I'm amazed that it only took me until the next opportunity to try it with other insects - flies, bees, hornets - to discover that it worked with them as well, and so for the past few years I've managed to live with all sorts of insects, including bathroom spiders and beetles, without killing them. In fact, I've come to feel a small degree of affection for the ones who cross my path. In fact, I even rescue some from confinement and take them outside.

I might never have achieved a peaceful relationship with insects if I hadn't read that newspaper piece about the millers and yuccas. Very likely I'd not have thought to try talking to a species I'd loathed for so long. Over my lifetime, I've read many books about the natural world, and with each one my respect and wonder have increased. I've listed a few of them that especially moved or enlightened me in the "References" section. This is the poem I mentioned earlier:

The Miller Moths

It's a hot year
And it was a warm winter.
The millers are out in thousands,

Disturbing the twilight.
Their flight is gibberish,
Like television with the sound off.

They fly with desperate intensity
But no sense of direction,
Bashing into solids until they

Trap themselves behind a window blind
And bat their lives away.
Grey as true death,

Intense and insane as real life,
Two purposes only:
Survive long enough to reproduce,

And pollinate the yucca flowers,
Those phosphorescent candles
Whose light stays on the hillside

Even after true night falls.

    I'd long before decided I didn't want to kill creatures other than insects. The first bird I ever shot was the last, and I don't remember now when I last caught and killed a fish. I've yet to become a complete vegetarian, but I'm getting close. The more I read of what more and more scientists discover and publish about the natural world, and the shorter my time left to live in it, the closer I feel to it, and the less disposed I am to exercise my so-called "dominion" over any part of it.

    Passages like these, from Peter Wohlleben's admirable *The Inner Life of Animals,* may yet make me abandon my lifelong addiction to pig meat: "....Over time, the pigs in the experimental group [at the wonderfully named Swine Innovation Center in Sterksel, at Holland's Wageningen University] came to associate music with particular emotions. And now things got interesting, for other pigs were added that had never heard such sounds and therefore had no idea what they meant. Despite this, they experienced the same emotions the musical pigs experienced. If the musical pigs were happy, the newcomers also played and jumped around; in contrast, if the musical pigs were so scared that they urinated on themselves, the newcomers caught the feeling and exhibited the same behavior. Pigs clearly can experience empathy. They can pick up on the emotions other pigs are feeling and experience those feelings themselves - a classic expression of empathy." I'm sure that if I'd worked in the Swine Innovation Center for very long, I would have lost my bacon Jones - those "musical pigs" jumping around would have taken care of it. They may yet.

    Among my daughter's generation, I find a handful who've rejected the mindless rapine and abstract savagery of Capitalist "culture," and my hope for a future lies with them, and with their children. I observed in "Vacant Lots" that Nature expects some losses. That doesn't mean that Nature won't correct the fundamental errors of species who live in it. As my state burns today, I'm watching the beginning of one of those corrections. I'm so sorry that we've left our children and grandchildren and their living companions with this immense due bill. We really did believe you could get something for nothing.

My other comfort is the astonishing resilience of Life itself, which was best illustrated, for me, by the rapid return of life to Mt. St. Helen's after it blew:

Lupinus Lepidus

The firestorm that swept a swath
of Mount St. Helen's clean
left nothing alive. Nothing.
Nothing but a pumice field,
lifeless and dry as old bones,
devoid of any sustenance.

Within a year, though, within
a year, life had begun again,
insects blew in on the wind
and died and left phosphorus
enough for a vagrant lupine
to take in, and root, and live,

giving more nitrogen than it took,
beginning to create a soil
for other plants and for itself,
and food for more insects.
And so it goes, as Vonnegut observed:
In the midst of life, we are in death,

and in the midst of death we live.
A tough business, life.
Tougher, it seems, than anything.

Acknowledgements

The Twins:
Thomas Perry, *Blood Money,* Random House, 1999 [232-233]

Free Thinkers:
Helen L. (Bloore) McCollum and Jean R. McCollum, *The McCollum Family,* unpublished pamphlet
Patrick Murfin, "Vashti Cromwell McCollum: Advocate for Church/State Separation," http://www.harvardsquarelibrary.org/unitarians/mccollum.html]
Henry Reed Stiles, M.D, *The Stiles Family in America / Genealogies of the Connecticut Family,* Jersey City: Doan & Pilson Printers, 1895. Currently available and searchable on the internet at: heritagebooks.com/mm5/merchant.mvc?Screen=PROD&Store_Code=HBI&Product_Code=CD3523&Category_Code=C1 - 7k)
Cameron Rogers, *Colonel Bob Ingersoll,* Doubleday, Page & Company,1927
Ingersoll, Robert G., *The Gods and Other Lectures,* Self-Published,1874

The Chain of Cashel:
Willison, George F., *Saints and Strangers,* Reynal&Hitchcock,1945
H. Allen Smith, *To Hell in a Handbasket,* Doubleday,1962
Bruce Chatwin, *The Songlines,* Viking,1987
John Carey, ed., *Eyewitnesses to History,* Harvard University Press,1988

More Fun Than Fun:
Walter Kirn, "The Autumn of the Multi-Taskers," *The Atlantic,* November, 2007

War All the Time:
Juan Bosch, *Pentagonism: A Substitute for Imperialism,* Grove Press,1968
General Smedley D. Butler, *War Is a Racket,* Feral House, 2003
Herbert A. Philbrick, *I Led 3 Lives,* Grosset&Dunlap,1952
Jules Henry, *Culture Against Man,* Random House,1963
George F. Willison, *Saints and Strangers,* Reynal and Hitchcock,1945
William Bradford, *Bradford's History of Plymouth Plantation,* Wright&Potter,1901
Kurt Vonnegut, *Fates Worse Than Death,* Putnam,1991
Dalton Trumbo, *The Time of the Toad,* Harper&Row,1972
Dr. Hunter S. Thompso, *Fear and Loathing on the Campaign Trail,* Straight Arrow,1973
J. Glenn Gray, *The Warriors,* Harcourt, Brace,1959
William Pfaff, "Confessions of a Green Beret," *Commentary,* January,1970
Bella Fromm, *Blood and Banquets,* Harper&Brothers,1942
Richard Overy, *Interrogations,* Viking Adult,2001

Boring Repetition:
Kurt Vonnegut, *A Man Without a Country,* Seven Stories Press, 2005
Francis Russell, *The Shadow of Blooming Grove,* McGraw-Hill, 1968
Clive James, *Cultural Amnesia,* Norton, 2007

Ronald Wright, *A Short History of Progress,* Canongate Books, Ltd., 2005
James Moore, Wayne Slater, *Bush's Brain,* John Wiley&Sons, 2003
Matthew Josephson, *The Robber Barons,* Harcourt, Brace,1934
Rudolf Hoess, *Commandant of Auschwitz,* World Publishing Company,1959

Million Dollar Bills

Joni Mitchell, "Big Yellow Taxi," *Ladies of the Canyon,* Reprise Records,1970

Killer Virus
Jerry Mander, *Four Arguments for the Elimination of Television,* Morrow,1978
Andrew Weil, *The Natural Mind,* Houghton Mifflin,1972
Kriegel, Robert J., Patler, Louis, *If It Ain't Broke, Break It!,* Grand Central Pub,1991
Gordon Kahn, "It's Deductible," *The Screenwriter Volume 1, Number 5,* 10/1945
E.M. Forster, "The Machine Stops," *The Eternal Moment,* Sidgwick&Jackson,1928
George Orwell, "Pleasure Spots of the Future," *The Collected Essays, Volume IV,*
        Harcourt, Brace & World,1968
Peter Sacks, *Generation X Goes to College,* Open Court Publishing Co.,1996
Milan Kundera, *Slowness,* HarperCollins,1995
Moshe Feldenkrais, *Awareness Through Movement,* Harper&Row,1977
Kurt Vonnegut, "Flowers on the Wall," *Fates Worse Than Death,* Putnam,1991
Dietrich Bonhoeffer, *Letters & Papers from Prison,* Macmillan,1972
James Hillman, *The Force of Character: And the Lasting Life,* Random House,1999
Dr. Hunter S. Thompson, *Generation of Swine,* Summit Books,1988
E.B. White, *One Man's Meat,* Harper's,1944
George Orwell, *1984,* Harcourt, Brace & Company,1949
Linda Simon, *Dark Light,* Harcourt, Inc.,2004
Neil Postman, *Technopoly,* Knopf,1992
cummings, e.e., *Complete Poems,* Harcourt, Brace, Jovanovich, 1972

About the Benjamins

Abraham Joshua Heschel,"The Spirit of Jewish Education." *Jewish Education,* Fall,1953
Robert Stone,"A Higher Horror of Whiteness,"*Best American Essays,* Ticknor&Fields, 1987
Dave Hickey, *Air Guitar,* Art Issues Press,1997
James Gould Cozzens, *The Just and the Unjust,* Harcourt, Brace and Co.,1942
Robert Frost, "Two Tramps in Mud Time," *Collected Poems,* Halcyon House,1942
Matthew Josephson, *The Robber Barons,* Harcourt, Brace,1934
Dan Wakefield, *Kurt Vonnegut Letters,* Delacorte, 2012
Earl Weaver, *It's What You Learn After You Know It All That Counts,* Doubleday,1982
Tony La Russa, *One Last Strike,* Morrow, 2012

First Aid

Plimpton, G.,ed, *Writers at Work, Second Series*, Viking,1963
Sue Mingus, *Tonight at Noon*, Pantheon,2002
Jerry Mander, *Four Arguments for the Elimination of Television,* Morrow,1978
Robert Lewis Taylor, *W. C. Fields: His Follies and Fortunes,* Doubleday,1949
Ed McBain, *Jack and the Beanstalk,* Holt, Rinehart & Winston,1984

An Imperfect Trial:
    While a few films - notably Roman Polanski's *Chinatown* - have come close to showing the realities of the criminal justice system in the United States, the great majority of films and television shows offer nothing but military/police state propaganda, some of it (*NCIS, Blue Bloods,* for example) extremely persuasive and moving, and all the more pernicious for its aesthetic "virtues." The reporting I've found over my lifetime that has most accurately portrayed what I've experienced of the criminal justice system and the people caught up in it in one way or another, has all been found in works normally described as "fiction." The novels and short stories of Nelson Algren, and the series of novels centered on Rocksburg, PA police chief Mario Balsic, by K.C. Constantine, all express the realities of "criminal justice" as well or better than other "non-fictional" books I've read, and serve as a powerful antidote to the puritanical, vengeful mindset much of our country suffers from.

Mother's Quarter:
Ivan Doig, *The Whistling Season,* Harcourt, 2006
Lewis Lapham, *Imperial Masquerade,* Grove-Weidenfeld,1990
Tim Gautreaux, "The Piano Tuner," *Welding With Children,* Picador,1999
Thorne Smith, *Rain in the Doorway,* Sun Dial Press,1937
Dr. Hunter S. Thompson, *Fear and Loathing on the Campaign Trail,* Straight Arrow Press,1973
George McGovern, *Terry,* Villard,1996
George Plimpton, *Mad Ducks and Bears,* Random House,1973

Some of My Betters:
John Nichols: *The Milagro Beanfield War,* Holt, Rinehart & Winston,1974
       The Magic Journey, Holt, Rinehart & Winston,1978
       The Nirvana Blues, Holt,1981
       American Blood, Holt,1987
       The Empanada Brotherhood, Chronicle Books, 2007
Jim Harrison, *The Beast that God Forgot to Invent,* Atlantic Monthly Press, 2000
Laura Pritchett: *Hell's Bottom, Colorado,* Milkweed, 2002
       Sky Bridge, Milkweed, 2005
       Stars Go Blue, Counterpoint, 2014
       Red Lightning, Counterpoint, 2015

David James Duncan: *The River Why,* Sierra Club Books, 1983
                The Brothers K, Doubleday, 1992
                River Teeth, Doubleday, 1995
                My Story As Told by Water, Sierra Club Books, 2001

Nelson Algren: *Somebody in Boots*. New York: Berkley Medallion, 1965
           Never Come Morning. New York: Four Walls Eight Windows, 1987
           The Neon Wilderness. London: Andre Deutsch, Ltd., 1965
           The Man With the Golden Arm. Garden City: Doubleday, 1949
           A Walk on the Wild Side. New York: Farrar, Straus & Cudahy, 1956
           Notes From a Sea Diary. New York: G.P. Putnam's Sons, 1965
           Nonconformity. New York: Seven Stories Press, 1996
Bettina Drew,   *Nelson Algren: A Life on the Wild Side*. New York: Putnam, 1989
Frank Thomas, "Brand You." *Harper's Magazine*, July, 1999
Dalton Trumbo, *The Time of the Toad*. New York: Harper&Row, 1972

Writing 1 - Juvenalia
George Orwell, "Pleasure Spots of the Future," *The Collected Essays, Volume IV,*
        Harcourt, Brace & World, 1968

Golden Voices:
Malcolm Cowley, ed., *Writers at Work,* Viking, 1958
      General Radio History
Dunning, John, *Tune in Yesterday,* Prentice-Hall, 1976 - an encyclopedia of all the vital facts about hundreds of radio shows of the 30s, 40s and 50s
Chuck Schaden, *Speaking of Radio,* Nostalgia Digest, 2003 - a fine oral history of the radio era, told by many of its creators - actors, writers, announcers, producers.
        Vic and Sade
Rhymer, Mary Frances, ed., *The Small House Halfway Up the Next Block*, McGraw-Hill, 1972
Rhymer, Mary Frances, ed., *Vic and Sade*, Seabury, 1976
Idelson, Bill, *Gibby*, Bear Manor, 2006
Idelson, Bill, *The Story of Vic and Sade*, Bear Manor, 2006
        Bob and Ray
Elliott, Bob & Goulding, Ray, *Write If You Get Work*, Random House, 1975
Elliott, Bob & Goulding, Ray, *From Approximately Coast to Coast*, Atheneum, 1983
Elliott, Bob & Goulding, Ray, *The New, Improved Bob and Ray*, Putnam's, 1985
Gillespie, Dan, *Bob and Ray. and Tom*, Bear Manor, 2008
Pollock, David, *Bob and Ray: Keener Than Most Persons*, Applause, 2013
George Gissing, *The Private Papers of Henry Ryecroft,* Thomas Bird Mosher, 1921

By Measure:

Robert Frost, "The Aim Was Song," *Collected Poems,* Halcyon House,1942
Nat Hentoff & Nat Shapiro, *Hear Me Talkin' to Ya,* Rinehart, 1955
Berton, Ralph, *Remembering Bix,* Harper&Row, 1974
Keith Jarrett, liner notes, *In the Light,* ECM 1033/34ST, 1973
Mezz Mezzrow, *Really the Blues,* Random House,1946
Dave Hickey, *Air Guitar,* Art Issues Press,1997
Clive James, *Cultural Amnesia,* Norton, 2007

The Salesman Rex:
Dr. Hunter S. Thompson, *Fear and Loathing on the Campaign Trail,* Straight Arrow Press, 1973
Philip Wylie, *Opus 21,* Rinehart, 1949
Hank Greenspun, *Where I Stand,* David McKay, 1966
Matthew Josephson, *The Robber Barons,* Harcourt, Brace, 1934
H.W. Brands, *American Colossus: The Triumph of Capitalism 1865-1900*, Doubleday, 2010
Larry Tye, *The Father of Spin,* 1998
Jules Henry, *Culture Against Man,* Random House,1963
Michael Lewis, *The Money Culture,* Norton,1991
Marilynne Robinson, The Death of Adam, Picador, 2005
Ralph Ellison, *Shadow and Act,* Random House, 1964

Memory Holes:
Kurt Vonnegut, *Bagombo Snuff Box,* Putnam, 1999
Bradbury, Ray, *Fahrenheit 451,* Ballantine Books, 1953
Dan Wakefield, ed., *Kurt Vonnegut Letters,* Delacorte, 2012
Lewis Lapham, "Shooting Stars," *Imperial Masquerade,* Grove-Weidenfield, 1990
Tim Dorsey, *Tiger Shrimp Tango*, Morrow, 2014
Linda Simon, *Dark Light,* Harcourt, Inc., 2004
Michael Larsen, *Uncertainty,* Harcourt, Brace, 1996
Jerry Mander, *Four Arguments for the Elimination of Television,* Morrow, 1978
George Orwell, *1984,* Harcourt, Brace and Company, 1949,

Baseball:
Danny Peary and Tom Clavin, *Roger Maris: Baseball's Reluctant Hero,* Touchstone, 2010
Ernest Hemingway, "Banal Story," *The Fifth Column and the First Forty-Nine Stories,* Scribner, 1938
Mark Fainaru-Wada and Lance Williams, *Game of Shadows,* Gotham, 2006
Jose Canseco, *Juiced,* Regan Books, 2006
        Vindicated, Simon Sportlight Entertainment, 2008
K.C. Constantine, *Bottom Liner Blues,* Mysterious Press, 1993

Sacred Vacant Lots:

Robert Stone, *A Flag for Sunrise,* Knopf, 1981
Jerry Mander, *Four Arguments for the Elimination of Television,* Morrow, 1978
Robert Stone, "A Higher Horror of Whiteness," *Best American Essays,* Ticknor&Fields, 1987

Peter Wohlleben, *The Hidden Life of Trees,* Greystone Books, 2016
Peter Wohlleben, *The Inner Life of Animals,* Greystone Books, 2017
Hal Borland, *Hill Country Harvest,* Lippincott, 1967
Bruce Chatwin, *The Songlines,* Viking, 1987
Gerald Durrell, *A Bevy of Beasts,* Simon&Schuster, 1973
Jean-Pierre Hallet, *Congo Kitabu,* Random House, 1966
N. Scott Momaday, *The Man Made of Words,* St. Martin's, 1997
Farley Mowat, *Sea of Slaughter,* McClelland&Stewart, 1984
Gary Paulsen, *Winterdance,* Harcourt, 1994
David Quammen, *Monsters of God,* Norton, 1997
Ivan Sanderson, *Animal Treasure,* Viking, 1937
Ernest Thompson Seton, *Animal Heroes,* Scribner's, 1905
Wendell Berry, *The Unsettling of America,* Sierra Club Books, 1982
David James Duncan, *River Teeth,* Doubleday, 1995
David James Duncan, *My Story as Told by Water,* Sierra Club Books, 2001
Annie Dillard, *Pilgrim at Tinker Creek,* Harper's, 1974
Annie Dillard, *Teaching a Stone to Talk,* Harper&Row, 1982
John Nichols, *Keep It Simple,* Norton, 1992
John Nichols, *On the Mesa,* Gibbs Smith, 1986
Leslie Marmon Silko, *Yellow Woman and a Beauty of the Spirit,* Simon&Schuster, 1996
Laura Hillenbrand, *Seabiscuit,* Random House, 2001
Robert Lawson, *Rabbit Hill,* Viking, 1944
Willa Cather, *My Antonia,* Houghton, Mifflin, 1918
Robert Frost, *Collected Poems,* Halcyon House, 1942
Mary Oliver, *New and Selected Poems,* Beacon, 1993
Jim Kjelgaard, *Big Red,* Holiday House, 2001
Sam Campbell, *The Seven Secrets of Somewhere Lake,* Bobbs-Merrill, 1952
Tony Angell, *The House of Owls,* Yale University Press, 2015
Elaine J. Struthers, *Chimpanzee Voices,* Self-published, 2013

www.ingramcontent.com/pod-product-compliance
Lightning Source LLC
Chambersburg PA
CBHW080356170426
43193CB00016B/2738